STATE OF THE ART

PAULINE KAEL

STATE OF THE ART

A William Abrahams Book

E. P. DUTTON   NEW YORK

All material in this book originally appeared in *The New Yorker*.

Copyright © 1983, 1984, 1985 by Pauline Kael
All rights reserved. Printed in the U.S.A.

Published in the United States by E. P. Dutton, a division of New American Library, 2 Park Avenue, New York, N.Y. 10016

Library of Congress Cataloging in Publication Data

Kael, Pauline.
    State of the art.

    1. Moving-pictures—Reviews. I. Title.
PN1995.K2527 1985   791.43'75   85-10368
ISBN 0-525-24369-0
ISBN 0-525-48186-9 (pbk.)

Published simultaneously in Canada by Fitzhenry & Whiteside Limited, Toronto

DESIGNED BY EARL TIDWELL
INDEX PREPARED BY TRENT DUFFY

10 9 8 7 6 5 4 3 2 1
COBE
First Edition

CONTENTS

AUTHOR'S NOTE

The title of this book is a deliberate break with my sexually tinged titles of the past. It seemed time for a change; this has not been a period for anything like *Grand Passions*. I hope that *State of the Art* will sound ominous and sweeping and just slightly clinical. In the last few years, the term has been applied to movies as the highest praise for their up-to-the-minute special effects or their sound or animation; it has been used to celebrate just about all the technological skills that go into a production. But what I try to get at in this collection of reviews from June 1983 to July 1985 is the state of the art of moviemaking.

In the 1970s, people who met me usually said something on the order of "You're so lucky—you get to go to the movies." In the 1980s, people are more likely to say "Do you have to sit through that stuff?" They're referring, of course, to the infantilization of movies in the 80s. Having sat through much of that bland, retro "stuff," I've tried to suggest what it's about. And despite the dubious state of the art, I think I've culled some pretty good pictures. Whenever people have asked what they should go to see, there has always been something to recommend— *Under Fire* or *Stop Making Sense* or *Yentl*, *The Right Stuff*, *Splash*, *All of Me*, *Moscow on the Hudson*, *Lost in America*, *Indiana Jones and the Temple of Doom*, *The Purple Rose of Cairo*, *A Passage to India*, *Iceman*, *Prizzi's Honor*, *Mrs. Soffel*, *Choose Me*, *Micki & Maude*, or *Once Upon a Time in America*, *Utu*, *The Makioka Sisters*, *The Shooting Party*, *Bizet's Carmen*, *The Home and the World*, or the full version of *The Leopard*.

Once again, I must express my gratitude to William Shawn, Editor of *The New Yorker*, and William Abrahams, now of Dutton, and my infinite thanks to my daughter Gina and her son William.

xi

SILLINESS

A comic's naked desire to make us laugh can be an embarrassment, especially if we feel that he's hanging on that laugh—that he's experiencing our reaction as a life-or-death matter. Steve Martin is naked, but he isn't desperate. (He's too anomic to be desperate.) Some performers can't work up a physical charge if the audience doesn't respond to them, but Steve Martin doesn't come out on a TV stage cold, hoping to get a rhythm going with the people in the studio. He's wired up and tingling, like a junk-food addict; he's like a man who's being electrocuted and getting a dirty thrill out of it. Steve Martin doesn't feed off the audience's energy—he instills energy in the audience. And he does it by drawing us into a conspiratorial relationship with him.

Pop culture is a relatively recent phenomenon. It's only in the last two decades that moviemakers have come along whose attitudes were shaped by the movies they grew up on, and whose subjects were often drawn from those old movies. And it's only in the past decade that a new generation of comics has been shaping its material as a satirical spinoff of the Catskill traditions they grew up on. The Steve Martin we see is a marionette, like the Devo punks; what holds the strings is the pop culture that he has processed. But he's not protesting the overload of his nervous system. His core is burned out, and he's a happy idiot, all spasms and twitches, and videotape for nerve endings.

When Martin comes onstage, he may do, say, just what Red Skelton used to do, but he gets us laughing at the fact that we're laughing at such dumb jokes. Martin simulates being a comedian, and so, in a way, we simulate being the comedian's audience. Martin makes old routines work by letting us know that they're old and then doing them immaculately. For him, comedy is *all* timing. He's almost a comedy robot. Onstage, he puts across the idea that he's going to do some cornball routine, and then when he does it it has quotation marks around it, and that's what makes it hilarious. He does the routine straight, yet he's totally facetious. He lets

I

us know that we're seeing silliness in quotes. There he is, spruced up and dapper in a three-piece white suit; even his handsomeness is made facetious. Steve Martin is all persona. That's what's dizzying about him—and a little ghoulish. He and some of the other comics of his generation make the *idea* that they're doing comedy funny.

It's as if Steve Martin's showmanship had two stages—as if first he came on and said, "Imagine a clod like me dancing like Fred Astaire." An old-style comedian would then fall on his face, or if he were Jack Benny fancying himself as Heifetz he'd produce one sour note after another. But Martin's steadfast concentration allows him, in the second stage, to do just what he said he'd do—he dances like Fred Astaire. I admired Steve Martin for the acting and dancing he did in *Pennies from Heaven*; what he did was more than a "stretch," it was a consummation, and he may have been so startlingly right in the movie because of the doubleness behind its whole conception. Possibly there was also an attempt to achieve some sort of duality in Martin's last picture, *Dead Men Don't Wear Plaid*—a spoof of detective movies which spliced together footage of Martin and footage from films of the forties. Carl Reiner, who has directed all three of Martin's star vehicles (but didn't direct *Pennies*), worked with dedicated craftsmen and achieved a smooth composite; even the sound levels were carefully matched. Reiner and the others must have become so proud of their workmanship that they didn't register what a monotonous, droning feat they were engaged in. They smoothed out their one big chance for comic friction—the contrast between old and new.

Almost nothing of the new-generation approach is visible in the Steve Martin of slapstick package movies, such as the first burlesque he starred in, *The Jerk*, and his new one, *The Man with Two Brains*. In these, he's not very different from the more frenzied and gaga of the older-generation comedians, yet he gives the impression of being fully realized. The pictures don't have the sheer wacko splendor of *Young Frankenstein*, but something as well thought out as *Young Frankenstein* might be a constraint on Martin. When he leers in *The Man with Two Brains*, he leers triumphantly, like a baby grinning and dribbling milk out of his first few teeth. The performance is shameless, stupid fun. Despite the sadness in his face, the comic character we see up there has nothing in his head but a warped, infantile élan. Martin is as physical a comic as I've ever seen; the Jerk is the perfect name for him—he moves convulsively, at angles, his body shooting ahead of his thoughts.

Essentially a series of skits, *The Man with Two Brains* is indefensible by any known standard of comedy form—or formlessness. It's not much of anything, but it moves along enjoyably and allows this Jerk to stay wired up for the whole picture. Sunny, grinning, lewd, he's Harpo Marx with a voice and without the harp—a Harpo whose id has chased out Art. As the world's greatest brain surgeon, he's an exuberantly dirty-minded kid. This surgeon, who's stuffed with pretensions, perceives himself as a man of the world, but he's a guileless innocent compared with the woman he swoons over—a flirty, dimply sadist who marries him for her convenience. Kathleen Turner, who was so laboriously steamy in *Body Heat,* comes alive in comedy; she coos with pleasure as she frustrates this fool. She's a wicked-witch sex goddess who keeps him tense and frazzled. The story ideas in *Two Brains* aren't as inventive as the material in *The Jerk,* but that was an ugly-looking picture, with stumblebum pacing. (Martin was funny in it despite its dead spots and the tedium of his falling over things.) *Two Brains* at least has a look. Michael Chapman was the cinematographer, and his work has a graphic vitality that's unusual for a comedy; it certainly helps the gags, because we're kept alert between them. And Carl Reiner seems to be developing a bit of grace: the actors surrounding Martin are pleasantly subdued. David Warner plays a mad doctor in an offhand, distracted manner; it's consistent with the pastel colors of the live human brains that he keeps in candy jars. Some of the gags don't seem quite pointed enough—Warner's coin-operated transformer (for his laboratory machines that implant human brains in gorillas) doesn't get anything more than a smile. And the last, fat-bride sequence is hopeless. But the picture has at least one inspired love scene (between Martin and a brain, in a rowboat). And Martin himself—whatever he does—has the fascination of a man moving in an energetic trance.

This movie has the kind of maniacal situations that are so dumb they make you laugh, and since much of what children find hilarious has this same giddiness, they'd probably like the film a lot. But it also has the kind of raunchiness that may worry their parents (though it will probably just make the kids giggle). It has an R rating, so the kids may need their folks to get them in. That's a pickle.

□

Silliness is also the chief charm of *Octopussy,* the fourteenth (and least elegantly titled) of the James Bond movies. It's part parody and part travesty, and it's amiably fatigued. Those of us who keep going to the Bonds (even after the last two, the apathetic *Moonraker* and *For Your Eyes Only*) have probably become resigned to Roger Moore. He doesn't move particularly well, and, at fifty-five, he doesn't move very fast, either. We know (and his sheepish, self-deprecating manner tells us that he knows we know) that he has been playing the role because the producer couldn't find anybody more exciting. He still goes through (some of) the motions of a modern swashbuckling hero, but he gets most of his effects now by the spark in his worried, squinched-up eyes. He may not be heroic, but he's game. And he rises to the occasion of his one first-class joke. It's part of a sequence that might be a spoof of *Raiders of the Lost Ark*: running just a few steps ahead of a hunting party that's out to get him, he encounters a series of standard old-movie dangers, including an attack by a deadly animal. Moore lifts his index finger in the Barbara Woodhouse style of disapproval and subdues the beast with a single word.

The picture rattles along. It's not the latest-model Cadillac; it's a beat-out old Cadillac, kept running with junk-yard parts. (I never thought a Bond movie would actually resort to a suffering man in clown's makeup.) The director, John Glen, seems to lose track of the story, and neither he nor the writers (George MacDonald Fraser, with Richard Maibaum and Michael G. Wilson) appear to have thought out the women's roles. Magda, a mysterious, tall, greasy-lipped blonde (Kristina Wayborn, who played Garbo on TV), has an amused manner; she seduces Bond, then disappears without any explanation, and when she turns up again he barely gives her a nod. The naughty, chic perversities that are promised by the title and some of the décor are left to our minds—as if the moviemakers had no idea they'd planted them there. As the title character, the beautiful amazon Maud Adams is disappointingly warm and maternal—she's rather mooshy. At one moment, Octopussy is a leader, and the next moment she's a dupe, who doesn't know what's going on around her. The role is a washout, and the performance is so smiley-innocuous that when she leads Bond to her octopus-shaped bed it must be to lie back against the pillows and have a nice cup of tea and milk. But this is a joke book of a movie, set against a tourist-paradise India (it seems to be all palaces), and Glen keeps the small jokes humming. As an exiled Afghan prince, a dissolute schemer, Louis Jourdan doesn't have much to do but look annoyed, though he has one sly bit—he puckers up when he pronounces the amazon's name, giving it an ironic caress. Some of the other villains are more prominently displayed. There's a bright, blue-eyed English actor, Steven Berkoff, who plays the fanatic Russian general

4

Orlov. When Orlov speaks English, he takes a gleeful pride in his own precision, and listening to him wrap his tongue around English syllables is one of the slaphappy pleasures of this movie—he's like the mad Russians who were popular on American radio in the thirties. Kabir Bedi, a handsome Anglo-Indian actor—a monument of a man, who towers over Roger Moore—has a fine villainous curve to his mouth; as the prince's major domo, he looks alarming even when he isn't doing a thing. Among the lesser villains, I rather liked the identical David and Tony Meyer, who have the perfect profession for twins: they work for a circus, throwing knives at each other. There's also an agreeable appearance by the famous Indian tennis star Vijay Amritraj, who plays an agent assisting Bond; you won't have any trouble spotting him— he's called Vijay, and he smacks a pursuer with a tennis racquet.

Octopussy is probably the most casual of the Bonds. It features a chase sequence in a crowded marketplace with a great camera angle on a camel looking up and doing a double take as an automobile flies over its head. In some ways, *Octopussy* is more like the Bob Hope and Bing Crosby *Road* comedies than it is like the Bonds. (Among Bond's disguises here are a gorilla suit and an alligator outfit that doubles as a boat.) The pet octopus that the amazon keeps is a pretty little thing— blue, with markings so discreet that you might expect to find them on decorator sheets. What this woman is doing with a harem full of cuties (who are sometimes dressed as slave girls) isn't clear; at times they appear to be a feminist sisterhood, with Octopussy as their den mother. When they're forced to use their skills in the martial arts, they overpower their male enemies very sweetly, while moving about in gracefully choreographed patterns.

The movie is a little schizzy. It gives us Bond as a gorilla and as a gator; it gives us Bond swinging on ropes in the forest while yodelling like Tarzan. This Bond slides down a bannister while firing a machine gun and travels in a balloon equipped with a bank of television screens so he can monitor the action below. But the moviemakers also have him deliver a virtuous speech expressing anger at the possibility that thousands of innocent people will be killed if the atom bomb that Orlov has planted goes off. It's as if a teacher had been entertaining us with crazy stories and then reprimanded us for laughing. You can feel a collective slump in the audience.

Flashdance has Cuisinart movie technique: the perfection is in the slicing, not the food. The girl can't dance, but she's got a face. No problem: the moviemakers put her face on another girl's body—a dancer who moves so fast you can't see whether she's even got a face under her frizzy curls. And the strobe editing makes her even faster. This dancing doesn't go the way a body goes; this dancing goes the way an eggbeater goes.

The girl is eighteen, and working-class Catholic, like Rocky, and Tony Manero, and the girl in *An Officer and a Gentleman,* and she's proud. She's all alone in Pittsburgh, but she's got a dream. She's a welder by day and a dancer at night, and though her dances look choreographed down to each flutter of the frizz, we're meant to understand that they're an explosion of her instincts. But she doesn't want to dance this "natural" way. In her dream, she's a ballerina, handed bouquets, like a princess. The music throughout is synthesizer pop—some of Giorgio Moroder's throbbing specials along with bits of other whiplash disco songs (including some that were already on the charts); basically, the movie is a series of rock videos. When this girl dances in a neighborhood beer joint, the neon-framed stage looks like the latest design for a convention center. The picture has Vegas sound, thumping, thumping. Our wistful heroine has a darling smile, which is deployed very carefully during a long, provocative eating scene, with bits of lobster hovering on her perfect lips. Hot is in. And she isn't the only girl. For this picture, the producers have put together a prime collection of rumps: girls' rumps, but small and muscular and round, like boys'. These androgynous buns are kept busy at an ice-skating rink, at a body-building workout in a gym, and on the streets, where everything pulses, and a group of boy dancers perform on the sidewalks, spinning on their backs like tops. (Richard Colon, one of this group of black "breakers," who do the only real dancing in the movie, is so fast that he isn't subjected to the chop-chop editing—he's allowed to perform in his own time.)

The picture is a lulling, narcotizing musical; the whole damn thing throbs. It's a motorized anatomy lesson, designed to turn the kids on and drive older men crazy. It's soft-core porn with an inspirational message, and it may be the most calculating, platinum-hearted movie I've ever seen. *Flashdance* is selling the kind of romantic story that was laughed off the screen thirty years ago, and then made a comeback with *Rocky I, II,* and *III.* Life is simple for the courageous. Our poor little girl wins her young, handsome boss—the owner of the steel mill. It's O.K. for him to be rich, because he worked his way up from poverty (with record-breaking speed), and she wins him because she sticks to her principles and is true to her vision—yes, she really is going to become a ballerina. (You may think it a little late for her to start taking her first ballet classes, but she's been dancing every night in her dreams, so who needs practice?) The public is buying this picture; millions of people probably don't see anything wrong with it. They may even think that the critics are panning it because it's too sexy for us, and—God help us—too gritty and honest for us cocktail-swilling urban sophisticates.

Flashdance is like a sleazo putting the make on you. It gives a hard sell even to the heroine's confessions to her priest. How tender she is, how dewy-eyed and passionate. She confesses that she has been thinking of sex, and—oh, yes—she told a lie. This girl is all underdog, and she's got a real, scene-stealing dog besides. The dog's soulful expressions have more depth than anything else in the picture.

June 27, 1983

TIME-WARP MOVIES

hen we go into the theatre to see *Superman III*, we know that whatever else happens we're still going to have the pleasure of seeing a man fly without an airplane and without wings. But when I (for one) came out of the theatre it was with the distinct feeling that if the director, Richard Lester, had been able to deprive us completely of this pleasure he would have done so—not because he didn't want us to have a good time but because he loses touch with the simple, basic elements of his material. For roughly the first forty minutes of *Superman III*, during which Richard Pryor as Gus Gorman, who has been a flop at every job he has ever had, discovers that he's a computer wizard, Lester provides an agreeable mixture of the grandiose and the everyday. Our expectations are aroused: he must have some tricks up his sleeve. And he does, but the scattered impulses behind the movie cancel each other out.

Superman/Clark Kent (Christopher Reeve), who grew into a touching character in *Superman II*, is presented here as a blank—he's whatever is needed to fit the gags. Clark Kent is a bore with a simpering grin, and Superman has been doing his good deeds for so long that the people of Metropolis are jaded and take him for granted. Clearly, he needs a change, but it doesn't come from within. Richard Pryor's Gus, who has used a computer to embezzle from the conglomerate he works for, is caught by the boss (Robert Vaughn) and ordered to work out the ingredients of kryptonite—the only substance that can destroy Superman. Gus isn't that much of a wizard, though; the computer gives him all the ingredients but one, and so he fakes it, and the green chunk he hands to Superman, as if it were an award, is only near-kryptonite. It doesn't kill Superman; it demoralizes him, and he begins to perform dirty deeds.

What's strange about the movie is that the best things in it aren't developed, and what Superman and the other characters do doesn't seem to have any weight. Robert Vaughn's polished smarminess is scaled to television; his villainy doesn't fill the big screen, and when he tries to ruin the Colombian coffee crop or succeeds in stopping the world's flow of oil, Lester treats what happens so flippantly that nothing appears to be at stake. Vaughn's harridan sister and business partner—Annie Ross as the black-haired, witchlike Vera—might be something left in cold storage since the era of the Munsters. And a potentially amusing bosomy blonde, a floozy-intellectual named Lorelei Ambrosia (Pamela Stephenson), just sits around. Lester may think that these women are gags just in themselves—there are no payoffs. And when Gus hands Superman the chunk of green near-kryptonite, Superman doesn't have any idea what it is—it's as if he'd never seen *Superman* and *Superman II*.

Despite the film's anti-mythic tone, it's entertaining (in the early part) when we see Superman perform heroically. There's a dangerous fire in a chemical plant, and the firemen have no water. Superman freezes a lake and flies it over the site; the fire melts the ice, which turns into rain and puts out the fire. This comic-book fairy-tale fantasy is funny and enchanting—this, in essence, is what we've come to see for the third time. But although Lester had a hand in the first film and directed the second, he steps on our reaction here—he doesn't give us time to be exhilarated. He keeps his light, objective touch, which at times is indistinguishable from directorial indifference. Too many scenes are treated as if they were just obligatory, and because of that air of indifference, verging on disdain, the movie's sight gags and special effects—even the biggest ones—aren't particularly exciting. The splashy scenes that we look forward to don't seem to show up, because Lester has devalued them; everything feels marginal.

So when the soul-sick Superman is being prankish or surly—putting out the Olympic torch or straightening the Leaning Tower of Pisa or punching a hole in a tanker and causing an oil spill—we don't know how to react to this lecher with stubble on his chin and a soiled-looking cape. A funky, sexy-sheik Superman could have audiences squealing with pleasure, and a Superman with a vendetta against the world could be awesomely neurotic, but the movie has no sooner suggested the possibilities than it drops them. (When he sits alone in a bar, boozing and exploding bottles by flicking roasted almonds at them, we get more of a sense of how dangerous—and attractive—Superman could be than at any other time. The bad Superman has burning dark eyes; he looks like an Etruscan warrior.) We're not intended to take what happens to Superman as a genuine psychological crisis; the picture even loses track of the near-kryptonite. We're not intended to care about the victims of his spite. We don't know what we're meant to respond to.

It's a real loss that Clark Kent is shunted offscreen during these sequences, because we miss him—we wonder how he feels about what's going on. (Is he suffering? Or has he turned bad guy and told off his fellow-workers at the *Daily Planet*?) At last, Superman's headachy conflict with himself becomes so intense that he splits into two: a scene that needs to be crazed and funny—if only because the two identities are already split in our minds, so that we've been waiting for Clark. But what we get is a conventional battle of the titans, like John Wayne and Randolph Scott pounding each other in a frontier saloon. The setting here is an automobile junk yard. Superman keeps throwing Clark Kent into grind-up machines and demolishing him; he kicks him unconscious, and Clark keeps coming back for more punishment, like Wile E. Coyote in a Road Runner cartoon. It isn't comic, though, and it isn't satisfyingly worked out, either, but there's at least some psychological resonance in this battling, and when Clark Kent triumphs the scene is affecting. (We've come to trust him more than we trust Superman.) There's nothing to redeem the film's final big brawl when the healed, integrated Superman, who is once again at the service of mankind, goes up against a monster computer that Gus has designed and Vaughn has had built. Like Luke in *Return of the Jedi*, Superman is repeatedly fried by zigzag bolts of electricity.

Lester hasn't gone back to the heaviness of *How I Won the War* or the disaffection of *Petulia*, and he doesn't do the obvious subverting that he did on his *Musketeers* pictures, but he undermines the mystique

9

of Superman as an ideal father image and an ideal self-image. (Lester almost seems to think that he's letting the material subvert itself.) There's an idea here: that Superman is a victim of his own do-gooding and needs to be liberated—needs to discover that he has the same impulses and drives as other men. But this violates all the information we have stored up about him, which starts with the given that he isn't human—he's superhuman. We can accept the bad-guy Superman as a casualty of kryptonite, but the notion that when Superman is idealistic and helpful he's an asexual Mr. Square violates our memories of what was charming about Christopher Reeve's performance in the first two films. There was deadpan wit in Superman's impersonation of the clumsy, inept Clark Kent; here he doesn't seem to be in on the joke. And it doesn't make any sense that when Clark Kent goes back to Smallville to his high-school class reunion, everyone except Lana Lang (Annette O'Toole), who, we're told, has always had a crush on him, treats him contemptuously. In the first *Superman*, the schoolboy Clark Kent was physically strong and he was always considerate and sweet—why would he have been unpopular? Lester wants us to see Clark as a nerd and Superman as a virtuous clod, but all that does is drain the mythic life out of the movie. By not allowing the people on the screen to be enthralled by Superman's flights and miraculous rescues, Lester puts himself in the position of pooh-poohing the movie's special effects, and pooh-poohing the hero. He robs the picture of its chance to stir the viewer's imagination. He may also (out of impatience, or a willingness to sacrifice story points to pacing) have truncated episodes—such as Clark Kent's reëntering Lana Lang's life—which are left suspended. Annette O'Toole (who has an American-goddess profile) makes Lana's small-town-girl infatuation with Clark seem perfectly natural. She's the only member of the cast who appears to believe in her role yet stays in a comic-book frame. As Brad, the fifties-style jock who wants to marry Lana, Gavan O'Herlihy is believable, too, especially when he tells Clark Kent he hates him for being so nice, but O'Herlihy doesn't have the knack of comic-book style.

The logistical horrors of directing actors around special effects that are put in later may help to explain why Lester can't give this movie anything like the visual shimmer of many of his earlier films. And those effects may also be part of the reason he can't give it his jazzy, leapfrogging editing style. *Superman III* doesn't have much of a look, and the editing clumps along. (When a movie is heavy on special effects, you don't get much for forty-two million dollars anymore.) But all those technical problems don't explain why Lester, who tosses off a number of lovely visual gags, also uses so many labored tricks, such as a forties-style montage showing the results of Gus's fiddling with his computer: it ends with a man at the breakfast table opening his monthly statement from Bloomingdale's and shoving a half grapefruit in his wife's face. Lester does better with a gag sequence—a chain of mishaps—that sustains life for us during the lengthy opening credits, but the sequence doesn't have anything like the zest of the similar gag at the start of Richard Rush's *The Stunt Man.* And this attempt to get the film moving is marred by the credits themselves, which come sloshing up from the bottom of the screen and disrupt the action.

Lester, and the scriptwriters, David and Leslie Newman (who have been involved in all three films), are working with an insane disadvantage: they're trying to fuse two incompatible or, at least, conflicting legends. Christopher Reeve isn't the star of *Superman III.* Richard Pryor is. He's the box-office insurance that the producers, the Salkinds, bought for four million dollars. According to the Newmans, they and Lester dreamed up the idea (along with everyone else who was planning a new movie). And so, of course, once Pryor agreed, the Newmans tried to shape the story around him. At times, it isn't clear whether the action we're watching is in Metropolis or in Smallville, and at other times the central characters are apparently wandering in various directions around the Grand Canyon. What makes the picture seem so addled is the need to bring Gus and Superman together. They never do get to have a dramatic confrontation, and they don't actually become enemies—or friends, either—but Lester keeps so much fringe action going on that viewers don't have a chance to question what Pryor and Superman, who don't even belong to the same era, are doing in the same movie.

There's no way that this clean-language, family picture could use the Richard Pryor who used to do a ''Supernigger'' routine (which was spun off Lenny Bruce's ''Superjew''). When Pryor puts on a pink shawl in imitation of Superman's red cape, he's rather forlorn. What the film uses is Richard Pryor playing off his rich white master (Vaughn) in the scaredy-cat way that Mantan Moreland and other earlier, eye-rolling black comics did. Pryor's Gus isn't a villain; he only works for the villain. (And he does everything but steal chickens and have his hair shoot up straight 'cause he's 'feerd of ghosts.) He cringes and acts cowardly, and, yes, the audience laughs and finds him endearing. (Pryor as a computer genius doesn't ring any bells; I wondered why the moviemakers hadn't tried the ploy of using Pryor to wise up Superman, or as the demoralized Superman's tempter—that way he wouldn't have had to be so limp, and he and Superman could have had more scenes together.) Pryor doesn't give a bad performance, but it's a hesitant and bowed performance, as if he were trying not to be noticed. And it's a one-joke role. Gus's mind is so fogged in that he does everything he can to please his slimy master; it's pretty close to the end of the movie before he—ever so tentatively—shifts his allegiance. First, his boss totes him; then Superman (literally) totes him. He never does go out on his own. And when Superman is flying with Richard Pryor they look the way they do in the ads for the movie that show Pryor openmouthed and pop-eyed with terror. The romance is gone; the flying has become just another gag.

In *Trading Places*, Dan Aykroyd plays a snooty young blue-blood who runs a Philadelphia brokerage house, and Eddie Murphy plays a con man–beggar who disguises himself as a blind, legless Vietnam veteran. The two don't exactly trade places; they're traded, by a pair of heartless, rich old brothers (Ralph Bellamy and Don Ameche) who have made a heredity-versus-environment bet—something we've been spared in movies of the past few decades. *Trading Places*, which was written by Timothy Harris and Herschel Weingrod and directed by John Landis (*Animal House, The Blues Brothers*), is reminiscent of the kind of "classic" that turns up on TV at Christmastime, and it looks like a Christmas classic on a TV set that needs adjusting. It's drab. It's also eerily arch and static. Landis must think that he's achieving a mock-thirties formal style; for the first hour he italicizes each scene, fixing it in place as if he wanted us to take an inventory of every detail. He seems to be saying, "I'm smarter than this." It gets to the point where you may want to stand up in the theatre and say, "Yeah? Prove it." The picture is pompous—the setups are so rigid I wanted to kick the camera to get it moving.

The comedies of the thirties and forties from which this movie was hatched were often based on Broadway plays, and they carried over stage devices, such as the valet-butlers with impeccable diction who were a great convenience to playwrights. (Preston Sturges parodied this tradition in *The Lady Eve*, where Henry Fonda's valet—William Demarest—talked like a gangster gargling and was indignant when told to stay in his place.) The recent hit *Arthur*, which was derived from the same movie period as *Trading Places*, gave us John Gielgud as a valet father figure, and now we've got Denholm Elliott, coddling and grooming first Aykroyd and then Murphy. (Elliott hasn't been given the lines he would need to make anything of the role, but when the camera gloms onto him he obliges with little grimaces.) One snag in antique dramaturgical devices such as butlers to populate an empty stage and manipulative millionaires to put a plot in motion by toying with men's lives is that they push a movie into a time warp, and this one, with its stodgy look, suggests no period of the past or the present. And when Eddie Murphy speaks in modern slang he has a startling effect. He's the only person in the movie who belongs to our era, and he's a man of the eighties only in his speech. What he does in this movie is totally circumscribed by the plot mechanics.

The trajectories of the two men's lives—the representative of white privilege sinking into crime and craziness while the black con artist rises to the heights of the establishment—are crosscut. The new, young scriptwriters don't have the built-in clocks that the best screenwriters of the thirties had. Aykroyd's descent to bumhood is rather blurry, and each time the movie cuts back to him he doesn't seem to have deteriorated by more than two minutes. Murphy, on the other hand, whips through his initial changes, but then he has a nasty, humorless sequence in which he invites the people from a seamy ghetto bar to his town house for a party and promptly throws them all out, because some of them don't use ashtrays, or coasters for their drinks, and a couple of the women are dancing topless. From the way this sequence is directed, you get the feeling that the con man has learned the value of fine possessions, and that the ghetto crowd would wreck any decent place they got into. That can't be what was intended, can it? But the audience laughs contentedly. In a crude, dogged way, the movie has a sense of humor: it keeps telling you how terrific its sense of humor is. And it has that big, chugging structure working for it: the whole apparatus picks up some speed toward the end and comes to a rousing, slapstick finish, with the younger guys rich and the old skinflints punished. The audience appeared to like it.

This may seem like the attitude of a killjoy, but I wish the audience had groaned, because Landis's timing is deadly—he makes everything obvious. And he doesn't do much for his actors. Aykroyd uses one fairly effective comic shtick: he plays rich by keeping his face tilted up, the nose high, sniffing purer air, like a snobby dog in a cartoon. (Amusingly, it's the very same trick that Don Ameche is still using for his rotten-rich character.) And Aykroyd the broker has a suggestion of a flabby, insecure boy who wants the praise of his employers—it makes him rather touching. Confusingly, though, he's less appealing when he's on the skids. Dan Aykroyd is all exteriors; he's big and beefy, and, inspired as he has often been on TV, he doesn't seem to have a strong personality. (That may be part of why he's such a great impressionist.) I think he really is insecure playing the Harvard-educated young pup in three-piece suits, and we respond to the nervousness under the bluff of assurance. But when this plutocrat is stripped of everything and he turns into a low-comedy slob in loud plaids or a Santa Claus suit, Aykroyd falls back, relieved, on TV-sketch acting; he's no longer a character, and we have no particular feeling for him. Eddie Murphy's new-style savvy carries *Trading Places*, but this is only his second movie and he's already just one step away from being in a niche. Murphy is like a child performer who's too accomplished. His cockiness is uncannily knowing; he gets to your reflexes, like those Vegas veterans who make you feel that you're enjoying them even while you're pulling back. This isn't a man possessed; this is a man who knows his audiences—he plays completely off their expectations. (White people couldn't really learn anything of what it is to be black from Eddie Murphy; he's playing off their ideas of what it is to be black.)

My most vivid recollection of *Trading Places* is of the faces of the two cops at the beginning who lift the supposedly legless con man off his rolling platform. His legs dangle in the air, but the two cops haven't been directed to laugh or to look puzzled or to have any particular reaction. They just stand there—two stone-faced, bewildered actors, who have no idea what's wanted of them—and we see them in closeup after closeup. Some of the people in the audience assume that the director is hip and knows what he's doing, so they resolve their embarrassment in chuckling.

□

To the letter writers who have asked why I haven't reviewed *Betrayal*, the answer is: Because I couldn't sit through it. My body wouldn't let me. The best I can do is explain why. In the very first images, people were leaving a party, and I wanted to go off with them rather than go into the hideously proper upper-middle-class house where the party givers were obviously going to be full of hate for each other. Inside, the wife was tidying up, and the husband was watching her. She slapped him, and he slapped her right back. She sat down in despair, then got up when their child, who had awakened, came in. I was already overdosed on Pinter, and the dialogue hadn't even started. I stayed long enough to learn that the three characters are engaged in semi-parasitic cultural work: the husband is a publisher, the lover a literary agent, the woman an art dealer. So we know what Pinter thinks of them right off the bat. And, as usual, Pinter's drama is in the pecking order, which keeps shifting. I was surrounded by a quiet, attentive audience. People were listening to the ping-ponging vocal rhythms as if to be certain of not missing a single sinister nuance. As if you *could*! Every grim, frozen syllable is lobbed into your lap, along with Pinter's patented pauses—those ticktock silences that (famously) reverberate with what isn't said. The three actors all had the stricken look that is proper to a Pinter play; he doesn't bother writing about anyone who's alive. And there's nothing else going on in this movie—once you've noticed how ugly the lamps are, you're left with the stiff, stilted talk that's so calculated it's a parody. If the lines ever overlapped, it would be cataclysmic. This story of adultery told backward is a perfectly conventional corpse of a play given a ceremonious funeral on the screen. It's from Beckett by way of Terrence Rattigan. Maybe not even from Beckett. When I deserted my post, the husband was acting superior and malevolent (in the Ian Holm game-playing manner), and the lover was being callow, and their eyes were darting as each watched the other's reactions. And I had got to the point of staring at their thin brown lips and wondering if the two actors had been made up with the same lipstick.

July 11, 1983

HYSTERICS

The banner line on the ad for *The Survivors*, the new Michael Ritchie film, starring Robin Williams and Walter Matthau, says, "Once they declare war on each other, watch out. You could die laughing." The advertisers might as well be saying, "We dare you to see this dud."

Everything about the publicity campaign for the picture has been at this level. (From time to time, you'll read about how a strikingly clever trailer or a TV commercial helped to sell a movie, but nobody writes about the ones that repel audiences the way a plague warning would.) I doubt if there's any way that the public perception of *The Survivors* can be turned around, but some people may discover the movie when it gets to HBO and the networks. (That's how a lot of people discovered Ritchie's *Smile.*) *The Survivors* isn't about two men declaring war on each other; it's about two New Yorkers without anything in common who become friends. The advertisers probably didn't know what to do with it because it's a comedy for grownups. That may strike them as a contradiction in terms: all comedies are now presumed to be fodder for adolescents (unless they have the runaway charm or star appeal of a *Tootsie*). I don't mean to suggest that adults will necessarily like *The Survivors*—I have several good friends who hated it—but simply that it isn't shaped for the teen-age market.

The Survivors may be too unpredictable for some people. There's a lot of unconventional humor in the writing, by Michael Leeson. (This is his first movie credit; he won awards for his work on the TV series "Taxi.") Leeson and Michael Ritchie may compound each other's faults: Leeson doesn't appear to be experienced in building a plot to a climax, and Ritchie (*Downhill Racer, The Candidate, The Bad News Bears, Semi-Tough*) tends to be at his sharpest—and most involved—in divertissements on a theme, rather than on the theme itself. This slapstick social satire may have needed someone more square than either of them to give it a center. The movie flits about, and there are spots where a viewer might nod off, but I enjoyed a surprising amount of it, and I think that Robin Williams' work in it transcends the film's flaws.

Williams plays Donald, a junior executive who gets fired on the same day that Matthau, as Sonny Paluso, the owner of a service station, loses his business. They meet at a lunch counter, where each man is trying to drown his sorrow in a cup of coffee. Being fired seems to have thrown a switch in Donald's skull, and when a masked holdup man (Jerry Reed) tries to rob the coffee shop he puts up such a squawk that Paluso goes to his aid, and together they disarm the bandit and, briefly, become media heroes. The whole experience of being fired and feeling helpless in front of the armed robber and getting on television turns Donald's head. He becomes gun-crazy, buys an arsenal, and goes off for a course of training in survival tactics at a camp in New England; he wants to learn how to be violent, so he can live in the wild and protect himself when the social order collapses. The comedy is in the contrasting natures of Donald and Paluso. Everything surprises Donald. He's a sweet-natured hysteric who overresponds to every stimulus. He has the nervous system of an infant; the transitions between mood changes aren't visible—he doesn't consider, he reacts. Paluso is the opposite. Nothing surprises him; he gives the impression of having learned all there is to know about survival (in the big city) long ago. He's cautious and jaundiced, with the kind of cynicism that used to be ascribed to Manhattan cabbies. And when the would-be robber (a sociopath with delusions of being a big-time hit man and of having killed Jimmy Hoffa) is released from custody and goes after the two men, Paluso tries to get Donald to behave rationally—i.e., cravenly—so they won't both be killed.

The best thing about this framework is that it permits Robin Williams to be himself and yet to be Donald. He acts with an emotional purity that I can't pretend to understand. Williams expostulates all through the movie; he sputters out his short-circuited thoughts. He seems to be free-associating twenty-four hours a day; you know that his mind is racing even when he sleeps. And this spritzing never seems false or prepared. He spritzes *in character*. It's like a child's stream of consciousness: you see him making mad comparisons and landing from mental leaps, but you never see him take off. A lot of the comedy comes from his being a grownup with this ranting little kid inside him.

One of the few times Donald slows down is when he's on TV doing an "editorial reply" and discussing crime and criminals. His squashed rubber face is intent. He has a veneer of reasonableness and he articulates impeccably, but what he says is carefully thought out gobbledygook. Smiling into the TV camera, with a clenched-teeth smile—a cross between a grin and a grimace—he has a faintly gloating expression, as if he's sitting on something and wants to keep it a secret. This is one of several monologues—each different in emotional tone—that he delivers in the picture. There's a great one in a telephone booth up in the woods; when he goes into the booth we know what he's going to do but we don't know how, and so we're like eager connoisseurs of lunacy. At this point, Donald feels he has become a master of gunmanship and the martial arts; he has an assurance we've never seen before as he reaches for the phone and sneeringly challenges the crazy robber to come up and fight it out. I don't think I've ever heard just one side of a sneering dialogue before. It's much funnier than hearing both: the macho braggadocio in a void is clearly nutty. Donald is turning himself on; he emerges from the booth triumphant.

Throughout most of the picture, Williams' Donald is a child in panic who needs to be soothed. (Sometimes he looks as if his teeming little head is about to burst.) The soothing is Matthau's function, and he gives a quiet, old pro's performance; he relies on his winces and his sleepy slouch, and he can't get in much trouble with that. But there's nothing particularly funny in the way he takes Donald's scrambled conversations in his stride. Matthau can't be budged—even Robin Williams can't budge him. The other characters in the movie are all loco, and Paluso's thinking man's strategy for survival in the city—cowardice—would come across as loco, too, if Matthau didn't seem so grand and imperturbable. Actually, it's more than that: he's implacable, and that's a little dreary. There are other weaknesses. The revelation that the leader of the survivalist camp is a phony and a con man is too easy a way to dispose of what he represents. (Besides, para-fascists who are honest to the bone are much scarier.) And the plot, for symmetry, could use considerably more of the third key character—Jerry Reed's bullying thug; we need to know more of what's going on inside his handsome hard head. Reed (better known as a country musician) has a fine maniacal presence here, and his performance is so promising that I regretted that there wasn't more for him to do. That was also true for several of the actresses —especially Kristen Vigard, as Paluso's sixteen-year-old daughter, whose spacy mixture of knowingness and childishness adds up to some new configuration that superficially, at least, resembles sanity. The movie does a pretty fair job of demonstrating that the way things are now you'd have to be wacko to be sane. And Robin Williams carries it along by his cock-a-doodle-doo eagerness. He uses his hairy, broad-chested, no-neck body for the naked "universal" emotions that mimes strive for, and he achieves them (in a speeded-up form) without attaching big labels to them. He may be that rarity, a fearless actor.

When stories like the ones that were told on the Rod Serling TV show "The Twilight Zone" grow up, they become Borges fables—metaphysical hoodwinks. I didn't expect (or want) *Twilight Zone—The Movie* to be Borgesian, but I did rather hope that John Landis, Steven Spielberg, Joe Dante, and George Miller—the four young directors who are paying homage to the TV series—would tease us with more artful macabre games than the ones of the old shows. It's a naïve (and dubious) sort of tribute that sets out to do essentially the same thing with the implicit expectation of doing it better; what they've given us is simply a remake.

The original shows, which ran from late 1959 to 1964, and have been in rerun ever since, were ingenious partly because of how economically they got their effects. There were few characters—sometimes no more than two, or even one, and rarely more than eight or nine. They were ordinary people—little guys, anonymous Americans—and the meagrely furnished shows had a sort of cardboard realism. This was cottage-industry sci-fi fantasy. For the first two seasons, the half-hour shows were budgeted at sixty thousand dollars each; that meant one day for rehearsal and three days for shooting. (The budget sometimes got so tight that for a while the directors weren't allowed to use film; they had to use videotape—which in its early years was a miserable medium—and stage the shows the way live television plays were staged.) By necessity, the mysterious was made homey, almost comforting. Sometimes it might seem as if Rod Serling's message were that the U.S.A. was so democratic that demons visited even the common man. Serling was always trying to make a statement about the human condition; it generally turned into a lesson in how to be a good neighbor. The shows—there are a hundred and fifty-six of them—packaged an endearingly corny mixture of supernaturalism and civics. There are probably millions of people who as kids learned the clichés from "The Twilight Zone."

The new movie takes off like a breeze, with Dan Aykroyd and Albert Brooks—hitchhiker and driver—in a car at night on a dark country road, passing the time by playing trivia games, quizzing each other about the theme music for old TV series, and inevitably getting to "The Twilight Zone." Written and directed by John Landis, this prologue is a beauty, but the happy rush of fright we get from it has to sustain us for a long stretch, because the first two episodes are embarrassments. The first, which was suggested by some of the old shows (rather than adapted from them, like the three others), is a painfully blunt sermon on the evils of racism and prejudice. The central character, a loudmouthed bigot, is played by Vic Morrow, who, along with two Vietnamese-American children, was killed in a helicopter accident during the filming; that may be why we don't get the turnaround that we expect—when this bigot, after experiencing the terrifying plight of being a Jew trapped by the Nazis in occupied Paris, and a black chased by a lynch mob in the South, and a Vietnamese gunned down by G.I.s in a paddy, would metamorphose into a decent person. I assume that the moviemakers considered the possibility of dropping this segment, but that its writer-director, Landis, who was co-producer (with Spielberg) of the whole film, probably felt that it would be a memorial to Vic Morrow—that he wouldn't have wanted his last performance to be scrapped. It is, after all, a starring role in one-fourth of an A-budget movie. And there's nothing the matter with his scowling bad-guy performance, except there's no shading in it —that would probably have come with the twist.

The episode has no real ending, but that isn't what makes it so awful. What does is that the production is overscaled for its dinky, dull idea. Probably the quality that makes the original shows tolerable is their bareness; their emptiness is eerily restful, and viewers extend good will to Rod Serling's preaching because of the amateurish, tacky, school-play look. The black-and-white photography doesn't suggest the sixties—it's an indefinite past, a synthesis of thirties and forties and fifties, when everybody was Eisenhower-gray. Here, as soon as we see crowds on the screen and elaborate camera setups, Landis's thin pretext of a script collapses. With big colored images on a movie screen, and even images of Vietnam, the characters, who talk like throwbacks to that gray age, don't make any sense. This section is like an unconscious parody of the old shows; its straightness is a deadweight on the viewer's head.

In some ways, the lump of ironclad whimsy directed by Spielberg, which follows, is a worse embarrassment. It's about how through their willingness to engage in youthful play a group of people in a home for the aged become children again (which the moviemakers regard as a great break for them). And as if the whole idea (it's adapted from the 1962 show "Kick the Can," written by George Clayton Johnson) weren't darling enough, a good-fairy black man, played by Scatman Crothers, has been added, so that he can bare his choppers and smile angelically for what certainly feels like eternity. (A friend commented, "I guess we're going to have to accept *Song of the South* as another of Steven Spielberg's formative experiences.") There are a few pleasant jokes involving the old people's voices, which they carry over into their new kiddiehood. (Selma Diamond's whiny, nasal rasp is a perfect match for the little girl it comes out of.) But this is a coy and twinkling piece of work. Having become children, the people can go back to their aged bodies with "fresh young minds"—like the sugarpuss minds of the moviemakers who worked on this segment? With the gloppy rich music, and what might be (laughingly) described as the ensemble acting, the tone here is sentimental-comic, and horribly slick. It's as if Steven Spielberg had sat down and thought out what he could do that would make his detractors happiest.

The third segment, directed by Joe Dante, from a script by Richard Matheson, is loosely based on the 1961 show "It's a Good Life," from a short story by Jerome Bixby. It's a risky attempt at using a style derived from animated cartoons for an insidious, expressionist effect, and after the two latent parodies it's a relief to see something that—unresolved as it is—is at least clearly and unmistakably a parody. There are so many startling good things in it—one of them is the alert, graceful Kathleen Quinlan as a strong-willed young schoolteacher—that I wish it were fully successful, but the half hour seems long. Matheson, who wrote a number of the original shows, hasn't lived up to his own formulation that "the ideal 'Twilight Zone' started with a really smashing idea that hit you right in the first few seconds; then you played that out, and you had a little flip at the end. That was the structure." There's more than one smashing idea here; there's also a misleading prelude, and then the ideas (which don't quite complement each other) pop up, hit you, and recede. No one seems to have known how to get this segment started, and it dwindles away, as if no one knew how to finish it, either. (It badly needs a little flip.) The theme is how horrible life might be if a ten-year-old boy (Jeremy Licht) could run everything just as he liked, on the basis of what he has learned from TV, and this may be too fertile a subject for the half-hour form; there are also too many different kinds of parody (mostly of television and of acting, but also of American child-centered family life) buzzing around in the material.

This Looney Tunes segment is eccentric and unsettling; it has a couple of spooky images—one of the boy's mute older sister, who has had her mouth wiped off her face (so she can't talk back to him), and one of a cartoon rabbit who is skinned and fanged. He could give you the screaming meemies. And there are some tingles. For example, we catch a glimpse of the isolated house (where most of the action takes place) in a TV cartoon, and this house—Victorian, with a parking lot—has a long hallway that's a cartoon version of the passageways in *The Cabinet of Dr. Caligari.* There may even be a tingle in the fact that Kevin McCarthy, who plays the boy's guffawing Uncle Walt, has an obvious affinity for cartoon-style acting, and his big jaw and huge teeth look just right here. And a little bell rings when we meet the boy's family, because we already know them and their double takes from the cheery, bland characters these actors have played in family-centered sitcoms; it's a while before we recognize that they're so frightened they're hysterical. The notion of the boy's controlling people and turning them into two-dimensional figures in a cartoon world is powerfully creepy; somebody has slipped acid into our lemonade. Joe Dante and his helpers (one of them is the animator Sally Cruikshank) have created an insane atmosphere, and for those people in the audience whose childhood included a TV set that was always going this half hour may reawaken all sorts of childhood feelings. Dramatically it doesn't work, but the pieces are almost all there and you can put it together afterward; it's better when you think it over than when you're watching it.

Matheson lives up to his formula for an ideal "Twilight Zone" in the fourth episode, which is a reworking of his script for the 1963 "Nightmare at 20,000 Feet," and, with the Australian George Miller (the director of *The Road Warrior*) in charge and John Lithgow as star, the result is a classic shocker of the short form—something that ranks with the Alberto Cavalcanti segment of *Dead of Night*, the one with Michael Redgrave as the ventriloquist. Miller can't get any distance from his subject: almost all the action takes place in the confines of a plane during a storm, and most of it in the tight space where Lithgow, as Valentine, is seated squirming and wriggling, sick with fear. The whole episode is about this one passenger's freaking out. (Redgrave's ventriloquist was coming apart, too, and Matheson and Miller may be paying their respects to *Dead of Night* by including among the passengers a little girl with a ventriloquist's dummy.) Working within strict spacial limits, and with Lithgow almost always on camera, Miller builds the kind of immediacy and intensity that Spielberg built at the high points of *Jaws*. Miller's images rush at you; they're fast and energizing. And it's in no sense a putdown to say that the short format is perfect for him. The mechanical virtuosity he sustains here would be too overwhelming in a full-length movie—it would seem inhuman. Here, Lithgow makes everything credible. You're never aware of his pumping himself up; hysteria seems to come naturally to him. He does something that's tough for an actor to do: he shows fear without parodying it and yet makes it horrifyingly funny to us. And when you see an actor with this kind of finesse working inside such bizarre material, the finesse itself is outlandish and makes us laugh.

John Lithgow is six foot four, and he's built large, and cuddly, like a Teddy bear. Onscreen (and on the stage, too), he has a special gift for far-out characters, such as the transsexual Roberta Muldoon in *Garp*. Lithgow domesticates flakes; he lets us observe which screws are loose and which are fixed firmly in place. Valentine, the respectable author of a book on computer microchips, is about as far out as a role can get. Valentine has been shaking too much to shave; he has soft stubble on his chin. Those who are subject to anxiety attacks may have a double anxiety attack when they recognize that an attack is starting. Valentine is soaked in cold sweat. He isn't fat, but he's fleshy, and when the sweat pours he's like an animal in terror—a baby-faced ox. And he's writhing with shame because he can't control himself. He knows that the other passengers and the stewardesses (who had to help him back to his seat after he'd panicked in the john) think he's distraught, and maybe they think he's crazy. What else would account for the squalling sounds he has been making, or the way he has been twisting himself on the tiny seat, like a human pretzel? And now, looking out his window, he thinks he sees a form outside, skittering about on the wing of the plane. Peering through the wind and the heavy, sleeting rain, he can't be sure if it's an animal or a person. The other people on the plane look where he points and see nothing. Can it be just an illusion—a projection of his fear? Abject and humiliated as he is, sedated by the head stewardess and trying to act rational, he nevertheless has a compulsion to see what's out there. He lifts his drawn window shade. The shadowy gremlin is attacking the plane, clawing at the wing and tearing out an engine.

Lithgow's performance is like a seizure; the art is in the way he orchestrates it emotionally. With his white face all scrunched up, and anxiety burning out his brain, he takes us with him every step of the way, from simple fear to dementia to stupor, and every step is funny. Valentine never stops embarrassing himself. It's a comic orgy of terror.

July 25, 1983

ANYBODY HOME?

*Z*elig, the new picture by Woody Allen, is a lovely small comedy, but it can't bear the weight of the praise being shovelled on it. If it's a masterpiece, it's a masterpiece only of its own kind; it's like an example of a nonexistent genre, or a genre from another country— something mildly eerie that feels Eastern European, about a man who's on the verge of disappearing and finally he does. Allen had a vertiginous, original idea for a casual piece, like his Madame Bovary story, and he worked it out to perfection. The film has a real shine, but it's like a teeny carnival that you may have missed—it was in the yard behind the Methodist church last week. Insignificance is even its subject.

The son of an Orthodox Jewish actor, Leonard Zelig (played by Allen) wants to be safe, accepted, liked; being a nothing himself, he takes on the characteristics of whatever strong personalities he comes in contact with. In the faddist twenties, his freakish transformations (which are beyond his conscious control) make him a celebrity—he becomes the rage. The movie, which is in the form of a documentary about Zelig, the Human Chameleon, is worked out meticulously, using trick effects that put Allen into old newsreels and stock footage, as well as into expertly faked footage that looks old. Mia Farrow, who, like Woody Allen, is seen only in simulated found bits of film, plays a young psychiatrist, Dr. Eudora Fletcher, who tries to cure Zelig, and, falling in love with him, is loyal even when the press and the public turn against him. And this mock documentary, which is an intricately layered parody, includes interviews "today" with people who knew him, including the elderly Eudora (played by Ellen Garrison), who reminisces about him, in her levelheaded way. And it has its guest-star savants. In a takeoff of *Reds*, Allen uses modern cultural figures—such as Susan Sontag, Irving Howe, Saul Bellow, Bruno Bettelheim—as "witnesses" to Zelig's career, and they each interpret that career in terms of their specialty. (A few of them are perhaps too self-aware—too smiley about satirizing their own ideas. But Woody Allen has got one thing exactly right: as soon as they talk in abstractions we tune out on what they're saying.)

The picture is thoroughly charming. It's quick and deft and it races along. I admired the delicate care with which it was made, I kept smiling happily, and I laughed out loud once, at something so silly I wasn't sure why it got to me. But when I see comparisons with *Citizen Kane* in the papers, I don't know what the writers are talking about. When you went to the movies in the pre-television days the picture would come on right after the newsreel. And at the end of the newsreel in *Citizen Kane* the picture does start up. At the end of the newsreel in *Zelig*, the picture is over. I felt good, but I was still a little hungry for a movie. There's a reason *Zelig* seems small: there aren't any characters in it, not even Zelig. It's a fantasy about being famous for being nobody. Zelig is played humbly and gracefully; Woody Allen never disrupts the movie's smooth, neutral surfaces—at times he's as meek and abashed as Stan Laurel. Even when Zelig has taken on the black skin of a jazz trumpeter, or the blubber of a fatty, or the profile of a Mohawk Indian, he isn't really strong or sure of himself. There's something frail and shy—and still—about him in any guise. He's emotionally mute.

Zelig is an end-of-the-alphabet man, the one who comes last, and he's so anonymous that he can be everywhere. He melts into any situation. Yet whether he's on the field at spring training in Florida waiting his turn at bat after Lou Gehrig and Babe Ruth, or innocently causing a fracas by showing up next to Pope Pius XI on the balcony at St. Peter's, or peeking from behind Hitler on the stage at a giant National Socialist Party rally, he's always looking into a camera, looking for himself. The movie is so densely about a man's obsession with himself—with his misfortune, his nothingness—that it's suffocatingly sad to think about. (Maybe that's why it suggests an Eastern European sensibility.) One of the newsreel announcers tells us that Zelig continues to "astound scientists" who observe his transformations, and for a while eminent doctors use him like a guinea pig; his half sister takes him away, and she and her husband put him in sideshows, exhibiting him as a freak, like the Elephant Man. We see him at one zero point when the doctors are conducting experiments on him: He's sitting by himself in a hallway, "a human cipher," eating a hard, unbuttered roll that has been handed to him. People walk past on their errands without registering his existence; he barely registers it. Woody Allen is poignant here in the way that Chaplin was often poignant, and it's creepy, because you feel that these rich, gifted, accomplished writer-director-comedians who have won their artistic freedom, who have many friends and are attractive to lovers, who are admired the world over, are showing you the truth of how at some level they still feel utterly alone and lost, like wormy nothings. And you don't know how to react to it. *Zelig* is fastidiously controlled and dry, but at the core—that lonely figure chewing dutifully, without pleasure —it's bathed in tears. Yet that, too, is presented fastidiously.

This film is an unusually gentle, modulated comedy. It could be rambunctious, what with Zelig having not just one but two ticker-tape welcomes to New York, and inspiring Jazz Age songs and dance crazes, and all of this coming to us as part of the stylized, hyperbolic past that we see in old newsreels. But Allen plays everything off against Zelig's sad nothingness. It's an ingenious stunt. Like the unbuttered-roll scene, which is totally visual (its strength comes from the placement of the walkers-by in relation to the camera), the whole movie has been thought out in terms of the film image, turning American history into slapstick by inserting this little lost sheep in a corner of the frame. (The effect is something like what you get when you read *Ragtime*.) Allen couldn't have told the story of Leonard Zelig any other way—the pathos would have been crushing. It's the fakery that dries it out and keeps it light. Zelig is always just glimpsed, and the movie darts on. It's incredibly artful; it's all touches—like the enlightened-modern-woman expression on Eudora's face as she publicly smokes a cigarette. The clothes, the paraphernalia seem exactly right yet funny—the care that has gone into the trivia is itself absurd. The movie is said to be about modern man's anxiety and his quest for identity, about conformism, the emptiness of celebrity, the fickleness of the public, etc. And it *is* about all these themes, but it's very "real"; you don't have to have read Kafka or worried about existential predicaments to get it.

Zelig has a literary precursor—Melville's Confidence Man, whose appearance also kept changing, but Zelig is the Confidence Man without a game (and without the author's passion). Zelig has relatives, too, such as Chekhov's Olga, in "The Darling," who changes to suit her husbands, and Toto, in the Zavattini–De Sica film *Miracle in Milan,* who tries to make physically afflicted people feel better by imitating their afflictions. Woody Allen's originality is in shafting the almost universally accepted idea that everyone is someone. His movie is a chiding demonstration that everyone is not someone. That's real subversion. (At least a third of all Tin Pan Alley lyrics may be shot to hell.) Allen doesn't build up any rage about it, or much hilarity, either. Even the hysteria that might be expected to accompany such drastic role confusion as Zelig's is missing; Zelig's nothingness is simply a given—an idea that Woody Allen gets to play with. And he puts it through its permutations.

At one level, the picture is a skewed fairy tale about a patient winning his shrink: she's the best person in the world, she cares for you, she's faithful to you and follows you all over the globe to help you. And the movie is at its most inventive and its wittiest, I think, when Mia Farrow's Eudora is having difficulty treating Zelig because he, with his adaptation mechanism, thinks that he, too, is a psychiatrist. She devises a strategy to get through to him. Since she cannot convince him that he isn't one, she does it indirectly—she tells him that she is a sham, an impostor, that she has been deceiving him and isn't really a psychiatrist. Zelig is visibly upset, and we see his distress as he begins to feel that he's an impostor, too. But her cleverness backfires: his only way of dealing with his agitation is to disappear.

Throughout the movie, Zelig keeps disappearing, and Woody Allen's conception of him is of a very withdrawn, recessive person. Though Eudora pursues Zelig and there's an apparently happy resolution of his troubles—he learns to use his disorder and, presumably, gains an identity—that doesn't quite jibe with what we see. Mia Farrow, perhaps the most thin-skinned of actresses—luminously so—is unearthly, weightless, a Peter Pan. She has refinement in her bones. And hand in hand she and Woody Allen play together with tactful ease. She has never seemed more finely chiselled or more beautiful, but she wears huge specs and her slender face seems to disappear behind them. She's the invisible shrink. I got the feeling that Woody Allen as director was changing her, making her more like himself—that he was making her recede. And that she, like a chameleon, was becoming as faded and indistinct as he is. But she also changes him. She doesn't challenge him (as Diane Keaton did in her pictures with him); she frees him from stress, and he comes up with fresh, delicate scenes, like the one in which, under hypnosis, he murmurs, "I love you," and then, in a whimper, "You're the worst cook . . . those pancakes. I love you . . . I want to take care of you. No more pancakes." When he's with her, they're both childlike, withdrawn, far away. The whole picture goes by so fast and the people are at such a remote distance that it seems evanescent, and though the aged Eudora is still around to be interviewed, Zelig seems to have vanished—evaporated. He should be back, though. The term "Zelig" will probably enter the language to describe all the nonpersons we meet.

Bill Miner is one of nature's noblemen. His hair and his thick mustache are turning white; his face is weathered, and his eyes are bright pale blue. They shine with joy of life, and he makes us feel that we can read his emotions in them. This is the sort of outdoors face that inspires trust, a face with "character." (It's amazing how often con artists have this clear-eyed, guileless look—it helps to account for the way voters are taken in by the snake-oil salesmen they elect to office.) *The Grey Fox* opens in 1901, when Bill Miner (Richard Farnsworth) is released after thirty-three years in San Quentin. He had been let out twice before, in 1870 and again in 1880, but had barely sniffed free air when he got into trouble again and was returned to prison, where he served his full time. (He might have been eligible for parole if he hadn't continually tried to escape.) Now he's a living anachronism, a legendary stagecoach bandit—the outlaw whom William Pinkerton, the head of the notorious agency, credited with initiating the call "Hands up!"—released into the twentieth century.

There may never have been photographs of trains more exultant than the shots here of the old Northern Pacific steaming through mountain forests. This mechanical chugging, rolling beast makes its own cloud formations as it carries Bill Miner north to the Puget Sound area to see his sister. A courteous old gentleman, Miner has no reason (yet) to hide his background, and when a fellow-passenger, a drummer selling a labor-saving gadget, a mechanical apple peeler, asks him what line he's in, he replies that he's "between jobs," and when he's asked what he did, he says, "I robbed stagecoaches."

The Grey Fox isn't a lament for the last of a breed. Miner isn't hostile to the new technology that has antiquated him—he's fascinated by it, and he buys an apple peeler. In this movie, the objects that represent twentieth-century ingenuity and "progress" are infused with the wonder they had for the people who first set eyes on them. In 1903, Miner, who has been working for a living and feeling degraded by it, as if he'd stooped beneath his class, goes into a Seattle nickelodeon and sees his first movie. It's *The Great Train Robbery,* and it transforms his life. We see the light from the screen on his face as he realizes that there is a way for him to adapt his professional expertise to the new era. One man in the theatre can't contain his enthusiasm; he's so charged up that he jumps to his feet and fires his gun. Miner's exhilaration takes a quieter form; his eyes are dancing, but he's thinking. When the picture is over, he goes directly to a store to buy a Colt revolver, and we see the gleaming dark metal as he touches it, feels its heft, spins the cylinder. The way the cinematographer, Frank Tidy, lights the Colt you see the beauty in its deadly craftsmanship. And Miner respects it as the tool of his trade; with this small, compact gun a man is grandly equipped to cry "Hands up!"

There were sixty-three train robberies recorded in the United States and Canada between 1870 and 1933. (Movies and TV have, of course, made us feel as if there were thousands.) Thirty-three of them took place before 1914—the year Bill Miner died—and he was definitely responsible for six of these, and was probably involved in a few others. He was only sixteen, in 1863, when he robbed his first Pony Express, but he was about sixty when he robbed his first train. So he had to be a busy, agile old fellow. He was also dignified and smart, and he never killed anybody. In British Columbia, where he fled after the Pinkertons got on his tail, he became a folk hero—the Gentleman Bandit, the Grey Fox. For a period, he lived there, pretending to be a mining engineer, in and around a town called Kamloops.

This first feature directed by Phillip Borsos (at twenty-seven, after a number of highly regarded documentaries) is based on a script by John Hunter that stays fairly close to the historical accounts. It concentrates on Miner's stay in Kamloops, where he came to know a cultivated woman, a free-lance photographer whose life was to be entwined with his. He's in the local newspaper office when he first sees Kate Flynn, a suffragette and "free spirit," with thick curly auburn hair that's like frazzled brain waves pushing against her ladylike big hat. She is telling off the editor for his refusal to print a letter she has written to him about women's not being paid what men are for the same jobs. At first, Jackie Burroughs, the celebrated Canadian stage actress who plays the role, is a little irritating, as if she's trying for the mannered spunk of Katharine Hepburn but is slipping down to Cloris Leachman. She very quickly— maybe it's Kate's awareness of her own foolishness, maybe it's her big, toothy, sensual smile—won me over. Also, I realized how badly the movie needs Jackie Burroughs' flamboyance—she gives it some artifice, and some musk. Richard Farnsworth, who was born in Los Angeles in 1920 (and has a definite resemblance to the actual Bill Miner), was a stuntman for more than thirty years in Hollywood, until he began to get speaking parts in the seventies—the best known is that of the arthritic ranch hand in *Comes a Horseman* who needs a kitchen chair to mount his horse. (He was recommended to the Canadians who made this movie by Coppola, and it is presented under the aegis of his Zoetrope Studios.) Farnsworth is a superb camera subject, and I don't think we ever feel that he isn't doing enough here. He has an almost lewd, secretive grin and a lulling sexual presence. He can certainly play cagey. But Jackie Burroughs is an actress and accessible; Farnsworth is an icon and inaccessible. His acting is almost all in the way he attracts the camera, and without Jackie Burroughs to spark things—the two of them do some highly photogenic flirting—the picture might be too stately. (It might, in fact, seem like a silent film.) In their first encounter, at the newspaper office, Kate exits telling the editor that he has "the mentality of a grocery clerk," and the editor proves she's on target by saying, "Nothing wrong with her a husband wouldn't fix." Actually, it's what's right with her that a man would probably try to fix, and though Miner's eyes glisten in response to her anger at social injustice, when they become lovers she is more subdued (which seems to prove the editor right), and her role diminishes. The picture could have used more of her warmth, and additional scenes between the two. One problem: the scriptwriter doesn't fill in the historical gaps in Miner's life, so we never find out how he became this civilized, sensitive man or a lover who would appreciate this free-thinking woman. Even plot points—such as how the Pinkertons track him to Kamloops—aren't filled in.

Though the influence of *The Great Train Robbery* in altering the course of Miner's life is just an entertaining supposition—and I rather doubt if the canny Bill Miner we see here needed a movie to show him the true path—Borsos returns to footage from it toward the end of *The Grey Fox*, when a pursuit scene from the 1903 film (shot in the forests of New Jersey) is intercut with Miner's attempted escape from a posse. I think it's too obtrusive a device; it interposes the filmmakers' intentions between us and the story, and it turns *The Grey Fox* into some sort of mystical tribute to movie mythology and the photographic image (though the scenes from *The Great Train Robbery* are run in wide-screen). It's almost as if Borsos and his collaborators were saluting themselves. But I doubt if any of this really bothers anybody, because there's so much to look at.

Frank Tidy, who is British, has the cinematographer's credit on Ridley Scott's *The Duellists*, and his work here is equally spectacular. This picture has the most lovingly photographed rain since *McCabe & Mrs. Miller*, and there are wonderful scenes with snow on frozen dark-green grass. The images are dense and ceremonious. Even the extras and bit players have the air of awkward formality that we associate with an earlier era; the men got up in old Mounties uniforms stand stiffly, as if the coarse wool were itching them. The actress who plays the sister isn't well directed, and her plucked eyebrows may make you think of a "What's wrong with this picture?" contest. And Jackie Burroughs wears modern eye makeup with her period clothes. But the whole movie has a sense of occasion. As a Western, it isn't as much fun as last year's *Barbarosa*; it isn't fulfilled dramatically. But then it isn't exactly a Western. Borsos replaces the familiar landscapes of Hollywood Westerns with his own interpretation of the Pacific Northwest. The story of the "badman" is told by means of historical facsimiles and through the use of authentic-looking locations that suggest the damp chill of the British angry-young-working-class-hero films circa 1960. The shots often have the stabbing eloquence of old photographs—especially those of starved, underpaid workers.

Unlike the conventional Western, *The Grey Fox* gives honest hard work a bad name. When Miner reaches the farm of his sister and her husband, he earns his keep by picking oysters from the Puget Sound mud flats, and it's bleak drudgery. You feel as if the row of rain-soaked pickers must have chilblains right through to their souls. And each job Miner gets is grinding misery; the employers are mean, petty exploiters, cheating their workers in every way they can. When the Kamloops police corporal (Timothy Webber) asks Kate Flynn to take a picture, it's of the slaughtered family of a Chinese worker—presumably he couldn't feed them and killed them to end their suffering. (The movie is like the book

Wisconsin Death Trip with a romantic bandit as its center.) Miner acquires the confederates he needs for his holdups as if he were bestowing the gift of independence on them. After a robbery, Shorty (Wayne Robson), a stumpy little boozer Miner has liberated from exploitation in a lumber mill, can't believe his luck—he's got real money, even if they have to bury it for a while. Much of the movie is tinged with irony, but Borsos might be a left-wing rhapsodist with flowers blossoming from his temples. He puts a gold frame around Bill Miner without revealing a thing about him. Borsos himself seems to be taken in by the nobility of Miner's countenance; this old robber looks courtly even when he's stealing a farmer's horse—his manner suggests regret at the incivility of his action. In this movie, robbery is the only honorable profession for a man of style. Borsos appears to have a dandy's approach to crime and injustice, but he's an inspired image-maker. *The Grey Fox* somehow manages to be an art Western without making you hate it.

August 8, 1983

FRAMED

Set on an idyllic English estate in the summer of 1694, *The Draughtsman's Contract* was written and directed by Peter Greenaway, a British filmmaker whose previous work was in non-narrative forms, and though he's working with narrative here, the film is a formalist tease—a fantasia of conceits about perspective, and about the relationship between the artist, his art, and the world. The artist in this case is a punctilious draughtsman, Mr. Neville (Anthony Higgins), who lives in one manor house after another, producing, for the owners, a series of topographical drawings of their holdings. The matronly Mrs. Herbert (Janet Suzman) requests him to come to the Herbert estate to do twelve drawings in twelve days as a present for her husband (who will be off whoring in Southampton). Mr. Neville demurs, but she presses him and he accepts her offer—on condition that he will have "the use" of her body. She agrees, and the contract is drawn up and signed. Upon his arrival, he takes out his optical grid and, looking through the attached view-finder (as if he were a movie director), selects his twelve vistas of the house and grounds, and orders that on the appointed days these views be kept free of intrusion. But when he sits down to work, unexpected objects—a ladder, a shirt, a pair of boots—keep marring his line of vision. Annoyed at these blemishes on his chosen landscapes, he includes them in the drawings anyway—out of a mixture of literal-mindedness and pique. The film is designed so that we keep comparing Neville's drawings of the grounds with the photographic images of those grounds, and there's a definite suggestion of Antonioni's *Blow-Up* in the mysterious blots, which, it turns out, are evidence of the murder of the absent Mr. Herbert—evidence that points to the draughtsman, the arrogant plebeian outsider, as the murderer.

The movie is a lesson for (or a joke on) the draughtsman, who, limited to his single perspectives, isn't aware of what's going on. Neither—for quite a stretch—is the audience. The beginning is a Hogarthian vaudeville show—it's a series of comedy blackouts—and although a number of clues are planted in the prissy-mouthed, cadenced speeches about defecation and other cloacal concerns, we're not likely to register the import of what is being said. The speeches are so arch and twitty they seem to be pitched higher than a dog whistle, and the people talking are popinjays in perukes shaped as geometrically as the shrubs at Marienbad. If *Last Year at Marienbad* had been directed by Joseph Losey, it might have been much like this movie, which sits on the screen like an implacable pastry. After it's over, you may not find it difficult to piece together the rough outlines of what Peter Greenaway is doing, but while you're watching it you may be too busy fighting off sleep to care. What kept me awake was the fun of seeing perhaps a third of the audience slumbering so peacefully. (It's in an East Side art house—nobody snores.) It seemed to me that people took their little sabbaticals at four or five distinct times; they didn't miss anything vital. *The Draughtsman's Contract* puts you in a narcoleptic trance even if you're paying attention. Some of its idiosyncrasies may sound amusing—for example, there's a naked man jumping about from one pedestal to another, serving (as I have read that some men actually did serve in the period) as a living statue. But Greenaway's impishness congeals, because there's no dramatic motor in the sequences. A movie for him is a set of theorems to be demonstrated by

32

tableaux. His mind may be active, but his camera is dead, and so are his actors.

If this stultifying picture is being received with the kind of respectful seriousness that marked the reception of some of Losey's films (such as *The Go-Between*), it may be because audiences can see it as a revelation of the disgusting true natures of the landed gentry, and because it makes everything to do with sex ugly. There must be junkies for English-upper-class movies (just as there are Nazi-movie junkies)—people who want to see over and over again the gardens, the halls, the finery, and the politesse, and, of course, the poisonous, warped behavior. Nobody has put together a more vicious, dispassionate crew of schemers than the unproductive bunch at the Herbert establishment; their everyday life is like a weekend in the country, and they expend their small energy plotting—they don't intend to lose an ounce of their privileges. The men's faces are powdered to match their wigs, and their costumes are so stiff and ornate I kept expecting the actors and the costumes to disassociate and go their own ways. Mrs. Herbert and her daughter, Mrs. Talmann (Anne Louise Lambert), who draws up her own sexual contract, wear towering headpieces that look like skyscrapers designed in old Cathay. There's an element of class revenge when the draughtsman, who is garlanded in a wig of lavish black curls that puts Loretta Lynn to shame, orders Mrs. Herbert to assume the positions that he requires for whatever means of access strikes his whim. He pulls her heavy brocades open contemptuously in one scene, and the poker-faced woman may stir an empathic reaction when she comes back to her chambers after a session with him, gagging. Intercourse has nothing to do with pleasure here: it's about who is using whom—it's about power. And the foolish young Mr. Neville mistakenly thinks he has some.

The women stoop beneath their class because they're trying to hang on to their property. Mrs. Talmann hopes to produce a male heir and save the estate from being managed by her fool of a husband. In this movie, as in so many other movies with an ideological slant, the poor are potent, the rich desiccated. The virile artist, Mr. Neville, will be used, and then punished for his effrontery. Since the characters are stylized monsters, it's startling when Greenaway lets this victimization fantasy go the full masochistic course. The reprisals against Mr. Neville are very fast and brutal, and the sudden burst of Jacobean violence disrupts the film's attempt at Restoration-comedy artifice. The violence seems to be saying, "Did you think all this was only a game?" Of course we did, because, despite the lurking seriousness, Greenaway's tone was so superior. Now he switches to "realism"—a move you might have thought beneath him.

What's beneath him from beginning to end is, apparently, the whole idea of motivation. By having all the characters involved in Mr. Neville's entrapment, he ducks out on solving the murder mystery of who killed Mr. Herbert and who hatched the plot against the draughtsman. Greenaway simply pins it all on the rotten upper class.

Underneath this film's mannerisms and hauteur, it's a very conventional, calculating movie. The surface, though, may seem closely related to painting and to literature. You stare at fixed views of English gardens and listen to remarks that sound as if the characters had rehearsed them all day. And when Greenaway wants to introduce symbolic objects—first a pomegranate and then a pineapple—the characters underline the symbolism. (Mr. Neville is offered what must be the most significant pineapple since the Twyla Tharp dance film *The Catherine Wheel*.) And precise explicit social chatter is now highly valued by educated moviegoers; the audience often perks up when characters talk like books. Eric Rohmer has prepared the way, but he's light-years away from *this* stuff. With Rohmer, you don't feel the chill of a metaphysician breathing down your neck.

Greenaway (who himself did the drawings) presents the draughtsman as a lover of landscape who is attacked and destroyed by those who love only property. If Greenaway doesn't show Mr. Neville so much as a twinge of sympathy, this may be because he believes he's subverting bourgeois aesthetics by not allowing his characters any emotions beyond vanity, greed, pettishness, and lust. Subversive or not, there's an honorable tradition behind this approach to character. But if you see a production of *Volpone* you know what Ben Jonson is getting at; there's nothing abstract about it. With Greenaway, you have to contend with so many kinds of abstraction that there's no human comedy left in the material; he has deliberately squeezed it dry. Yet there's no clarity in the abstractions, either. When we see the landscapes through the metal grid, the effect is perfectly pleasant, but no big perceptions jump to mind. What the movie has to say about art and framing doesn't add up to anything overwhelming. You can *get The Draughtsman's Contract* and still feel that *getting* it isn't enough.

□

A friend of mine does a great Sylvester Stallone—he does Stallone reciting Edgar Allan Poe's "The Raisin." What can be done about

34

this mock writer-director-producer-actor? He has become the stupidos' Orson Welles. Stallone turns everything into a fight, and *Staying Alive*, his sequel to John Badham's *Saturday Night Fever* (1977), with John Travolta once again playing the dancer Tony Manero from Brooklyn's Bay Ridge, is a weirdly stripped-down-for-action musical. Stallone doesn't bother much with characters, scenes, or dialogue, and he runs out of story in the first eight minutes. He just puts the newly muscle-plated Travolta in front of the cameras, covers him with what looks like oil slick, and goes for the whambams. The publicity has centered on Stallone's remaking of Travolta's body—getting him to pump iron and develop a chest that's a modified version of his own. (What for? Dancers don't need the big, body builders' muscles that Travolta has now. What would they do with them—lift ten-ton ballerinas?) I didn't know there was that much the matter with Travolta's body. He looked pretty jazzy coming down the street in *Saturday Night Fever*, and he wasn't a bad disco hoofer. Now that he's all built up, he doesn't do any dance numbers that we might enjoy—he's too busy spinning and prancing in split-second flashes to music that's trying to pound the audience into submission. Travolta still has his star presence; he holds the screen more strongly than ever —but too flagrantly, because Stallone doesn't give the other performers a chance. Stallone has somehow projected his own narcissism on Travolta, who's in danger of turning into a laughingstock if he doesn't put some clothes on and stop posing for magazine covers as though it were Hiawatha Night at the O.K. Corral.

Staying Alive, in which Tony gets his big break and becomes a Broadway dancing star, is a cross between *Flashdance* and *Rocky III*. But, in their own sleazo ways, those movies work—*Staying Alive* doesn't. (It works only at the box office.) Stallone is lazy: he doesn't pilfer from out-of-the-way places. He stays on the main road from *All That Jazz* via *A Chorus Line*, and on to *Fame*. And his repertory of gimmicks is so limited that each of his *Rocky* movies has essentially been a remake, while several sequences here are like homages to dear *Rocky*. There's a single good idea in the movie—but, maddeningly, it isn't developed. Tony has an only modestly gifted dancer girlfriend, who works as a chorus girl; waiting for her backstage, he watches a woman dancer (Finola Hughes), the British star of the show, and is awed by the woman's artistry. He's suddenly hit by the aphrodisiac qualities of talent and success; his eyes light up with excitement, and he tries to get to know her. Since he's still struggling to become an artist, it makes perfect sense that he would be drawn to other artists—it's evidence of the depth of his commitment. Mediocrity would be a horrible thing to a man trying

35

to become as good as he possibly could. But Stallone proceeds to turn the woman artist into a condescending, promiscuous rich bitch. (Her skyscraper apartment is a deluxe lair where she seethes venomously.) This way, Stallone can stick to his *Rocky* formula: the hero and the heroine must both be underdogs. Tony must learn to appreciate the qualities of his over-devoted, hardworking Jackie (rhymes with "lackey"), who is modelled on Rocky's ever-loyal Adrian. Jackie is played very appealingly by Cynthia Rhodes, who has a velvety singing voice, and I kept waiting for Tony to notice that if Jackie wasn't a great dancer she could at least sing. But Stallone seems fixated on the idea that a driven good-Catholic boy like Tony (who wears a king-size cross around his neck) needs an untalented woman. The details are equally repugnant. For example, a slinky, metallic *zhoom* sound whooshes across the pulsating track now and then; it turns up first with Bob Mackie's credit for some of the costumes—the S-M tatters worn in the Hell scenes near the end. And it isn't enough for Stallone to do a Hitchcock-like appearance, bumping into Tony on a city street—he has Tony recognize him and do a double take.

Julie Bovasso, who once again plays Tony's mother, has a couple of remarkable moments. She seems almost to have internalized Travolta's face, and in one scene she and Tony, whose self-esteem is at a low point, sit very quietly facing each other across the kitchen table, and they are uncannily alike—mother and son, with matching anxious eyes. There's a suggestion of a Samuel Beckett character in her despairing silence. In another scene, Julie Bovasso, sitting in the theatre on the opening night of Tony's Broadway show—*Satan's Alley*—delivers a dumb line with such pure, innocent surprise that she makes us laugh despite the awful numbers from the show that we have been watching. *Satan's Alley*, which is supposed to catapult Tony to stardom, is so close to the modern-day *Faust* that is parodied in *The Band Wagon* that I waited for the famous shot of that *Faust* laying an enormous egg, just before the audience emerged ashen-faced, as if stricken by a wasting disease. But Sylvester Stallone imagines that his vision of the sweaty agonies of Hell, staged in a cellblock socked in by what looks like heavy ground fog, is a triumph. We in the movie audience are stricken, all right, but luckily we get a last-minute reprieve: about two minutes of Travolta on the street moving to the "Stayin' Alive" music from *Saturday Night Fever*. If it weren't for that, I don't know whether audiences would have the strength to crawl out of the theatre.

Stallone was born too late and has missed his vocation. If the studio system were still in operation, he could be the man in charge of transformations. Whenever the studios wanted to punish a star, they could give him to Stallone. A Timothy Hutton might emerge as the Incredible Hulk; Sissy Spacek might be built up to be a dominatrix like Lisa Lyon and scare us all.

August 22, 1983

SEX AND POLITICS

A moviegoer can vegetate fairly comfortably at Eric Rohmer's innocuous sex roundelay *Pauline at the Beach*. Rohmer's psychological observations are so precise and tiny and he is so distanced from his six characters that the film has a cooling effect. There's no danger here of not understanding everything the six are up to. Rohmer doesn't just show you—he also tells you. In fact, he tells you more than he shows you. You listen to the chat or read the subtitles, and feel "civilized."

Rohmer has an amazing gift for finding (or creating) actors who embody the observations that he wants to make, and, with the help of the cinematographer Nestor Almendros, he establishes a loose, summery atmosphere that the characters fit right into. (The lighting is the best work by Almendros that I've seen in several years.) The six convey a sense of ordinary, ongoing life. The belle of the beach, the voluptuous blond fashion designer Marion (Arielle Dombasle—she was the heroine's friend in *Le Beau Mariage*), is a self-centered divorcée with an unpleasant tinkle in her voice. She seems to take pleasure in her own affectations —she flirts coyly, touching her face and shoulder with a fluttering hand as she talks of wanting to "burn with love." Rohmer tells us what he thinks of her by showing her walking away from the camera in a tight, wet silver-gray bathing suit that's squeezing her: she's Venus with rear cleavage.

The fatuous Marion does her burning with Henri (Féodor Atkine), a tall, suave, fortyish stud who's like a slinkier Trintignant with the high-cheekboned sexual arrogance of a Yul Brynner. He's amused when she lands in his bed on their first date. (The next day, she once again walks away from the camera—this time her bottom is center screen.) Henri is impressed by her beauty but sees through her pretensions— she's of purely transient interest to him. Pierre (Pascal Greggory), a handsome blond wind-surfer, has known Marion for years; he thinks that he has earned her love by his devotion, and he can't understand why he has never got very far with her. He hangs around her like a puppy playing guard dog. She urges him to date Pauline (Amanda Langlet), her dark-eyed, fifteen-year-old cousin, who has been put in her charge for a few weeks, and she advises Pauline to gain some sexual experience by going out with him, but Pauline finds a boyfriend on her own—Sylvain (Simon de la Brosse), who is about her age—and without any ado they become lovers.

The incident that creates the bedroom-farce misunderstandings is a casual sexual matinée. While Henri is in his bedroom with a sexy work-ing-class girl—a candy seller from the beach (played by an actress known simply as Rosette)—Sylvain dashes upstairs to warn him that Marion is on her way. Trying to spare Marion any humiliation, and hoping to avoid a bad scene, Henri pushes the candy girl and Sylvain into the bathroom. When Marion sees them, she assumes that the matinée has been theirs, and eventually, through Pierre's self-righteous snitch-ing, Pauline hears of it and is wounded.

We know what Rohmer thinks of Pauline—her bathing suit fits her nymphet behind snugly, with nary a wrinkle or a crease. Pauline is natural and truthful; she hasn't learned adult subterfuges. The film begins with a French proverb translated as "A wagging tongue bites itself," and Pauline, who is the moral center of the movie, doesn't carry tales. She listens to Marion deceiving herself and switching from one attitude to another as she tries to manipulate Henri. Pauline takes in what people say and what they do; she doesn't add to the talk with what she has heard. Rohmer treats the lovemaking of Pauline and Sylvain as pure and uncorrupted. And now the selfish adults, with their stupid games, have spoiled this playful, perfect first love.

Rohmer serves it all up with exquisite control—all the low-key con-versations and the soft sounds of the wind and of steps on gravel. The nuances seem exactly right: there's a thin veneer of chic over everybody, and nothing looks forced, though I wish that Henri didn't have to spell out the limitations of Marion's physical attraction and explain that he found the fuddlebrained candy girl sexier. But does anybody who isn't a senile sentimentalist really believe in these "natural" adolescents who go to bed together without a stab of fear or self-consciousness—without even any coaxing or promises or pimples? Rohmer's adults delude themselves; his children see clearly. Their love is a state of grace from which adults fall away. *Pauline at the Beach* is frivolous, yet it has this phony moral built into it. And people in the crowded theatre chuckle their approval of Rohmer's wisdom. They seem to accept his judgment of the characters. I don't think I've ever before seen a director score points with an audience by treating a mature beauty's curvy behind as vulgar and a pubescent, undeveloped girl's behind as the ideal. The movie is a daisy chain woven by a prig. The little girl is our moral instructor.

□

For about the first fifteen minutes, *Risky Business* has a lively, off-beat quality. At seventeen, Joel Goodsen (Tom Cruise), a virginal and not too smart high-school senior, is equally worried about what college he'll get into and when and how he'll make out with a girl. His parents go off on a week's vacation, and he's left alone in their expensive ersatz-Colonial house on the North Shore of Chicago. Goaded by a schoolmate, he phones for the services of a call girl named Lana (Rebecca De Mornay). Up until her arrival, Joel is desperate, horny, and ingratiating—especially when he dances by himself to a Bob Seger record. Imagining himself a rock star dancing, he's a charmingly clunky dynamo. (At times, he's like a shorter Christopher Reeve, and the film seems to be raising the question "Can nice boys be sexy?") But once Lana glides in, murmuring, "Are you ready for me?," the movie shifts into an enamelled dream-time in which this flowerlike young call girl gives the kid sinfully sweet erotic satisfaction and helps him make a pile of money besides. The picture becomes visually glib and so smooth that at first I assumed it would all turn out to be a joke—I waited for Joel to wake up. After a while, I waited for the writer-director, Paul Brickman, to wake up. But this languorous, glossy professionalism—mated to jangling electronic mood music by Tangerine Dream—was apparently what he was after. From Lana's entrance to the end, the film keeps its creamy-dreamy soft-core porno look, and everything is dark and slightly unreal.

Risky Business aims to be hypnotically sexy, but it's overdeliberate and vacuous. Directing his first feature, Brickman (who wrote *Citizens Band* and the forthcoming *Deal of the Century*) is a control freak. He makes Lana's scenes with Joel as much of a turn-on as he can without actually showing anything anatomical (he might have set out to top *Body Heat* in this), but there are no incidental pleasures in *Risky Business*—there's nothing but the one thin situation. It's all Joel's rite of passage into hipness; he grows up sexually, and financially, too, when Lana turns him into a pimp and his home into a bordello for one big, lucrative night. He has been attending a seminar workshop on free enterprise; Lana makes an entrepreneur out of him. The film's point of view is that Lana's whoring is a hot girl's practical and honest approach to business, that her street-smart materialism is cleaner than the snobbish, hypocritical materialism of Joel's parents: the father with his punctiliousness about his platinum Porsche, the mother with her panicky fears about her dumb bric-a-brac, and both with their anxiety about their son's getting into the "right" (i.e., Ivy League) school, so he'll be on the path to success.

There's a stale cuteness in the idea; it's like a George Bernard Shaw play rewritten for a cast of ducks and geese. Joel gets to fulfill his daydreams about having sex and making money, and Paul Brickman gets to fulfill his daydream about making what he probably regards as a serious satirical comment on American affluence. Joel becomes an Example, and he loses whatever likability he had as a goofball kid; Cruise isn't allowed enough emotions to sustain the performance. Joel's schoolmates are similarly drained of personality (when they play cards they're just junior versions of their fathers, and that seems funny until you realize that the film means to indict them for it), and his parents never had any. The Goodsens are an upper-middle-class Jewish family who are like Wasps, only more so. The exteriors were shot at a Highland Park house just around the block from the one used in *Ordinary People*.

The only person in the movie who is left with any trace of individuality is Rebecca De Mornay's purringly seductive Lana—a vision created out of men's desires, yet distinctive, too. She's mysterious, supple—a golden blonde with an inward-directed smile, like Veronica Lake, but taller and with a greater range of expressiveness. This young actress has an original way of playing a prostitute. Her face never opens up to Joel or to us. She's calculating; she has something going on in her head beyond what she's saying—she might be thinking of the move after the next move. Somehow, Rebecca De Mornay—this is her first major screen role—makes the coolheadedness that Brickman has written into the character seem bewitching. But, of course, Brickman never takes Lana out of fantasyland; she isn't permitted to emerge as a character—she has no motives or feelings beyond what serves his purpose. Lana has to be a sensuous creature who enjoys her work, and prostitution here isn't a sad, rotten business—it's just a shade "risky." The picture is centered on this tiresome lie, which appears to satisfy some deep vanity in men. It's one of the invincible lies that keep going so long they gather moss and turn into fables.

During the past few weeks, the book *The Rosenberg File*, by Ronald Radosh and Joyce Milton, has been widely reviewed by people who expressed surprise that the authors came to the conclusion that Julius and Ethel Rosenberg were indeed guilty of conspiring to give atomic-bomb information to the Soviet Union but that their execution, on June 19, 1953, was a terrible injustice. This conclusion is now being discussed in the press as if it were something totally new—as if people in the fifties, governed by their political prejudices, believed the Rosenbergs to be either spies who deserved to die or innocent martyrs. I went to my bookcase, and within ten minutes I had found essays on the Rosenbergs by three writers—Harold Rosenberg, in *The Tradition of the New*, Robert Warshow, in *The Immediate Experience*, and Leslie Fiedler, in *An End to Innocence*—all dating from the early fifties and all saying substantially the same thing as the Radosh and Milton book. Harold Rosenberg wrote, "What shocked fair-minded people was the objective factor of the disproportion between the crime as charged, and for which the defendants were convicted, and the death penalty. . . . Granted that the Rosenbergs were justly convicted, and I don't question that, they did not seem to deserve the electric chair." And these writers showed an understanding of the manipulative possibilities in the case. These are Warshow's calm opening words, written in 1953: "Julius and Ethel Rosenberg were not put to death for their opinions, but from their side, clearly, they died for their opinions nevertheless. And not only did they choose to give up their lives: each sacrificed the other, and both together sacrificed their two young children." And Leslie Fiedler wrote of the contrast between the Rosenberg case that came to trial early in 1951 and the symbolic, propagandistic Rosenberg case that got its start in the Communist press later that year, in which the couple were depicted as the victims of a frameup because they were "progressives" and Jews. Soon they were discussed all over the world as political prisoners and compared to Dreyfus, Sacco and Vanzetti, and the Scottsboro Boys.

41

The new movie *Daniel,* directed by Sidney Lumet, from E. L. Docto-row's script based on his 1971 novel *The Book of Daniel,* is about that symbolic Rosenberg case. It was clear from the quasi-modernist novel that Doctorow wasn't naïve about the Rosenbergs but that he was let-ting himself go emotionally—that he loved the energy and anguish that Jewish persecution stirred in him. And he went right for the torn, bleed-ing heart of the matter: the novel centers on the emotions of the two young children orphaned by the electric chair and (less powerfully) their struggles as adults to come to terms with their political legacy. The book is an upsettingly personal fantasy that plugs right into the persecution fears and victimization fantasies that the case excited—particularly among American Jews but also among much of the gentile left. Docto-row's book is so charged with painful feelings that it's sadistic to the reader. He uses the Rosenbergs' deaths to fire his furnace. It's a mussy, mixed-up, passionate book—demagogic and harrowing.

The movie is all those things, too, except it's not passionate, and so it doesn't carry you along. Whenever Sidney Lumet gets into one of his chronicles of agonized morality—such as *Prince of the City* (1981) or *The Verdict* (1982)—it seems as if his normally high energy level sinks, and the melodramatic materials he's working with thicken and become clotted. *The Verdict* at least followed a relatively straight line, but *Daniel* jumps back and forth among four decades shot in slightly differ-ent color ranges, and nothing takes hold now or then or in between. It's one of the most emotionally fragmented films I've ever seen. Or didn't quite see. For Lumet, chiaroscuro appears to be a sign of seriousness; everyone lives in the dark. Lumet is once again working with the Polish cinematographer Andrzej Bartkowiak. The two of them received consid-erable praise for the "Caravaggio" lighting of *The Verdict*—but why should anyone want to do a modern courtroom drama in Caravaggio tones? *The Verdict* was dim and looked posed. This picture often looks plain ugly, as if there were barnacles on the lens; even when the action is outdoors, it has the gummy drabness of institutional life.

Daniel—in which Timothy Hutton plays the title character, the son of the "Isaacsons," and Amanda Plummer plays his driven-mad younger sister, Susan—is meant to take its form from Daniel's quest for the meaning of his dead parents' lives. He has jeered at his sister's political activism and has become a rigid, tight academic—a graduate student at Columbia who even gives his young wife a bad time. Disliking himself, he goes back over the events of his childhood, hunting down people who were involved in the Isaacson case, and asking questions. But this doesn't provide any impetus to the scenes, because it isn't clear what he hopes to find out. He never asks the straightforward question "Were my parents spies or weren't they?" And so he never gets to the question "If they were spies, how was it that they were fooled into thinking that what they were doing was for the good of mankind?" The movie doesn't move —it agglomerates. The hollow quest is carefully rigged with digressions and overcomplicated by narrative devices. As if the material weren't agonizing enough, from time to time we get Daniel in closeup—sometimes just his eyes and nose and nose hair filling the screen—as he narrates gory particulars of the different means of execution that have been used in various countries throughout history. (You can bet that drawing and quartering gets its full share of attention.) We also see perhaps half a dozen sequences with the actors in dumb show, their arms waving like semaphores, while Paul Robeson's voice rolls across the soundtrack in songs that have been selected for their special relevance to what Daniel sees or remembers as he crisscrosses the country. It is a secret rarely let out: rich as Paul Robeson's voice was, he was a very monotonous singer. These songs all sound the same. (And boy, could this movie use something jazzy to pace it.)

As the sister, Amanda Plummer is photographed cruelly. She seems sallow and shrivelled and rodentlike in her initial scene; I could hardly look at her, and I barely registered what she was saying. But her words were repeated in a voice-over a little later, and I was struck by how eerily delicate her vocal rhythms were. In her second scene, I was prepared for the way she was photographed, and she seemed to transcend it—she brings a lyrical, otherworldly intensity to Susan's madness. The other performances range from Lindsay Crouse's fine, strong Mrs. Isaacson to Mandy Patinkin's grotesquely hyper Isaacson. I don't know what Lindsay Crouse is playing—Doctorow doesn't create characters; he has his own patented cutouts—but she plays well. She's a flesh-and-blood presence, and she's convincing as a politically involved woman of her time. Even her accent seems right. Patinkin, though, is like a crazily overenthusiastic football coach; a lot of the time, the camera seems much too close for what he's doing, and at other times we simply have no preparation for his manic cavorting. Hutton, meanwhile, grows ever hairier. He's swathed in so much beard that the only feature he has left to act with is his pretty blue eyes, and they become a little disconcerting, because they don't quite match up with the eyes of the various little kids who play Daniel in the earlier decades. (As an infant, Daniel looks as if he'd grow up to be Charles Laughton.) It's terrible to pick at details like this, but the movie is so unwieldy and so many platforms are mounted that details may be all you actually take in.

There are large quantities of performers in this movie. Ellen Barkin, for example, turns up as Daniel's wife and makes a striking impression in her few minutes of screen time. She fares better than most of the other women playing Jewish roles; the middle-class characters, in particular (such as Carmen Matthews, as the defense attorney's wife, and Maria Tucci, as Daniel and Susan's foster mother), are subjected to brutal long takes in which they expose their cold, ungenerous natures —they're like spiders presiding over their dark apartments. Mostly, we get a flash of the actors, perhaps in a closeup; then they'll turn up in a scene or two, and disappear. And it's impossible to know why they're in the movie. The only time we know for sure is when they're black, because then they're there to display their nobility and the Isaacsons' love of them—as when Mrs. Isaacson embraces a black prison matron before sitting down in the big chair. Her last act on earth is thus a demonstration of solidarity. What will people who don't know anything about the Rosenberg case and haven't read the novel make of the movie? If they get anything at all, it will probably be the idea that the Rosenbergs were killed because they were Jewish and because they believed in social justice. Social justice is what their spiritually reborn son commits himself to at the end, when he and his wife and baby boy take part in a peace rally. This is his parents' legacy to him. It's almost a sick joke, considering that it was the Rosenbergs' fervid dedication to principle that made them susceptible to Soviet manipulation. (There's another—even sicker —joke here: the rally footage is from the June 12, 1982, disarmament gathering. The parents gave the bomb to the Russians, and the son protests its use.)

The movie comes to us with all sorts of disclaimers in the press: Lumet says that it isn't about the Rosenbergs, that it's the story of the "thawing" of Daniel, who "buried himself with his parents—froze emotionally, intellectually." And this, I think, is supposed to exempt *Daniel* —which, of course, *is* about the Rosenbergs, and uses them to trigger viewer responses—from the obligation to make sense of the material. It was always possible to be sane about the case—as the Radosh and Milton book is, and as the writers I cited and many other people were at the time—but not if you saw the Rosenbergs as innocent martyrs to the cause of social justice. That is, however, the easiest way to get a response. *Daniel* isn't interested in sorting things out. Its confusion feeds a strain of public hysteria and a fear of anti-Semitism. Poor Mandy Patinkin—one moment he's lifting his arms in a dance, as if he were getting ready to play Tevye in *Fiddler on the Roof,* and not long afterward he's being strapped in the chair, and the juice comes on and his body is rattling. Then Lindsay Crouse goes through her strapping in and rattling, but she's got more life in her than he does, and she needs more juice. She has got to rattle again. Is there any purpose in this except to make Jewish audiences quake and weep and feel helpless?

September 5, 1983

A BAD DREAM/A MASTERPIECE

Coming right after Jean-Jacques Beineix's directing-début film *Diva*, *The Moon in the Gutter* may be a shock, but it's the kind of excruciatingly silly movie that only a talented director can make. (Hacks don't leave common sense this far behind.) The trashy chic of Delacorta's novel *Diva* (which was written like a script) gave Beineix something to play with. This time, he takes the 1953 American novel *The Moon in the Gutter*, by David Goodis, as the basis for a romanticized tragic vision. With Gérard Depardieu in the frayed T-shirt of a poor, honest working-man and Nastassia Kinski in spangles "created by Marc Bohan for Christian Dior," and the two of them gazing soulfully at each other across a chasm of class distinctions, the picture cries out for giggles and hoots. Yet Beineix's damn talent gets in the way, so you can't even have a good time razzing it.

The opening words of the narrator are enough to give you a premonitory pang: "In a port nowhere in particular, in a dead end in the dockside area, a man came nightly to escape his memories." This man —he's a stevedore—is called Gérard, and that's the only simplifying step Beineix permits himself. Gradually, we pick up the idea that Gérard is obsessed with the death of his sister, who killed herself after she was raped. It takes a long time to get the reason for his moping straight, because the images of his sister traipsing along at night in the water-front area in spiky high heels and a starlet's shimmery wisp of a gown certainly don't suggest the pure, virginal girl he talks about, the one who took her own life because she felt defiled. (Beineix doesn't seem to have much interest in representational details.) For most of the movie, Gérard lunges from table to table in a waterfront dive that features two haglike painted whores out of the Expressionist past dancing together, and he stares meaningfully into the faces of drunken men who he imagines might be the rapist. Two of the prime suspects appear to be his father and his brother, so naturally we begin to think that there's some Freudian hanky-panky going on: Was Gérard himself in love with his sister? Is he himself the criminal he seeks? The way Beineix works here, it's not for him to show us what's going on—it's for us to wonder. In an interview in *Film Comment,* Beineix explains Gérard's swinish, slobby brother (played by Dominique Pinon, the small blond killer in *Diva* who looks like a mutant) and Gérard's besotted father (Gabriel Monnet) in these terms: "The character of the brother stands for the *idea* of a brother, and that of the father for Father, rather than his own parent." Put that in your pipe and smoke it.

Gérard also has a standard-issue fiery, tempestuous, but loving girlfriend, Bella (Victoria Abril), who, through a quirk of casting, has a black mother (Bertice Reading). The role of Bella was initially scheduled to be played by the black American actress Diahnne Abbott, and that probably accounts for the black mother; presumably, when Beineix re-cast the role he was carried away by his idea of an indefinite, universal place inhabited by people of unspecified backgrounds and didn't think mother and daughter needed to match up. It may also come as a surprise to the audience that a stevedore who goes to work on the docks every day is so poor and deprived that he lives in a decorator shanty—it's rag-strewn, with what might be burlap sacks dangling from the walls. Gérard and Bella and their relatives are the lower-depths poor, doomed to live in crumbling hovels. The rich moon-goddess Kinski, who has the bewildering Anglo-Saxon name Loretta Channing, lives "uptown," in a sumptuous mansion, with her dissolute-dude brother, Newton Channing (Vittorio Mezzogiorno). Loretta has glazed, zombie eyes, and she may be Gérard's wish fulfillment. She doesn't talk like a person—she talks like the essence of femme fatale. She seems to come from the world of the movies, by way of Coppola's *One from the Heart,* and this has to be deliberate.

Beineix takes movie conventions and clichés of the past as iconography and creates a fake-poetic world for himself. If we supply the name Marseilles for his stylized nameless port, it's because it's based on the Marseilles of the French films of the thirties, just as the decent, trapped

Gérard is based, primarily, on the decent, trapped Jean Gabin of those films. Gérard is an ordinary "little" man reaching (hopelessly) for the moon. He and the other characters come from movies processed by Beineix's memories and imagination. They're movie myths masquerading as mysterious characters. And so they don't talk; they make utterances—gnomic Freudian utterances such as "There's no such thing as chance."

Like Scorsese when he called our attention to the fake grove of trees in *New York, New York* as if to shout, "Look, I'm shooting on a studio set, just the way the directors in the forties did!," Beineix shows off the studio-made look of his alley, his warehouses, his wharf. The movies made in the old Hollywood studios used their sets and their lighting to create an atmosphere that would intensify the power of the story. Beineix—like Scorsese before him, and like Coppola in *One from the Heart* and *The Outsiders*—makes the audience conscious of his style. He's celebrating the poetry of the movies, which for him is the poetry of artificiality. So Nastassia Kinski is posed like Hedy Lamarr in *Algiers*; she's the unattainable—the moon that shines on poor Gérard down there in his Brando T-shirt in the *film noir* gutter. Of course, when you're playing the moon there's not much you can bring to your role; Kinski is used like a wax figure—she's tilted this way and that, her lips parting, her neck flung back. And Victoria Abril's Bella, who tosses her curls and gives off heat, is like a parody of generations of sensual, jealous spitfires —Rita Moreno redux. The music is an exaggeration of Hollywood's old soaring and slurping scores—the kind that make you wince during revival showings. The whole movie is layered; you can see the detritus of dark-shadowed French tragedies of the thirties and American films of several decades, and it's made in thick, nocturnal color—the color of a bad dream.

Beineix is fond of saying things like "In my film, the filmmaker reflects on his own art" and "The entire film is an attempt to stop time. . . . This is what an artist does—freezes a moment in time and explores it." At Cannes, in May, where *The Moon in the Gutter* was first shown, he informed the press that his film was "a symphony of images." In the *Film Comment* interview, he said, "It's a film that talks about institutions, about the rich and the poor, without being interested in either wealth or poverty. It shows the existential suffering of two human beings (Depardieu and Kinski) which comes out of the gap between them —he, who lives in the gutter, and she, who comes from fantasy-land." Temporarily, at least, Beineix is a master of foolishness. I think he means all the hundreds of ready-made phrases that pop out of his mouth, such as "There is no story. It's symbolism." He's right about that, alas. How else can you explain Gérard's giving his father (or Father) a violin for a birthday present, when the shaky old boozer not only doesn't play the violin but can barely stand up?

What it comes down to is that Beineix doesn't have the impulse simply to represent; his impulse is to represent representations. André Téchiné, who made *French Provincial* in 1974 and *Barocco* in 1976, also worked in a layered style and with movie-derived characters, but his films were lighter, more illusionist in manner. Beineix is suffocatingly passionate about what he's doing, and this is what trips him up: his material is so far removed from actual experience (and is so familiar) that it can't support the weight of his emotions. The film becomes both oppressive and stupid.

In the sixties, the recycling of pop culture—turning it into Pop Art and camp—had its own satirical zest. Now we're into a different kind of recycling. Moviemakers give movies of the past an authority that those movies didn't have; they inflate images that may never have compelled belief, images that were no more than shorthand gestures—and they use them not as larger-than-life jokes but as altars. Beineix and Scorsese and Coppola become worshippers of film, and their filmmaking religion leads them to re-representation. Like the humbug Wizard of Oz, they rig up overblown, monumental effects to impress us or scare us; the effects ultimately point to the little guy pulling the levers—the little guy behind the curtain who is trying to put on a big show. These directors are so proud of their manipulation of images—they're so caught up in the filmmaking process, and have so much emotion invested in it—that they expect their re-representations to wow people. They can't understand why audiences are cold. But audiences are cold for the best of reasons: the new "mythic" films are made up of images without substance. The directors' "larger-than-life" stylization is empty.

In *The Moon in the Gutter*, the actors are not supposed to be anyone in particular. They're supposed to evoke, and what Beineix wants them to evoke is all those classy bad ideas he cherishes. Gérard, according to Beineix, is supposed to be "seeking to reconcile himself with his other half, his better half." How on earth does an actor show you that? He can't; all he can do is what Depardieu does—wander about somnambulistically. The actors in *The Moon* are helpless, because the movie isn't about their characters' emotions—it's about Beineix's swooning response to the earlier movie stars that they are standing in for. Although Depardieu is in the Jean Gabin role, he doesn't actually suggest Gabin; he's been in too many Depardieu roles for that. And he has a special problem: something in him has been sucked out by so much exposure to the camera. The volatility that made him seem raw and funny in *Going Places* has been lost. He hasn't turned into a bad actor, but he has become a pro, and "sensitive" in a dull, pictorial way. His edges are smooth, and though he gives conscientious performances, they all seem to be in just about the same range. (The only surprise in *The Moon* is the crude, loud sound of the black mama's—or Mama's—speeches; the actress is made to sound like someone bellowing in a TV commercial.)

Having cancelled out the actors, Beineix is left alone with his effects. Against all odds, he can sometimes engage us by imagery that isn't about anything in particular. This is especially true of the sequence with Gérard and the other dockhands at work loading and unloading cargo. The men and the equipment are stylized silhouettes, abstractions of men at work. Maybe we watch these compositions so intently because we've never seen anything quite like them—and because for a moment we're spared the warmed-over romanticism. From time to time, there are dazzling flourishes, such as the exterior view of the cathedral where Gérard and Loretta go for some sort of dream marriage ceremony: it's perched on top of a cliff, and its improbability gives the scene an awesome craziness. (Beineix's victories here are the equivalent of an actor's magnetizing us by his reading of a menu.) Beineix is a real technician, and he knows how to make images flow into each other, even though he's working with a palette that suggests manufactured rot. *The Moon* is primarily a nighttime movie, yet the highlight color is green—a thick green shellac with hallucinogenic overtones. (Asked by an interviewer to explain his color scheme, Beineix replied, "Color is a vibration that stems from our unconscious." Talk about humbug wizards!) The rapist wears red shoes, and the red of the raped girl's blood is as lacquered as Loretta's lipstick and her sleek red roadster. The picture is color-controlled to look poisonous, yet it undeniably has its *own* poisonous look.

In the street outside Gérard's family hovel, there is a brightly colored advertising billboard with the slogan "Try Another World." Beineix puts it in scene after scene; it's his big irony—that honest workers like Gérard can't win in *this* one. But a viewer can get fed up with the bad news. After a while, I thought the poster should have said "Try Another Movie."

It's deeply satisfying to see, finally, Luchino Visconti's magnificent 1963 film *The Leopard* in Italian, with subtitles, and at its full length—three hours and five minutes. It had been cut to two hours and forty-one minutes when it opened in this country, in a dubbed-into-English version that didn't always seem in sync, and with the color brightened in highly variable and disorienting ways. Now the movie has its full shape, and it couldn't have arrived at a better time. The new movies—especially the new American movies—have reached a low, low point. And here is a work of a type we rarely see anymore—a sweeping popular epic, with obvious similarities to *Gone with the Wind.* Set in Sicily, beginning in 1860, it's *Gone with the Wind* with sensibility—an almost Chekhovian sensibility. It doesn't have the active central characters that the American epic has; there's no Scarlett or Rhett. But it has a hero on a grand scale—Don Fabrizio, Prince of Salina, played superlatively well by Burt Lancaster. And it's so much better at doing the kind of things that *Gone with the Wind* did—showing you how historical events affect the lives of the privileged classes—that it can make you feel a little embarrassed for Hollywood. *Gone with the Wind* is, of course, a terrific piece of entertainment; *The Leopard* is so beautifully felt that it calls up a whole culture. It casts an intelligent spell—intelligent and rapturous.

The Visconti epic is based on the posthumously published, best-selling novel by Giuseppe Tomasi di Lampedusa—an impoverished Sicilian prince, like his hero. (The Lampedusa coat of arms bore a leopard.) The movie isn't what we normally call "novelistic," though; everything comes to us physically. Visconti suggests Don Fabrizio's thoughts and feelings by the sweep and texture of his life. The fabrics, the medal-laden military uniforms, the dark, heavy furniture, the huge palaces, with their terraces and broad marble staircases, and the arid, harsh landscapes they're set in are all sensualized—made tactile. Burt Lancaster has always been a distinctively physical actor, and this is a supremely physical role. We know the Prince by his noble bearing and the assurance of his gestures—they're never wasteful. He's at ease with authority; you can believe that he's the result of centuries of aristocratic breeding. There's grandeur in the performance, which Lancaster has acknowledged he modelled on Visconti himself (who, though not a Sicilian, was a count whose family titles were among the oldest and most noble in Europe). It is not merely that the Prince is in tune with his surroundings. They have formed each other: he and the Salina country palazzo basking in the yellow light outside Palermo are one.

The Prince's estates have dwindled, money is running low, but he keeps up the family traditions. He's not a romantic—he's a realist. He'll protect aristocratic values for as long as he can, and he'll do his best to protect the future of the Salina family—his wife and seven children, his nephew—and the household priest and all the other attendants. He bends to the times only as much as he needs to. In 1860, Italy was in the middle of a revolution. Garibaldi and his followers—the Redshirts— were trying to unify Italy and free the south and Sicily from Bourbon rule. The Prince's favorite nephew, the spirited, gallant Tancredi (Alain Delon), goes off to join Garibaldi; he goes with the Prince's blessing and a small bag of his gold—the Prince understands that the Bourbons will fall. He's a man with few illusions, a man of sense who suffers fools all the time and tries to cushion his impatience. When Garibaldi lands on Sicily with an army of about a thousand men, and there are skirmishes in the streets of Palermo, the Prince's neurasthenic wife (Rina Morelli) becomes hysterically frightened—she's a whimperer—and he, recognizing that they may be in danger, takes her and their brood to safety at the family holdings across the island in Donnafugata. Along the way, the servants lay out a picnic—they spread a vast white linen cloth, and dish after dish, while the grooms take care of the horses. (Corot should have been invited.) At Donnafugata, the Prince leads the procession of his people, weary, and covered with dust from the road, into the cathedral. Seated in the Salina family pews, they're like corpses—petrified, deadwood figures.

The movie is about the betrayal of Garibaldi's democratic revolution, and about the wiliness of opportunists like Tancredi. ("Black and slim as an adder" was how Lampedusa described him.) Tancredi makes his reputation as a heroic fighter while he's an officer with Garibaldi's Redshirts, but as soon as power shifts to the Mafia-dominated, middle-class landgrabbers, he changes into the uniform of the new king—*their* king, Victor Emmanuel II, from the House of Savoy. He doesn't so much as blink when he hears the gunshots that mark the execution of the last of Garibaldi's loyal troops. The young Delon is perhaps too airy for the role. With his even features, small teeth, and smooth cheeks, he's a very pretty art object, perfectly carved. He'd make a fine, spry figure in an operetta, but he doesn't have the excitement or force to give Tancredi's actions the weight they might have had. (This Tancredi is as shallow as that other opportunist—Scarlett.) But the film is essentially about the Prince himself—the aging Leopard—and how he reacts to the social changes.

Lancaster provides the film's center of consciousness. We see everything that happens through Visconti's eyes, of course, but we feel we're seeing it through the Prince's eyes. We couldn't be any closer to him if we were inside his skin—in a way, we are. We see what he sees, feel what he feels; we know what's in his mind. He's fond of—and a little envious of—Tancredi, with his youth and verve. The Prince—he's only forty-five, but forty-five was a ripe age in the mid-nineteenth century—has perceived what the result of the revolution will be: the most ruthless grabbers will come out on top. There's a despicable specimen of the breed close at hand—the rich and powerful mayor of Donnafugata, Don Calogero (Paolo Stoppa), who is eager to climb into society. The Prince has a daughter who is in love with Tancredi, but the Prince understands that this daughter—prim and repressed, like his wife—is too over-protected and overbred to be the wife Tancredi needs for the important public career he's going after. And Tancredi, who has nothing but his princely title and his rakish charm, requires a wife who will bring him a fortune. And so when Tancredi is smitten by Don Calogero's poised and strikingly sensual daughter, Angelica (the lush young Claudia Cardinale, doing a bit too much lip-licking), the Prince arranges the match. (All this is presented very convincingly, and it's probably silly to quibble with a masterpiece, yet I doubt if a warmhearted father—and especially one sensually deprived in his relationship with his wife—would be so free of illusions about his daughter. And it seemed to me that he was more cut off from his children—one of the striplings is played by the very young Pierre Clementi, who has the face of a passionflower—than a man of his temperament would be, whatever his rank.)

Lighted by the justly celebrated cinematographer Giuseppe Rotunno, the movie is full of marvellous, fluid set-piece sequences: the dashing Tancredi's goodbyes to the Salina family when he goes off to join Garibaldi; the picnic; the church sequence. The original Italian prints may have had deeper brown tones and more lustrous golds—some of the scenes have a drained-out look—but there's always detail to exult in. Each time the Salina family assembles for Mass or for dinner, it's a big gathering. Some of the smaller, less opulent sequences are ongoing political arguments, like the ironic dialogue between the Prince and the timid worrywart family priest (Romolo Valli), or between the Prince and a family retainer who is his hunting companion (Serge Reggiani, overacting). This poverty-stricken snob, who's loyal to the Bourbons, is shocked that the Prince would approve of his nephew's marrying a girl whose mother is "an illiterate animal." The political issues that the film deals with are, of course, simplified, but they're presented with considerable cogency, and they're very enjoyable. Of the smaller sequences, perhaps the most dazzling is the conversation between the Prince and a petite, intelligent professorial gentleman (Leslie French) who has come with the official request that he stand for election to the Senate. (Victor Emmanuel II is a constitutional monarch.) Here, the Leopard—refusing the offer —shows his full pride. It's the most literary passage in the movie; it's the rationale of the script: the Prince explains the Sicilian arrogance and torpor, and how he and the land are intertwined. I doubt if any other director has got by even halfway with a fancy dialogue of this kind, yet it's stunningly successful here. Lancaster has held his energy in check through most of the performance; now he comes out blazing, and he's completely controlled. He has a wild, tragicomic scene, too, when the weasel-eyed Don Calogero comes to discuss Tancredi's proposal to his daughter. The sickened Prince listens to him, and then, in a startling move, picks up the little weasel, plants a quick, ceremonial kiss on each cheek to welcome him into the family, and plunks him down. It happens so fast we barely have time to laugh. Don Calogero's greed shines forth then in the satisfaction with which he enumerates each item of the dowry he will bestow upon Tancredi; it's as if he expected the Prince to cry "Hosanna!" for each acre, each piece of gold.

Probably the movie seems as intense as it does because the action isn't dispersed among several groups of characters, the way it usually is in an epic. We stay with the Prince almost all the time. Except for the fighting in the streets, there's only one major sequence that he isn't in —an episode in which Tancredi and Angelica wander about in unused parts of the rambling Salina palace in Donnafugata. The Prince's absence may not be the reason, but this episode doesn't seem to have any purpose or focal point, and it's also the only time the film's tempo seems off. Whenever the Prince is onscreen—whether in his study, where the telescopes indicate his interest in astronomy, or in the town hall, controlling his distaste while drinking a glass of cheap wine that Don Calogero has handed him—we're held, because we're always learning new things about him. And in the concluding hour, at the Ponteleone Ball—certainly the finest hour of film that Visconti ever shot (and the most influential, as *The Godfather* and *The Deer Hunter* testify)—it all comes together. At this ball, the Salinas introduce Angelica to society—to all the many Sicilian princes and aristocrats. Visconti's triumph here is that the ball serves the same function as the Prince's interior monologue in the novel: throughout this sequence, in which the Prince relives his life, experiences regret, and accepts the dying of his class and his own death, we feel we're inside the mind of the Leopard saying farewell to life.

Everything we've seen earlier, we now realize, was leading to this splendid ball, which marks the aristocrats' acceptance of the parvenus who are taking over their wealth and power. (The poor will stay at the bottom, and—in the Prince's view, at least—will be worse off than before; the new ruling class will not be bound by the tradition of noblesse oblige.) The Prince, alone by choice, wanders from one mammoth ballroom to the next, observing all these people he knows. Tancredi and Angelica have their first dance, and the Nino Rota score gives way to a lilting waltz by Verdi, which had been discovered just before the film was shot; Visconti was giving it its first public performance, and a piece of music may never have been showcased more lavishly. Visconti (and perhaps his helpers) certainly knew how to stage dance sequences. (The movie was edited in a month, yet the rhythmic movement of the whole film is intoxicatingly smooth.) Soon the crowded rooms are stifling and, with the women fluttering their fans, look like cages of moths. The Prince, strolling away from these overheated rooms, sees a bevy of adolescent girls in their ruffles jumping up and down on a bed while chattering and screaming in delight—overbred, chalky-faced girls, like his daughters, all excited. In a room where people are seated at tables feasting, he glances in revulsion at a colonel covered with medals who is boasting of his actions against Garibaldi's men. He begins to feel fatigued—flushed and ill. He goes into the library, pours himself a glass of water, and stares at a big oil—a copy of a Greuze deathbed scene.

It's there, in front of the painting, that Tancredi and Angelica find him. She wants the Prince to dance with her, and as she pleads with him their bodies are very close, and for a few seconds the emotions he has been feeling change into something close to lust. He envies Tancredi for marrying for different reasons from his own; he envies Tancredi for Angelica's full-blown beauty, her heartiness, her coarseness. He escorts her to the big ballroom, and they waltz together. It's Angelica's moment of triumph: he is publicly welcoming her into his family. He is straight-backed and formal while they dance, but his thoughts are chaotic. He experiences acute regret for the sensual partnership he never had with his wife, and a nostalgia for the animal vitality of his youth. His intimations of his own mortality are fierce. After returning the shrewd, happy Angelica to Tancredi, he goes to a special small room to freshen up. Coming out, he sees into an anteroom—the floor is covered with chamber pots that need emptying. Eventually, the ball draws to a close, and people begin to leave, but a batch of young diehard dancers are still going strong: they're hopping and whirling about to livelier music now that the older people have left the floor. The Prince arranges for his family to be taken home, explaining that he will walk. When he passes down the narrow streets, he's an old man. The compromises he has had to make have more than sickened him—they've aged him. His vision of the jackals and sheep who are replacing the leopards and lions ages him even more. He is emotionally isolated from his wife and children; he no longer feels any affection for the sly-faced Tancredi. He's alone.

The Leopard is the only film I can think of that's about the aristocracy from the inside. Visconti, the Marxist count, is both pitiless and loving. His view from the inside is not very different from that of Max Ophuls in *The Earrings of Madame de . . .* —which was made from the outside (though it was based on the short novel by the aristocratic Louise de Vilmorin). Ophuls' imagination took him where Visconti's lineage (and imagination) had brought him, and he gave us a portrait of a French aristocrat by Charles Boyer which had similarities to Lancaster's performance. But we weren't taken inside that French aristocrat's value system with anything like the robust fullness of our involvement with Lancaster's Leopard. If it weren't for the Prince's wiry, strong, dark-red hair and his magisterial physique—his vigor—I doubt if we'd feel the same melancholy at the death of his class. The film makes us feel that his grace is part of his position. We're brought to respect values that are almost totally foreign to our society. That's not a small thing for a movie to accomplish.

September 19, 1983

ON GOLDEN SWAMP

Ⓒ*ross Creek*, an account of a woman's struggle to become a writer, is given a supernal glow by the director Martin Ritt. The picture seems to be suffering from earthshine: everything is lighted to look holy, and whenever the score isn't shimmering and burnishing, nature is twittering. It's all pearly and languid, and more than a little twerpy—it's one long cue for "Oh, What a Beautiful Mornin'." Loosely based on Marjorie Kinnan Rawlings' semi-autobiographical tales about what she learned during her years in an orange grove in the Florida swamps, the movie opens in 1928. We're meant to admire Mrs. Rawlings (Mary Steenburgen), a Northerner, for her courage in leaving her home and husband and going down to Florida to write. But the script doesn't give even a hint of why she bought the grove (sight unseen), or why she thinks she'll find more propitious conditions for writing gothic romances in the subtropical marshland than she had in her bedroom or her study in New York. The filmmakers view her as a feminist ahead of her time—a heroine who gives up a soft life and goes out on her own to face hardships. Yet the way they tell the story, she's almost immediately equipped with everything she has cast aside. When her jalopy gives out before she arrives at her property, it's said to be in hopeless condition, but the courtly and handsome hotelkeeper Norton Baskin (Peter Coyote), who drives her to her tumbledown shack, shows up again a day or two later bringing the car, which has been repaired so that it looks sparkling and new. Meanwhile, friendly neighbors have been dropping in, and Mrs. Rawlings has hired a young black woman, Geechee (Alfre Woodard), to clean and cook, and field hands to take care of the crops. The house is already transformed; it's gracious and orderly, and she's at her typewriter, with a potted gloxinia blooming nearby. She's ladylike, and the local people do everything for her. So what's so heroic about her—beyond her managerial skills?

The film's central peculiarity is that Mary Steenburgen doesn't make contact with the audience. Our emotions circulate among the other characters; they never land on her, and it's because she's so withdrawn. She has a tight, little-girl voice, and she seems to count to ten before she speaks; her eyes narrowed, she looks at the person she's going to say something to, and we have to wait until she says it. I think she wants us to see that Mrs. Rawlings is a determined woman who doesn't speak lightly, and that she observes everything around her and takes it in—stores it for her art. But the movie dies many deaths during her ten-beat considerations. She's playing in "real time," and everyone else is playing in heightened, theatrical style; the other actors take us out for a ride, and she keeps putting the brakes on.

Her character isn't appealing in other ways, either. Mary Steenburgen has traded in her softness for a frosty, patrician manner. And with crisp hatbrims that come down to her eyes, and her expression pinched and vinegary, Mrs. Rawlings is a Mary Poppins even when she's belting down a shot of corn liquor. She treats that tall, charming Norton Baskin abominably. But he must see in her what the filmmakers see (and what they fail to show us), because he keeps coming back. And he's certainly a resourceful fellow. He doesn't just get cars repaired; he flushes Maxwell Perkins out of the swamps. Perkins (Malcolm McDowell) explains that he has been visiting "Ernest in Key West," and before dinner he sits down to read Marjorie's latest effort, her breakthrough story, "Jacob's Ladder," which, of course, isn't a gothic—it's about the lives of backwoods people—and Perkins tells her he'll publish it.

Ritt and his collaborators seem to have adopted a child's-storybook women's-liberation approach. Actually, Marjorie Kinnan Rawlings and her husband, Charles, bought the Florida grove together and lived there for about five years before they separated. And all these "giving" people! In the movie, Geechee follows her mistress's example: she learns to be independent. Luckily for Mrs. Rawlings, she goes right on cleaning and cooking. (Independence seems to make her a perfect, loving servant.) In the book *Cross Creek*, Geechee is a hopeless, tormented drunk who wanders off, and she and the other characters don't do much without expecting something in return. It's a readable, toughminded book, filled with people who, according to the author, are "a blend of the true and the imagined." One of its weaknesses is the homey sententiousness about "the land" which mars a few paragraphs of the opening and closing chapters; this high-toned guff is just what Mary Steenburgen is given to recite in voice-over. Most of the movie is sun-coated and sugar-cured. It's the development of a writer according to the Waltons.

Something about centering a picture on a heroine seems to lead Ritt to Disneyfy his men. In his *Norma Rae*, both Beau Bridges and Ron Leibman were emasculated; here Norton Baskin, the character based on Mrs. Rawlings' second husband and widower, has no apparent interest in life except to be supportive of this wonderful woman, who keeps rejecting him. Peter Coyote (he was Keys in *E.T.*) has a Jiminy Cricket charm, and he manages to suggest an amiable, gentlemanly insolence; he's a spiffy fellow for a woman to turn up in the swamps (or any other place). But he has been sprinkled with pixie dust. The only man in the movie who has any strength as a character is Rip Torn as Marsh Turner —a Cracker on a grand scale and too powerful for sweetening. Rip Torn is off and running before Mary Steenburgen finishes her ten-point count. Cobbled together out of several people in the book (and probably intended to represent the spirit of the place itself), Marsh Turner figures in a subplot, which is basically a revamped version of Mrs. Rawlings' book *The Yearling*. He's a father who loves his daughter (Dana Hill) so much that he lets her make a pet of a fawn, even though he realizes that the grown deer will endanger the family's food supply.

Ritt shows his flair for melodrama in his handling of the hyperemotional entanglement between father and daughter. The scriptwriter, Dalene Young, piles most of the film's dramatic action into these scenes, and Rip Torn and Dana Hill work together with what looks like spontaneous frenzy—you believe in his passion for her, and she's almost as far into her character as she was in *Shoot the Moon*. (She was so very bad in her starring role in the TV production of *The Member of the Wedding* that her performance here is a return to grace.) In the past, Torn's emotions have generally been twisted, and he has often had a mean, hipster's glint. His meanness was fun; it was tonic. But his being *on* was sometimes the essence of his acting and of his characters. They fed off being on—that's what made them seem sadistic, sharklike. Self-hate was Rip Torn's specialty. Here, he's essentially decent; he's untwisted, and you see more sides to him than in his usual roles. There's a warm, free-flowing stream of emotion in his performance; both the character and Torn himself seem capable of sorrow (and of generosity). As Marsh Turner, he wears a feather in his hat. He's a gallant, responsible husband and father who's also a grandstanding rowdy. Then, within a few minutes of screen time, he turns into a weeping, broken man; drunk and in despair, he throws an empty liquor keg through a shopwindow in town; returning home, he bangs things in misery, breaking up furniture. Marsh Turner's emotions rear up very large, and he simply discharges them—when he's bashing chairs or tables, it's like brushing a tear away. It's a rampaging role, but Torn doesn't seem to be afraid of anything, and he gives his character a pleasure in performance—something that American actors rarely do. He endows this backwoods man with his own love of whooping it up in front of people, and with an awareness of the impressions he makes. It's a demonstration of a wild-man actor's art— he lets us see how rage and tears verge on each other. It's crazy, great acting, and the picture would be stone cold without it.

You can't really dislike *Cross Creek*. It's lulling, in a semi-stupefying way. You sit there staring at this prestige item that might have been planned to open at Radio City Music Hall for Easter Week circa 1935. Alfre Woodard brings some speed and urgency to Geechee's first conversation with Mrs. Rawlings, when she insists that she be hired. And Ritt handles the low-key scenes involving a white handyman, Tim (John Hammond), and his bedraggled wife (Toni Hudson) with a sure—if slightly mechanical—touch. (The Tim episode is like a classic yet shopworn short story.) Yet even what is well done feels out of whack. I think what keeps it that way is the misconception of the central figure—envisioning her as a muted, passive artist who soaks up the local color, and leaving us to watch her soak. It may be an impossible-to-play role; the heroine never deepens or takes hold. At the end, she says that she has become a part of Cross Creek, but to us she's still an outsider. Mrs. Rawlings—that's what the people in the movie call her—comes across as a lyrical stiff.

The remarkably ugly ads seem to be trying to suggest radiant respectability: they show the heroine peering out from a background of blotches and lily pads, and they describe the picture as "The true and compelling story of Marjorie Kinnan Rawlings, Pulitzer Prize winning authoress of *The Yearling.*" That sad, misbegotten word "authoress" is emblematic of everything that went wrong with the movie.

About halfway into the Australian comedy *Lonely Hearts*, the shy Patricia (Wendy Hughes) is sitting in a tea room with the eager, eccentric Peter (Norman Kaye), and she looks out the window and says that she loves Melbourne in the winter. And her comment may bring you up short, because it makes you realize that you haven't registered where or when the film is taking place. *Lonely Hearts* is burdened by that title and, much worse, by its nondescript look and dreary, crabbed cinematography. The exteriors are as cheerless as the orange-brown interiors. This is a movie in which you have to settle for the acting and the odd flyspecks of humor. Wendy Hughes, who looks a bit like Joan Hackett here, starts out with her straight dark hair solemnly parted in the middle and tucked behind her ears. She is perfectly in control of her performance: she's a beautiful woman acting plain, and she is skillful enough to put across every nuance of Patricia's sexual repression. Patricia is a bank clerk in her thirties who wilted before she bloomed. Now she has moved away from the parents who intimidated her, taken an apartment of her own, and got herself a therapist. She's still wearing proper-schoolgirl clothes (jumpers and shirtwaist dresses), and she moves with an agony of self-consciousness, but she has signed up with a dating service.

That's how she meets Peter, a forty-nine-year-old piano tuner who has just been liberated by the death of the invalid mother he has been caring for. Norman Kaye, a stage and TV performer making his film début here, doesn't always ring as true as Wendy Hughes does, but then he doesn't hit as many familiar notes as she does, either. (She gives the standard fine-actress-playing-dowdy-aging-virgin performance.) Norman Kaye is playing an individual whose traits don't add up the way character traits in movies usually do. Peter has a furtive, childlike prankishness in him, and that's what keeps the movie alive. Norman Kaye is an unpredictable actor, who takes a lot of quirky, vagrant chances. He plays Peter with a ruddy, mottled complexion, and his face is an uncharted maze of tics and wrinkles, topped by a hairpiece that's like Pagliacci's hat. The total effect is surprisingly genial and attractive. Peter is most likable, I think, in the scene at a rehearsal of the amateur theatrical group he has brought Patricia into; sitting behind his friend the director (Jon Finlayson) and watching the atrocious acting of his amiable, innocent brother-in-law (Jonathan Hardy), he leans forward to make a comment, pressing his head down on his friend's shoulder to hide his giggles.

The budding romance between the timorous Patricia and the whimsical bachelor doesn't put too much of an emotional squeeze on us, because although the core material is moist the film's humor is dry and sometimes darting and sneaky. The movie is very casually strung together. It's an Australian variant of the comfy-cozy Ealing comedies of the fifties, but it doesn't have their precise construction or their sharply pointed wit. It moves from one small slapstick diversion to the next. The director, Paul Cox, who wrote the picture with John Clarke, falls back on such standbys as that little-theatre group, which helps to fill the big void in the script. There's not much story. Peter's work as a piano tuner allows the director to follow him into homes and institutions, and every place has some potty people or is good for a gag or two. So are the places that Peter and Patricia go to on their dates. (The director may feel virtuous about the film's dun-colored drabness; it may tie in with his conception of realism and how ordinary people see things.) At times, Cox may appear to be staging a ''Candid Camera'' show, but he whisks the principal actors in and out, and keeps the bit players busy. Peter always has another piano to tune or the theatre group has a crisis, and the film keeps bopping along. It's mildly satirical, mildly romantic, and mildly engaging.

If I'm stingy in my praise, it's because the people in the movie have been constricted so that we can like them. Patricia and Peter accept their ordinariness and aspire only to the happiness of simple, unassuming people. Their modest, desperate hopes are for what is clearly within their reach, and so we can smile complacently at their efforts. Their aspirations are scaled to flatter the audience: our smiles are like giving them a pat on the head.

October 3, 1983

THE SEVENS

The *Right Stuff* gives off a pleasurable hum: it's the writer-director Philip Kaufman's enjoyment of the subject, the actors, and moviemaking itself. He's working on a broad canvas, and it excites him —it tickles him. Based on Tom Wolfe's 1979 book, the movie is an epic ramble—a reënactment of the early years of the space program, from breaking the sound barrier up to the end of the solo flights. It covers the years 1947 to 1963, especially the period after 1957, when government leaders, who felt they'd been put to shame by the Soviet Union's sorties into space, rushed to catch up; they initiated Project Mercury, assembled a team of official heroes—all white, married males—and began to exploit them in the mass media. Henry Luce, the founder of *Life*, which had perfected the iconography of a clean-living America during the Second World War, bought exclusive rights to all NASA coverage of the space program and put the newly selected astronauts under contract; *Life* then presented them and their wives as super-bland versions of the boys and girls next door. The movie contrasts the test pilots who risk their lives in secrecy with these seven publicly acclaimed figures who replace the chimps that were sent up in the first American space capsules. They're synthetic heroes, men revved up to act like boys. Walking in formation in their shiny silver uniforms, the astronauts, whose crewcuts give them a bullet-headed look, are like a football team in a sci-fi fantasy. But they're not quite the square-jawed manikins they pretend to be; creatures of publicity, they learn how to manipulate the forces that are manipulating them. They have to, in order to preserve their dignity. They're phony only on the outside. Their heroism, it turns out, is the real thing (which rather confuses the issue).

As the lanky Sam Shepard embodies him, Chuck Yeager, the "ace of aces" who broke the sound barrier in 1947, evokes the young, breathtakingly handsome Gary Cooper. And Yeager and the other test pilots have a hangout near the home base of the U.S. flight-test program: a cantina in the Mojave Desert, with a wall of photographs behind the bar —snapshots of the flyers' fallen comrades. Presided over by a woman known as Pancho (Kim Stanley), the place recalls the flyers' hangout in the Howard Hawks picture *Only Angels Have Wings* and the saloons in Westerns. Shepard's Yeager is the strong, silent hero of old movies —especially John Ford movies. On horseback in the desert, he looks at the flame-spewing rocket plane that he's going to fly the next morning, and it's like a bronco that he's got to bust. Kaufman uses Sam Shepard's cowboy Yeager as the gallant, gum-chewing individualist. He has some broken ribs and a useless injured arm when he goes up in that fiery rocket, and he doesn't let on to his superiors; he just goes up and breaks the sound barrier and then celebrates with his wife (Barbara Hershey) over a steak and drinks at Pancho's. He expresses his elation by howling like a wolf.

Even if the actual, sixtyish Chuck Yeager, now a retired Air Force brigadier general, weren't familiar to us from his recent appearances in TV commercials, where he radiates energy and affable good-fellowship, we can see him in the movie (he plays the bit part of the bartender at the cantina), and he isn't a lean, angular, solitary type—he's chunky and convivial. Sam Shepard is playing a legend that appeals to the director. He's Honest Abe Lincoln and Lucky Lindy, a passionate lover, and a man who speaks only the truth, if that. This legendary Yeager has too much symbolism piled on him, and he's posed too artfully; he looms in the desert, watching over what happens to the astronauts in the following years as if he were the Spirit of the American Past. Sam Shepard's Yeager appears in scenes that have no reason to be in the movie except, maybe, that Phil Kaufman has wanted for a long time to shoot them. (The worst idea is the black-clad death figure, played by Royal Dano, who, when he isn't bringing the flyers' widows the bad news or singing at the burial sites, sits at a table in Pancho's, waiting.) Kaufman must assume that the images of Yeager will provide a contrasting resonance throughout the astronauts' sequences. But Sam Shepard isn't merely willing to be used as an icon—he uses himself as an icon, as if he saw no need to act. And he can't resonate—he isn't alive. The movie is more than a little skewed: it's Kaufman's—and Tom Wolfe's—dreamy view of the nonchalant Yeager set against their satirical view of Henry Luce's walking apple pies. This epic has no coherence, no theme to hold it together, except the tacky idea that Americans can't be true, modest heroes anymore—that they're plasticized by the media.

Like Tom Wolfe, Phil Kaufman wants you to find everything he puts in beguilingly wonderful and ironic. That's the Tom Wolfe tone, and to a surprising degree Kaufman catches it and blends it with his own. The film's structural peculiarities and its wise-guy adolescent's caricature of space research all seem to go together to form a zany texture. It's a stirring, enjoyable mess of a movie. Kaufman plays *Mad*-magazine games, in which the woman nurse (Jane Dornaker) testing the astronauts is a comic ogre with a mustache and the space scientists are variants of Dr. Strangelove—clowns with thick German accents. (Scott Beach, who plays the Wernher von Braun figure, wears a wig that sits on his head like a furry creature that took sick and died there.) Counterculture gags are used for a sort of reverse jingoism. When the scientists get together to celebrate their victories, they sing in German. When Lyndon Johnson (Donald Moffat) can't understand what von Braun is saying, he's a Lyndon Johnson cartoon, and the dialogue has the rhythm of a routine by two old radio comics. Most of the low comedy doesn't make it up to that level; Kaufman has a healthy appetite for foolishness, but his comic touch is woozy—some scenes are very broad and very limp. (Even Jeff Goldblum, as a NASA recruiter, can't redeem all the ones he's in.) And there are coarse, obvious jokes: the astronauts come on to the press like a vaudeville act—playing dumb and giving the reporters just what they want—while the Hallelujah Chorus rises on the soundtrack. The action zigzags from old-movie romance to cockeyed buffoonery to the courage (and exaltation) of men alone in tiny capsules orbiting the earth at eighteen thousand miles an hour. Kaufman relies on the contrasts and rhythms of the incidents to produce a cumulative vision, and it doesn't happen. The picture is glued together only by Bill Conti's hodgepodge score. But a puppyish enthusiasm carries it forward, semi-triumphantly. And the nuthouse-America games do something for it that perhaps nothing else could have done: they knock out any danger of its having a worthy, official quality, and they make it O.K. for the flights themselves to be voluptuously peaceful.

The flights—a mixture of NASA footage and fictional material, with marvellous sound effects—are inescapably romantic. Working with the cinematographer Caleb Deschanel (*The Black Stallion*) and with the San Francisco avant-garde filmmaker Jordan Belson, who does special visual effects, Kaufman provides unusually simple and lyrical heavenly scenes. As a scriptwriter, he may try to come in on a wing and a prayer, and as a director he may have too easygoing a style for the one-two-bang timing needed for low comedy, but he's a tremendous moviemaker, as he demonstrated in *The Great Northfield, Minnesota Raid* (1972), *The White Dawn* (1974), *Invasion of the Body Snatchers* (1978), and *The Wanderers* (1979). He has a puckish side; it comes out here in a rather unshaped deadpan joke using Australian aborigines to account for the mysterious "celestial fireflies" that Ed Harris's John Glenn reports seeing. Kaufman's re-creation of the middle and late fifties is realistic and affectionate without any great show of expense. (He was able to fake most of the locations in the San Francisco area, which doubles here for Florida, Texas, Washington, D.C., and New York, and Australia, too.) And he doesn't take the bloom off space by knocking us silly with the grandeur of it all. *The Right Stuff* has just enough of Jordan Belson's tantalizing patterns and rainbow fragments to suggest the bliss that Chuck Yeager felt high above the desert and that the astronauts experience while they're inside their spinning capsules. Strapped in and almost immobile, John Glenn is also the beneficiary of a magical effect that he himself can't see. The lights from the equipment that are reflected in the windows of all the astronauts' helmets hit him just right; we see two tiny lines of jewelled lights streaking down his face, one from each eye. "Astro tears" the movie crew called them. (They suggest Jesus in space.)

Phil Kaufman makes it possible for some of his characters to show so many sides that they keep taking us by surprise—especially Ed Harris's John Glenn, the strict Presbyterian, who probably comes the closest to fitting *Life*'s image of an American hero. This Glenn, who reprimands his teammates for their willingness to oblige astronaut groupies, and is grimly humming "The Battle Hymn of the Republic" to keep himself together as he sits trussed up in his capsule, hurtling back into the earth's atmosphere, is perfectly capable of using patriotism as a put-on: at the Mercury team's first big press conference, in Washington, he assumes the role of spokesman, flashes his quick, big smile, and is real pleased with himself. Blond and blue-eyed, and, at thirty-two, considerably younger than John Glenn was at the time, Ed Harris has some of the bleached pallor of Robert Duvall, and when he's sitting out in space, loving it, his pale-eyed, staring intensity may remind you of Keir Dullea's starchild face in *2001*. But Harris has a scary, unstable quality that's pretty much his own. He holds his head stiff on his neck, and he's the kind of very still actor who can give you the willies: he often has the look of someone who's about to cry, and a flicker of a smile can make you think the character he's playing is a total psycho.

Your feelings about Harris's Glenn are likely to be unresolved, except in Glenn's scenes with his wife, Annie (played with delicate, grinning charm and mischief by Mary Jo Deschanel, the actress wife of the cinematographer). In an early scene, Kaufman establishes that they have an understanding of each other that goes beyond words. It has to, because the enchanting Annie is a stutterer who can't get a sentence out.

Her husband knows how to read every blocked syllable; the two of them are so close they communicate almost by osmosis, and even when she's making fun of his gung-ho wholesomeness he giggles happily, secure in the intimacy they share. Then, on the day of his scheduled flight, the NASA people ask him to talk to his wife on the phone and persuade her to "play ball" with the television newscasters who are outside the Glenns' house waiting to come in and interview her. Vice-President Johnson is also out there, in his limousine; he wants to come in to reassure her on TV. On the phone, she's distraught—she can barely speak her husband's name. But he intuits what she's trying to say; it's as if he could read her breathing. She faces terrible humiliation—she wants to know if she has to let them all in. Glenn has the single most winning speech of the whole three-hour-and-twelve-minute movie when he tells her that no, she doesn't have to let anybody in. And, good Presbyterian that he is, he manages to express his rage at the networks and the politicians without ever using a cussword (which is a feat comparable to her non-verbal communication—they're both handicapped). The scene is perhaps the wittiest and most deeply romantic confirmation of a marriage ever filmed. When Glenn is back on earth and the two of them are riding in a ticker-tape parade in his honor, they're a pair of secret, victorious rebels.

The movie probably has the best cast ever assembled for what is essentially a docudrama—although a twenty-seven-million-dollar docudrama, and one with an individual temperament, isn't like anything we've seen on TV. Scott Wilson appears as the test pilot Crossfield, and Levon Helm is Ridley, Yeager's mechanic. Pamela Reed brightens up the scenes she's in; she's all eyes as Trudy, the secretly estranged wife of the astronaut Gordon Cooper. And I felt my face twitching, as if I were about to laugh, whenever Dennis Quaid's Gordo was on the screen, because he has a devilish kid's smile, with his upper lip a straight line across his face. Quaid plays Gordo as a self-reliant, tough kid—a wised-up Disney boy, the savviest Huck Finn there ever was. When he gets his turn in the heavens—Cooper makes the last solo flight into space—his split-faced grin is perhaps the standout image of the film. He's cynical and cocky—a materialist in every thought and feeling—and so when his face tells us that he's awed by what he sees, we're awed by what we see in his face. It may seem ungrateful to point out the results of realism, but most of the actors playing astronauts are martyred by their haircuts; their features look naked, their noses as big as a bald eagle's beak. Scott Glenn, who plays Alan Shepard, has gone even further than the others. He looks a little like Hoagy Carmichael, but he seems to be deforming himself; if this is meant to be an aspect of the astronaut's character, it isn't delved into. Scott Glenn has got so wiry, gaunt, and muscular that his skin appears to be pulled taut against his bones, and when he laughs his whole face crinkles, like a hyena's.

If we're often preoccupied by the men as physical specimens, this has a good deal to do with the subject, but it may also be because we're not sure how to interpret their meaningful glances at each other. Are we intended to see comradeship there, and mutual respect, or do the expressions mean "They're buying it!" or "This is the life!" or "My head is numb"? We in the audience are put in the position of being hip to what's going on even when we don't really get it. What, for example, are the astronauts thinking as they watch old Sally Rand do her feather-fan dance in their honor in Houston in 1962? (The dancer who impersonates her is, blessedly, younger and more gifted.) The jazzy hipness in the film's tone comes down to us from Tom Wolfe—it's an unearned feeling that we're on to things. Probably Kaufman thinks that he's conveying a great deal more to us than he is. Certainly he's trying to "say something" when he cuts Sally's fan dance and the expressions of the astronauts watching her right into footage of Sam Shepard's Chuck Yeager being brave again (and still unsung). But he's making points on an epic scale rather than telling an epic story. He hasn't dramatized what he wants to get at; he has attitudinized instead—setting the modern, hype-bound world against a vision of the past that never was. Though it's a docudrama and some incidents are included simply for the record, *The Right Stuff* is drawn not from life but from Tom Wolfe's book and Kaufman's nostalgia for old-movie values.

The mishap that the astronaut Gus Grissom (that terrific actor Fred Ward) is involved in gives us, briefly, something solid that makes us feel very uncomfortable. As the film presents it, the gloomy-souled Grissom panics during the splashdown of his capsule and is desperate to get out. The helicopter that is to pick up the capsule is hovering overhead, maneuvering into position. Though the film doesn't make it absolutely clear, when the hatch blows open and Grissom climbs out (and the capsule sinks) the implication is that he opened it. He claims that it simply malfunctioned and opened by itself, but clearly the NASA people don't accept his account, because he receives considerably less than a hero's welcome, and his wife, Betty (Veronica Cartwright), feels horribly let down by the second-rateness of the ceremonies in his honor. I wish that Kaufman had followed through on the disturbing, awkward quality of this incident, which grips us at a different emotional level from the other scenes. I realize I'm asking for a different kind of movie, but if he'd taken

66

a different approach to the Gus and Betty Grissom episode he might have opened up some of the implications of the phrase "the right stuff" that have bothered me ever since Tom Wolfe's book came out.

Yeager is, of course, the movie's archetype of "the right stuff"—the model of courage, determination, and *style*. The astronauts don't have an acceptable style, but the movie half forgives them, because, as it indicates, this isn't their fault—the times are to blame. The men themselves have the guts and the drive, and they win Kaufman's admiration. But then there's Fred Ward's Gus Grissom, who may at a crucial moment have failed to demonstrate "the right stuff." Isn't this all painfully familiar? Doesn't it take us back to the Victorian values of *The Four Feathers* and all those other cultural artifacts which poisoned the lives of little boys (and some girls, too), filling them with terror that they might show a "yellow streak"?

Being far more of an anti-establishmentarian than Tom Wolfe, Kaufman probably felt that he had transformed the material, but he is still stuck with its reactionary cornerstone: the notion that a man's value is determined by his physical courage. You'd think that Kaufman would have got past this romantic (and perhaps monomaniacal) conception of bravery. (With this standard, whatever you fear becomes what you compulsively measure yourself by.) I assume that people who are jellyfish about some things may be very brave about others. And certainly during the counterculture period there was a widespread rejection of the idea of bravery that this film represents. According to Wolfe, "the right stuff" is "the uncritical willingness to face danger." Yet the film's comedy scenes are conceived in counterculture terms.

The movie has the happy, excited spirit of a fanfare, and it's astonishingly entertaining, considering what a screw-up it is. It satirizes the astronauts as mock pilots, and it never indicates that there's any reason for them to be rocketing into space besides the public-relations benefit to the government; then it celebrates them as heroes. As a viewer, you want the lift of watching them be heroic, but they're not in a heroic situation. More than anything else, they seem to be selected for their ability to take physical punishment and accept confinement in a tight cylinder. And about the only way they can show their mettle is by *not* panicking when they finally get into their passive, chimp positions. (If they discover that they're sick with terror, they can't do much more about it than the chimps could, anyway.) It's Yeager who pronounces the benediction on the astronauts, who tells us that yes, they *are* heroes, because they know (what the chimps didn't) that they're sitting on top of a rocket. (I imagine that the chimps had a pretty fair suspicion that they weren't frolicking high in a banana tree.) If having "the right stuff" is set up as the society's highest standard, and if a person proves that he has it by his eagerness to be locked in a can and shot into space, the only thing that distinguishes human heroes from chimps is that the heroes volunteer for the job. And if they volunteer, as they do in this film, out of personal ambition and for profit, are they different from the chimp who might jump into the can eagerly, too, if he saw a really big banana there?

Anyone who believes himself to have been a revolutionary or a deeply committed radical during his student-demonstration days in the late sixties is likely to find *The Big Chill*, which opened the recent New York Film Festival, despicable. And if the advance publicity for the film has led you to expect a serious, "personal" movie about how the late-sixties campus activists have adjusted to becoming the kind of people they used to insult, you may find it pretty offensive. It's no more than an amiable, slick comedy with some very well-directed repartee and skillful performances. It's overcontrolled, it's shallow, it's a series of contrivances. But there are pleasures to be had from this kind of wise-cracking contemporary movie that you can't get from anything else.

Directed by Lawrence Kasdan, who wrote the script with Barbara Benedek, it's set in South Carolina, where a group of seven former friends from the University of Michigan gather for the funeral of Alex, the campus radical who brought them together, and who has now, after years of flailing about disconsolately, slit his wrists. The movie is, nonetheless, lighthearted from the start. It may pretend to be about "life," but it's really about being clever (even the title tells you that), and about the fun of ensemble acting. It begins with a little game-playing: glimpses of two pairs of hands—one pair with sexy long red fingernails —as they adjust a man's very spiffy clothes. The man turns out to be the corpse being dressed. This amusingly callous, slightly tawdry gag, planned so immaculately that it suggests a parody of *American Gigolo*, sets the film's tone. (It's a shame that Alex's old friends don't get to admire his fancy duds, but it appears that he was accoutred for us, not for them—it's a closed-coffin ceremony.) After the funeral, the friends —all in their mid-thirties—feel the need to be with each other again. They bury the sixties (which Alex symbolizes) and then dredge them up to talk about. The out-of-towners stick around for the weekend, at the spacious home of the only two of the old group who married within it; the husband, who has done well in the running-shoes business, is played by Kevin Kline, and his wife, a doctor, by Glenn Close. These two are also the happiest of the seven surviving friends. Kline (who, for the first time, relaxes in front of the camera and comes across as a character rather than an actor) is a man of substance here, a quick-witted fellow who adores his kids and feels no guilt about making money. He doesn't look back, except musically; the sixties for him are the rock 'n' roll records he loves, which we hear throughout the movie—"Joy to the World," Aretha Franklin's "A Natural Woman," the Stones, the Band, and so on. His wife had a long emotional attachment to Alex and a brief sexual one, and she's torn up by his death, but she's a warm, nurturing woman, and will be fine.

As soon as you see how warm she is, you begin to see the film's flabby side—the seven characters are like a psych major's sexually integrated version of a forties bomber crew. The pleasures of *The Big Chill* are the pleasures of the synthetic; it's all tricks, but craftsmanlike, exemplary tricks. Glenn Close's opposite number is JoBeth Williams, the dissatisfied wife of an advertising executive, a tough bitch who means to leave him and nail the most famous of the group—Tom Berenger, a TV star, who is dissatisfied in his own way (he seems to be in a state of suspended animation) but is not about to be nailed. She's furious when, ever so gently, he turns her down. The likable Mary Kay Place has perhaps the worst role: she's a lawyer who gave up on her idealistically motivated legal-aid job and went into corporate law. Unmarried, disappointed with everything she has been involved in since her college days, she wants a child and hopes to conceive one this weekend by one of the old friends she loves and trusts. Mary Kay Place brings a soft, self-deprecating wryness to the part, but it still reeks of cheap poignancy, which is compounded when the man who is her first choice—William Hurt—turns out to have been made impotent by the wounds he suffered in Vietnam. This device should probably be marked "Property of Hemingway" and retired, but, still, working with it, Hurt gives the best performance of his young movie career. As a man who lives by dealing drugs and is his own chief customer, he looks doughy and unhealthy, as if he'd lost touch with his own life. He's quiet, and maybe because he isn't acting all over the landscape and commandeering our attention, he's very appealing. The seventh, Jeff Goldblum, a writer for *People* and a man of stunning superficiality, takes himself very seriously. His tall, gangling body, his pointed head, and his scowling face and bobbling

Adam's apple are all involved in whatever he's saying; he's a living cartoon—a man who wrinkles his forehead to think. This is probably the best-written role that Goldblum has had since the 1978 *Invasion of the Body Snatchers,* and he gives his fatuous remarks a huffy delivery that makes him the butt of his own lines; his huge eyes, behind specs, never let on that he knows he's funny. He's got a real comic creation here: a worrywart, a young old geezer.

There are nifty details in this movie, such as the name of the chain of running-shoe stores that Kevin Kline has built up (Running Dogs—remember the revisionists of the Chinese Revolution?), and Kline's little son's knowing the lyrics of the sixties songs. Sometimes details are punched up too mechanically: cuts to Hurt's single earring or to Mary Kay Place's young-professional outfit, for example. At times you may feel as if the cutting followed the script exactly—as if you were seeing a blueprint. And there's an early montage of the characters reacting to the news (the big chill) and packing their suitcases; it's a guerrilla tactic —to expose these people before we even meet them. A little later we get a montage of them unpacking, and even glimpses of what's on their night tables. And it's too cute, with items like an anthology of Kafka. The movie might have been inspired by a screenwriting manual that tells its purchasers to make lists for each character: What's he reading? What kind of clothes does he wear? What would he pack for a trip? Yet the film's details help you past the obviousness of most of the roles—the women's especially, and also Berenger's. He's not bad at all; his apologetic narcissism is rather touching—with his bushy blow-dried hair and thick mustache, he's a sheepish ringer for Tom Selleck. But he really has only one terrific scene: when the whole group rushes to the TV set to watch the opening credits of his hit series "J. T. Lancer"—which show him as the daredevil hero, leaping from one hazard to the next—and he's compelled to look. The film is often weak when two people go off and bare their souls, but the group scenes have snap and proficiency, and they show Kasdan's flair as a director.

Most directors are at a loss when they try to shoot ensemble scenes, and John Sayles, when he made the 1980 *Return of the Secaucus 7*— a sixties-reunion film with a similar houseparty structure but an unslick tone—didn't seem to have any idea of how to use the camera as an active participant, pinpointing what was going on. Kasdan keeps the camera jumping for the gag (the way Sydney Pollack did in *Tootsie*), and in the ensemble scenes you can almost hear the crackle as he hits the effects he wants. There's also an eighth person—an observer—in the house with the group: Meg Tilly plays the young girl with whom Alex was living at the time of his suicide. She's ten to fifteen years younger than the others, and, with her small, delicate features and wide-apart almond eyes, she seems to stand for a generation born shell-shocked and wise—or is it stoned and empty of anything but matter-of-fact considerations? Her role is perhaps too conceptual, and there probably should be a little more going on in the character, but she's an extraordinarily lovely presence. *Secaucus 7* had an outsider in some scenes, too: the local fellow, Howie (played by Sayles himself), who hadn't gone off to college—who'd married and was raising a family. Howie had what the others, with their hipness, had lost, and he made us aware that the Secaucus 7 were all childless and unrooted. Here, Meg Tilly makes us conscious of how articulate the whole bunch is. It's easy to see why Alex turned to this restful girl—she's a refuge from ideas—and it's very pleasing when she and William Hurt find a rapport.

The remarkable thing about this movie is that the actors don't destroy themselves even in their maudlin moments. Glenn Close has an icky "generous" scene toward the end—she makes it work by the sheer silliness of her expression. Whenever Kasdan tries for depth, the movie is phony, but a lot of the time it manages to turn phoniness into fun— which is in a long if not so great Hollywood tradition.

October 17, 1983

IMAGE MAKERS

In the opening scenes of *Under Fire*, rebel soldiers in Chad are trying to move a caravan of elephants carrying crates of weapons across a patch of open field, and Nick Nolte, as Russell Price, a photojournalist, trots alongside, snapping pictures of the ponderous beasts and the drivers sitting way on top of them and their freight. Suddenly, a helicopter gunship appears, blasting, and the scene turns into a horrifying shambles of elephants running and men shot down as they scurry for the bush. Wherever he is, the big, blond Russell Price goes on taking pictures. He is covered with cameras; they're his only luggage, and they swing as he moves. He switches from one to the other, and with each small click of the shutter we see—in a freeze-frame that is held for just an instant—what he has shot. The director, Roger Spottiswoode, a Canadian-born Englishman who's thirty-eight now, began working in London studios at nineteen and already had several years of experience, including work as an editor on Sam Peckinpah's *Straw Dogs*, when he came to live in this country, in 1971. He edited two more Peckinpah films and Walter Hill's *Hard Times*, worked with Karel Reisz, first as editor, then as second-unit director and associate producer, and also wrote the first draft of *48 Hrs.* before he got a chance to direct (with *Terror Train* and *The Pursuit of D. B. Cooper*). He was ready—maybe more than ready—for *Under Fire*. It has been made with breathtaking skill. Price's photographs—those freeze-frames, most of them in black-and-white, some in color, and each with its small, staccato click—fix the faces, the actions, the calamities in our memories, and the film is so cleanly constructed that they have a percussive effect. They're what *Under Fire* is about.

When Price hitches a ride on a truck carrying rebel troops out of the area, he's not the only American (or the only blond) among the black men. Oates (Ed Harris), a mercenary with the grin of a happy psychopath, sits among the rebels thinking he's among the soldiers of the government that's paying him. Price sets him straight, and he chuckles; he doesn't care who he kills anyway—it's his sport. When Price gets back to his hotel, the foreign press corps—which includes Claire (Joanna Cassidy), a radio reporter who is just breaking up with her lover, Alex (Gene Hackman), and Alex himself, a celebrated war correspondent and Price's closest friend—is preparing to move on to the next big trouble spot, Nicaragua. And we realize that what we have seen is, essentially, the prologue. But we have already grasped the most important thing about Price, who risks his carcass as a matter of course: he's an image man. And, seeing through his eyes as he clicks the shutter, we intuitively recognize how good he is at what he does. There's a purity about his total absorption in images. Price doesn't even have to do the kind of interpretation that the reporters do; he doesn't have to try to make sense of things. Nolte's loping, athletic grace as he moves alongside fighting men adds to the feeling we get that Price is an artist and an automaton, too. His whole body is tuned up for those clicks. He couldn't explain why he shoots when he does; he simply *knows*. And Nolte has what is perhaps an accidental asset for the role: his eyes are narrowed, as if by a lifetime of squinting through cameras, and his eyelids look callused.

It doesn't take long to grasp that Price and Claire and Alex regard their lack of involvement in what they cover as part of being professionals. They are observers, not participants, and they're proud of it. It's the essence of their personal dash and style—the international form of the swaggering cynicism of *The Front Page.* They all risk their lives with a becoming carelessness. But that's almost the only thing they have in common with the heroes and heroines of old Hollywood movies. One conspicuous difference is that they're grownup people in their forties; Alex may even be fifty.

The movie is set in 1979, during the last days of the rule of General Anastasio Somoza, the dictator-president whose family was put in power and kept there by the United States. And in a sense the Sandinist revolution—the imagery of it—is the star. This is trompe-l'oeil moviemaking, with Mexican locations in Oaxaca and Chiapas dressed up in the shantytown building material of Nicaragua (uncut beer-can sheets), and the political graffiti and the pulsing, hot colors—turquoise and flaming pink. The young Sandinistas who dart through the streets in striped T-shirts, with bright handkerchiefs masking their faces, have the street-theatre look that is so startling in the book *Nicaragua,* Susan Meiselas's 1981 collection of photographs of the insurrection. Spottiswoode knows not to make realism drab; there's dust and anger everywhere, but the country is airy and alive with color. Produced at a cost of eight and a half million dollars (Nolte and Hackman worked for much less than their usual fees) and with only fifty-seven shooting days, the film is a beautiful piece of new-style classical moviemaking; everything is thought out and prepared, but it isn't explicit, it isn't labored, and it certainly isn't overcomposed. No doubt the cinematographer John Alcott, whose speed is turning him into a legend—he's the man who doesn't bother with light meters, he just looks at the back of his hand—gave it its tingling visual quality. The dialogue is exciting, too. The script, by Ron Shelton, working from a first draft by Clayton Frohman, is often edgy and maliciously smart. Terry Southern at his peak did no better than the lines Shelton has written for Richard Masur as Somoza's American publicity expert —the man trying to improve Somoza's "image"—as he offers condolences to the lover of a correspondent murdered by Somoza's troops: "Jesus Christ, a human tragedy. What can I say?" (Shelton was a professional baseball player for some time; he has been writing scripts for three or four years, but except for some rewrite work he did on *D. B. Cooper,* this is the first to be filmed.) What gives the movie its distinction is that the articulate, sophisticated characters don't altogether dominate the imagery. The Nicaraguans (some of them played by Mexicans, others by Nicaraguan refugees in Mexico) aren't there just to supply backgrounds for the stars.

With its concentration on the journalists—the outsiders—*Under Fire* is a little like Peter Weir's *The Year of Living Dangerously*, but visually and in its romantic revolutionary spirit it's more like the Cuban scenes in *The Godfather, Part II* and Gillo Pontecorvo's *The Battle of Algiers* and *Burn!* Spottiswoode isn't inflammatory in the way that Pontecorvo is, but in his more subdued impassioned manner he presents the case for the 1979 revolution—the one that the United States government has been trying to undo by backing the insurgents known as contras or anti-Sandinistas. (I assume that the title of the film comes from the words of Augusto César Sandino, the leader of a peasant army, who was murdered in 1934: "It is better to die as rebels under fire than to live as slaves.")

The revolutionaries, with their poetic peasant faces, are presented in a grand, naïve, idealized movie tradition. Anger doesn't make the Sandinistas mean or violent, and there's no dissension among them. (It's how we want to think revolutionaries are.) They don't have any visible connections to the Communist powers, either. Even so, this is one of the most intelligently constructed political movies I've ever seen. Its fictional inventions serve a clear purpose. Although the Sandinistas have always been led by a group, the story posits a single leader—Rafael— who gives the people hope. Rafael is featured in the graffiti—his face is the emblem of the revolution—but he has never been photographed, and the story involves the attempt of Price and Claire to find him, and the various forces that manipulate them before and after their search. One of these forces is a wily Frenchman, Jazy, who works for the C.I.A., and, as played by Jean-Louis Trintignant, he's a suave, lecherous imp. You know he's a dangerous little sleazo (he says he works for everybody, and he probably does), but he's also knowledgeable and witty. And when Somoza's men throw Price in the clink "for taking too many pictures" and kick him around, it's Jazy—a pal of Somoza's—who gets him released. Jazy is the kind of pal of Somoza's who amuses himself with Somoza's leggy young mistress, Miss Panama (Jenny Gago). The General himself is played by René Enriquez (of "Hill Street Blues"), who in fact is a Nicaraguan and was acquainted with Somoza. His performance is a finely nuanced caricature: this Teddy-bear Somoza deludes himself that he's an aristocrat with thousands of years of tradition behind him. He has perfected a form of infantilism—he sees only what he wants to see and hears only what he wants to hear. He's so locked in himself he's like a product of inbreeding—a genetic idiot who thinks he's a grandee.

The corrupt environment creates tensions in the gentle, affable Price: anger at the way Somoza's bullies treated him, and deeper anger at the way they brutalized the priest he shared a cell with. And something happens that upsets him so much that, photogenic as it is, he momentarily forgets to take a picture. When he and Claire are on one of their trips trying to find Rafael and are being escorted by Sandinistas, he sees the mercenary Oates hiding. Oates is out of his skull; he's an obscenity. (He stands in for all the mercenaries running loose in Third World countries.) But Price, being a journalist and regarding himself as "neutral," doesn't reveal Oates' presence. Then, as he and Claire are walking along and talking to their young Sandinista guide—who wears a Baltimore Orioles cap, because the Nicaraguan Dennis Martinez is on the team—Oates kills the kid. It's a spiteful, showoffy murder, and Price knows he could have prevented it. He's sickened; he's full of grief and disgust. It's Claire (whom he loves) who points out to him that he didn't take a picture; the artist-automaton broke down and behaved humanly, and that night is their first together.

When Price and Claire reach Rafael's hiding place and Price is asked to perform a crucial service for the rebels, he is emotionally prepared. He is asked to fake a photograph for them, and he does it, though this is a betrayal of his art and, if it becomes known, will almost inevitably wreck his reputation. Events then move very quickly. Shortly afterward, Price discovers that a whole series of photographs he took (just for himself) of the unmasked Sandinistas at Rafael's headquarters have been stolen and are being used by the demented mercenary Oates—a one-man hit squad—to identify the rebel leaders. Even Price's pure images are being polluted; they're being used every which way. They're marking his subjects for extinction.

Before Price came to Nicaragua, he was an overgrown small boy playing with what he loved to do: take pictures. (And this is why Nolte is a perfect choice for the role. He can be dumb, unthinking, oxlike, yet with a controlling intelligence and a central sweetness and decency.) In Nicaragua, where somebody's using you all the time, Price is in a new situation. Detachment can have hideous results, as he saw when the Orioles lover was killed. Whatever Price's misgivings as a professional photojournalist with a reputation for integrity, and whatever the effects of the action on his future, when he fakes the picture to help the Sandinistas he isn't destroyed by doing it—he's humanized. He is letting himself be governed by his own core of generosity. These are the terms of the movie, in which Price the photojournalist is a metaphor for movie director. Making movies, this picture says, isn't about purity. It's about trying to suggest the living texture in which people make choices that may—from an academic point of view—appear unethical, crazy, wrong.

The movie fills our heads with images of people under fire. There are terrified peasants and Somoza's equally terrified national guardsmen— probably peasant boys who signed up because they were hungry. At one point, Price and Claire are in a car in a provincial town, and the driver panics when guardsmen direct him to stop; he backs up, and, with guardsmen firing at them, Price and Claire jump out into the street and try to hide. There's not much sense to anything that happens during the insurrection. Peasants in dirt streets stare at a shiny big automobile in flames. Refugees in the provincial city of León mill in the streets trying to escape the national guardsmen who are shooting at them, and they're simultaneously attacked by planes. In some neighborhoods of Managua, guardsmen fire into the flimsy beer-can shacks, and shoot everything in the streets that moves—even squealing pigs. It's in this sequence that the movie reënacts the 1979 killing of Bill Stewart, the ABC correspondent, at a national-guard checkpoint in Managua. After kneeling and holding his hands out, to show that he had no weapons, Stewart was told to lie down, with his arms over his head, and was then—for no particular reason—shot, while his cameraman went on photographing the scene. I hadn't been aware of how that footage had stayed in the back of my head for four years, but at the movie, as soon as I saw the guardsmen standing there in the street, and saw one of the characters mosey up to them to ask directions, I knew what was coming; Stewart's death was still so vivid that this reënactment almost seemed to be in slow motion, and, with Price's shutter-click frozen frames, in a sense it was. The killing has an eerie inevitability about it. *Under Fire* isn't just reproducing a famous incident here, it's making us conscious of the images we've got stored up. It brings the Nicaragua of countless news stories right to the center of our consciousness. We knew more about the place than we thought we did. And Jerry Goldsmith's spare, melodic score (one of the best movie scores I've ever heard) features a bamboo flute from the Andes with a barely perceptible electronic shadow effect—a melancholy sound that takes you back. It tugs at your memories.

There's a good reason, I think, for the use of grownup people as the principal characters. These grownups aren't surprised or scandalized by what they see, and their lack of surprise is part of the unusual quality of *Under Fire*. There's no gee-whizz acting. After Hackman's Alex— who has been "hanging in there" with Claire, hoping she'll change her mind about wanting her freedom—decides to head back to the States and take the anchorman's job he has been offered, Claire says goodbye to him and watches as he goes off in the taxi that's taking him to the airport. Partway down the street, Alex sees Price walking up; he jumps out, and they hug each other. As he goes off again in the cab, Claire and Price both stand watching as it becomes smaller down the street and heads toward the hill in the distance. It's a beautiful shot, and expressive, too, because nobody (the audience least of all) wants Hackman to go. He's totally believable as a network's choice for anchorman—it's the quality in him that makes him so valuable to the movie (and picks up its energy level when he returns). Hackman seems leaner here than in his last films, and he's faster—he's on the balls of his feet. As the famous Alex, he maintains a surface jauntiness—he's professionally likable. But Alex has ideas ricocheting in his head, and whether he's sitting down at the piano in a Managua night club and singing or just basking in his celebrity he's never unaware of what's going on around him. He's always sizing things up—taking mental notes. He has an expansiveness about him; he's full of life (the way Jack Warden was in *Shampoo*). The three major characters have to be people who have been around, because outrage is not the motivating emotion of *Under Fire*, as it was in, say, Costa-Gavras's *Missing*. Spottiswoode and Shelton may be appalled, but they're not shocked. And they're not interested in presenting characters going through the usual virgin indignation. The United States has been setting up or knocking down Nicaraguan governments since 1909; the movie can hardly pretend to be showing us things we don't—at some level—already know. *Under Fire* is about how you live with what you know.

Joanna Cassidy, who has the pivotal role, is a stunning woman with a real face, and as Claire she has a direct look—the kind of look that Claire Bloom's characters have sometimes turned on people, and that Jane Fonda has had in her best roles. Joanna Cassidy is tall (Trintignant looks really petite when he's next to her), and as Claire she has the strength of a woman who's had to set her jaw and keep her smile for long stretches. Claire has had to be tough, and toughness deeply offends her. She has been struggling to keep some softness. The film catches her at a key time in her physical development. Running through the streets, she moves with extraordinary grace, and you certainly know why Price takes pictures of her sleeping nude. But her job has yielded her everything that it's going to. She has an almost grownup daughter, whom she talks to on the phone and on tapes—she would like to be with her. This is a time in her life when doubts have settled in. The foreign press corps, like the mercenaries, jump from one chaos to the next; they go where the armaments shipments are going. They keep the people at home "informed," but to the people they descend on they must seem like powerful celebrities who could change things if they would just tell "the truth." Claire is doing her job almost automatically now, and her mind has a roving eye. When Price's automatic-response system fails him—when he doesn't take a picture of the dead kid right next to him—it's a change in him she can respond to. None of this is spelled out for us; it's all there in Joanna Cassidy's performance and in Nolte's response to her physical presence. As Price, he doesn't use the low, growling voice that he had in *48 Hrs.*, and his beefiness is all sensitivity. Nolte never lets you see how he gets his effects. His big, rawboned body suggests an American workingman jock, but he uses his solid flesh the way Jean Gabin did: he inhabits his characters. He's such a damned good actor that he hides inside them. That's *his* sport.

I have been wondering why some members of the press show so little enthusiasm for this picture. (It certainly couldn't be more timely.) Possibly the movie ladles too much guilt on journalists. (The mercenary who has been poisoning Price's life bids him a cheery farewell—"See you in Thailand.") But I can think of only a few scenes that aren't brought off and only one that's clumsily staged: the last appearance of Trintignant's fascinatingly crisscrossed Jazy. Three frightened young Sandinistas who have come to his house to kill him wait around while he explains his political rationale to Price—his fear of the future Communist takeover. I think there's something in *Under Fire* that's bugging the press the way it was bugged a couple of years ago by *Absence of Malice*. Price's faking the photograph and accepting the penalties that will follow may be bewildering to the run of journalists who make decisions about what to report on the basis of their own convenience and advantage all the time. Since they do it unconsciously, they can easily be aroused to indignation at Price's conscious act. Maybe they know that they wouldn't do what he does, and they think that that means he's morally inferior to them. And maybe, like other professional groups, they don't like movies about them that don't glorify them.

Spottiswoode could be a trace too sane; the actors go as far as they can with what they've got to work with, but possibly he doesn't go quite far enough (and neither, possibly, does the script). Spottiswoode doesn't have the wild, low cunning that the great scenes in Peckinpah's films have—he doesn't spook us. But he does everything short of that. In its sheer intelligence and craft this is a brilliant movie.

October 31, 1983

HAIR

eart Like a Wheel is a biographical movie about the drag
racer Shirley Muldowney, who has won the National Hot Rod Associa-
tion World Championship three times. The director, Jonathan Kaplan,
and the writer, Ken Friedman (associates from their days at New York
University), don't glamorize their heroine—played by Bonnie Bedelia—
or try to turn her into a feisty, female Rocky. The film is an open-eyed
look at what it cost Shirley Muldowney to win out over men in what was
previously considered the domain of macho daredevils. And the feeling
of authenticity that it gives you is likably modest and sensible. Kaplan
gets his details right; the blue-collar people on the screen appear to be
accurately observed, without interpretation. Heart Like a Wheel is the
type of B picture in which the characters say flat, emotionally neutral
things in situations that seem to call for hyperventilating excitement.
This kind of affectlessness is sometimes praised as realism and as art.
But there's also a cost that Kaplan and Friedman pay: the film's "objective" surfaces don't yield much to us beyond the facts of the characters'
lives. Heart Like a Wheel has a B-picture sensibility. That's what's good
about it, and that's what makes it not good enough. What's on the screen
is like the raw material for a terrific movie, but if you try to assemble
it in your head you may discover that there's an awful lot missing.

At the opening, the child Shirley—perhaps four or five—is in a car
with her father, the honky-tonk singer Tex Roque (Hoyt Axton), who is
casually speeding on back roads. She feels carsick, and he knows how
to cure her. He puts her on his lap, and, with his big, burly arms around
her, she takes the wheel; when she gets the sense of controlling the
movement, she feels better—she loves it. When the car hits a bump in
the road, it seems to fly through the air; she's exhilarated and he's
gleeful as they ride together over the dark asphalt. The film jumps ahead
about twelve years, to 1956. Bonnie Bedelia is Shirley as a sixteen-year-
old Schenectady high-school girl marrying a gas-station attendant, Jack

79

Muldowney (Leo Rossi), a tall, well-built hot-rodder who's a whizbang mechanic and dreams of having his own garage. Shirley is at the wheel when they speed away from the church, and soon afterward the slender, delicate-looking bride picks up a drag-racing challenge that the groom doesn't think he can handle, and, driving his car, she wins.

The movie is about Shirley Muldowney's involvement with cars and men. And since it's a rare sport in which a woman competes directly with men, the picture has unusual overtones. In the years of her marriage, Shirley works as a waitress, and Jack, who works in a filling station, tools up the cars she races. They have a son, who goes along with them to the small-town competitions. It's a close family, with Jack apparently proud of his wife's driving ability—until she wants to move into the world of big-time professional racing. He thinks she's making a fool of herself, and accuses her of neglecting him and the boy, and then, fed up (and drunk), he smashes her dragster. That's the end of the marriage: they grapple and hit each other, and, with the child watching from an upstairs window, she clonks him on the head with a hefty flashlight and takes off.

The movie sticks to a biographical format, observing her progress year by year as she joins up with a champ, Connie Kalitta (Beau Bridges), wears hot pants as her trademark, and becomes a racing star, known as Shirley "Cha Cha" Muldowney. Her adolescent son (Anthony Edwards) works as part of her crew, and when she breaks with Connie she goes on alone (with the son, now full grown). The biographical material could have used more shaping, but the film is engrossing all the way through. Kaplan doesn't appear to have the sureness in domestic scenes that he has in the outdoors. The Oedipal mysteries that are hinted at seem a bit too symmetrical: when Shirley's son breaks in on a fight she's having with Connie, the three bodies become entangled, and the son (perhaps unconsciously trying to keep his mother from leaving him again) hits Connie with a wrench. Kaplan, a graduate of Roger Corman's action school, who directed seven earlier pictures and four for TV, is much more confident in the race-track scenes, especially after Connie and Shirley, having broken up, compete against each other (and our emotions are divided). While the movie was going on, I kept mulling over Shirley Muldowney's life, thinking that with just a twist here and there she would come across as a mean bitch who sacrifices the men who love her just for the satisfaction of winning races. And I respected the fact that Kaplan and Friedman were making what appeared to be (and often felt like) a feminist movie about a working-class woman who was fighting men on their own turf. Yet the picture left me feeling a little blank.

Bonnie Bedelia's role spans Shirley's life from sixteen to forty, and she's a highly competent actress, but I didn't know anything about Shirley Muldowney when the picture was over. I felt that I knew Beau Bridges' Connie Kalitta. Bridges brings dazzling radiance to characters like this rowdy, all too lovable philanderer; he shows you the fellow's insides in the flash of a nervous smile. His Connie is a stocky, blobby guy who's totally impulsive; he makes sense as a drag racer. Shirley doesn't. Why would a wary, suspicious person—a planner and pusher who thinks everything out—become addicted to a suicidal sport that takes place in five-to-six-second bursts of activity? Connie lives on his instincts. After an accident in which Shirley has been badly injured, she comes to the track, and a man grabs her by the arm—the arm that has been burned. Connie goes completely ape. He lunges at the man, hitting him hysterically; you can feel his wanting to kill the guy for inadvertently giving her more pain. It's perfectly apparent that Connie loves Shirley and admires her; you can also see that he's a skirt-chaser who humiliates her without meaning to. She feels let down by him; he violates her monogamous standards. Yet his roving eye is part of his radiance; he's always true to himself—to his impulses. And he means to give pleasure. Sitting there, I couldn't fault him for being duplicitous, but I didn't have to live with him. (He's that real, that close.)

There was someone else in the movie I knew—Hoyt Axton's Tex Roque, who's earthy and congenial and doesn't want his daughter Shirley to be any man's victim. Axton is a marvellous, unforced actor. As Tex Roque, he has gusto in his canny eyes and grinning face; he loves the life he's living. That's part of what's missing from Bedelia's performance: her acting is so tightly controlled that she has no zest. (Her body never moves without her conscious consent.) Bonnie Bedelia's high, rounded forehead and her childlike features made her seem forlornly pretty when she played Bruce Dern's poor, pregnant young wife in the 1969 *They Shoot Horses, Don't They?* Since hers was the only soft face in that picture, she was able to get by with a little-match-girl display of hopefulness and courage; she sang "The Best Things in Life Are Free" in a sweet, clear voice, and hearts melted all over theatre floors. She was soft again and even prettier in 1970, when she played the bride in *Lovers and Other Strangers.* Now, in her first starring role, she seems determined to show her strength. But actors show their strength when they let go; Bedelia keeps herself on a short leash with a choke collar. We don't see any of the child's exhilaration in the woman. Drag racing is a fulfillment of nothing we can detect in her character; it appears to be a career she has chosen and pursued methodically. (Running an orphanage in a Dickens novel might be more in her line.) What Bedelia gives Shirley is a dry and precise irony—which shines in a Christmas sequence, when she talks to her ex-husband on the phone, and then does a radio interview, also on the phone, with an interviewer who doesn't know the first thing about her. Bedelia has a smiling glitter as she talks to this fool on the radio. Shirley the champ is intensely aware of not getting the recognition that she thinks her accomplishments entitle her to, particularly at a time when women in more genteel sports are being celebrated. She resents the Cha Cha image, which she can't shake off. She's so hard and bitterly amused that the price she pays for being a champion seems like another form of victimization.

The moviemakers avoid sentimentality by not bringing their heroine to life. At times, what Bedelia's Shirley does has no meaning for us—it just seems as if she's doing it because that's what the real Shirley Muldowney did. And there's a detail that struck me as a beautiful (passed-up) opportunity to reveal something about her. Throughout the picture, Shirley wears a succession of elaborate, fake-looking black hairdos. They're as bizarrely stiff and ornamental as the ones on the women singers at the Grand Ole Opry, and they make her look like a dragon lady in a comic strip. (Her forehead is generally concealed.) I assume that this is an imitation of the real Shirley, and, to do the moviemakers justice, they may have felt that certain things are better left unexplained, because they're just too paradoxical to account for. But it isn't that kind of explanation that's needed—it's simply some illumination of the conflicting impulses in this woman. These heaping hairdos keep appearing on her, like a blight, and since we never go into her dressing room or see her primping or instructing the women at the beauty parlor, we have no way of knowing what weird notions of femininity they serve. Is it that the men she meets are more comfortable around women who look a certain way—that the men relate to what's unnatural, and that the thick, stiff curls make it possible for Shirley to feel accepted? Wouldn't it give the film's Shirley Muldowney more dimensions if we could see that unlike college-educated professional women who ask to be accepted for what they are, Shirley the hot-rod champ is still trying to pass as a classy belle? And *does* she pass? Does she get any pleasure from it? Or does it add to her feeling of loneliness and isolation?

In its own, limited terms, there's not much wrong with this movie. Kaplan stages plenty of action sequences (of the kind that action-film enthusiasts call "existential" and "cinematic"); he avoids dramatic climaxes (of the kind that these enthusiasts disparage as "theatrical"). And this can make a movie seem honest and authentically American—none of your highbrow stuff. Shirley's hardness can be seen simply as what happens to a woman who bucks a sexist society. Sometimes, the less insight a movie offers, the less it offends people. *Heart Like a Wheel* is probably being praised more for what it isn't than for what it is.

The film has one truly striking image that goes way beyond the verisimilitude that Kaplan and Friedman are after most of the time. Bonnie Bedelia's performance has been concentrated in her eyes; Shirley's intelligence shows in the way she takes in everything going on around her. Then she staggers out of her big crash in flames, and her son runs out to her. He looks into the charred helmet, and only one eye is visible—one terrified eye in a scorched patch of face, with even the eyelashes gone—and he stares into that trapped eye, trying to make contact with her, trying to assure her that she'll be all right. It's a great scene. It may even speak to the issue that is buried in the movie. There is a reason Shirley Muldowney hasn't become more famous for breaking the sex barrier in hot-rod competition. For the best of motives, women (especially young mothers) have not been eager to compete in thrill sports like drag racing. When Shirley's son—who will soon be the only man left in her life—stares into that smoking helmet, the scene exposes the superficiality of most of the film's treatment of Shirley Muldowney's determination to be the fastest hot-rodder of them all.

Educating Rita is no more than a two-character play—a duet —"opened up" a bit for the screen, but the lines have surprise and wit, and Michael Caine, who is one of its two stars, has become something of a phenomenon. He gives each new role everything that he can—if necessary, he's a show all by himself. Luckily, he gets some help here. He plays a dispirited college professor—a once promising poet who now poses as a boozehound and a burned-out slob. He tries to conceal his mediocrity by carrying on as if he were Dylan Thomas. Rita, played by Julie Walters (for and partly about whom the role was written), is a street-smart young hairdresser in Liverpool who signs up for literature tutorials in the Open University and is assigned to him. She wants the education that he, with his doctorate and his fancy turns of speech, has decided is worthless. He enjoys her quick mind, her slang, and the yowl in her voice. He thinks she has a more honest perception of things than his book-fed, upper-class students do; she's funny and eager to learn, and he delights in her alertness and her tattiness—a miniskirt and a maxi-coiffure and high heels that rattle on the university's old cobblestones.

Julie Walters' performance may be too "set" for the camera (she played the role on the London stage for about seven months), but her inflections are funny in unexpected ways. Rita is Julie Walters' role in the way that Billie Dawn in *Born Yesterday* was Judy Holliday's role; you enjoy these performances, knowing how worked-up they are. At first, Julie Walters seems tiny, with a pinched, doll's mouth, and she reminded me of Barbara Harris; then her brassy-waif quality suggested Shirley MacLaine, and before long she recalled a whole collection of funnygirls. (She has good fast timing.) Willy Russell adapted his own play, and some of the opening-out scenes he has provided actually work (this almost never happens); the director, Lewis Gilbert, has an affectionate touch here. The material isn't sustained—Rita, like Billie Dawn, is inevitably less entertaining after she's transformed. And there are scenes that sort of wobble around, such as the one in which Rita gives an educated, false response to the professor's poetry, and he sees right through what she says. And there are foibles, such as the professor's giving Rita a dress that we don't see him buy and never see her wear —what's it doing in the movie? But none of this matters much, because of Caine. About half an hour into the film, the professor is in a rage, and Rita says something hilarious out of the blue, and he breaks up—he can't help himself. The way Caine plays the scene, you'd swear she took him totally by surprise. Later, after Rita has been devouring the learning she is offered, the professor realizes he doesn't have much more to give her, and he becomes anxious, and jealous of the students she spends time with. His last trump card is Blake—he looks forward to teaching her Blake in the fall. When she comes back from summer school in the country and he realizes she has already "done" Blake, he is devastated, crushed. The news is tragic to him—he can barely comprehend it. He seems to turn red all over; he has been cheated out of giving her the last gift he had to offer. Their teacher-student relationship is finished prematurely—he isn't ready to accept it.

Michael Caine is the least pyrotechnical, the least showoffy of actors. He has prodigious ease on the screen; it's only afterward that you realize how difficult what he was doing is. His role here is a masochistic one, but Caine transcends that aspect of it. The professor's anguish at having nothing left to give Rita is also his recognition that he has lost his last vestige of superiority. For years, he hasn't been able to give form to his thoughts—they've been eating away at him, bloating him. We can see his impotence in his pink-rimmed, blurry eyes. He's crumbling from within. Somehow, Rita is the one person who reaches him, and after he accepts her token gift to him—she trims his beard and cuts his hair—he looks bewildered but years younger. His smirking terror is gone. This is a master film actor's performance. The goal of Caine's technique seems to be to dissolve all vestiges of "technique." He lets nothing get between you and the character he plays. You don't observe his acting; you just experience the character's emotions. He may be in acting terms something like what Jean Renoir was in directing terms.

November 14, 1983

THE PERFECTIONIST

Barbra Streisand's *Yentl* is rhapsodic yet informal; it's like a gently surprising turn of phrase. Set in the thriving Polish-Jewish communities of an imaginary, glowing past, the movie has its own swift rhythms. Its simplicity and unity are somewhat reminiscent of Jacques Demy's *The Umbrellas of Cherbourg* (1964); perhaps that's because the composer Michel Legrand wrote the scores for both, and the songs carry both films' emotional currents (though in totally different ways). Adapted from the Isaac Bashevis Singer story "Yentl the Yeshiva Boy," the Streisand film tells of a young woman who grows up in a tradition-bound community in which bright boys—yeshiva boys—live to study Torah. Coddled and prized, they sit at their books all day long, memorizing and reciting, debating moral issues, and attempting to fathom the unfathomable. Women are excluded from scholarship, but Yentl has a passion for religious study—she thinks it's the only way of life that's worthwhile. And so when her widower father (who has secretly taught her) dies, she dresses as a boy, sneaks away at night and goes off to enroll in a yeshiva in a distant town.

The beginning of *Yentl* is shaky. Streisand wants to make sure we get the idea that women are kept in ignorance, and she's a trace insistent. And the end is, I think, a flat-out mistake. But most of *Yentl* is, of course, its middle, which is glorious; it's like that of the story, though with different shades of humor. Yentl, a woman crowding thirty, passes as an adolescent student and feels like one. She's carefree and goofy; she has found herself—as a boy. (Yentl in disguise is definitely a boy, not a man. That's how the masquerade was conceived by Singer, and it works for Streisand the way it did for Katharine Hepburn when she passed as a boy in *Sylvia Scarlett*.) You can believe that the people in the Jewish quarter accept this smart, smooth-faced student, who has taken the name of Anshel, as male, because she isn't so very different from a lot of precocious, little-shrimp kids who seem to grow only in the head. Anshel is a sprite: as the yeshiva student, Streisand doesn't have an image of Barbra Streisand to play, and she lets herself be this slender and defenseless kid showing off his knowledge. When Streisand is playing a character, it releases something in her—a self-doubt, a tentativeness, a delicacy. She seems physically lighter; her scale is human, and you can share something with her that you can't when she's planted there as Streisand (and seems domineering). The basic concept of this movie lets her release herself, and as the yeshiva boy she's giddy and winsome.

Her singing voice takes you farther into the character; the songs express Yentl's feelings—what she wants to say but has to hold back. Her singing is more than an interior monologue. When she starts a song, her hushed intensity makes you want to hear her every breath, and there's high drama in her transitions from verse to chorus. Her phrasing and inflections are so completely her own that the songs make the movie seem very personal. Her singing has an ardent, beseeching quality—an intimacy. And her vocal fervor lifts the movie to the level of fantasy.

Streisand sings with such passionate conviction that she partly compensates for the sameness of Legrand's tunes. A few of them are exciting in context, but "This Is One of Those Moments" and "Tomorrow Night" are so dull they seem to be all recitative, and Legrand's music simply doesn't have the variety, the amplitude, to do justice to Yentl's full emotional range. The Alan and Marilyn Bergman lyrics don't rise to the poetic richness of the occasion, either; songs such as "No Matter What Happens" and "A Piece of Sky" are tainted with feminist psychobabble and Broadway uplift. Streisand's eerily way-out-there-by-itself voice soars, striving to achieve new emotional heights, and the music is on a treadmill. But as the director Streisand does graceful tricks with the songs. She uses them to take the audience through time and space. Yentl begins a song, and it continues in voice-over as the action races ahead. The songs are montages and comedy routines, too, with images of what Yentl is singing about edited to the rhythm of the music. During the song "No Wonder," a dialogue scene takes place while Yentl/Anshel sings a wry, funny commentary on it, and it's all brought off rather softly, without fuss. As a musical, *Yentl* conveys the illusion that the songs simply grow out of the situations—which isn't altogether an illusion.

The movie loses its sureness of touch now and then, but it's unassuming. It's a homey, brightly lighted fantasy. Yentl's teacher papa (Nehemiah Persoff) has the apple cheeks and jolly gray beard of a Yiddish Kris Kringle. And when he dies and she leaves home, a big bird who represents his spirit hovers overhead, accompanying her on her travels. The place Yentl grew up in, the inn where she breaks her journey, the town where she passes the examination and is accepted as a yeshiva student—they all have the familiarity and the pastness of places we know from folktales. Only the big, clanging gates of the Jewish quarter, which are closed at night, seem unusual, and it may take a second or two to register what they are, because the movie doesn't emphasize the specific nature of its folklore. It takes it for granted. (In a scene in which Yentl, dressed as a boy, pays for a ride on a farmer's wagon and then isn't allowed to climb on board, the point that the people on the wagon are gentiles who are pulling a trick on her isn't fully shaped for the audience, and some moviegoers may be mystified.) But *Yentl* isn't a sweet, tame musical. Coming out of that ornery, mischievous Singer story, it couldn't be. There's a running theme in Singer: human beings keep trying to flirt with God, hoping that someday a line of communication can be established, but sex always gets in the way. Their wonderful good intentions are thwarted by the tingle of the groin.

Dressed as a boy, Yentl is no longer resentful of male privileges, and for the first time she feels attracted to a man. At the inn, just after she has left home, she meets the virile, bearded Avigdor, played by Mandy Patinkin (who makes the impact here that he failed to make in *Ragtime* and *Daniel*). Avigdor is friendly and warm. He's also charged up sexually. After years of the repressed life of a yeshiva student, he can hardly wait to be married to the luscious ripe peach who is pledged to him. Yentl, who is aroused by his sensual fever, accepts his suggestion that she come to his yeshiva, and when, as Anshel, she is accepted there and is considered a prodigy, Avigdor's eyes sparkle with pride. He plays big brother to her, and she becomes his study partner.

Maybe the magic of this Singer story (and of many of his other tales) is that the folkloric characters have been imbued with a drop of D. H. Lawrence's blood, yet they live in a time when confusing sexual urges are explained as the work of demons. "Yentl the Yeshiva Boy" is a folktale told by a sly trickster: its elements don't stay within the conventions of folklore. (It's as if the story were a river, and fish were trying to jump out of it.) Things take a turn toward the disturbing in "Yentl the Yeshiva Boy"; they become quite turbulent. There's darkness on the one hand and ribald comedy—even sex farce and burlesque—on the other, but the storyteller remains imperturbable.

In the movie, when Avigdor's fiancée, Hadass (Amy Irving), a beauty out of the erotic pages of the Old Testament, enters the picture, it becomes a series of dilemmas and metaphors. The three principal characters look at each other with longing, and sometimes with fear and bewilderment. They can't sort their emotions out. Avigdor, not knowing that Anshel is a woman, feels a closer companionship with her than he has ever known with anybody else of either sex. When Hadass's father cancels the wedding and Avigdor is distraught, Anshel, his confidant, shares in his pain. And the brooding, pitiful Avigdor, having lost Hadass, and loving his friend Anshel, wants Anshel to marry her; that way, Avigdor won't feel he has totally lost her. He threatens to go away if Anshel doesn't agree to the plan. Meanwhile, Hadass, whose love for the burly, strong Avigdor is a mixture of attraction and terror, begins to love Anshel for his gentleness —Hadass has found a "man" she doesn't feel afraid of. The baffled Yentl, who sees in Hadass everything that she herself didn't want to be and couldn't have been—who sees that Hadass is like a slave girl when she's around men—is jealous of her and at the same time touched by her. Hadass's submissiveness is mysteriously sultry. And Yentl/Anshel—as if in a trance, thinking to hold on to Avigdor and also captivated by Hadass—asks for her hand in marriage.

One moment, Yentl is a yeshiva boy, taking pleasure in being the smartest kid in the class; the next moment, she's got herself in a fix. There's only one end to this story, and it's the one that Singer gave it: Yentl must go down the road in search of another yeshiva. She is condemned to the life of study that she has chosen (and a Chassidic scholar can never learn enough). It isn't difficult to figure out the thinking behind the film's ending, in which Yentl, restored to women's clothes, goes off to America, where, presumably, freed from the binding traditions of the

Old World, she can live as a woman and still continue her studies. The thinking is that you have to give the movie audience hope. (And there's even an attempt to show that Hadass will be changed by her encounter with Yentl/Anshel—that, Lord help us, she has had her consciousness raised.) Streisand tries to turn a story about repressed, entangled characters into a sisterhood fable about learning to be a free woman. She tries to transform a quirky folktale into a fairy tale. And it feels almost like a marketing choice.

But this is by no means a playing-it-safe movie. It's a movie about restrictive social conventions and about internal conflicts—about emotions and how they snarl you up. There are no chases, no fistfights or fights of any other kind. The picture is closer to the sensibility of the Ernst Lubitsch musical comedies than it is to films such as *The Turning Point* and *Rich and Famous*. And even when the characters' sex roles are blurred—when they're lost in a multitude of roles—Streisand as director keeps them all clear. Her vision is sustained—until the end. The closing shipboard sequence seems a blatant lift from the "Don't Rain on My Parade" tugboat scene in *Funny Girl*; it feels like a production number, and it violates the whole musical scheme of the movie. It also has Streisand wearing immigrant chic and playing the Streisand image. This misstep must have come from an excess of virtue. Streisand wants to give the audience an educational and spiritual message. She wants Yentl to be—gulp—a role model. Where Streisand's instinct as an artist fails her is in her not recognizing that Yentl exists on a magical plane, and that the attempt to make her a relevant, contemporary heroine yanks her off it. The script, by the English playwright and television writer Jack Rosenthal and Streisand, prepares for this ending by placing the action in 1904, but the Chassidic life that the movie shows belongs to an earlier, make-believe past. At the start of the film, a book peddler calls out "Storybooks for women! Sacred books for men!" By 1904, the novels—*War and Peace*, perhaps, or *Anna Karenina* or *The Brothers Karamazov* or *Middlemarch* or volumes of Dickens or Balzac—might have had more to tell Yentl than she could get out of the sacred texts. (A girl who couldn't study Torah may not have known how lucky she was. When Yentl sings defiantly "Where is it written what it is I'm meant to be?" the answer is: In those sacred books that she's so high on.) This musical creates its own frame of reference; its spirit is violated by earnest intentions. Streisand wants to create a woman hero, but when you read Singer, Yentl isn't the hero—the story is. And at its best the movie is the hero, too.

Streisand's long obsession with the material is well known; she began thinking about the story as a possible film in the late sixties, and bought the screen rights in 1974. Whatever the box-office results, her instinct was sound. It *is* the right material for her. And now that she has made her formal début as a director, her work explains why she, notoriously, asks so many questions of writers and directors and everyone else: that's her method of learning. And it also explains why she has sometimes been unhappy with her directors: she really did know better. *Yentl* is never static or stagy; the images move lyrically. The same intuitions that have guided Streisand in producing her records and her TV specials have guided her here—and taken her into some of the same traps. But, even if you object (as I do) to the choice of songs on her records and the manner of those specials, they're highly professional. Within her own tastes, she aims for perfection. Shooting on Czech locations and in English studios, and with the cinematographer David Watkin, Streisand has made a technically admirable movie, with lovely diffuse, poetic lighting and silky-smooth editing. And she brings out the other performers' most appealing qualities. It's a movie full of likable people. Steven Hill, who plays Hadass's father, gives marvellous line readings, and he has something of the same gnomish charm as Nehemiah Persoff's Papa; they're the elders as a child sees them. And Amy Irving's Hadass has a comically human dimension. The half-closed eyes of this slave princess as she serves dinner make her look as if she were deep in an erotic dream, but they are actually the result of her having had to be up at dawn to buy the fish. Her sleepy, plaintive beauty is the perfect foil for Yentl's skinny, anxious face. When Amy Irving just stands there, with her mass of thick, curly dark-red hair and with ornaments dripping from her head and body, she seems to be overcome by her own heavy perfume. She's dopey and she's sumptuous—she's the image of what women have wanted to be freed from, yet can't help wanting to be.

Streisand and Amy Irving play off each other with a kind of rapport that you don't see in movies directed by men. They have a scene in which Hadass, now in love with Anshel, tries to help him conquer his physical timidity—tries to seduce him—and Yentl is in pain as she backs away. It's a deeply ambiguous scene; thought went into it, as well as care. And toward the end of the film Streisand and Patinkin play a bedroom scene in which Avigdor, who has been sexually attracted to Anshel in the vagrant moments when he wasn't sick with love for Hadass, shows the limits of his understanding of a woman's needs. The scene is simply different from scenes conceived and directed by men; it has a different flavor. Avigdor is revealed as essentially a big, sweet Jewish hunk who could never accept a woman as an equal, and when he and Yentl part, the tapering, feminine hand she holds up in farewell puts a seal on his blindness. The whole movie has a modulated emotionality that seems distinctively feminine. That's part of why the independent-woman-on-her-way-to-the-new-land ending is so silly. There is something genuinely heroic in the mixture of delicacy and strength that gives this movie its suppleness. Within the forty-one-year-old star-director are the perfectly preserved feelings of a shy, frightened girl of twelve. She's also shockingly potent. So was Colette—and there's a suggestion of her in the Yentl who runs her fingers over books as if they were magic objects.

Bob Fosse's *Star 80* is about the degradation of everything and everybody. Fosse shows us skin and sleaze from fancy camera angles. The movie is based on Teresa Carpenter's "Death of a Playmate," in the *Village Voice*, and other accounts of the murder of the *Playboy* playmate Dorothy Stratten by her estranged bodybuilder husband, Paul Snider, a pimp and a two-bit promoter, who, after killing her, sodomized the corpse and then shot himself. Fosse, who wrote the script and directed, uses the case as evidence that murder is inherent in pornography and that the whole world is scummy. The central character, Snider (Eric Roberts), is a loser and a slime; he has False Values, and he's wacko besides. Roberts, who gave a tender, thoughtful performance opposite Sissy Spacek in Jack Fisk's *Raggedy Man*, uses a wet, mushy voice here, and he makes you feel the man's squirminess and rage. He gets the film's central idea across: that Paul Snider represents a mutation of the *Playboy* "philosophy," and that it's his frustration at not becoming a success like his idol, Hugh Hefner, that's driving him crazy. But Fosse, apparently deliberately, makes him loud and monotonous. He starts too high—shouting, and twisting his face—and as the movie goes on he sweats more and more, and the vein in his forehead does bumps and grinds. Dorothy, played by Mariel Hemingway, is so malleable she's a nothing, a big dummy. As Fosse has written the role, she's insultingly stupid. That seems to be a prerequisite for the small amount of sympathy allotted her. Mariel Hemingway tries hard and has a touching quality, but she's all wrong for the part —she's simply not a Bunny type.

There's no suspense: we know what's coming. But Fosse uses his whole pack of tricks—flashbacks, interviews, shock cuts, the works—to keep us in a state of fixated dread. Each time there's a cut to Paul spattered and smeared with Dorothy's blood—which happens at frequent intervals—the music screeches "Look!" There isn't even an early good-times period when Dorothy and Paul have something going between them; everything is ugly from the start. (Dorothy's mother, as played by Carroll Baker, is the only character who isn't on strings; she has some substance.) There's an incredible arrogance about this movie: Fosse must believe that he can make art out of anything—that he doesn't need a writer to create characters, that he can just take the idea of a pimp murdering a pinup and give it such razzle-dazzle that it will shake us to the marrow. But his razzle-dazzle is like Paul Snider's loud, flashy clothes and the grease in his hair. And Fosse's ideas aren't much better than Paul's, either. Every time Dorothy's picture is taken, the sound of the camera is like the sound of a gun being cocked—the photographers are killing her by inches. Other samples of Fosse's conceptualizing: When Dorothy acts in a cheapo movie, she bites a blood pellet at the wrong time and gets her face messy; when Paul kills her, he blasts her in the face with a shotgun. When Dorothy has her picture taken by a professional photographer for the first time, she's posed against a wall decorated with graffiti; when Paul uses his shotgun on her, her blood drips from a huge blowup of her face on the wall, recalling the graffiti.

In *All That Jazz*, Fosse forced you to look into his cut-open chest; now he's got more bloody innards to show you. The way he presents the movie, there's nothing at stake: Mariel Hemingway's Dorothy doesn't seem to have any depth and isn't meant to have any talent. And Paul is a pathetic, failed flesh-peddler. There's nothing else visible—just other forms of flesh-peddling at the *Playboy* mansion and the movie studios. That seems to be the film's meaning: that there's nothing at stake in the entire world, and nothing to do but be bloodied by it. *Star 80* is like a pointlessly gruesome update of John Schlesinger's *Darling*, with the very latest in smug self-hatred. Fosse has gone so far that the question arises: Can a movie get by with total disgust for its subject? Fosse piles up such an accumulation of sordid scenes that the movie is nauseated by itself.

November 28, 1983

RETRO RETRO

Sitting in the theatre where *Terms of Endearment* was being previewed, and listening to the sniffles and sobs of the audience that only a few minutes before had been laughing, I flashed back to *Penny Serenade* in 1941, the picture in which Irene Dunne and Cary Grant as a young married couple stood by helplessly as their little adopted daughter died. And I watched as, once again, the survivors overcame their pettiness and selfishness and showed the strength they had in them; they demonstrated their American middle-class (white) moral fiber. This is a real-life-tragedy movie that leaves you no choice but to find it irresistible. It's exactly the kind of bogus picture that will have people saying, "I saw myself in those characters." Of course they'll see themselves in *Terms of Endearment.* James L. Brooks, who directed it, guides the actors with both eyes on the audience.

He works this way in perfect sincerity. Brooks was one of the two collaborators who thought up "The Mary Tyler Moore Show," and he and three other fellows put "Taxi" together; as a writer-producer on those series (and others), he developed a sixth sense for what makes TV-watchers laugh. An enthusiastic reviewer said of the characters in *Terms of Endearment,* "You would be happy to spend several more hours in their company." That's exactly how you feel about the best half-hour series shows. They're entertaining in a random, eccentric way; you have no idea what will happen next. The acting has a comic-strip frame around it; it's stylized and comfy. The actors are out to please you and keep you coming back for more. And you want to like them. The characters they play represent our own notions of who or what we would be *if* (if we were snobs or buffoons, or whatever). Sometimes watching a character is like watching our alter ego going at a problem. Often the cleverest characters set themselves up for the line that demolishes them. (Of course, they're not really demolished: they continue to have lives after the commercial.)

In *Terms of Endearment,* which Brooks adapted from the 1975 Larry McMurtry novel, he keeps the audience giggling over the same kind of ramshackle comedy. Shirley MacLaine is all tics as Aurora Greenway, a snappish, compulsively neat widow tending her house and garden in the prosperous River Oaks section of Houston—a Southwestern Scarsdale. Aurora is a little dotty: in our first view of her, she's climbing into her sleeping infant's crib to make sure the baby hasn't died. Everything about her—her pert little expressions, her pinchedtight mouth and narrowed eyes, her standoffishness, and even the pair of devoted suitors who hang around for years—is quaint. This isn't meant as a putdown of Shirley MacLaine's performance; I don't know how else the role could be played. Aurora doesn't exist except as a pixie horror to string gags on. She's a cartoon: a rich skinflint with a blond dye job and pastel frills. Surely she's not meant to be believable? She's a TV-museum piece, like the characters in "Mary Hartman, Mary Hartman" or "Soap"; she's warped. And so is the pie-eyed lecher who's her next-door neighbor—a former astronaut named Garrett Breedlove, played by Jack Nicholson. (It's only in the world of TV comedy that characters *have* next-door neighbors.) Spanning thirty years in the lives of the cantankerous Aurora and her straightforward daughter, Emma —played from adolescence on by Debra Winger—the movie is one droll payoff after another, with Nicholson kept on the sidelines until Emma, married and with a child (and another on the way), moves to Iowa with her husband, and, after a time, Aurora and Garrett Breedlove have an affair.

It's a screwball, sitcom affair, but Brooks pulls some sleight of hand and "real feelings" come out of it. Aurora falls in love with Garrett the guzzler, but—in the psychiatric hand-me-down vernacular—he isn't ready to make a commitment. Aurora is, though, and the emotion she feels for him helps her become human; when tragic illness strikes her family, she shows her mettle. I think I hated *Terms of Endearment* the most when the grief-stricken Aurora embraces her longtime servant, Rosie (Betty R. King), who shares her misery. Greer Garson in her Mrs. Miniver drag was only a shade more noble. When Aurora and Rosie hug each other—sisters under the skin—the audience is alerted that Aurora is really a good person, and from then on she becomes useful and considerate. As the Second World War movies taught us, the function of adversity is to build character.

All this retro-forties virtue piled on the cartoon underpinnings of TV comedy shows might seem utterly nuts if it weren't for Debra Winger. The movie is a Freudian story of role reversals between mother and daughter, told in a slaphappy style. Most of the time, Aurora is a vaude-ville joke—she's the mother who's always phoning her daughter at the wrong moment. She refuses to attend her daughter's wedding, but phones her bright and very early the next morning. I didn't feel much love or any other connection between MacLaine's brittle Aurora and Winger's fluid Emma. They don't have the uncanny similarities—the vocal tricks, the syntax, the fleeting expressions—of real mothers and daughters. I'm not sure what Brooks meant to show us, but what comes across is Aurora as a parody of an anti-life monster and Emma as a natural woman—a life force. The two actresses might be playing in two different movies. Debra Winger—as she did in *Urban Cowboy* and *An Officer and a Gentleman*—gives you the feeling that she's completely realized on the screen. There's a capacity for delight that is always near the surface of her characters (and she never loses track of what turns them on). The adolescent Emma (in braces) has a husky, raucous voice and a lowdown snorting laugh; this is not a standard ingénue. Winger heats up her traditional-woman role and makes it modern by her aban-don. She floods the character. When Emma's two little sons give her a bad time and she fights with them, she's direct and all-out; she's totally involved in this power struggle with her kids, and they know it. While Aurora overgrooms even her back-yard garden, and the flowering bushes look cramped and forced (they're as contorted as the little statues stuck among them), Emma lives in the disorder of three children, dilapi-dated houses, not enough money, and a college-English-teacher husband (Jeff Daniels) who's having an affair with a graduate student. The predic-tions that Aurora makes when she tries to talk Emma out of marrying the handsome lunkhead—he's like a big, floppy stuffed animal—turn out to be accurate, but what Aurora doesn't foresee is that Emma will be fulfilled in the marriage and the kids. Emma thrives on the semi-con-trolled chaos of family life; she accepts messes—life is messes. All this is in Debra Winger's performance; she's incredibly vivid, and she has fresh details in her scenes—details like spotting a zit on her husband's shoulder while she's lying in bed next to him, talking to her mother on the phone. But Emma has been made too heartbreakingly wonderful. She's an earth mother, of course, with some sort of supernal understand-ing of Aurora, and when she has her third child she gives birth to her mother—her little girl is a tiny ringer for Aurora. The way that Emma is presented she's a glorified ordinary woman—a slob angel.

Brooks does some cramping and forcing of his own when he cross-cuts between Aurora's first date with the astronaut and Emma's extramarital romance with a timid bank officer (John Lithgow, as a jumbo-size shrinking violet). The two relationships may be vaguely parallel, but they take place in different time frames, and the film cuts back and forth between actions that are a few minutes apart and actions that are days or weeks apart. This is the clumsiest patch of the movie, although there are other sequences that don't come off—such as a trip to New York that Emma takes. And there are characters who don't come off—such as those perennial suitors, who seem to follow Aurora around just so she can be bossy with them, and Patsy, Emma's friend from her school days, who suggests the New York trip. (Patsy seems to be waiting around for her running gag to be given to her, and she never gets it.) But most of the time Brooks' TV-trained intuitions are more than adequate to what he's doing here—extending half-hour gag comedy to feature length by the use of superlative actors who can entertain us even when the material is arch and hopped-up.

The movie gains its only suspense from keeping Jack Nicholson waiting in the wings for almost half its running time. After eleven years of living next door, Garrett asks Aurora out to lunch; four more years pass before she accepts. By that time, you're so primed that his every kidding leer rocks the theatre. When he comes on to her in the Nicholson lewd, seductive manner and tells her that she brings out the devil in him, it may sound like the wittiest, most obscene thing you've ever heard. The years have given Nicholson an impressive, broader face, and his comedy has never been more alert, more polished. He isn't getting laughs because of his lines; he's getting them because of his insinuating delivery. He has one inspired nuance: when Aurora accepts his invitation to lunch, this flabby old astronaut glances up at the heavens as if to ask, "Why did you make me so sexy?" Whatever Nicholson does—lick his lips, roll back his eyes, stoop slightly, or just turn his head—he keeps the audience *up*. There's a charge of fun in his acting; he lets you see the bad boy inside him. When Garrett stands, stripped to his trunks, in Aurora's bedroom, it isn't just the flab hanging out that makes him funny—it's that he stands like a dirty-minded little kid who hasn't yet learned to suck in his gut, and an old sex warrior who can't be bothered.

There's nothing visually engaging in the movie except the actors. I liked the way Shirley MacLaine flung herself about in a hospital scene: Aurora has a tantrum because the nurses have failed to bring a suffering patient a scheduled painkiller, and you feel the emotions that Aurora has had to suppress suddenly exploding at the only target she can find. (This tour-de-force scene was the one time Aurora's rambunctiousness seemed to have any subtext.) I liked the desolate look on Lithgow's yearning face when Emma says goodbye to him. There are enjoyable bits all through this movie; a staggering amount of contrivance has gone into it, and when all else fails, Nicholson's sparse hair sticks out at the sides of his head, or something else is surprising and screwy. Brooks does perhaps his best directing with the two small boys (Troy Bishop and Huckleberry Fox) who play Emma's sons—Tommy, at about ten, and Teddy, at about six. The boys don't like a lot of what goes on between their parents, and they show it. On the other hand, Brooks is shameless about exploiting the children's emotions to jerk tears from the audience. The picture isn't boring; it's just fraudulent.

In this début film, Brooks appears to be a genuinely clever fellow with an inspirational psychology. Aurora, who has tried to keep life out, finally welcomes it. And, of course, Garrett Breedlove, the potbellied satyr, has to become a responsible guy. Brooks was probably attracted to the McMurtry novel because McMurtry's people are eccentric in a way that's supposed to make them lovable and forgivable, and Brooks, who added the character of Garrett, has made him in the same mold. Garrett is like those wastrel British aristocrats in the pukka-sahib pictures: when the crisis comes, his fundamental decency rises to the surface; he straightens up and does the right thing. He and Aurora are good Americans.

Terms of Endearment is being compared to two high-prestige, award-winning pictures—*Ordinary People* and *Kramer vs. Kramer*— and though *Terms* is both tackier and livelier than they are, the comparison is apt: it, too, is pious. And the piousness is integral to the whole conception. If *Terms* had stayed a comedy, it might have been innocuous, but it had to be ratified by importance, and it uses cancer like a seal of approval. Cancer gives the movie its message: "Don't take people for granted; you never know when you're going to lose them." At the end, the picture says, "You can go home now—you've laughed, you've cried." What's infuriating about it is its calculated humanity.

Carroll Ballard's landscapes are peerless; they achieve a kind of superreality. His great scenes have a sensuous, trancelike quality; the atmosphere seems outside time. And in his first feature, the 1979 *The Black Stallion*, this distilled atmosphere made it possible for a simple boy-and-animal story to be transformed into something mythological.

The boy's sense of wonder—his way of finding the mysterious in the ordinary—recalled *Pather Panchali*, but there were also elements of Arabian Nights fantasy that suggested the 1940 Korda production of *The Thief of Bagdad*, without the theatricality. *The Black Stallion* is a magical fusion; a friend of mine said that when he saw the picture he felt that he was rediscovering the emotional sources of mystery and enchantment.

I have been following the course of Carroll Ballard's filmmaking since the early sixties, when I saw a short he made as a student at the U.C.L.A. film school; that little movie and some of his work later in the sixties already showed traces of his ecstatic eye. The documentaries that he did for the United States Information Agency—*Beyond This Winter's Wheat* and *Harvest*—were breathtaking, with layered images that suggested one horizon above another, as in a Morris Louis painting. And he did the rollicking *Pigs* in 1967, and in 1969, for the Pasadena Humane Society, *The Perils of Priscilla*, about a lost cat, seen from the point of view of the terrified animal trying to find its way home. Then, in 1970, he made the celebrated *Rodeo*. The visual imagination Ballard brings to the natural landscape is so intense that his imagery makes you feel like a pagan—as if you were touching when you're only looking.

Ballard's gifts are awesome; so are the risks of filtering an ecological story through his sensibility. His second feature, *Never Cry Wolf*, from Farley Mowat's autobiographical book, is a failed classic—unspeakably beautiful but unsatisfying. It's about Tyler (Charles Martin Smith), a young biologist working for the Canadian government, who is sent to spend a year in what Mowat calls "the desolate wastes of the subarctic Barren Lands." Tyler's mission is to find a way to get rid of the wolves that have supposedly been devastating the caribou herds; this is of some urgency to the government, because the hunters are complaining that they're not getting their share. The facts that Tyler collects indicate that these hunters, rather than the wolves, are slaughtering the herds, but the proof is so difficult to photograph that the viewer is dependent in large part on Tyler's explanatory narration.

The movie fails as an adventure story: it simply doesn't have a dramatic core. It needs a more stirring script; the first hint of trouble comes when the pilot (Brian Dennehy) who flies Tyler to his icy destination engages in fancy philosophical talk—you feel you're in the hands of amateurs. The picture also needs a central actor with a greater range (and some depth). Charles Martin Smith was the Toad in *American Graffiti*, and he was very likable as one of the three Crickets in *The Buddy Holly Story*. He has a boyish quality, and Ballard must have felt that audiences would identify with him, especially since Tyler starts out as what in Westerns used to be called a tenderfoot. But the boyishness that comes through here is not the kind that people are eager to identify with—Smith's Tyler is crabbed, plodding, and, at the start, ineffectual. The performance feels thought out in advance. In the beginning, Smith is deliberately dopey; then he drops the dopiness—and Tyler is just a dull, well-meaning fellow. He's dull even when he behaves heroically. And—what's crucial here—there's nothing natural about the performance, and no sense of discovery in it.

The cruel fact is that more wolves would have helped; wolves that were more accommodating would have helped, too. The animals on the screen just don't seem eager to act out their roles, and they're not strong in the grandeur department—they look sort of scroungy. Children who went to see *The Black Stallion* could believe in that mythological horse because Ballard had fully created him; the wolves here are never characters. Despite the names that Tyler gives them, they have no discernible personalities, and nothing really happens between Tyler and the wolves. These long-legged creatures with tiny, sharp eyes are playing out a script of their own devising.

Ballard's theme is the magic to be found in nature. From the way the movie turned out, it appears that when he couldn't get magic out of Smith or out of the wolves he fell back on the snowscapes. In *Stallion*, you knew whose imagination was being fired—the child's. Here there's a lot of free-floating transcendence. It doesn't serve the prosaic story, but it certainly holds you. It holds you even though you may forget what the movie is trying to be about. Everything that Ballard (working with Hiro Narita as the cinematographer) shoots seems new, and it has a distinctive, shimmering purity. The only disadvantage of this is that since the essence of what Tyler learns is that wolves actually serve the ecology of the area, the movie's luminous vistas can give you the uncomfortable feeling that you're being handed a high-minded flower child's view of nature. Tyler tells us that the wolves actually keep the caribou herds strong—that they cull out only the weak and the diseased. If he had explained that the wolves aren't fast enough to run down the healthy caribou and so usually kill only the sick, we might not have had any trouble believing it. But the way the film's rationale is presented, it's as if the wolves were good Darwinians, mindful of the health of the caribou herds.

Visually (and aurally, too), the film is magnificent. Tyler is set down alone with his food and equipment in a flat expanse so icy, bare, and vast that it makes you laugh. He's a speck on a lunar landscape—a gigantic

99

stage for a Beckett play, with infinity right there around him. And every crunching footstep is magnified in this cold vastness. The noises, recorded by the sound editor Alan Splet (who worked with David Lynch on *Eraserhead* and *The Elephant Man*), aren't familiar; they belong to this plain of ice, and they seem to come at you from a distance, grow louder, crash, and then echo in waves. They're funny and terrifying, and the wolf calls have the wonderful eeriness you want them to have. Ballard knows how to use space and sound for a deranged, comic effect. In the film's climactic sequence, when Tyler wakes up to discover that the caribou herds are running past and this is his chance to see what the wolves will do, Ballard has him dash in naked among the animals. He's like a tiny boy in the midst of the rushing crowd of beasties. There's an idea here, all right—a realistic hero. What there isn't is an exciting hero. Tyler is always a speck in this big movie; when he talks about his insignificance, we believe it.

December 12, 1983

A DE PALMA MOVIE
FOR PEOPLE WHO
DON'T LIKE DE PALMA MOVIES

Al Pacino's Tony Montana is small and mean. The slash of a scar that runs through one eyebrow and down across the cheekbone seems to go right to his soul; there's something dead in his face—as if ordinary human emotions had rotted away, leaving nothing but greed and a scummy shrewdness. As the central character in the new *Scarface*, directed by Brian De Palma from a script by Oliver Stone, he scrambles up the rungs of the Miami drug world the way that Paul Muni, as an Italian immigrant, climbed to the top of the Chicago bootlegging business in the 1932 *Scarface*. Modelled on the career of Al Capone, the 1932 film, like the other prototypical gangster pictures—*Little Caesar* and *The Public Enemy*, both of 1931—was set during Prohibition. The basic story fits right into the early eighties: the new Scarface is a Cuban, one of an estimated ten thousand inmates of jails and mental institutions whom Castro, having his little joke, deported to the United States in 1980, when President Carter (briefly) opened the doors to Cuban refugees. Tony Montana boils with resentment because other people have a soft life, and more money than he has. "Me, I want what's coming to me," he says—"the world and everything in it." He's an angry, vindictive killer, and he sees America as the land of opportunity.

For the first three-quarters of an hour, the film is garish and intense. With Giorgio Moroder's synthesizer music pulsating and with shots of the arrival of the "Marielitos" (the Cubans who set out from Mariel Harbor), it feels like the beginning of a new-style, post-*Godfather* gangster epic—hot and raw, like a spaghetti Western. The swaying movements of music and image suggest a developing delirium. In these lushly ominous early sequences, the·American immigration officers spot Tony for what he is, and they put him and his pal Manolo (Steven Bauer) in a detention camp. We see the sadistic murder that the two of them carry out in order to buy their freedom, and then the first drug deal that Tony handles, which turns into a bloody massacre. These two sequences are planned and edited with staccato, brutal efficiency; De Palma seems to be adapting his techniques to naked melodrama, chain saw and all. (The massacre is awesome—a slapstick comedy of horrors which just goes streaking by.) And our first encounters with the other characters raise our expectations. Frank Lopez, the Hispanic-Jewish kingpin of the Miami drug trade, who takes a fancy to Tony, is like any number of movie producers: as played by Robert Loggia, he's a big, beefy windbag who enjoys being expansive and handing out paternal advice. Frank's bored girlfriend, Elvira, a Wasp junkie with silken blond hair and a mannequin's cool, is played by Michelle Pfeiffer, a funny, sexy beauty who slinks across the screen—she's the Platonic ideal of classy hooker. And Frank's henchman, Omar, an anxious pockmarked creep who has a big laugh for his boss's jokes, is played by the whirlwind F. Murray Abraham; he manages to look like a shark here, and every time he appears in a scene, its energy level jumps.

The film is fine until it gets into the 1932 story. The original *Scarface* unfolded rapidly; the scenes went bambam fast. In this 1983 *Scarface*, the same scenes are played languorously, in stately, pseudo-*Godfather* style, as if something were going on in the characters—as if they had an interior life and were going to grow or change. Just when De Palma needs every trick he can come up with, he gives up on "style" and goes straight. The original had a core of wit, but Oliver Stone's script just seems to touch the old bases, and after those showy early sequences De Palma tromps through the stock situations; nothing else he does has the rash brilliance of that Mack Sennett chain-saw sequence. His handling of the minor actors may be better than ever (Arnaldo Santana has a scene as Ernie—a flunky who expects to be killed and then isn't—that any actor could be proud of), and he works in a lot of little zaps, and always provides you with something to look at. It's the stuff up front that's sluggish. When Howard Hawks, who directed the 1932 film, and Ben Hecht, who wrote the script, decided to give their Al Capone and his sister the incestuous passions of the Borgias, they were having a nose-thumbing good time. This new film lingers over Tony's possessiveness about his sister, and is so obvious about it that the picture manages to make incest seem dated. Mary Elizabeth Mastrantonio, who plays the fiery sister, has a great camera face and is clearly raring to give a performance, but she's stuck with scenes that refer back to the mores of 1932. When Tony's mother (Miriam Colon)—a bone thrown to the moralists—goes through the standard poor-but-proud speech, telling him how worthless he is, the episode has an echo-chamber effect. If the actress faltered in her lines, the audience could prompt her.

De Palma may have felt that he could stretch himself by using a straightforward approach—something he has never been very good at. But what happens is simply that he's stripped of his gifts. His originality doesn't function on this crude, ritualized melodrama; he's working against his own talent. In desperation, he seems to be trying to blast through the pulpy material to something primal, and it isn't there. He keeps attempting to whip up big animalistic scenes, and then plods through them. And as the action rolls on, F. Murray Abraham is bumped off, and then Loggia (along with Harris Yulin, who turns up as a self-satisfied crooked narc and does perhaps the best work he's ever done on the screen). And the piquant Michelle Pfeiffer—she hunches her beauti-ful skinny shoulder blades when she's inhaling coke—doesn't have enough disdainful, comic opportunities.

After a while, Pacino is a lump at the center of the movie. His Tony Montana has no bloom to lose, and he doesn't suggest much in the way of potential: heights aren't built into him. Nothing develops in Pacino's performance. This is a two-hour-and-forty-nine-minute picture with a star whose imagination seems impaired. He wants to show us what an ignoramus this big-shot gangster is, and the role becomes an exercise in loathsomeness (on the order of De Niro's performance in *Raging Bull*), without internal contradictions or shading. Pacino isn't a lazy actor, and sometimes he comes up with invention that's really inspired —like the way Tony, who's all eyes for Elvira, bobs around her on the dance floor. It's the only time he seems youthful: Elvira wriggles by herself, grinding her pelvis ever so slightly—this is her notion of sophisticated dancing—and he bounces about like a horny country bumpkin. (Pacino was also inspired in the contorted, ugly dancing he did in *Cruising*.) But most of the time here he goes through the motions of impersonating a dynamo while looking as drained as he did at the end of *The Godfather, Part II*. He has no tension—his "dynamic" movements don't connect to anything inside him. Then he gives up the fake energy, and this is supposed to stand for Tony's disintegration. He's doing the kind of Method acting in which the performer wants you to see that he's living the part and expects you to be knocked out by his courage in running the gauntlet. Pacino is certainly willing to go all the way with Tony's drunken and drugged-out loutishness. But he may be too comfortable with it; he's sodden.

There was a major difference between Paul Muni's Tony in *Scarface* and both Edward G. Robinson's Rico in *Little Caesar* and James Cagney's Tommy Powers in *The Public Enemy*: Tony wasn't likable. It was his jabbing, phallic drive—the sheer "I want" force of the man—that made him exciting to watch. Stone and De Palma have retained this idea; likability is left to Steven Bauer, as Tony's loyal friend Manolo (the role played by George Raft in the 1932 version). Bauer, a bilingual Cuban-American in his mid-twenties who appeared in the eighteen-episode public-television series "Qué Pasa, U.S.A.?" under the name Rocky Echevarria, brings the picture a nifty mixture of businesslike murderousness and lover-boy sweetness. You can hook in to his character, and you may experience a pang when Manolo is killed. But Pacino is not the darting, energetic gangster hero who scores and scores. He's hollow from the start—he seems to have to act to look alive. And you don't feel a thing when Tony is finished.

This *Scarface* has the length of an epic but not the texture of an epic, and its dramatic arc is faulty: Tony is just starting to learn the ropes, and then, sated with wealth and dope, he's moldy. He seems to get to the top by one quick coup. We need to see more of his rise and how he managed it—how he built his organization and won the loyalty of his men. And we need to see his triumph. We miss out on the frightening exhilaration of Tony's winning his crown; there's no satisfaction for Tony or for the audience. We don't even get any of the gangster conspiracies that we might enjoy. The middle of the movie is missing. We get the aftermaths but not the capers. And Pacino seems to shrink with power; he looks as if he's about to disappear in a puff of coke.

Pacino has several scenes in which he's practically buried in money —we are given to understand that it's coming in so fast that it's a joke. And he also has scenes in which he's covered in cocaine: Tony dunks his face in it, or just shoves his snout in it. This, too, is a joke—the whole movie is a joke about consumerism (and capitalism). Tony gets everything he wanted—an estate with a tiger on the grounds, an enormous sunken tub for his bubble baths. The grandiose visual effects include a blimp with the words "The World Is Yours" spelled out in lights; it appears in the sky on the night that Tony disposes of Frank Lopez and lays claim to Elvira. The same words—they were the motif of the 1932 film, also—appear on the lamp (a globe of the world) that lights the Pompeian entranceway of the mansion that Tony and Elvira live in after they're married. The joke is how shallow he is, how degraded. He's a pig rooting around in money and cocaine, and, as things go wrong, he snorts more and more. (This could be a summary of how some movies are made now.)

Probably all this excess is intended to be satirical—snorting coke turns into a running gag. But the scenes are so shapeless that we don't know at what point we're meant to laugh. The ludicrousness that the moviemakers are showing us can't be sorted out from the ludicrousness of the movie itself. When the quick-tempered Elvira, who has regarded Tony as filth since the first time she saw him, suddenly throws a drink at him, and says accusingly, "Can't you see what we've become!," her line is a howler. And when Elvira complains of the boringness of Tony's constant use of a seven-letter obscenity it's like a criticism of the picture. The obscenities here *are* boring; they're used in the enervated way they were in *Rumble Fish*—the lines sound as if the actors were making them up. And in a picture with Ferdinando Scarfiotti as the visual consultant and such extravagant theatrical effects as rooms and terraces that are pastel abstractions, a painted mural of a tropical paradise on Frank Lopez's office wall, and home furnishings that suggest Roman Empire Art Deco, the flat, stunted language seems almost campy, like the language in the Maria Montez–Jon Hall–Turhan Bey epics. What is a moviegoer supposed to be thinking about while listening to Elvira's impassioned "We're losers, not winners" or hearing Tony say of Elvira, "Her womb is polluted"? (He also comes up with some variant of "You touch my seester, I keel you.")

The movie turns funny through a curdled, unfunny blowsiness.

Tony doesn't even spit out his expletives anymore; he slurs them. Elvira accuses him of not being much of a lover, and he sprawls in his bubbles in his big tub watching TV and muttering, "I don't need nobody." This isn't the usual *La Dolce Vita*, you're-never-happy-when-you-get-what-you-want movie. Tony is progressively immobilized. He lolls in the circular tub, and the camera rises high above him—he's a cigar butt in a bird's-eye view of an ashtray. The camera has to move because *he* isn't going to move. The dialogue doesn't move the scenes forward, either, and the action slows to next to nothing.

Tony is such a coked-up dullard that many of us in the audience—especially women—may lose all interest in him. His lassitude is our lassitude. But the moviemakers expect us to care about him because of their conception of his force. Near the start, Tony tells Frank Lopez that "the only thing that gives orders in this world is balls." And Tony, as he keeps demonstrating by his brutality, has "steel in his balls." That's what separates him from the other gangsters: he's fearless. This fearlessness—the *cojones* of a hit man—is the only explanation that the movie offers for Tony's rise in the world. And because he isn't afraid of anybody he dares to speak his mind. In a restaurant full of white-haired fat cats—a Wasp millionaires' stronghold—he yells, "You don't have the guts to be what you wanna be! You need people like me. You need people like me so you can point your fucking fingers and say, 'That's the bad guy.' "

Tony may sound almost passive; he may dribble saliva. But this is the film's message (or rationalization): that Tony is an honestly brutal businessman—he isn't a hypocrite like the Wasps. There's even the suggestion that he's better than they are because he isn't afraid to do his own killing. (The film's message is like a sociopathic moron's interpretation of Robert Warshow's thesis in his famous essay *The Gangster as Tragic Hero*.) The restaurant sequence is especially tinny, because the Establishment millionaires and their ladies are the usual Hollywood dress extras, and their polite, aghast expressions (and anonymous, helpful buzz) give them a stiff, Pop Art stuffed-dummy look. They're in a time warp. This isn't just a sloppy piece of filmmaking, though—it's the only piece of rabble-rousing that I've ever seen in a De Palma movie. When Tony, the drunken, corrupted peasant, tells off the old rich, he appears to be speaking for the writer and the director. And from the film's point of view he knows the truth about power and how it works. (It may be that Stone and De Palma got into these cheap distortions by using the movie business as their model for the world.)

The picture is peddling macho primitivism and at the same time making it absurd. Tony's sister does a creeping-hellcat seduction number on him, and he doesn't respond. She empties a gun at him, and her bullets can't kill him (or don't, anyway); he gets more vital as he's pumped full of lead. It takes men to shoot him down—in a rampaging, *White Heat* finale that involves an army of assassins and fills the screen with corpses, without generating much excitement.

At the beginning, we're led to expect that something terrible will happen, and what happens is that the director's concentration seems to fall apart, and his energies are dispersed. Maybe in giving up his artistry De Palma was trying to identify with Pacino's performance, and trying to persuade himself that the methods he was using here were more honest, more truthful than the way he'd worked on his other pictures. But Pacino's Tony has nothing to reveal. *Scarface* is a long, druggy spectacle—manic yet exhausted, with De Palma entering into the derangement and trying to make something heroic out of Tony's emptiness and debauchery. The director is doggedly persistent—compellingly so— but the whole feeling of the movie is limp. This may be the only action picture that turns into an allegory of impotence.

December 26, 1983

BUSYBODY

Meryl Streep gives a very fine performance as Karen Silkwood, considering that she's the wrong kind of actress for the role. Since she has reached great heights of prestige, and many projects are offered to her, she's the one who's making the wrong choices—she is miscasting herself. There's a scene in *Silkwood* in which Karen and the other employees of the Kerr-McGee plutonium and uranium fuel plant near Crescent, Oklahoma, are having lunch, and Karen, who likes to titillate her co-workers by showing them how freewheeling she is, nuzzles close to one of them—Drew (Kurt Russell), her lover—rubs his bare upper arm with her fingers, and then, swinging her hips and moving from table to table, starts to take a bite out of somebody else's sandwich. Meryl Streep imitates raunchiness meticulously—exquisitely. She does a whole lot of little things with her hands and her body; she's certainly out to prove that she's physical, and she seems more free here than in her other starring roles. But she hasn't got the craving to take that bite. If the young Barbara Stanwyck had grabbed the sandwich, we'd have registered that her appetite made her break the rules; if Debra Winger had chomped on it, we'd have felt her sensual greed. With Streep, we just observe how accomplished she is. She chews gum and talks with a twang; she tousles her shag-cut brown hair; she hugs herself; she eyes a man, her head at an angle. She has the external details of "Okie bad girl" down pat, but something is not quite right. She has no natural vitality; she's like a replicant—all shtick.

Karen Silkwood, who worked at the plant for two years, was contaminated by radiation—she had plutonium in her lungs—and might have died of cancer if she hadn't been killed in 1974, at the age of twenty-eight, in a car crash. She was on her way to a meeting with a *New York Times* reporter when her car veered off the road and into the concrete wall of a culvert. According to the legend that has sprung up, she was murdered because she was about to "blow the whistle" on Kerr-McGee and had documents to give the reporter which would have backed up her allegation that the mineral-resources conglomerate was not meeting quality standards in the production of plutonium fuel rods for the government, and was falsifying its records. (She had already presented thirty-nine claims of health-and-safety irregularities to the Atomic Energy Commission, which investigated her charges and confirmed more than half of them.) The most dramatic events in the various accounts of Karen Silkwood's life are circumscribed, because they're in contention (probably forever); there's no definitive version of what happened. As a result, the movie is a series of suggestions and insinuations and evasions.

What *can* be dramatized is the character of Karen Silkwood, and that could be enough, because, unlike storybook heroes and heroines but like many actual heroes and heroines, she was something of a social outcast. (As Simone Weil noted, it was the people with irregular and embarrassing histories who were often the heroes of the Resistance in the Second World War; the proper middle-class people may have felt they had too much to lose.) Karen Silkwood drank and popped pills and liked to play around. She had given her three small children over to their father, and at the time of her contamination she was going with Drew and sharing an apartment with a lesbian co-worker (called Dolly here, and played by Cher). She was—perhaps obsessively—centered on her duties as a member of the union's negotiating committee and worked gathering evidence to support her charges. She was a maze of contradictions, and a spirited actress could have made us feel what her warring impulses came out of. A woman who gives up her children is horrifying to many of us; we want to understand the sexual needs or the passion for freedom that drove Karen Silkwood to it, and how these emotions tied in with her union activism and the courage she showed in going against the company.

Meryl Streep sensitizes the character and blurs her conflicts. She plays Silkwood in a muted and mournful manner—Karen's sad, flirty eyes show the pain of a woman who doesn't quite understand how she lost her children, and can never get over it. She's haunted by her loss; she's fine-boned and fragile—a doomed, despondent woman with many an opportunity to smile mistily through incipient tears. And, returning to the screen after an interval of eight years, Mike Nichols, the director, soft-pedals everything around her. Kurt Russell is a marvellously relaxed, easy actor, and his talent comes through, even though he's used mostly for his bare chest and his dimples. Cher, who showed a likable toughness and directness in *Come Back to the 5 & Dime Jimmy Dean, Jimmy Dean,* is used as a lesbian Mona Lisa, all faraway smiles and shrugs. She has a lovely, dark-lady presence, but Dolly is a wan, weak role. In the film, Karen and Drew and Dolly live together in a small, rickety house, and both Drew and Dolly are in love with Karen; it's hard to know why, except that Karen is played by the picture's star. (They love Karen the way everybody in *An Unmarried Woman* loved Jill Clayburgh.) "I can't stay away from you," Drew tells her, and he demonstrates the very latest in gentle, good-animal lovemaking. And Karen has a scene sitting in a porch swing and holding Dolly and comforting her, because she can't love Dolly the same way Dolly loves her. By that time, the movie has refined a potentially great woman character and turned her into a neurasthenic object of sympathy and adoration.

Unable to take a stand on what happened and provide a set of villains (or of misunderstandings of accidents), Mike Nichols has made a passive advocacy film—it raises suspicions of many kinds of nuclear-age foul play, and everything is permeated with paranoia, hopelessness, and death. The movie is so cloudy and unfocussed that its high points are the moments when Karen's radiation sets off the plant's alarm and she is forced into a high-pressure shower—it suggests a concentration camp—and scrubbed down with an abrasive brush. That's when she's at her most helpless, and it may be the only time we in the audience identify with her.

The movie has a sad, depressive sting. It's absorbing because we know that many companies are in fact criminally careless about employee safety, and that when employee complaints are publicized, and accusations start flying back and forth, the plant may quietly close down. So we understand the fearfulness of the other workers, and their resentment when Karen—literally a busybody—sits around making notes. But the movie is gutted—it's aesthetically frightened and faded. Mike Nichols' work is erratic throughout. There are good performances by Craig T. Nelson, Ron Silver, E. Katherine Kerr, Sudie Bond, Josef Sommer, Fred Ward, and several others, but almost every one of them has a scene that gets frozen or hokey—Fred Ward is turned into a wooden Indian. The cinematography, by Miroslav Ondříček, is discreetly poetic, with the plains and the petrochemical plants and the people all in uneasy relationships with each other, but every now and then Nichols calls for a cloying, calendar-art-sunset lyricism that temporarily destroys the visual texture. There are melodramatic posturings by the implied "bad guys" which belong to an altogether different style of storytelling, and when the workers at the plant turn against Karen they could be posing for illustrations of a pamphlet on how capitalism whips workers. The dangling implication that Dolly somehow betrayed Karen to the Kerr-McGee managers is particularly unsettling; a scene in which Karen questions her and she acts guilty is out of "The Twilight Zone." It's hard to believe that the script—by Nora Ephron and Alice Arlen—could have had so many loose ends, and no finish. (The end of the film is chopped short. It must have been a special problem, partly because *The China Syndrome* borrowed what is widely believed to have been Silkwood's murder for its highway-chase sequence.)

Some scenes appear to relate to passages that were edited out. My favorite glitch comes about two-thirds of the way through the picture: When the simple, pragmatic Drew is fed up with Karen's spending so much time on union activities, he quits his job at the plant and wants her to quit, too, and come away with him. But she's all involved in her fight. She claims that he doesn't care if everybody at the plant is poisoned, and he leaves her, saying, "Don't give me a problem I can't solve." As he goes out to his car, he is followed by a large, devoted dog whose existence we hadn't registered before, though we did once see Drew—rather bewilderingly—pouring kibble into a dish. (This sequence ends with a wildly unlikely but very fetching romantic conceit: Drew comes back in, his face melting, and, taking Karen in his arms, he says, "I loved it, baby," before driving off. Men screenwriters would have been much less likely to have a man break up an affair in a manner so gratifying to a woman.)

Soon company officials come to the house that the three have shared; they find traces of plutonium there and accuse Karen of having deliberately contaminated herself so she could hurt Kerr-McGee. Karen reels off an elaborate explanation of how she was poisoned, and her words don't have the weight of thought. The scene is an embarrassment: Are we meant to think that she's lying, or is it just that Streep lost hold of the character? It's as if no one on the set were listening. Or watching, either; Karen's accuser looks at her with a blank stare of the kind that used to be called "pitiless." And there's an awful scene a little later, after the walls have been stripped down and the house evacuated: Drew comes back and wanders through the empty rooms in some sort of reminiscent daze, and he takes the front-door key as a souvenir—it's like something out of *Random Harvest* (M-G-M, circa 1942). The capper to the director's uncertainty is the song Karen sings, first onscreen and then in voice-over at the abortive end. Meryl Streep has a tender, scratchy singing voice, a little like Buffy Sainte-Marie's; her singing has more emotional lift than her acting—it's the only suggestive element in her performance. But "Amazing Grace"! It's the safest, most overworked song in contemporary movies.

There's no vulgar life in *Silkwood* except for Diana Scarwid's Angela, a cosmetician in a mortuary who has an affair with Dolly and lives with the three for a while. Scarwid does a vaudeville turn that rouses the audience from its motion-picture-appreciation blues. Standing ramrod straight, and with her bottom packed into pastel pants, she gets laughs out of her tight walk; she gets laughs out of lines that have no laughs. She prolongs syllables and twists meanings—she sounds like Jean Harlow as a Valley Girl. Scarwid seems to be the only person connected with the movie who isn't worried about not being artistic enough. (When she and Kurt Russell are bitching at each other, they're a terrific team.) And it's a lucky thing that Angela the cosmetician is around to ply her professional skills on this movie, because *Silkwood* is a stiff.

Meryl Streep has been quoted as saying, "I've always felt that I can do anything." No doubt that's a wonderful feeling, and I don't think she should abandon it, but she shouldn't take it too literally, either. It *may* be true for her on the stage, but in movies even the greatest stars have been successes only within a certain range of roles. Katharine Hepburn didn't play Sadie Thompson or Mildred Pierce, and Ginger Rogers didn't appear in *The Swan.* Anna Magnani didn't try out for Scarlett O'Hara, Bette Davis wasn't cast as the second wife in *Rebecca,* and Garbo didn't break her heart over not doing *Stella Dallas.* Part of being a good movie actress is in knowing what you come across as. My guess is that Meryl Streep could be a hell-raising romantic comedienne. (A tiny dirty laugh comes out of her just once in *Silkwood,* and it's funkier and more expressive than any of her line readings.) She has the singing voice for musical comedy, and the agility and crazy daring for knockabout farce. And maybe she can play certain serious and tragic roles, too—she was unusually effective in her supporting role in *The Deer Hunter.* But in her starring performances she has been giving us artificial creations. She doesn't seem to know how to draw on herself; she hasn't yet released an innate personality on the screen.

□

Lubitsch abandoned his famous light touch when he made the melodramatic burlesque *To Be or Not To Be,* in 1942. The actors gave noisy, effusive performances, probably because they were so gleeful at having the chance to make fools of the Nazis. And getting back at Hitler may have given Lubitsch such a charge that he thought everything the actors did was sidesplitting. All that the picture has going for it is a sort of crude, tireless enthusiasm. (It was made at a time when a lot of people thought that if you showed how ridiculous the Nazis were they would —magically—lose their power.) The new version, produced by Mel Brooks, has nothing to take the place of that anti-Nazi rambunctious-ness, and no new point of view. Set in Poland at the time of the German invasion, this *To Be or Not To Be* is still the story of a theatre troupe that outwits Nazi officialdom. Directed by Alan Johnson, who was the choreographer on several earlier Brooks films, it's a mild farce—benign but not really very funny. Johnson doesn't seize his opportunities to work up a head of steam. You know very early that you're not in the hands of a filmmaking wizard: during an air raid, you hear the conversa-tions of the actors as they scurry down to the basement shelter, and there isn't a single line that makes you laugh or relates to the plot. It's just filler—dead time. Comedians such as José Ferrer and Jack Riley appear in supporting roles, but the semi-new script, by Thomas Meehan and Ronny Graham, doesn't give them enough gags; the tall, dazed Christopher Lloyd has a good moment or two, but the only one who keeps his energy up high enough to give the picture a real boost is Charles Durning—he seems able to tune in to some private madhouse in his head.

The roles once played by Jack Benny and Carole Lombard—the husband and wife who run the theatre and are its stars—are now filled by Mel Brooks and Anne Bancroft, and the surprise is that she's the picture's chief asset. With her thick, dark curly hair cut short, pencil-line thirties eyebrows, a broad, lascivious smile, and her body jiggling in silver lamé, she's spectacularly sexy. Her dialogue is barely adequate, and at times her smile gets a little glassy and her expression says that she's floating, waiting to be told what's wanted of her, but she sustains the loose, invitational manner of a woman who is bored with her little putz of a husband and is eager for some action. (Her backstage dallyings with a young Polish bomber pilot—Tim Matheson—are timed to coincide with her husband's recitation of the "To be or not to be" soliloquy onstage.) There's a friendly warmth about Bancroft's vamping; she seems more at ease in the general silliness than Brooks does. It's not really *his* silliness: the Jack Benny role hasn't been fully reconceived for him, and he has to rush around in one disguise after another, pretending to be a whole series of Nazis. He loses the particular maniacal sophistication of Mel Brooks—he's like any other actor rushing around to keep a movie going. Brooks' plight reminded me of how ordinary the Marx Brothers were when they appeared in roles that hadn't been written for them, in the movie version of the Broadway farce *Room Service*. They didn't cut loose, and neither does Brooks.

The high spot of the film comes in its opening number—Brooks and Bancroft singing "Sweet Georgia Brown" in Polish. But even that number could have used more raucousness. It's a trace too bland, and it depends too heavily on Bancroft's dazzling smile and shimmer and shake. The two other musical numbers are duds. So are many of the plot-complication scenes, especially the ones featuring James Haake as Bancroft's dresser—a fey homosexual who wears flowered silk wrappers and matching shorts. When the Nazis come to arrest him, he tries to hide among the chorus girls onstage. The director doesn't seem to know whether the scene should be played for laughter or suspense or pathos. It's a mess. And the picture's be-kind-to-Jews-and-homosexuals tone is icky. The scenes centering on Jews being hidden in the theatre are awkward, because if the Jews are hiding in the basement, what does that make the actors on the stage? The implication is that Mel Brooks is a Polish Catholic. That's a first.

January 9, 1984

VANITY, VAINGLORY, AND LOWLIFE

here are two high spots in *The Dresser*, the film version of Ronald Harwood's play about an old Shakespearean actor-manager (Albert Finney)—a knight of the theatre who is touring the provinces with his dilapidated company during the Second World War—and his dresser (Tom Courtenay). In the first, the stage assistants and company members and Norman the dresser are in the wings banging drums and shaking clanging metal, trying to create a loud enough storm to satisfy the old man—they call him Sir—who is onstage playing Lear. And a cold, disagreeable member of the troupe (Edward Fox), a limping actor-playwright who despises Sir and has refused to help, is disgusted by the lack of professionalism of these noisemakers; he gets into their midst and clangs away enthusiastically, showing them how it should be done. In the second, which takes place in Sir's dressing room during the intermission, a young stage assistant (Cathryn Harrison) comes on to the aged warrior, hoping to obtain an acting job; she tells him she feels "the power and the mystery" in his room, and he lifts her up in his arms, testing her weight, feeling how much lighter she'd be as Cordelia than his wife—his Lady Wife, he calls her—who is growing a bit portly. Finney brings a wonderful mock gravity, charged with tumescent lewdness, to the flirtation. When Sir is excited, you can practically hear his rusty old machinery grinding and creaking.

There's also a lovely moment or two with Lockwood West as a heavy-set, elderly actor who must substitute for the (smaller) actor scheduled to appear as Lear's Fool and is stuffed into the Fool's motley: bulging out pitifully, he receives his last-minute instructions from Sir with such trembling eagerness to perform well that your heart goes out to him. I wish that this movie, directed by Peter Yates from Harwood's somewhat restructured adaptation of the play, were a comedy about the glorious, berserk life of the theatre, because in fond, light moments like this one we feel exactly what we're meant to feel, and more. And Finney is marvellously straight-faced and righteous when, as Sir, he reminds the company that the spotlight must always be on him. He's polished and funny in the opening scenes, in which the troupe is completing its engagement in a small city, with *Othello*; he pounces on his lines, caressing his vowels. Sir's humble bow to the audience is a masterpiece. So is his curtain speech, in which he refers to his Lady Wife but doesn't single her out from the company; nothing is allowed to distract attention from him. In the train station, his grand manner with his walking stick as he points the way for the others to follow him could hardly be bettered. And when he sees that the train that is to carry them all to the next town on their itinerary is pulling out, he thunders "Stop that train!" in a voice that resounds in the huge station like the voice of God. (The train stops.) Finney can gasp for breath so loud that he could be mistaken for a snorting bull; he has amazing sounds coming out of him—maybe the most stupendous vocal sounds in movies since Nicol Williamson's Merlin in *Excalibur*. And he brings humor to the role in the way he lets Sir's bombastic, declamatory style onstage carry over into his conversation; he's onstage all the time. He also has an arresting quiet scene: with the help of some ingenious lighting, this actor who's only forty-seven manages to look wasted and flabby in Sir's portable bathtub—an old man physically exhausted. More typically, he's batting his blue eyes dolorously, and his voice is honeyed with self-reverence, as he announces, "I'm a spent force. My days are numbered."

Almost everything in *The Dresser* is good except what relates to its theme: the symbiotic relationship of the grand old trouper and his dresser. The play and the script are written mostly from the point of view of the flyweight dresser, who cajoles and teases and mothers the old man, and keeps him going. Harwood, as a young actor, served for a while as a dresser to the touring actor-manager Donald Wolfit (who is probably best known to American moviegoers for his appearance as the rumbling-voiced tycoon with bushy eyebrows in *Room at the Top*), and there's an element of unconvincing fantasy at the core of the material. It's as if Winston Churchill's valet were to write a book about how he held his adored master together, pouring energy into him and enabling him to unite Britain to fight the Nazis, and then a film were to be made depicting Churchill's life just as the valet described it—a saga of dependency. Finney and Courtenay have to keep showing us the supposedly deep bonds between them, and pointing up the metaphor of Lear and his Fool. Courtenay's Norman is always hopping about, mincing and fussing, and talking, talking—cheering the old man on by performing for him. And it's a piece of choreography that Courtenay patented before he got near the camera. He played the role in Manchester when *The Dresser* opened there, in 1980, and again in London and on Broadway, and his interpretation has lost whatever connection it may once have had to Norman's emotions; it's externalized and rhythmic—it's all dried up.

Courtenay's performance is so practiced that the material becomes confusing. I wasn't sure if Sir, when he gets wildly distraught in the marketplace of the city where he is to play Lear in the evening, was going through routine shenanigans or a major crisis. And when that night he seems unable to summon the will or the strength to make his first entrance onstage I couldn't tell from Courtenay's flutterings whether Norman was used to Sir's being this much of a wreck or whether this was supposed to be the first (and, as it turns out, the last) breakdown. From Courtenay's responses, he appears to have seen it all a thousand times before. This is partly the director's fault. Yates (who has a background in the theatre himself) may have been so charmed by working with such accomplished actors as Finney and Courtenay that he failed to "make it new."

The movie is claustrophobic, and not because most of it is set on-stage or backstage but because the conception seals off the possibilities—Sir's death is all that can happen—and because there's a hot-house artificiality to the central relationship. I didn't believe in Norman's pure (though jealous) devotion to his master; it doesn't even go with Courtenay's tight face and his peevish, asexual tics. (I waited for the eruption of the poisonous resentment and malice that I assumed were lurking just beneath the fawning manner.) And I didn't believe in the subplot about the twenty-year unrequited passion that Madge (Eileen Atkins), the stage manager, is supposed to have for Sir. Madge is what in this country would be a Jane Alexander role; she's a construct—she gives you her whole character in the first closeup, and then gives it to you over and over again. What all this comes down to is that Harwood's real cleverness—which includes using the wartime bombing of Britain to give an element of gallantry to Sir's Shakespearean touring, and using the sound of an air raid to spur him on to give his greatest performance—hits too many hollow notes. And though Finney is often commanding and almost always witty, we never get a substantial enough taste of Sir's Lear; without that, Finney's performance lacks the final zing that it needs. It becomes a little less than titanic—rather amorphous, in fact.

But what's off-putting about *The Dresser* is that it's conceived as a tribute to Norman. "Shall we make an effort?" he says to Sir, who collapses against him sobbing. In the film's view, great actors are incorrigible, demented children; they need these dedicated, smothering servants. And the picture itself has a lot of Norman's pinched oppressiveness. There's a suggestion in the material that an English child needs an English nanny—which couldn't be more untrue.

□

A reasonably accurate test of whether an action movie is racist: Do the white heroes slaughter people of color in quantity, either affectlessly or triumphantly? This test isn't foolproof. In *Raiders of the Lost Ark*, Arabs are casually dispatched—it's as if the hero were skeet shooting—but the tone is clearly a parody of old-movie conventions, and I wouldn't call the picture racist. Thoughtless, maybe, but not racist. *Uncommon Valor*, a realistic action fantasy in which a group of Vietnam veterans get together for an expedition into northern Laos to bring out the missing-in-action men from their unit who have been slave laborers for ten years, *is* racist. The Communist soldiers are depersonalized; they're presented in much the same terms as the Japanese in Second World War films such as *Bataan* (1943). They're little yellow-peril targets. The plot mechanism that makes the movie effective is that the ex-Marines who undertake the raid—they're like a dirty half-dozen plus one, their leader, a former Marine colonel (Gene Hackman)—have been haunted for a decade. They can't forget the men who were left behind. And, with the United States government spying on them and trying to stop them, they're misfits, rebels, underdogs.

Directed by Ted Kotcheff, whose last film was the 1982 *First Blood*, a piece of primal pulp with Sylvester Stallone as a mistreated Vietnamvet Green Beret, *Uncommon Valor* is very shrewd about the chip on its shoulder: these tough guys who risk death to save their buddies are put before us as the kind of men who made our country great—and as men whom our country no longer has a place for. The colonel's obsession with the Marines classified as missing in action (his son is one of them) has resulted in his being forced into an early retirement; most of the others haven't been able to adjust to civilian life, because of their shame and their feeling of dishonor. In the film's nightmarish opening sequence, set in Vietnam in 1972, we see several of them running and climbing aboard the helicopter that is going to take them out; the rest of the men in their unit, carrying their wounded, are running toward it, with North Vietnamese soldiers right behind them, when the order is given and the aircraft takes off. We see the horror in the faces of the men being lifted into the air as they look back at the friends they're abandoning.

The colonel spends years tracking down the whereabouts of those forsaken men; at last, he obtains an aerial photograph of the prison compound in Laos where they've been spotted, and goes to round up his son's buddies—the Marines who got away—and persuade them to join him. It isn't hard: he gets a little initial resistance from a former major (Harold Sylvester), a black man who's now an executive, but most of them (Fred Ward, Reb Brown, and Tim Thomerson) are so plagued by Vietnam that they're rootless and welcome this mission. One of them— the bearded, half-crazed Sailor, played by the heavyweight prizefighter Randall (Tex) Cobb—is as ungenteel as you can get; a self-destructive biker who walks like a gorilla, he can hardly wait to go. With money supplied by an oil magnate (Robert Stack) who, it turns out, has a son among the missing, the colonel arranges to have a full-size model of the camp built in Texas. He and the men go into training there, and rehearse the raid. It's exciting to watch a group of men plan a life-or-death action, and then see what happens when they try to carry it out. These men figure that they'll have just three minutes to pick up the prisoners and get out.

At first, I was puzzled about why Gene Hackman was playing the colonel—who could be a gung-ho, wonderful-guy John Wayne hero—in such a dogged, almost impersonal manner. During the toughening-up period, there's horseplay among the six men, but the colonel isn't one of the boys, and there are no jokes about his being fifty. (Hackman, who as a young man spent five years in the Marines, looks hale enough to keep up with the others.) The essential difference between Hackman's performance and what John Wayne might have done in the role is that a John Wayne hero would have been so patriotically fired up that he would have enjoyed the killing he had to do to accomplish his mission. He would have brought a pop grandiloquence to the action sequences. And though the picture might have been a bigger hit, many of us would have rejected it as kids' stuff and perhaps laughed at how John Wayne was redeeming our national honor by winning the Vietnam War for us. Hackman's colonel treats soldiering in a businesslike way; his no-non-sense performance may even be a little more colorless than it needs to be. But he offers a range of held-in, adult emotion that you don't expect to see in an action film. The colonel is a fair-minded, rational, bitter man, with the hell of waiting etched in his face—the capture of his son has drained his life of any relaxation. He offers a terse explanation of why the politicians don't want to get the missing-in-action men out: because the war was lost. Wayne would have said that with sarcastic disgust. Hackman's disgust is internalized; he says it harshly, matter-of-factly. The politicians want to forget all about the war and the men who were sent to fight it. There's enough recognizable truth in this to soften the audience. Working from a script by Joe Gayton, the twenty-seven-year-old son of an Air Force sergeant, the director plays on the general cynicism about the government, and the feeling that though there may be American prisoners of war still alive in Southeast Asia, the politicians have written them off.

The film doesn't offer any explanation of why a small group of Americans would be used in Laos as a work detail under heavy guard. Vietnam is short of food and money, but it has a considerable labor surplus, and, with recent reports of a Labor Coöperation Treaty between it and the Soviet Union, and hundreds of thousands of Vietnamese being sent to work in Siberia, it seems likely that the Vietnamese government would want to trade any American prisoners for goods or money rather than go to the expense of hiding them and guarding them. But whether or not there's any basis for believing that there are Americans held as slave laborers, the movie is very canny in how it exploits our cynicism about the United States government's denials.

In *Uncommon Valor*, the government isn't seen as an expression of the will of the people, anymore, but as something completely cut off from them. The seven men, who have been psychically scarred and ignored—these men whose feelings aren't sanctioned by the government—express the people. The men who were lifted out by helicopter at the start are very appealing in the way they relate to each other; there's something they don't speak about but share. What they did last time left them feeling impotent; they're going back, and this time they're going to do it right. They're all low-key, except for the flamboyant Sailor. And, in the movie's terms, their defiance of the government—they keep going even after the C.I.A. fingers them to officials in Bangkok and their weapons are confiscated—is enough to make their mission honorable and make them heroes.

The film shows us Communists holding Americans prisoner and treating them cruelly; what's implicit is that the Communists are doing it because they're evil. It boils down to this: we know these seven Americans and we're touched by them; we don't know the men they're killing (or what they may have suffered). And so, during the weird, quick chaos of the actual raid, the audience has the pleasure of cheering each time a Vietnamese or Laotian soldier is bumped off. The exultant, patriotic American music on the soundtrack during these attacks adds to the audience's good feelings. Here, finally, is a movie about our heroes in Vietnam. The cheering is racist and childish, yet somehow not deeply offensive. It's as if the audience were saying, "This is how it should have been."

Uncommon Valor depends on the vainglorious idea that seven ex-Marines can take care of almost any number of foreigners. And it sets up typical action-movie ploys: The raiding group has a young, inexperienced member (Patrick Swayze), whose reasons for joining up are different from those of the others; probably the true reason is that the picture needs a juvenile lead so that the younger audience will have someone to identify with. And the film includes three heroic, anti-Communist guides who help the men over the border from Thailand into Laos. The movie is nowhere more fake than in its handling of these three spirit-of-the-good-Asian-people characters: an old man (Kwan Hi Lim)— Gunga Din with a gun—and his two strong, resourceful daughters (Alice Lau and Debi Parker). Introduced to "balance" things, sexually as well as racially, they are supremely courageous, and as inhuman as the evil Communists who have enslaved our American boys. John Milius was one of the film's producers, and it has overtones of his pop mythologizing, but Ted Kotcheff doesn't go in for big flourishes. He makes just one exception: Tex Cobb's wildman, called Sailor because he used to "take a lot of red wine and uppers and sail away." Sailor is all flourish; he could be a sentimental cartoon of the bearded, bearlike Milius. And, maybe because Hackman's colonel is so locked in his determination, the film really needs Cobb, whose performance is playful and uninhibited. Alone on the screen doing free-form tai chi in silhouette during the closing credits, he's an endearing figure—a big, slobby satyr. (He couldn't be more unlike the lean, relatively hairless Asians.)

Starting with its easily forgotten title (taken from the words of Admiral Chester Nimitz inscribed on the Marine Corps War Memorial in Arlington, Virginia: "Uncommon Valor Was a Common Virtue"), this movie is peculiarly understated, and maybe that's part of why it's so effective. It isn't a solid piece of work, like *Under Fire* or *The Dogs of War*, but it moves on a strong emotional current. The cinematography, by Steven H. Burum (he was the second-unit man on *Apocalypse Now* and recently did *Rumble Fish*) and Ric Waite (*The Long Riders, The Border*), and the smooth authority of the editing, by Mark Melnick, undercut the cheap jingoism. And Ted Kotcheff's directing has probably never been so assured. *Uncommon Valor* takes you by surprise. You don't expect this unheralded action movie to be as enjoyable as it is. And maybe the secret is that it isn't too obstreperously rousing. Kotcheff keeps the grandiosity in check. When the colonel first goes to see the ex-Marines, he finds that one of them (Fred Ward) has become an artist; this poor fellow's tortured wire sculpture is meant to reveal the state of his soul and tell us that he'll join up. Kotcheff makes the point yet glides right over the gaudiness. And the picture isn't virulent. Hackman's matter-of-factness tones it down; his face, glimpsed in flashes and in the background, gives it levels of feeling beyond sloganeering. Besides, the raiders don't all get out alive, the colonel's hopes aren't all fulfilled, and the picture doesn't milk the homecoming scenes. *Uncommon Valor* benefits from being small-scale. It's a middle-of-the-road right-wing fantasy. At its best, it's also an expression of the pain caused by the war we lost.

𝕾*udden Impact,* with Clint Eastwood appearing as Dirty Harry Callahan of the San Francisco Police Department for the fourth time, might be mistaken for parody if the sledgehammer-slow pacing didn't tell you that the director (Eastwood) wasn't in on the joke. The picture was one of the top hits of the holiday season, and maybe that has some dire meaning, but, once inside the theatre, at least some of the ticket-buyers were whistling and wisecracking. *Sudden Impact* features integrated scum—mostly black or swarthy, with many of indecipherable origins (Portuguese? Black Irish?), but with a few blonds salted among them. Once again, Harry—who doesn't have to wait for crimes to be reported but catches criminals flagrante delicto, and saves the state the cost of a trial by convicting them on the spot, with bullets —has been too efficient for the weak-kneed, lily-livered San Francisco politicians (liberals, all of them). So he's sent out of town to track down leads on a murder case; he drives to the picturesque coastal city of San Paulo (actually, Santa Cruz), where he's also besieged by robbers, sadists, killers. America has gone to hell—Harry can't cross a street without interrupting some heinous crime.

The murderer he's on the trail of is played by Sondra Locke, who, it turns out, is a saintly executioner, much like him; she's taking care of her quota of scum, and might just as well be called Dirty Harriet. The script conveniently provides a trauma in Harriet's past; she and her younger sister were hideously raped—and throughout the movie we get flashbacks to the leering, sweating faces of the rapists. The trauma is convenient in that it helps to account for Sondra Locke's frozen-faced inexpressiveness. But Eastwood, as director, makes the mistake of giving us a flashback to the pre-rape Harriet, and she's as blank then as now. Actually, Sondra Locke may be on to something. What expressions would be appropriate to this movie? By out-deadpanning Clint Eastwood, she comes across as the one and only right woman for him. But she takes a lot of beating and raping here, as she has in other Eastwood productions. And Harry is the only character who is glorified; he keeps coming back after the villains think they've killed him, and in one resurrection, at night at the amusement park on the beach, he walks slowly toward the villains, like the cowboy hero of a Western, with the boardwalk lights forming a halo around him. The picture is like a slightly psychopathic version of an old Saturday-after-noon serial, with Harry sneering at the scum and cursing them before he shoots them with his king-size custom-made "44 Auto Mag." He takes particular pleasure in kicking and bashing a foul-mouthed les-bian; we get the idea—in his eyes, she's worse than her male associ-ates, because women are supposed to be ladies. Eastwood's disap-proval of her impropriety sits a little oddly in a movie with sub-barnyard jokes about a little bulldog's hindquarters and a laugh-fest centering on a man shot in the genitals and a frankfurter covered with ketchup. It's the obviousness of everything in *Sudden Impact* that may be putting it over. The main sadistic, rotten villain looks at Harriet and says, "The bitch is mine." When you see a merry-go-round with a unicorn that has an outsize horn, you wait to see this guy land on it; naturally when he does, you applaud or hoot. Eastwood's movie-making might be euphemistically described as basic.

January 23, 1984

VULGARIANS AND ASCETICS

In the nineteen-seventies, Woody Allen, the first post-Freudian movie comedian, channelled his own anxieties and obsessions into his clowning. He was the first to use his awareness of his own sexual insecurities as the basis for his humor, and when he turned psychodrama into comedy he seemed to speak—to joke—for all of us. Moviegoers felt themselves on insiders' terms with the neurotic Woody Allen hero, who reflected their defenses, their feelings of insignificance, their embarrassing aspirations. But the culture has changed: Woody Allen no longer tells us what we think of ourselves. A wall has come down between him and us: in *Broadway Danny Rose*, which he wrote, directed, and stars in, he's on the other side, with the rest of the comedy specialists, beating against it, trying to make us laugh. It's as if he'd been blessed with perfect pitch for reaching audiences and had then become tone-deaf. No one has yet replaced him in the national consciousness, although after *My Dinner with André* came out, there was talk around the colleges that Wally Shawn would be the Woody Allen of the eighties, and there have been flurries of audience identification with John Belushi, Richard Pryor, Bill Murray, Steve Martin, Eddie Murphy, and even, after *Risky Business*, Tom Cruise.

Woody Allen is the spirit of the seventies incarnate, but he's also a determined guy, and he has developed something that may make him successful in the eighties: a fair amount of commercial know-how. The star of *Broadway Danny Rose* is not the Woody Allen we all felt ourselves to be (or, at least, to have a close connection with). As Danny Rose, Woody Allen isn't hip and he isn't dizzy with angst; the picture doesn't have any specifically modern themes. Danny is a small-time booking agent, a mild, patient fellow who nurtures his more promising clients until they're on the brink of stardom, at which point they invariably leave him and sign up with a big-time agent. The movie has close ties to the pictures that used to be made from Damon Runyon's Broadway stories or, sometimes, were simply based on his characters—*Little Miss Marker, Pocketful of Miracles, Guys and Dolls, Bloodhounds of Broadway, A Slight Case of Murder*, and perhaps two dozen others. They were about racketeers and entertainers with hearts of gold who had unlikely nicknames and spoke in a stylized tough-guy vernacular—Damon Runyonese. These lowlifes seemed to know nothing of the world beyond Broadway; they were a bit stunted, but were regarded with great affection, rather like the way Coach is regarded on the TV series "Cheers." Woody Allen himself isn't full of affection, though; he's spinning a tale without having any particular involvement in it, except, perhaps, in its *King of Comedy* underlayer—its condemnation of what it views as the scurviness of our time. *Broadway Danny Rose* seems "worked up," and though it's moderately entertaining and has some good fast talk and some push (it isn't as attenuated as Allen's 1982 *A Midsummer Night's Sex Comedy*), nothing in it feels easy or natural.

Danny Rose is Mr. Goodness-and-Poignancy. He lacks the deviousness and the blow-your-own-horn brashness to prosper; he's an agent without a conniving bone in his body. Woody Allen's Zelig was nobody in history; Danny Rose is nobody in show business. He's a little schmo in loud plaids, but he's also a virtuous man. The new Judas in his life is Lou Canova (Nick Apollo Forte), a barrel-chested singer in his forties with a dimply, piggy, Vegas smile and a voice to make musicians shudder. A has-been trying for a comeback, he suggests the least talented aspects of Buddy Hackett and Tony Bennett. In his first movie appearance, Forte is completely convincing as a ruffled-shirt vulgarian sweating with sentimentality. As the story is told to us, by Sandy Baron sitting at a table in the Carnegie Delicatessen with an assortment of fellow-comics (Corbett Monica, Morty Gunty, Jackie Gayle, Will Jordan, and others), Lou Canova is having a hard time balancing the demands of his career, his wife, and the woman he's hooked on—Tina, the brassy blond widow of a mafioso. Lou feels he can't live without seeing her. So when Danny has him booked to appear at a benefit at the Waldorf he insists that Danny go to New Jersey to pick her up and bring her to the benefit as if she were Danny's date. Danny's ordeal as he chases after the infuriated, balky Tina, trying to persuade her to accompany him—while hit men chase after the two of them—is the centerpiece of the film.

The audience's first sight of Tina is something of a shock, and her every subsequent appearance produces a faint ripple of disbelief, because this ruthless tough dame who chews gum with a vengeance, talks with a nasal Brooklyn accent, and has a teased-stiff mop of curls that come down to her big dark glasses is played by a padded-out Mia Farrow.

It's like seeing a Harpo wig and a Hart Schaffner & Marx suit on a statue by Donatello; she's a work of art in disguise, her face hidden. There's just one shot of Tina—looking in a bathroom mirror, with a towel around her head—that reveals the finely modelled Mia Farrow. The rest of the time, Tina is in motion, talking incessantly, and she sounds so much like Louise Lasser (who was married to Woody Allen and appeared in a couple of his early films) that the performance throws a curve into the material. Mia Farrow is certainly different here, but you can hardly see her, and her playing against type doesn't do anything special for the movie; it just makes you stare at Tina's mouth and chin—you look for signs that Mia Farrow is really lurking under the fright wig and shades.

Although the manner of this movie is deliberately raucous, and the decision to film it in flat, grainy black-and-white suggests that Allen may have wanted to give it a strangeness (as if it weren't happening now) and the feel of a takeoff, the material is rather unformed. It's larval, like Danny. The story's satirical underpinnings are never brought up top, and there's an element of something like cowardice—although it may be just nice-guyism—in the way that Allen shies off whenever there's a chance for something sharp. If you plotted a graph of the show-biz character traits that were the diametric opposites of Woody Allen's traits, you'd probably find that Lou Canova had them all, and the comedians at the Carnegie Deli, with their grating voices and gargoyle grins, had plenty of them. But though Woody Allen knows how repulsive Lou Canova's act is, Danny Rose doesn't. He isn't permitted to have either taste or consciousness. "God bless ya, darling," he may say nervously to an old lady who's detaining him when he's in a hurry. When he uses the phrases that are the stock-in-trade of cheesy entertainers, he wobbles somewhere between weaseling and spreading joy. The picture has a curdled, Diane Arbus bleakness.

Danny, with his *chai* (a Jewish life-and-luck charm) on a chain around his neck, is going to be sweet and dull forever—a kind, considerate person. The story is set, retrospectively, in an indefinite period; it's told as if Sandy Baron, the narrator, were in 1983 talking about a legendary figure of the past, but from the visual and verbal clues that we pick up, Sandy Baron seems to be in 1983 talking about 1982. *Broadway Danny Rose* may be meant to be a timeless fable; it comes across as a toothless fable. I wanted to hear Lou Canova's wife say something that would clue us in on what living with this singing oaf must be like. I wanted to know why the oaf was so madly in love with the squawk-box Tina. I wanted Danny's novelty-act clients (the woman who plays tunes on water glasses, the stuttering ventriloquist, the blind xylophonist) to say something so weird and redemptive that it would dispel the suspicion that we were supposed to laugh at them, lovingly, for being hopeless, elfin losers—while dear Danny Rose was adding to his goodness quotient by serving them Thanksgiving dinner. (It's a scene out of Dickens.) Allen leaves us in the uncomfortable position of waiting for laugh lines and character developments that aren't there. But he plugs up the holes with gags that still get laughs; he remembers to pull the old Frank Capra strings, and he keeps things moving along.

This is the only time a Woody Allen picture has made me feel that he was writing down—trying for a crowd pleaser. The 1959 English musical satire *Expresso Bongo*, with Laurence Harvey as a scrounging Soho booking agent, covered some of the same ground, but it had zest. The agent that Harvey played wasn't Mr. Virtue; he didn't turn the other cheek. In *Broadway Danny Rose*, the dimness of the images begins to merge with Danny's dimness. Woody Allen isn't all there in Danny. He has left out the hostility that made him famous, and the imagination and freak lyricism, too. As Danny, he's a Chaplinesque moral presence in a world of Catskills comics and Mafia hoods. Danny is a little cloying, and so is the movie. Agents can have a good cry.

□

The Italian film *Basileus Quartet*, written and directed by Fabio Carpi, is about the monastic life of a celebrated group of classical musicians. ("Basileus" is the Greek for king.) The story begins with the heart attack, during a concert, of the elderly first violinist, Oscar, played by François Simon—whose performance, cut short though it is, is the wittiest stretch of the movie. He does a ripe parody of the sniffs and tics of a hypersensitive fiddler. Oscar is really into the music—his eyelids are fluttering, his mouth is sucked in with prissy passion. He isn't just making music, he's responding to the music, and this is, of course, all tied up with the fact that a violinist absorbs the vibrations of his instrument in his cheek and neck. One part of him is listening to the music he's playing to make sure he's doing it right, and another part is responding in a way that the audience can't. The result—a violinist's seeming to swoon with ecstasy—gives him a special romantic appeal. (If you question this ecstasy, ask yourself why Isaac Stern's face always reflects a private bliss.) The story that Carpi tells is dependent on the romance inherent in classical fiddling.

Oscar's quartet has been together for thirty years, and at first the survivors, who are in their fifties—Michel Vitold as a repressed homosexual, and Omero Antonutti and Hector Alterio as repressed heterosexuals—think that Oscar's death means the end of the group and the beginning of new lives. They have no money worries; they can do as they like. But these men, who have been touring for decades and have no family except the quartet itself, feel lost on their own. And when Edo (Pierre Malet), a twenty-year-old virtuoso with long ringlets, flaring nostrils, and the animal sensuality of a young Nureyev, presents himself as the only man who can replace Oscar, they audition him and their problems are solved. They don't even have to make the decision to go on as a group; Edo's turning up makes it for them. *Basileus Quartet* is, in a way, like *Death in Venice* with three Gustav von Aschenbachs, or, perhaps, three men who represent different aspects of Aschenbach.

The writer-director very carefully builds the irony that the three aging men grasp: they have led emotionally impoverished lives—they have given up everything for their musical careers—but Edo denies himself nothing, and his music does not suffer. The others observe, and see what they've missed. Edo breathes heavily when he fiddles; women can't take their eyes off him. He meets their eyes, and the trysts are settled. As the quartet travels through Italy, France, Switzerland, and Austria, Edo—the darling, the pet of the three proud papas—has his pick of the beautiful women of Europe. He drinks, gambles, smokes pot, has an affair with a woman terrorist whom the police are tracking; he loves excitement. The life in him is, of course, too much of a shock to the other men, and, with no ill will on his part, he brings them to grief. One goes mad, another is destroyed, and the third is broken in spirit.

Fabio Carpi is by no means a great or original filmmaker, but the movie is pleasing. Though it was an inexpensive production (under five hundred thousand dollars), *Basileus Quartet* is calm, distanced, deep-toned; the men live well wherever they are, and the interiors seem as richly varnished as their instruments. They frequently perform at private musicales in palazzos and villas. (Alain Cuny—surely one of the most absurdly magnetic of all bad actors—is the host at a couple of their concerts, and his big, square head fills the frame.) But at heart this is a story about three aging monks regretting their wasted lives. (That's what I found disappointing about it: we may never get to see another movie about a string quartet, and this one turns out to be less interested in music and musicians than in demonstrating the perils of asceticism.) A fourth moper turns up when Hector Alterio bumps into a friend from his youth—Gabriele Ferzetti (he was the sell-out architect hero of *L'Av-*

ventura), who's weary and bitter. There's even a fifth: when Omero Antonutti goes to visit the woman he once loved, she's all gall and wormwood, and scathingly angry about her supposedly ruined face (though she looks fine-boned and elegant). With all these handsome, prosperous people complaining about being older than they used to be, the movie really should be a comedy. I don't mean to suggest that Carpi has no humor, but he's somewhat too measured and solemn in his approach. One Aschenbach may be tragic, but three? In *The Sea Gull*, when Masha says, "I'm in mourning for my life," it's funny. Here three men are saying it in unison, like a vaudeville team; the other characters who are introduced are also saying it. But Carpi doesn't see the joke.

The picture sags when the yearning old homosexual played by Vitold deludes himself that Edo is his lover, and chides the young musical and sexual prodigy about his naughty bad habits or breaks in on Edo when he's with a woman. Vitold's role is a literary cliché, with no surprises. What gives the film its sustaining interest is the faces of the actors—two of them in particular. Seeing Antonutti as the brutal father in *Padre Padrone* and as the peasant leader in *The Night of the Shooting Stars*, I never imagined that he could be at his ease in dapper evening clothes. And Hector Alterio, the Argentine who has starred in Spanish films such as *The Nest* and *Cría!*, is even more resplendent. These two—both with trim, lordly beards—bring the film force and dignity; the rounded domes of their high foreheads and partly bald heads loom in the wood-panelled rooms. If you're going to give a movie Old Master lighting, these are certainly the actors to soak up the light.

But the movie is essentially thin; the situation isn't rooted in anything. These aging musicians seem to have no contact with other musicians, no shoptalk, no insane anxieties about their instruments. They don't argue about the merits of other musicians or listen to the latest recordings. They don't even bitch about the acoustics of the halls they play in. All is gloom and empty lives. What's left out is what the men's music has meant to them. Anyone who has ever played chamber music knows how deeply refreshing and convivial it can be. If Carpi wants to demonstrate the damage caused by denial of sensual gratification, he has certainly picked the wrong vocational group. Playing in a quartet is like being part of a socially approved orgy. That's why some musicians consider it the greatest form of music-making: it's all feelings.

February 6, 1984

COMEDY, EPIC, SITCOM

In *The Lonely Guy*, Steve Martin, thrown out by his girl-friend, falls into a subculture of Lonely Guys, and we accompany him as he enters this secret society of men who recognize each other. (It's like the closeted gay subculture of the fifties.) The fun of the movie is Martin's stumbling into this world of outcasts and his earnestness in trying to conceal the signs that he's one of "them." Martin, who can't quite believe the situation he's in, puts all his energy into finding a new girlfriend. He's only a temporary Lonely Guy, but on his first day of this new life he meets Charles Grodin, a listless, permanent Lonely Guy, who becomes his close companion. These two Manhattanites engage in a series of partly improvised dialogues that take place in Central Park and around the city. When they walk together, Martin, the dreamer, has a spring to his step; Grodin, who has stopped dreaming, drags himself along. A dumpy fellow who's losing his hair, he looks as if his brain were fogged in. He's the essence of droopiness. His shoulders are bowed down, and he seems to have sunk into his floppy pants; he might have been born holding a weighted shopping bag in each hand. Grodin creates the character out of practically nothing—out of inflections—and, with Steve Martin playing straight man to his fud, they're a manic-depressive team. They keep coming up with absurdist jokes, Martin by being desperately starry-eyed and hopeful, Grodin by his frowns—by being negative about everything. And Grodin can't be budged.

It's too bad that the secret world of the Lonely Guys isn't more fully worked out, with more contrasting species and types. Except for the Steve Martin–Charles Grodin teamwork, almost nothing carries over from one scene to the next, and most of the people in the cast are marooned, trying to look animated when they have nothing to do and nowhere to hide. The film is at its peak when Steve Martin, having found Iris (Judith Ivey), a girl with a yen for Lonely Guys, and then lost her phone number, goes up to the roof of his apartment house and despairingly howls her name. His call is like a signal; it sets off other Lonely Guys on the roofs of other tall buildings, who howl the names of their own lost loves. It's as if Martin had discovered another wrinkle in the lives of Lonely Guys, and for a minute New York City is like a gothic village of howling tomcats. There are other scenes that stand out. The first time Martin goes into a restaurant and asks for a table for one, all heads turn toward him and a spotlight follows him as the maître d' seats him. At a costume party on a cruise ship, Martin, who's dressed as Charlie Chaplin, with derby and walking stick, loses Iris to a swinger (Steve Lawrence); he turns his back to the camera and for an instant recaptures the mood of the silent clowns as he walks out of the film frame with the Chaplin lonely-little-fellow walk, twirling his stick. At home in his apartment, Martin waters his plants and talks to them while Grodin, who's visiting, reads the obits in the newspaper, looking for the names of Lonely Guys who have killed themselves. ("This one's thirty-three.") Often, the execution of a gag is crude but you can still laugh at the idea; there's a sneezing-in-bed routine that could have been a classic if it had been given more care. The movie is flimsy, though. We don't find out why Martin's girlfriend throws him out or why Iris has a soft spot for Lonely Guys, and after Grodin has defined himself as a perennial reject he acquires a last-minute womanfriend. *The Lonely Guy* is generally likable, but it makes you feel as if you were watching television. At times, you *are* watching television: celebrities such as Merv Griffin, Loni Anderson, and Dr. Joyce Brothers drop in, the idea being that their appearances are automatically good for a laugh.

Adapted from Bruce Jay Friedman's 1978 *The Lonely Guy's Book of Life*, the picture was directed by Arthur Hiller, who is the opposite of a perfectionist. (His last movies were *Romantic Comedy*, which started pushing up daisies in its first shots, and the ineffable *Making Love*.) Watching some of the parts of this film that fizzle—the scenes with Martin at the greeting-card company where he works as a writer, or the scenes with Steve Lawrence surrounded by hordes of adoring women—I had the feeling that Hiller plows through a comedy script, shooting it diligently, right on schedule, whether the gags work or not. And then he begins the next picture. The script here—it's by Ed Weinberger and Stan Daniels, from an adaptation by Neil Simon—calls for Lonely People to jump off bridges and buildings, and the way that Hiller and his cinematographer, Victor J. Kemper, set up the shots, the stunt men and women risking their necks might as well be sacks of sawdust. Steve Martin deserves better craftsmanship and a director with some whoopee in his soul. Martin isn't just breezing through his pictures; his mind is working, his physical agility keeps your spirits high, and he comes up with little refinements in the midst of broad slapstick. He has a way of pronouncing "lonely" so that the first syllable has an aching sound; you can hear the character's sympathy for the plight of the lonely. His heart goes out to these guys, and it goes out to himself.

□

El Norte is about the flight of two oppressed, terrorized young Guatemalans—Rosa (Zaide Silvia Gutierrez) and her brother Enrique (David Villalpando)—who travel from their Mayan village in the highlands, which probably hasn't changed much since pre-Columbian times, to modern Los Angeles, where they pass themselves off as Mexicans and become part of the Hispanic cheap-labor force. Written by the director, Gregory Nava, and his wife, Anna Thomas, who was the producer, the film was made on a shoestring. It's an attempt at an epic, and in certain, dogged ways it *is* an epic; it's divided into three parts (set in Guatemala, Mexico, and Southern California), and it tries to cover all the bases—the typical difficult, wrenching experiences of Central American refugees. But it's an epic of the independent and underfinanced film movement, which means that moviegoers have to be willing to settle for humanistic aims and considerable amateurishness. The Navas (who met at the U.C.L.A. film school) couldn't shoot the Guatemalan section in Guatemala; they faked it in Mexico, and they didn't have the art directors and craftsmen to fake it magnificently. (They rely a lot on flute sounds to suggest the isolation of a mountain village.) Their Rosa and Enrique aren't Guatemalans, either; they're Mexican actors, and Enrique shows it. But the subject ties together with our own experiences of the Hispanics we see in menial jobs, and it gets to us, no matter how naïve or crude the moviemaking is.

The film's account of the mistreatment of the Indians, who pick crops under the eyes of an armed overseer, and of the violence that erupts—in which Rosa and Enrique's parents are murdered—has a ritual inevitability about it. It's a romanticized, idyllic life of oppression, with dignity, and the slender, quietly intelligent Rosa is very beautiful in her striped woven cottons and with a large jug of water on her head. We know that we're not in the hands of a great writer-director when the father, on his way to attend the labor-organizing meeting that will result in his getting killed, pauses to tell his fully grown son the story of how the rich men took their land away from them, and the son, after being told to go home to his mother, bows and kisses his father's hand, reverently. (In their own, non-Hollywood way, the Navas are shameless.) But in this folkloric section the stilted moviemaking is somewhat offset by the suggestion of García Márquez in the slightly hallucinogenic atmosphere: in the lavender light and some magical butterflies and an apparition or two. It's pasteboard García Márquez; it's merely part of the picturesqueness of the place, but it helps.

In the Mexico section, the Navas put Rosa and Enrique through a rapid series of ordeals. With the two of them learning how to deal with the authorities, fighting for their lives with a guide who means to rob them and kill them, and then having to crawl through a rat-infested sewer pipe to get across the border between Mexico and the United States, this is actually the best—the most straightforward—moviemaking. It's also the most conventional action-movie material. When *El Norte* reaches its richest possibilities—in Los Angeles—it gets bogged down in too many incidents that illustrate the perils in the lives of illegals but don't tell us much about these particular ones. Within a matter of days, Rosa goes from carrying water on her head to trying to operate an electronic washing machine in a Beverly Hills mansion. And she has a poignant quality: she seems insecure, smaller, lost. (Now the flutes on the soundtrack are her inner voice.) But Enrique—or Ricky, as he's called in the expensive restaurant where he works as a busboy—has nothing to draw us to him except his gullibility and his eagerness to please. Since the movie doesn't deal with America's role in the oppression that is driving Guatemalans to the north, its point must be to sensitize us to what they and other illegals in our midst feel and think, yet the movie doesn't enable viewers to see deeper into Enrique than the thoughtless Anglos on the screen do. If he's suffering any spiritual distress from leaping over centuries, we aren't aware of it. He looks simple to the people in L.A., and he looks simple to us.

Rosa and Enrique are used as representative characters, and it's on that basis that we can accept their lack of individuality, but then the didactic script pulls a shift on us. Rosa, who was attacked by rats in the sewer pipe, comes down with typhus, and here's the clinker in the film: her sickness prevents Enrique from grabbing his big chance—a job as a factory foreman in Chicago, and the legal status that will come with it. The director actually shows us the plane to Chicago flying off without him, and when *El Norte* starts operating on standard dramatic-crisis tricks the good will we bring to it dwindles. We may no longer feel any compunction about admitting to ourselves that it's uninspired. The

Navas want to be sure we get the great, resonant theme, and so Rosa, in her fever, with Enrique weeping at her bedside, tells us the lesson of the movie—that they are homeless at home and not accepted here. (This must come as a surprise to Ricky, who seems to have been adapting and making friends.) It *is* a great, resonant theme, though, and maybe that's why the film's ineptitude doesn't leave you feeling quite as empty as an ordinary mediocre movie does.

☐

Blame It on Rio is about father-daughter incest, in a disguised form. It's about a forty-three-year-old father's guilt and confusion because of his affair with his best friend's fifteen-year-old daughter, who is also his own teen-age daughter's best friend. Yet it's also meant to be a rollicking romantic comedy. The forty-three-year-old father is played by Michael Caine—he was born in 1933, and this picture seems to have aged him another ten years. I think this is the first time that I've seen Caine onscreen and taken no pleasure in his performance. He manages to give his flashy, "smart" lines a reading that makes them sound humanly plausible, but the result is counterproductive. His acting comes across as overemotional; the near-incest keeps him sweating and rushing about anxiously, and you just want him to get free of this picture—which is like a splurgy, risqué episode of "The Love Boat"—and back to sanity.

The scene that the movie never recovers from comes early. Caine and his pal, Joseph Bologna—they're British and American coffee executives who operate out of São Paulo—take their daughters (Demi Moore and Michelle Johnson, respectively) for a month's holiday in Rio, where the four of them share a villa. The girls go down to the beach, and when the men go there, too, ogling the bare-breasted women, they see the backs of two beauties, who turn, and their bare-breasted daughters come bobbing over to them, laughing at their discomfort and hugging them. It's as if a Doris Day–Rock Hudson comedy of the early sixties had gone topless. The movie mixes travel-folder footage of Rio that's colorful and showy in a rather insulting way—it seems designed for an audience of tired businessmen looking for tropical kicks—with these messy erotic-parental situations. The way the ripe-to-bursting Michelle Johnson is made up, she has the lewd expression that little-girl teases of six or seven sometimes get when they smear their mouths with lipstick; the moviemakers are obviously trying to launch her as a sex goddess, and trying too hard. They've got her snaring Caine on the beach at night after a Brazilian wedding celebration (macumba, and all that); she commands, "Make love to me," takes out her retainer, and wiggles invitingly.

Blame It on Rio was directed by Stanley Donen, and its executive producer was Larry Gelbart, who also wrote the final script, revising Charlie Peters' earlier version. (Claude Berri's 1977 film *One Wild Moment,* which has the same plot, isn't credited on the screen or in the publicity.) It's understandable that the moviemakers thought they were on to something, because they are, but it's not something they can handle in this touristy manner—and it may be that these particular moviemakers couldn't handle it in any manner. Most of *Blame It on Rio* is an attempt to squirm out from under its subject. The film goes on and on, prolonging Caine's misery. Bologna is enraged because his daughter tells him she has been having sex with an older man, but won't tell him who. He's obsessed with finding the man, and insists that his friend Caine be at his side. By the time Bologna is beating up strangers and reading his daughter's diary, the picture has degenerated into a smarmy sitcom. It oozes self-consciousness.

February 20, 1984

THE WOMEN

Entre Nous moves along in a relaxed and unruffled way as the French actress-turned-filmmaker Diane Kurys tells the story of two young married women in the nineteen-fifties who don't recognize how unfulfilled they have been in their marriages until they meet each other. In the preliminary scenes, set in 1942, Lena (Isabelle Huppert), a pretty eighteen-year-old redhead with a soft, curly long bob, has been arrested and brought to an internment camp for Jews in the Pyrenees. The camp is guarded by members of the French Foreign Legion, and one of them, Michel (Guy Marchand), writes her a note warning her that she may be deported to a Nazi camp and offering her marriage as a means of escape. She accepts. During the marriage ceremony, she discovers that he, too, is Jewish; she's incensed to learn that she won't have the protection of a gentile name. But she has no choice, and they hasten to the Italian border. Michel carries a small black suitcase with their possessions, and before they make it across the Alps and into Italy he's also carrying his exhausted bride, on his back. By 1952, the hardworking Michel has got himself his own garage in Lyons, and Lena, now the mother of two small daughters, has a fur coat, and a servant to do the cooking and cleaning. Lena meets Madeleine (Miou-Miou) at a school pageant. Madeleine, who comes from a moderately wealthy family, was an art student in 1942 and had married a fellow student, who was killed in a street skirmish between the students and the collaborationist police. (Miou-Miou lets out an impressive scream as her husband is torn up by bullets.) A widow at nineteen, Madeleine drifted into marriage with a sometime actor and sometime black marketeer, Costa (Jean-Pierre Bacri), and now she has a son at the school. Much more worldly than Lena, Madeleine seems somewhat dissociated from her own life; she seems to be walking through it, and her little boy, treated indifferently by his mother and made fun of by his father, is shy and scared of everything.

The two women become inseparable; they develop an intimacy that is based partly on their sitting around complaining about their husbands. For Lena, the friendship with Madeleine is like one long consciousness-raising session. She begins to see Michel as uncouth, as gross. Kurys, who collaborated with Alain Le Henry on the screenplay, presents the material in short, anecdotal scenes, skipping back and forth between incidents in the two women's lives as they struggle to define themselves. The two husbands are dark and hairy and grubby; they never look really clean. But Miou-Miou, a brunette here, with a short bob, is tall and elegantly slender in the long, full skirts of the early fifties, and she and Huppert are lighted and posed so that they are two heroic profiles, with taut neck tendons and beautiful chins. The men, who always seem to need a shave, are treated as lumps, as part of the common herd. The two women are romanticized and politicized; they're turned into feminist precursors.

The film is primarily about Lena's courage in leaving her husband, and in what has become known as "taking charge of your own life." After Michel has been driven half crazy by frustration at being closed out of Lena's new interests, she has the justification she needs to walk out on him, taking the children. At the end of the film, she and Madeleine (who left her own husband sometime earlier, had trouble holding a job, and went through a nervous breakdown) are about to open a dress shop in Paris, which will presumably thrive. There's no doubt that Lena is meant to be the heroine; the camera feasts on her determined little face. (Huppert, who's eager and responsive in her initial scenes, goes blank after a while and just stands stiff for the camera; when Lena is at her most heroic, Huppert seems totally outside the events of the story, as if she already knew the ending and were a little bored with it all.) The audience is cued, as it was at Paul Mazursky's 1978 *An Unmarried Woman*, to see the faults in the husband and the superiority of the wife. In one scene, Lena, who usually wears blouses with Peter Pan collars and prim, slightly boxy suits, puts on a clinging black cocktail dress that Madeleine has given her. Michel, who is supposed to be going out with her, tells her that she looks like a whore, and that her panty line shows; she wriggles free of her panties and leaves alone. There were cheers and applause from the audience I saw the movie with; you could practically hear the "Right ons" of the seventies. Kurys has shaped the scene like a cheerleader.

What's left unshaped is how Kurys feels about much of what she shows us. It's apparent that Michel has supported the family and built up his business without any help from Lena, who even leaves most of the child care to the servant. Lena is a proper bourgeoise who keeps her children in their place; she prizes refinement and respectability, and she doesn't like it when Michel roughhouses with the two little girls and makes up stories for them, or, at a picnic, galumphs around imitating an ape and uses his head to bat a ball. (How could kids not love a father like this?) Michel, a man with a capacity for enjoyment, has still got Lena on his back. He's married to an armored, frigid woman who, after she forms her attachment to Madeleine and discovers class, independence, and the arts, thinks herself above him. But this movie is not meant to be about a tight little bitch-princess with aspirations to culture. Kurys lets us see the two women's self-preoccupation and their unresponsiveness to their children, but this is all pushed to the side; it isn't given any weight. In one sequence, Lena and Madeleine take their kids out on an excursion, and Lena, busy talking to Madeleine, boards a bus, assuming that the kids are with them; after a while she notices that her older daughter is with Madeleine's son but her younger daughter is missing. Little Sophie has been left behind somewhere—Sophie, the five-year-old, who, we're told at the end, grows up to be the filmmaker herself. Diane Kurys shows her father slapping her mother on this one occasion: Michel slaps Lena for not caring enough about Sophie to keep an eye on her. Yet the incident is presented so as to call attention to Michel's oafishness rather than to Lena's negligence. She is somehow meant to be charmingly oblivious.

The psychology of the film goes in one direction; its sexual politics take it in another. What we see and what we're told we're seeing are in conflict. Michel is the only character that a viewer is likely to have any feeling for. Guy Marchand plays the role superbly, without any actorish fuss; Michel's furtive lecherous side and his outbursts are completely believable, and we can see that he made a tragic mistake when he proposed marriage to the pretty girl he'd never actually talked to. Lena will never love him, and she's so shallow that she may never understand the depth of his love for the children—he's completely enchanted when he's with them. Yet there is no apparent recognition on Kurys' part that Lena is a pill. Kurys doesn't dramatize what she felt about her mother *then*—at the time that she and her sister were taken away from their father. She has made a very peculiar kind of memory film; she identifies with her mother in a political, feminist way, yet it's the father who's loving and playful, and who's the suffering center of the raw, undeveloped material in the movie.

The director's idealization of Lena and Madeleine seems to be based on a traditional conception of women as being finer-grained and more sensitive than men, and this is joined to the seventies view of sisterhood. The two women—who live as if they were members of the leisure class —appear to be very casual about being taken care of; a cynical observer might suggest that their greater sensitivity consists in not doing anything to help the men, yet the director doesn't point this up. The husbands, working to provide for their families, are made out to be clods. Poor Costa, who's rebuffed or outsmarted in his every shady negotiation, keeps trying to be a wheeler-dealer. In one sequence, he borrows money to buy eighteen carloads of men's shirts, and they turn out to have only one sleeve; he sits at home at a sewing machine in a dark, cramped room, trying to turn each long sleeve into two short ones. Madeleine, who can see him from her bright, airy studio, doesn't commiserate with him, doesn't offer a hand; she isn't really in the marriage. Yet the scene is played not to show us her detachment but to show us his comic ineptitude. (He belongs in his sweatshop.) The film's feminism is so facile that we don't get any new perception of what women's relationships might have been like at that time. Is Madeleine's being upper-class gentile part of what Lena responds to in her? The movie doesn't give us a clue. And why is Madeleine attracted to the conventional-minded Lena—is Lena meant to have a vitality that Huppert didn't come up with? We don't get much insight, either, into why the apparently assured Madeleine couldn't function in a job and broke down. Nothing about her is revealed to us; she's a stranger until after her crackup, when she loses her composed look. Then she's pale, her face goes a little vague and glassy from confusion, and she's more like the Miou-Miou we know from Bertrand Blier's *Going Places*, Bellocchio's *Victory March*, and Alain Tanner's *Jonah Who Will Be 25 in the Year 2000* but without that Miou-Miou's infectiousness.

Entre Nous trivializes Lena and Madeleine at the same time that it romanticizes them. Their friendship seems to be about their great profiles and an interest in clothes. Nothing is going on in their heads that's different from what several generations of male movie directors have indicated. And they don't show signs of any physical, sexual pressure, either. "Why do I feel so at ease with you?" Madeleine asks Lena, and we never get an answer. Perched on a bed next to Madeleine, Lena says, "I feel like kissing you," but she doesn't do it. This is a movie about two women not having a lesbian affair. *Entre Nous* keeps teetering on the verge of a seduction scene that isn't there, yet that teasing possibility—suggested mostly by Madeleine's cool, knowing glances—gives many of the scenes their only tension. At the women's very first encounter, at the school, Lena realizes that Madeleine isn't wearing stockings, and gasps at her audacity; Madeleine runs a finger down her leg over her suntan lotion and then thrusts the finger under Lena's nose, giving her a whiff. After the dinner party where Madeleine meets Lena's husband for the first time, she whispers to Lena, "You're not made for each other"; she's flirting. And when she does a portrait of Lena she seems to be using traditional male-seducer blandishments. Early in the friendship, Madeleine begins suggesting that Lena leave her husband, and when the women meet secretly in Paris they dance together at a night club, while other patrons—their curiosity piqued—scrutinize them.

On the train to Paris, Lena lets a soldier make love to her. Describing the encounter to Madeleine, she explains that she didn't allow him to go "all the way"—and she had an orgasm, for the first time. Implicitly, male-female sex is low-class and unsatisfactory. If Lena had let the soldier go all the way, she wouldn't have had an orgasm. The film has a political commitment to women's friendship, and it comes very close to having a political commitment to lesbian sex—Lena and the soldier didn't do anything that the two women couldn't do—but Kurys doesn't develop that. She just keeps it lurking in the air, though the film's title in France was *Coup de Foudre*—love at first sight.

Are we perhaps meant to think that Madeleine breaks down because she couldn't quite have a love affair with Lena? Some of Madeleine's actions may look predatory, but there's a muteness about her. At several points, she seems about to "take" Lena, but she doesn't. Is this what wipes her out—her lack of sexual aggression? Certainly her breakdown wins the audience's sympathy—which she probably wouldn't have got if she had carried out the seduction. Lena's first venture into business, a boutique in Lyons that is financed by Michel, is called Magdalena—a marriage of the two women's names. Yet when Michel accuses the women of being dykes the accusation is treated as evidence of his low, limited mind, his incomprehension of the finer things. The two women appear to be above sex of *any* kind; their passivity is part of their superiority. (Those vulgar husbands are always trying to make out.) Kurys leads us to expect a sex relationship in order to hold our interest. (Nothing else seems about to happen.) But apparently we're supposed to think that whether or not the women are lovers is irrelevant to the changes in consciousness they bring out in each other. Lena and Madeleine are what used to be called soul mates; *Entre Nous* is about spiritual lesbianism.

Kurys doesn't build scenes dramatically or prepare for changes in the characters' behavior, and this lackadaisical flabbiness in the construction can be interpreted as lifelike. But we also keep waiting for moves that have been indicated, and they don't come. *Entre Nous* isn't really much of a picture. Kurys directs the sequences involving Michel and his daughters with all the affection and humor that one could wish for. She also gives Michel his due in his final scene; for a few seconds the film is flooded with emotion. But she's remarkably callous in her treatment of Madeleine's little boy; everybody ridicules him, and we're supposed to laugh at him, too. (He's made a pathetic clod, like the two husbands.) And there's something superficial and complacent in the tone of the movie: in the way it swings with the feminist party line of about five years ago—with what's taken for granted now, and has no threat in it. *Entre Nous* has no present-tense urgency; it's all the director's retrospective view. This may, of course, work to its commercial advantage. A battle-scarred audience may take pleasure in a film in which everything seems resolved. The only thing that's distinctive about *Entre Nous* is its veneer of post-feminism. Kurys achieves this restfulness by making a movie about sexual politics without sex.

The insipidness and the false leads all go back, I think, to a single cause: there's a deep and shocking violation of privacy in Diane Kurys' putting her interpretation of her parents' lives and quarrels and betrayals onto the screen. This movie depends on the filmmaker's revelation that Lena and Michel are her parents: that's how she can get by with her undramatized sequences. *Entre Nous* is presented under the guise of "This is how it was—it's real, it's life." There's a casual sort of chutzpah about the method. In presenting fiction minus the protective veils of fiction, Kurys is attempting to give birth to her parents; she's trying to re-create them for her own purposes. She takes possession of them, and then she tries to contort her feelings about the rigid, repressive Lena in order to make her a modern heroine. Kurys doesn't romanticize her mother out of love. You don't have to romanticize someone you love (as Kurys demonstrates in the father's scenes). And she doesn't do it out of rage. She romanticizes her mother for her own convenience.

Footloose is set in a mythical Midwestern community where everyone is white Protestant and there's only one church. Having this monopoly, the Reverend (John Lithgow) considers himself the town's spiritual leader, and he has been instrumental in passing various restrictive laws, including one against rock 'n' roll and dancing. His teen-age spitfire daughter, Ariel (Lori Singer), balks at the restrictions, but no one openly challenges the laws until Ren (Kevin Bacon), a high-school boy with a punk haircut, arrives in town from Chicago. A clean-living, courageous boy of the highest moral calibre, Ren is nevertheless misunderstood by the townspeople. Still, he manages to lead the students in a campaign for a senior prom. And, with Ariel's aid, he is able to cite chapter and verse from the Bible in support of music and dance.

Ten years ago, would anyone have believed this as the plot of an eighties musical? Directed by Herbert Ross, from a script by Dean Pitchford, who is best known for the lyrics he wrote for the songs in *Fame*, *Footloose* is so immaculately retrograde that the Midwestern town seems to be in a *Brigadoon* time warp; Ren, with his punk haircut, has stumbled into a peachy-keen fifties where high-school boys wear cardigans. The only memorable thing about this piece of neo–Andy Hardyism is the title sequence: an exhilarating short-short film featuring pairs of dancing feet in a variety of footgear. After that, there's one good brief scene: a little boy asleep in church is roused by his father, listens to a few words of the sermon, and goes right back to sleep. And there's an entertaining sequence in which Christopher Penn, as a sluggish hayseed—he's like a junior version of the nasal, frowning Charles Grodin in *The Lonely Guy*—is taught to dance by Ren, starting with getting rhythm in his hands. (There's a neat bit with Chris Penn and Bacon moving together, both wearing headphones attached to the same Walkman.) And Lori Singer has a startling, zingy radiance; she obliterates the other people on the screen—not a major feat, considering that Kevin Bacon has been made so smooth-skinned and well mannered that his grin is frozen on his face, and Lithgow, playing the glum Reverend earnestly and thoughtfully, as if he were a character in Ibsen, keeps bringing the film to a halt.

Footloose never really gets going; the moviemakers just exhaust one bad idea after another. They raid *Rebel Without a Cause* and give us a tedious game of chicken with the good lad Ren in one tractor and a big bad bully who has been dating Ariel in another. This rotten bully causes so many harsh, bloody fistfights that when we're finally on the homestretch, hoping for some dancing, and he turns up again, looking for another fight, there were groans in the theatre. Most of the action sequences seem bizarrely neurotic: Ariel deliberately risks her neck in stunts involving cars, trucks, and a train, and she provokes a nasty beating from the bully. My guess is that these were the moviemakers' passes at women's liberation; they exalt Ariel's death-defying battiness as if it were glorious bravado. But their machismo leaks through: as soon as this disturbed girl hooks up with Ren she seems sane as anybody, and a whole lot saner than the men who made the movie.

A musical can be forgiven almost everything else if it just has some good singing and dancing. But the singing here is only on the white-bread soundtrack, and the dance numbers are gymnastic specials. The kids seem to be warming up to dance rather than dancing, and in the hero's one big solo his movements are cut together with the movements of ringers. Just once, near the end, we see a dancer with his face in full camera, as he wriggles his shoulders and arms (the way Buddy Ebsen used to in the musicals of the thirties), and you can feel the people in the theatre rouse themselves, like that kid in church, and then, when the dancer disappears, sink back into apathy. Herbert Ross was a dancer himself. Doesn't he see that even with all the work done by the virtuoso editor, Paul Hirsch, the miracles of splicing aren't as entertaining as one eccentric dancer wriggling his shoulders? A lot of people must have gone through nerve-wracking labors and pots of money to produce these stupid wonders, and what's the point? The country is full of actor-dancers, and, like Bobby Di Cicco in the jitterbugging sequence of *1941*, they bring a movie an excitement that can't be faked. They have personalities; that's what these numbers produced in the editing room don't have. Footloose is what they're not. There's no freedom in the dances— they've been choreographed to death, chopped to pieces, and reassembled. For a viewer, it gets to be like watching programmed androids.

March 5, 1984

KING CANDY

Splash has a friendly, tantalizing magic. In the prologue, Allen Bauer, a quiet, moony kid of eight on an excursion ship off Cape Cod, hears a siren song and plummets into the water; before the child mermaid who yearned for a playmate can get a grip on him, he's pulled out. The little sea nymph looks back at him longingly, rubs the tears out of her eyes, and, with a pert toss of her tail, dives down into the deep. Twenty years later, Allen (Tom Hanks) is a tall, skinny fellow with curly dark hair that stands up above a rounded, childlike forehead; he looks vaguely like a question mark. Allen runs the family wholesale-produce business in New York; it's a frenzied, disaster-prone business, and Allen's older brother Freddie (John Candy) is delighted to let him run it —that leaves Freddie free to play. But Freddie also worries, because he loves Allen, and Allen—obscurely disgruntled—never seems to go crazy about a girl. It all changes one weekend when Allen gets into a funk at the wedding of one of his workers and, hearing the siren song again, heads up alone to Cape Cod. He falls off a tiny motorboat, which whizzes around, knocking him unconscious; when he wakes up on the shore, we see who has saved him—it's the full-grown, svelte young mermaid (Daryl Hannah), with long blond tresses and the iridescent color tones of a goldfish. She kisses him and disappears in the water.

Daryl Hannah—she was the murderous dancing doll in *Blade Runner*—is lithe and strong-shouldered, so that the tail and fins, which

141

elongate her body, seem to complete her. A mermaid's eyes must, of course, be blue, and Hannah has wide, piercingly blue eyes; she also has smiling curvy lips and the look of a beatifically sexy Nordic goddess, yet her flashing tail and fins are like a butterfly's wings—they're her most ravishing feature. But Allen doesn't see that part of her—not consciously, anyway. When this lovely nymph, whose scaly extremities are transformed into legs when she's on dry land, trails him to New York City, he's totally smitten by her but reacts to her unfamiliarity with American customs as if she were from another country, a stranger, rather than from a magical species, and strange. To Allen, she's like a dream of a Swedish au-pair girl.

Made by the team who were responsible for the 1982 comedy *Night Shift*—the director Ron Howard and the writers Lowell Ganz and Babaloo Mandel—along with, this time, Bruce Jay Friedman, *Splash* is the opposite of deadpan comedy. Even the bit players let you know how they feel, and Tom Hanks has the expressiveness of a little kid who can't hide a thing. When Allen is with his au pair, flickering shades of unbelievable joy cross his face, and he's so unused to simple pleasure it gives him tics. Ron Howard has been an actor for most of his thirty years, and he has a knack for bringing the sweetness out of his performers without lingering on it. He keeps a lot of activity going, and the produce market seems like a real place of business, with a bunch of raffish guys hanging around and Allen kept on the go every minute. (He barely has time to look at the aquarium he keeps in his office.) You get the sense that Allen isn't vitally interested in the business he inherited or in anything else, until he meets this amazing foreign girl and starts looking dazed. Daryl Hannah's unself-consciousness about being naked is the key to the film's charm; the mermaid is simply innocent of the ways of the world, and that includes clothing. She stares at Allen with undisguised adoration, and, of course, not being human, she's innocently sexy.

Ron Howard has a happy touch, and he's the first film director who has let John Candy loose. This gigantic, chubby Puck has been great in brief appearances (seventeen movies in the past five years), but the role of Freddie the playboy is the first role big enough for him to make the kind of impression he made in the SCTV shows and in his guest shots on "The New Show." John Candy is perfectly named; he's a mountainous lollipop of a man, and preposterously lovable. As Freddie, who carries a cooler with beer when he goes to play racquetball with Allen and appears on the court cradling a beer in one hand and smoking a king-size cigarette, he doesn't have a hypocritical bone in his body. When he encourages his brother to give in to temptation, he's not playing devil's advocate; Freddie the girl chaser gives in to his own giddiest impulses —he doesn't want Allen to be deprived. Candy has the same function here that Michael Keaton, the brainstorming hipster of *Night Shift*, had. He stirs things up and spars with Tom Hanks. As a bon vivant and man about town, Freddie takes an almost lewd pleasure in his own vanity; he fancies himself debonair and light on his feet, and he is. But he also makes you aware of his bulk by the tricks in his verbal timing: when Hanks has said something to him and you expect him to answer, his hesitation—it's like a few seconds of hippo torpor—is what makes his answer funny. There's a certain amount of aggression built into a frame as big as Candy's: he simply occupies more space than other people do. But Candy doesn't have anything like John Belushi's insane volatility or the gleam in his eyes that told you he was about to go haywire and smash things up; Candy is the soul of amiability—it's just an awfully large soul. Freddie is the older brother you always wanted to have. He's Falstaff at fourteen, and the picture probably wouldn't work without him; he doesn't add weight, he adds bounce and imagination.

There is a whole cartoonish side of the film, involving a nuthead scientist obsessed with finding a mermaid, and a different, quite horrible mad scientist who's eager to perform sadistic experiments on one; most of this involves a lot of chasing around, and basically it's dumb. But Eugene Levy, of SCTV, who plays the nut case, is inspired; his voice is a raspy, deep foghorn, and his wiry hair and his specs are so vivid they seem to have taken over the man. Levy exults in the comic-book eccentricity of the role; everything he does is insanely deliberate—every particle in his body waits for instructions from the paranoiac brain. (As the sadist, Richard B. Shull doesn't have much to do. Mercifully.) It's easy to see the reason for all this subplot busywork: the writers needed to supply danger and urgency to keep the film in motion, and demented scientists were the best thing they could come up with. (And this yock material may actually be a relief to the part of the audience that likes the familiarity of TV humor.)

Splash is frequently on the verge of being more wonderful than it is—more poetic, a little wilder. That verge isn't a bad place to be, but the movie doesn't go far enough with, for example, the mermaid's delight in her discovery of the sounds that street musicians make, and of earth music in general. There's a fine joke that's set in Bloomingdale's and involves Allen's pressing the heroine to tell him what her name is, and her letting out a series of shrill, rhythmic sounds that remind you of dolphins and whales. (Her quick mind is dolphinlike, too.) But though the moviemakers encourage their young hero to plunge into the unknown, too often they keep their own feet on the ground. The writing is likable and clever, but in limited ways, and the plot is an encumbrance—it doesn't release the possibilities in the theme, it shunts them aside.

Some scenes let you down. When the nuthead, who has been stalking the girl, spots her and Allen leaving a hotel where the President of the United States has been guest speaker at a fund-raising bash, he sprays her with water from a hose. She metamorphoses and is helpless on the sidewalk, a fish out of water, and is surrounded by press and photographers with strobe flashes. And Allen, who is separated from her in the melee, is stunned and somewhat repelled by her turning into a mermaid. This doesn't make much sense in terms of his character (he thought he saw a mermaid when he was eight, so he should feel vindicated), and it leaves a vacuum at the center of the film. Matters aren't helped any by his being thought to be a sea creature, too. He's caught and put in a tank in a back-room laboratory in the Museum of Natural History, and when the mermaid is brought in, wrapped in a net, and lowered into the tank with him, while the scientists observe them, he's frightened of her and doesn't go near her. The picture seems all balled up, because his confused emotions aren't what a magical story calls for; he fails the first test of his love—he's not imaginative enough to deserve this treasure. It isn't until he's let out and Freddie talks sense to him that he pulls himself together and the movie gets back on course (but nothing he does afterward quite makes up for the revulsion he showed). Meanwhile, the nuthead scientist sees her and is appalled at what he has done. She's huddled in misery at the bottom of the tank, tendrils of spun-gold hair waving around her in the water. She's like a Pre-Raphaelite illustration for a fairy tale about a princess in captivity; it's a lyrical image of total depression—she looks near death.

Allen finally goes to the rescue, and everything ends as it should, except that we're a little shorted on poetry even at the very last. We need to feel the contrast between the tank she was dying in and the oceanic freedom she returns to; we need to feel that she reënters a boundless magical realm. What we get is too modest, too confined. The underwater photography is dreamily satisfying, and Daryl Hannah moves like the glistening vision of mermaids that we all carry from childhood, yet more time is given to the cars chasing the car that takes her to New York Harbor than is given to the final mysteries of the deep. (There don't seem to be many.) And there's just one redeeming detail in that stupid car chase: the full blast of Eugene Levy's voice as he says "Move!" But the picture has a generous spirit: even this paranoid has a change of heart.

And the heroine's having a tail gives romantic love the edge it needs. *Splash* gives you part of a movie you've always wanted to see; it's entrancing enough to suggest how blissful it might have been. The day after you've seen it, you may find yourself running the images over in your mind, and grinning.

God, how I have come to hate car chases. They've become an empty ritual. In *Against All Odds*, it's a macho contest between Jeff Bridges in a Porsche and James (The Snake) Woods in a Ferrari; racing side by side, they play their game of chicken through heavy traffic on Sunset Boulevard. And it's so grotesquely pointless that the embarrassed director, Taylor Hackford, tries to salve his conscience by including an apology: Bridges, the narrator, tells us that it was stupid and he shouldn't have done it. The apology should take in the whole revved-up movie, which is of the "everybody uses everybody" genre, set in swank surroundings and outfitted with electronic music to make you twitch. It's a mystery thriller, but the only mystery is how Hackford worked up the energy to keep going from one hollow scene to the next, and its idea of thrills is to have the one likable person in the cast (Swoosie Kurtz) try to open a safe while she's being menaced by a Doberman. (If I never saw another fistfight or car chase or Doberman attack, I wouldn't have any feeling of loss. And that goes for Rottweilers, too.)

Some of the first reviews of *Against All Odds* have praised the gaudy chase—maybe because that's the only time in the movie that the reviewers were absolutely sure what was going on: i.e., nothing. Suggested by the 1947 Jacques Tourneur suspense film *Out of the Past*, which had a slight and rather vaporous plot centering on a cunning femme fatale (Jane Greer), *Against All Odds* runs hog-wild on plot. Lifting mostly from *Chinatown* and *North Dallas Forty*, it has so many convoluted double crosses that each time you're told what was "really" going on behind the scene you just witnessed you care less. The one thing the picture never lets you forget is that capitalist decadence permeates the society. The femme fatale is now Rachel Ward, who steals and kills, lies all the time, and makes love alternately to Bridges, a pro football player, and to Woods, a gamblin' man. But she isn't really a bad girl: it turns out (disappointingly) that she's just confused, from having grown up in a nest of vipers, with a real-estate-tycoon mother (played with considerable cool by Jane Greer) and a smoothly villainous stepfather (a hambone special by Richard Widmark).

Retro hipness is in the air now, and, like a lot of other directors, Hackford is trying to prove he's hot stuff. *Against All Odds* has some of the eagerness to impress that marked the 1981 Michael Mann picture *Thief*; it has the same cinematographer, Donald Thorin, with the impersonal bravura of his high-definition, overlighted shots, and it, too, comes close to being a parody of *film noir*. Some sequences should earn their place in the annals of camp. My first choice is the sex-and-sweat scene that takes place in a studio reproduction of an ancient Mayan steam house at Chichén Itzá. Bridges, who has been hired by Woods to find Rachel Ward so that she can be brought back, has instead, after much searching, found her in a fishing village and run off with her, and they've been going to one remote spot after another, giving us a tour of Yucatán and Quintana Roo, with special attention to such sites as Isla Mujeres, off Cancún, and the Mayan city of Tulum. But there they are, having sex high up in the jungle in the ruins of Chichén Itzá, and who should walk in on them but Alex Karras, the trainer of Bridges' football team. The love-in-the-ruins scene is pretty funny anyway. Bridges' musculature has become excessive (every position he takes looks like a pose for the Mr. Universe contest), and here in the steam house, with the inscrutable faces of stone deities peering down at them, he and Rachel Ward, naked and writhing together, seem to be gilded, like the dead girl in *Goldfinger*. When Karras casually trots in and just stands there, we're probably meant to think important thoughts, such as "There's no place for lovers to escape to in this corrupt world." But a hoot or a giggle is more to the point. Alex Karras—the man who punched out a horse in *Blazing Saddles*—looks as if he'd walked into the wrong movie; he's outclassed by these burnished love wrestlers and the fancy electronic zhooms and vroops on the track.

Probably Taylor Hackford, the director of *An Officer and a Gentleman*—who served in the Peace Corps, made investigative-reporting documentaries for the public-television station in Los Angeles which were highly regarded, and is married to Lynne Littman, the director of the nuclear-calamity movie *Testament*—is perfectly serious about *Against All Odds*. He may be more than serious: the scenes aren't shaped to get anywhere, so even though the movie hops about L.A. and Mexico, the effect is static—in the way that obsessional fantasies often are. Probably, as Hackford saw it—he commissioned the script (by Eric Hughes)—the Bridges character, trying to locate the girl, was a searcher-investigator entering a world where he didn't understand who was connected with whom. And this would mean an opportunity to expose the full extent of slick, modern corruption.

It's this seriousness, I think, that fouls him up—he wants to indict everything and everybody, and whip up a hot delirium. That impressive actor Dorian Harewood seems to be in the movie (as the gambler's flunky) just so he can learn that "nobody in Beverly Hills will ever do business with a black man." Saul Rubinek is a skillful comedian, but as a loathsome, coke-snorting lawyer who routinely sells out his clients he just makes you feel queasy. Even Jeff Bridges can't do much with his role; he's used as a set of waxed and polished pectorals, because the director is so far into his big subject that he's lost his perspective on character. And Rachel Ward, the celebrated model turned glamour star who's at the center of it all and is meant to be irresistible, must think that by not acting she communicates mystery; there's no way to know when the character is lying and when she's not—everything she says has equal weightlessness. As the secretary to the wormy lawyer, Swoosie Kurtz has only two or three minutes onscreen, but she gets a relationship going with the audience; she draws you in, so that you put yourself in her place. She's the only member of the cast who doesn't seem to have been pulped. Rachel Ward can't get anything going. She's like a teeny-bopper imitating Joan Collins, and people coming out of the theatre were saying, "She's not as beautiful as I thought."

March 19, 1984

HUGH HUDSON OF THE APES

What kind of a title for a movie is *Greystoke: The Legend of Tarzan, Lord of the Apes*? A pompous, foolish one. There can't be many people who will remember this triple title, or many theatres that are equipped with colons for their marquees, either. When Edgar Rice Burroughs wrote his first Tarzan novel, back in 1912, he managed with just *Tarzan of the Apes.* As people all over the world know, Burroughs' piece of kitsch has everything—adventure, mother love, romance. And as a subject for popular art it's close to perfection; forty-odd pulp movies haven't killed it. But Hugh Hudson, the director of *Chariots of Fire,* which won the 1981 Academy Award for Best Picture, was handed the plum of mounting a new, big version of Tarzan from a script by Robert Towne, and Hudson brought the project his unique mixture of pomp and ineptitude. In interviews, Hudson says such things as that the movie is about "how society lives, halfway between the apes and the angels, aspiring to go up yet coming from down there" and that it's about "self-discovery, lost innocence, evolution, coming to terms with evil, the use and abuse of the earth, and the delicate balance between our moral and physical beings." This man has too much on his mind to put together an exciting adventure movie.

Robert Towne's idea was to tell the story of the lost infant, John Clayton (who would inherit the title Lord Greystoke), in terms of what is known now about ape life, so that the movie could center on the infant's dependency on his ape foster mother, the boy's gradual discovery of the ways in which he was different from the apes, and the adult Tarzan's learning what it means to be human. The film was to be called *Greystoke,* because the ancestral home of the Claytons represented Tarzan's human heritage. Towne's script, which I've read, was marvellously detailed; it had sweep and a sense of wonder, and everything fitted together—you could visualize an epic with a beautiful, classical shape. Hudson hired Michael Austin to trim the script and rewrite it. Towne's conception exists now only in vestigial form; it's in some of the bits and pieces of Hudson's scraggly mess, and Towne uses a pseudonym in the credits—P. H. Vazak, the kennel name of the dog he loved, who's now dead.

It's unlikely that anyone will ever congratulate Hugh Hudson for seamless moviemaking. When Hudson sets something up, chances are there won't be any follow-through. Men who look like villains appear and are never seen again; the hero is given portentous advice that never has any application. After a while, you lose that sense of expectation which is one of the glories of big adventure films. Periodically, Hudson fills the wide screen with idyllic long shots of wiggling rivers and distant mountains, and sometimes a volcano, other times an orange ball in the sky; you wonder where this place is and why you never get any closer to it. (Did the cinematographer, John Alcott, take slides on his vacation?)

The maddening thing about this *Greystoke* is that everyone seems to be doing his job except the director. The actors playing the apes are very well made up (so that each has distinguishing features), and they comport themselves convincingly, but the director doesn't give them the extra few seconds of screen time that would fix their personalities in our minds and enable us to remember them. And although the apes themselves might be perhaps the chief attraction of the film—especially to children—he has made their scenes inordinately brutish. Burroughs said that the name Tarzan (which isn't actually used here) meant "White-Skin" in ape language. (Burroughs never set foot in Africa.) You're certainly aware of how exposed the infant's white flesh is. Hudson has his child Tarzan experiencing so much physical torment and humiliation —the apes are constantly batting him around—that young kids are likely to be horrified.

From infancy to adulthood, this Tarzan is more sufferer than hero. The young Frenchman Christopher Lambert, who plays the part, has a fine physique—he's muscular yet graceful—and he has a resemblance to Charlton Heston, with a fleeting suggestion of Brando. Lambert has been in several French films that haven't come over here, and he seems to be a competent, trained actor; he doesn't disgrace himself—he's never ludicrous (though he comes close in a seduction scene that he has been directed to play on all fours). But he's a charmless, unmagnetic Tarzan; you don't develop any special feeling for him. Hudson seems to have directed him to suggest Truffaut's *Wild Child,* but the beast in him is never very vivid—despite a full complement of scars on his face and body. Lambert has dark, deep-set eyes (which make him seem attentive yet remote), and his low eyebrows are almost straight lines; his normal expression here is a scowling wariness. You'd think a man who grew up among apes would have a sense of humor, but not this fellow. He's never allowed to be playful—not even in the second half, in what is probably meant to be Scotland, when he's wooing Jane at the banquet table at Greystoke, and his mimicking the warbling of a bird and the roaring of jungle cats could easily be part of a teasing game. The audience is dying to laugh, because, of course, there's an element of make-believe right at the heart of the story: Burroughs tapped our fantasy lives. But Hudson's approach is to make the film *prestigious.* He doesn't seem to understand that if viewers don't identify with Tarzan and laugh with him the story has no power.

The only performer who is clearly enjoying himself is Ralph Richardson, who plays Lord Greystoke, Tarzan's grandfather. This was Richardson's last screen appearance, and the old prankster comes up with one emotional flourish after another. It's a vigorous, cuckoo performance, and a source of joy. When his role ends (with the grandfather's death), the movie would have done better to close up shop, because its energy level sinks. One other performer comes through. Andie Mac-Dowell, an unconscionably beautiful American model turned actress, is a softly enticing Jane. Though this is her screen début, she's at ease, and Jane, who comes across as poised and well educated, seems to have been waiting all her life for Tarzan. It's an elegant romantic performance (even if she's dubbed); Hudson does appear to know how to present his heroines. (Alice Krige's flirting over a supper table was probably the high point of *Chariots of Fire*.) One actor makes a strong visual impression: Nigel Davenport, in a small part as a gun-happy British major, who is struck down by the arrows of pygmies while he's posing for a photograph with an ape he has shot. Davenport is an imposing replacement for C. Aubrey Smith.

The first half of the movie, in the jungle, is fairly absorbing; the material retains some of the momentum of Towne's plan, and there are images and scenes that carry some emotion: the boy Tarzan crying in his grief as his ape-mother dies; D'Arnot (Ian Holm), a Belgian member of an expedition that has been attacked by pygmies, lying wounded and feverish in a tree and seeing Tarzan for the first time, as if in a vision; Tarzan taking care of D'Arnot and feeding him grubworms; D'Arnot, in his recovery, humming, Tarzan copying his sounds, and D'Arnot embracing him as he recognizes that he'll be able to teach Tarzan to speak and one day they'll talk together. But somehow the movie never shows us the culmination of D'Arnot's dream: Tarzan never does use language very expressively, and when the picture was over I had a hard time remembering the timbre of Lambert's speaking voice. It's a disembodied sort of voice; he doesn't sound like anyone in particular—and that, of course, makes us feel even more detached from him. But then you feel detached from the whole movie. For one thing, you don't get a sense of where you are on either continent. And when Hudson gives you something like that humming scene it doesn't seem to occur to him that the song itself should have some meaning in the story—it shouldn't just be a nothing song for Tarzan to mimic.

What's essentially wrong with a director like Hugh Hudson, who comes out of the London world of TV commercials, is that he thinks he can transcend the kind of adventure picture that C. Aubrey Smith used to appear in, and he doesn't understand the mechanisms that made those movies work. Hudson may think it doesn't matter if he uses pieces of the Towne script and leaves out what they connected to. He gives us the big scenes without the steps that prepared us for them, and they're no longer big scenes—they're flat. When the expedition group that D'Arnot is part of finds the remains of the tree house where Tarzan was born, and where his parents' bodies lie rotted away to bones and dust, there's no awe or horror in the scene. And what should be a wrenching moment, with D'Arnot telling Tarzan that the ape who loved him and protected him wasn't his real mother, and Tarzan refusing to believe him—a confrontation in which you couldn't help knowing how Tarzan felt—is played backward, with D'Arnot complaining that Tarzan won't believe that the dead woman in the tree house was his mother, and you don't feel much of anything.

Hudson and, presumably, Michael Austin have concocted scenes where the tone is so obviously off that you may find yourself open-mouthed. When James Fox, as a churlish aristocrat who proposes to Jane and is rejected, takes out his anger on a symbolic counterpart of Tarzan, who seems to turn up for the sole purpose of being abused (you can fill in his identity for yourself: a mute? a stableboy?), Tarzan jumps down from the battlements of Greystoke castle and protects the victim, whereupon the aristocrat delivers himself of this injunction to Tarzan: "You have a lot to learn, jungle man!" And the picture seems to have got garbled when Tarzan—now Lord Greystoke, with an estate of many thousands of acres—surreptitiously releases an ape from the British Museum of Natural History and, instead of arranging to take the ape home with him or to take him back to Africa, ushers him out into the streets of London; when this impulsive act leads to the ape's death, we're meant to condemn "civilization." Even that hardly prepares a viewer for the full collapse of the film's tone when D'Arnot, who has been visiting his friend at Greystoke, suddenly makes a speech—this is at the turn of the century—denouncing "this absurd society." From then on, the movie simply loses its mind, and dribbles to a pathetically indecisive conclusion.

Hudson twists the story into knots in order to deliver his "statement" that apes are more civilized than people. He appears to believe that by giving us this gimcrackery he's turning pop art into high art. All he actually does in this movie is take the pleasure out of pop.

□

Opening at Christmas, 1942, *Racing with the Moon* is the story of two Northern California small-town boys (Sean Penn and Nicolas Cage) who are due to report to the Marines in six weeks. Penn, a slim, introspective kid with what are now called "caring" parents, falls in love with a new girl in town, played by Elizabeth McGovern, who is soon sweetly googly-eyed over him. Cage, his pal from childhood, is almost an orphan, and though he isn't big, he's a hulk; a lonely loudmouth and self-centered creep, he gets a girl pregnant and, in desperation, puts pressure on Penn to raise the money for an abortion. And Penn puts pressure on McGovern, whom the boys imagine to be rich. That's the whole movie. Nothing there, but nothing terribly wrong there, either. Richard Benjamin directed, from a script by Steven Kloves (who has just turned twenty-four and wrote it when he was twenty-two), and the picture is all of a piece. It's a little heavy on forties atmosphere, but it has a pleasant, reminiscent texture, and Penn continues to be remarkable. He's a juvenile lead who approaches his roles like a character actor —he creates young lived-in characters. The part here might easily have been played as "sensitive"—i.e., soupy—but he brings it emotional crosscurrents. He shows you a bright, if inarticulate, adolescent who's still partly attached to the rituals of his childhood but balks at being treated like a kid and has begun to enjoy the freedom of adulthood. And though this boy hasn't been provided with enough to say, Penn gives a great reading to the lines that aren't there. He does it with his reactions and his expressive movements; there's no busyness or waste, and you never catch him trying to create a character out of effects—you see the full person, with nothing closed off. Elizabeth McGovern has a slow response pattern that is lazy and sensual and—in a free-form way that's all her own—witty; she keeps you staring at the movements of her cherry-red lips. McGovern and Penn develop a quiet humor—they really seem to have something going. And as the kind of jerk that it's easy to have a sentimental attachment to, Nicolas Cage makes the most of his sheik's dimples, his hound-dog eyes, and his ace comedy timing.

Benjamin directs the three of them lovingly, so that the nuances they bring to their roles sustain our interest, and he blends in good small performances by the lively Shawn Schepps (as a girl that McGovern double-dates with), Carol Kane (as an agreeable flooze), Arnold Johnson (as a tattoo artist), and many others. Except for a sequence that creates a tense false expectation (out of *The Hustler*) that Penn, who plays the piano, is going to have his hands injured by the sailors he's shooting pool with, and a dumb scene with McGovern almost committing a theft, there's nothing that doesn't seem to fit in. Why, then, does the movie seem so slight and unsatisfying? (When it was over, I was in a relaxed, receptive mood, still waiting for something to start.) I think it's because we knew all this. There are no revelations about the period or the people.

There isn't a thing in *Racing with the Moon* that you can get excited about or quarrel with (except, maybe, such a trivial point as whether Penn's language is too modern when he expresses his disgust with Cage for treating the pregnant girl crudely). The script might be an exercise in conventional fine writing; it's a reminiscence based on earlier reminiscences. And the movie doesn't feel first-hand. It's too smooth, and it's square. When the two boys discuss how to raise the hundred and fifty dollars for the abortion, it's tedious; and when Penn watches the burial ceremony for a serviceman whose body has been shipped home the pensiveness of the scene is too carefully brought out; and though the love between Penn and his father (John Karlen) is "nice," it's clearly meant to be "nice." The picture is too conscious of its own deft touches, such as McGovern's brushing off Penn's arm after she has helped Cage's girl into the abortionist's office. This stuff becomes self-congratulatory, and we register it too approvingly.

In Hollywood a few years ago, it was considered axiomatic that over fifty-five miles an hour Burt Reynolds was a star. (Then he made *Stroker Ace*.) Sloshed, Dudley Moore is a star. *Arthur*—a huge success—was able to keep him happily stewed throughout. His new film, *Unfaithfully Yours*, takes too long getting him falling-down unconscious.

This new version of Preston Sturges' *Unfaithfully Yours* doesn't risk the calamitous box-office fate of the original, in 1948. Sturges' film was a great musical joke. Just after a world-famous and supremely arrogant symphony conductor (Rex Harrison) is given reason to believe that the young wife he adores has been unfaithful to him, he must step onstage to conduct works by Rossini, Wagner, and Tchaikovsky, and the three compositions inspire three different fantasies of how he will suavely and masterfully handle the situation, each fantasy being in rhythm with the music. When the concert is over, he fumbles through a slapstick mixture of all three. The new version, directed by Howard Zieff, from an ingenious script by Valerie Curtin, Barry Levinson, and Robert Klane, has an outward resemblance to the Sturges film, but the main idea—that the mood of the music affects the fantasy—is gone.

Now the conductor, played by Moore, fantasizes only while conducting the Tchaikovsky Violin Concerto, with his supposed betrayer, Armand Assante, as the soloist, and the concerto has no special tie to the action. The tone of this new movie isn't much like that of the original, either; it's a coarser piece of slapstick, partly because Zieff fails to give the characters a quiet minute or two. Richard B. Shull, who plays the part of the private detective played by Edgar Kennedy in the original, doesn't have a chance to be as touching and eccentric as Kennedy's music-loving detective was (even though, if my ear is to be trusted, Shull is the only actor in the cast who gets to speak a few lines from Sturges). It's the quiet scenes where we get to know the characters that make their other scenes work, but Zieff must be afraid that if he quiets down the picture will die. And so he directs with the frantic pacing of TV commercials, and we don't particularly care what happens.

Zieff's *Unfaithfully Yours* isn't a film that people are likely to laugh about for decades (as some of us have been doing with the Sturges version), or even to remember the next week; I didn't enjoy the picture until Moore began to get manic and apoplectic, but it does hold you—it isn't a total dud. Smoldering is Assante's thing, and his role here is to smolder. His bedroom-voice and sleek, well-pleased-with-himself manner are a serviceable contrast to Moore's sudden, violent self-doubt, and the idea of the conductor's thinking he's being betrayed by his own protégé and concertmaster is rather nifty. Albert Brooks, who plays the conductor's manager, is really brilliant; his dialogue—some of which, I gather, he himself came up with—gives the film a crazed, hip subtext. When he's onscreen, *Unfaithfully Yours* doesn't seem like a remake; it seems to be happening right this minute. There's also a chance for Richard Libertini to do a comedy turn as the conductor's Italian chef-barber-valet; Cassie Yates is just right as Albert Brooks' bored, straying wife; and a Hungarian singer, Magda Gyenes, adds giddy tempestuousness to a New York restaurant scene where Moore and Assante do an impromptu duelling-violins number.

Dudley Moore is at the center of things, and there's no question about it—when he's finally polluted, he's a slapstick virtuoso. But Moore isn't really an actor; he's a revue artist, and he's outside his roles. He dominates the screen partly because you're always aware of him as Dudley Moore. And because of that you may feel that he hasn't been as well protected by the director here (or by the script) as he might have been. When Rex Harrison's dapper, smugly-sure-of-himself conductor—he was formidable in the manner of Sir Thomas Beecham and Leopold Stokowski—felt betrayed, it was funny (and this remake was originally planned for Peter Sellers, who had a special flair for being cuckolded, as he demonstrated in the *Pink Panther* pictures). When Dudley Moore (who is almost forty-nine and isn't getting any taller) feels betrayed, he's rather too pitiable and elfin, and you get a little uncomfortable. This is emphasized by the writers' having made the conductor's bride, who's half his age, a glamorous Italian movie star, played by Nastassja Kinski.* This young actress is becoming more striking and assured—muskier, too—and it certainly would have helped if the movie had given the wife some reason to be as passionately in love with the conductor as she is; at one point, she jumps into the air at the sound of his voice, like an eager puppy. Moore is so dedicated to getting comic effects that in some of his dishevelled scenes he seems perfectly willing to suggest a sack of potatoes with hair on it—which can be funny but appalling, too. And he's needlessly infantilized at the end of the movie. In the last scene, the conductor collapses in front of his Park Avenue apartment house, and his wife picks him up and carries him inside. This may be some sort of first, but I didn't hear anybody laughing. By the time the film is over, you're not eager to see Moore again; he has been exploited here as if there were no tomorrow.

April 2, 1984

CIRCUS

A documentary shown on television a few years ago—Vladimir Rif's *When I Think of Russia*—ended with two transplanted artists, Baryshnikov and the poet Joseph Brodsky, talking together late at night at a party; they were probably a little drunk and definitely very sad, and what came across was the bond between them. They knew they'd never get over their sense of loss. I didn't think a regular movie—a movie with actors—could communicate the emotions of Russian expatriates in the

*Starting with this picture, she changed the spelling of her first name from Nastassia to Nastassja.

way that this glimpse did, but I was wrong. Paul Mazursky's *Moscow on the Hudson* does it. Mazursky has hit on just the way to go about it: with Robin Williams as his Russian saxophonist hero, he has made a comedy about a tragedy—about going away forever, about not being able to go home.

In the first part (which is in Russian, with subtitles), the sax player, the bearded Vladimir Ivanoff, who worships American jazz musicians, goes through his daily grind in Russia. He has a job in a circus band, lives among three generations of his family in a one-room apartment, and has to arrange to use a friend's place when he wants to be alone with his girl, who, before going to bed with him, hounds him to join the Party. Vladimir queues up automatically whenever he sees a line in front of a shop; he queues up even if it makes him late for rehearsals and he has to use half of whatever he's bought as a bribe, so that Boris, the K.G.B. man who supervises the circus, won't penalize him.

When Vladimir meets a friend who was a teacher before being sent to a mental hospital and now works paving streets, the friend asks, "Are you still with your music?" Vladimir says, "Still playing for tigers and bears." But he and the other band musicians love their instruments; you can see it in the way they hold them as they march, in close formation. (During a break, they sit close together, eating oranges.) Vladimir is a rumpled, uncomplaining survivor, accustomed to the endless lying and spying and toadying. He's also used to the temperamental outbursts of his friend Anatoly (Elya Baskin), the circus clown; Anatoly, who has the face of a clown even when he takes off his makeup, dramatizes his suffering—he cries out, "I hate my life!" Vladimir, who addresses his friend, with great courtliness, as "my dear clown," understands his emotion, but when Anatoly says that he has got to have his freedom and is going to defect when the troupe performs in New York, Vladimir doesn't want to take him seriously.

We know that Vladimir himself is going to defect, because the story is told as a flashback. In the opening scene, he's on a New York City bus giving directions to a Frenchman and saying, "It's pretty tough getting around here at first," with the look of satisfaction of someone who has mastered the bus routes. But we don't know how or why this fellow who loves his family (and adores his grandfather) will do it. By the time it happens—during the half hour that the circus troupe is given to shop in Bloomingdale's, on the way to the airport and home—we know Vladimir so well that it seems natural and inevitable. What makes him love his family deeply is what makes him lose them forever. Vladimir embodies the Russian tradition of the holy fool.

His passivity is deceptive; he has inner strength—he can't help feeling the truth. Given an opportunity to say no to the K.G.B., he can't resist it; he can't *not* defect.

Bloomingdale's—no more than a bit player in *The Electric Horseman*, where the store's name was used for a gag—is a star in both *Splash* and *Moscow on the Hudson*. Mazursky uses it as the hub of the New York world, and the plot radiates from this temple of the mouthwatering temptations of capitalist decadence. The script (by Mazursky and Leon Capetanos) is slyly and gracefully designed so that the people Vladimir encounters in the store during the dizzying few minutes it takes him to escape from the control of the K.G.B.—people whom we at first assume to be minor players—become the most important people in his new life. Vlad (as these Americans call him) walks into this capitalist cornucopia and finds friendship and love. A black security guard (Cleavant Derricks) protects him from the K.G.B. "You're in my jurisdiction," the guard tells the Soviet agents—the workers at Bloomingdale's talk about it as if it were a country. And when matters are settled the guard, who has offered to put Vlad up, takes him home to Harlem, where three generations of *his* family live together. A shark-faced Cuban immigration lawyer (Alejandro Rey), who happens to be shopping in the store during the defection, leaves his card. And Lucia (Maria Conchita Alonso), an Italian girl who works in the perfume department, becomes Vlad's steady date. Yet it doesn't take long before he discovers the isolation and paranoia of living in New York. The brutality of the city confuses him; in Russia, he says, he knew who the enemy was.

Nobody in New York wastes time offering Vlad sympathy, because there's nothing unusual about his plight. Perhaps the sneakiest, most original aspect of the movie is that just about everyone Vlad meets, except some of the black people, is foreign-born (or an out-of-towner). He starts as a busboy, hustles his way from one crummy street vender's job to another, drives a taxi, chauffeurs a limo; he studies English, saves enough money to buy a sax in a secondhand shop, and acquires an apartment in the East Village. And all this time he's surrounded by Puerto Ricans, Lebanese, Haitians, Iranians, Brazilians, Cubans, Vietnamese—every variety of Hispanic, Asian, and European. These "ethnics" are in the service jobs that white native Americans have scrambled out of, and they're on the streets hustling alongside him. They talk English mixed with their own languages, their lips twisting over the syllables in different ways. ("When you speak English, does your mouth hurt?" Vlad asks another immigrant.) He builds a new, makeshift family out of this disparate group, but it can't fill the void created by what he left behind. (The Russia of this movie is a country where the grandfathers look like Harpo Marx.)

Paul Mazursky's distinctive funky lyricism is in the scene with Vlad outside Bloomingdale's waving goodbye to the circus troupe in the chartered Liberty Lines bus that's taking them to the airport; he already knows that he has cut himself off from his own life. (And from then on there may be some extra moisture in his shining eyes when he laughs, or a smile will end a little abruptly.) The lyricism is in the way Vlad tries to dance American style; it's in the double joke of his pleasure at the first joke he makes in English. It's in the Old World politeness of his manner as he talks to an F.B.I. man, and in the courtesy he extends to a gay, whom he smiles at, taking him for another F.B.I. man. And it's in the delicacy of the scene in which a newly arrived legal émigré—a Russian Jewish young man, very shy and looking a bit like Kafka—brings Vlad a letter from his family. It's the magical element in some parts of the movie. You may be saying to yourself, "This scene shouldn't work, it can't work," while you're laughing because it's working. That happens when Vlad and Lucia are in the bathtub eating mu shu pork and fooling around while she studies for her naturalization exam and recites the Bill of Rights. And it happens again in the naturalization ceremony.

The film wins your good will by its comic rhythms (especially in the first half). It's shaped so that when the band, in New York, strikes up the circus march you're eager for both the circus and the escape, and then you're in Bloomingdale's (what a place to get lost in!), which turns out to be another circus. And Mazursky's instinct was really working for him when he paired Robin Williams with Maria Conchita Alonso, a Venezuelan beauty who's an unself-conscious cutup, like the young Sophia Loren, and has a glorious, full-choppered grin. Her Lucia is outgoing, independent, sunshiny; she has come to this country to make something of herself—she would like to be a newscaster. Robin Williams' Vlad is an anonymous Soviet man hoping for the creature comforts of a home and a family—a supplicant always. The bathtub scene, in which Lucia leans back against his furry chest while his furry arms enclose her, is physical in a way that disposes of the steam-house contortions of the lovers in *Against All Odds*. These two suggest real people.

That's the plain, open secret of what makes this movie so pleasurable: you get to know the people in it, and Mazursky shows you how normal it is to be a little crazy. (Alejandro Rey's Cuban, who seems to be gleaming with predatory intentions, turns out to be a decent fellow who has oversold himself on the natty Latin look.) In spirit, *Moscow on the Hudson* is like a more imaginative *Harry & Tonto*, with a mellowed style; Mazursky has become a far more skillful filmmaker, and his cinematographer, Don McAlpine, and the rest of his team help to give the picture a textured simplicity that is rare in a comedy. When you actually see Mazursky (he plays a tourist called Dave basking on a Florida beach and complaining about the rotten service at the hotel), he gives the film a manic zap—a heightened comic tension—that the other scenes don't have. What they do have is a smoothness—a relaxed appreciation of what the performers are doing, as if Mazursky were as surprised and exhilarated as you are.

Vlad is the most Chaplinesque of Mazursky's heroes. The term is often used as a putdown, but this film provides a reminder of the good side of Chaplin. There's nothing wrong with suggesting an ordinary reasonable man who doesn't want to cause any trouble, as long as he isn't pathetic about it, and Vlad doesn't slip into that—not even in the scene in Russia where he plays his sax for the circus animals, and definitely not in the scene in the East Village where he goes on playing despite the complaints of a neighbor but retreats farther and farther into his apartment and winds up in the water closet. Robin Williams' Vlad is sturdy and resourceful—that's what's touching about him. Robin Williams was extraordinary in his last picture (Michael Ritchie's *The Survivors*), and he gets better and better. He isn't a comic "doing" a Russian; he just plays a Russian, and it's as if he'd been born one. (I could have been fooled if I hadn't seen him before.) He has nothing of the pixillated Mork about him; his Russianized pronunciation of American names is just funny enough, and when he cries it's Russian style, starting around the mouth.

A few scenes are poorly acted—one in an Immigration office with a noisy black woman officer, and several involving Boris, the K.G.B. man, who's much too coyly aware of being a comic bad guy, and who turns up for a final hammy bow when we'd thought we were rid of him. There's also a misconceived scene—Vlad, alone and drunk, having a vision of his grandfather capering on the street. And one sequence seems truncated: when Vlad gets to sit in with the black saxophonist he idolized from records back in Russia the film cuts from their playing together to a scene of Vlad's despair afterward—presumably because his idol had not been enthusiastic about his work. We really need to get a sense of what the man told him; the way it is, we can't gauge if Vlad is over-reacting or if his playing is too derivative and his idol made that clear to him. These weaknesses are minor; the only larger one is the faltering of the film's rhythm (though not its mood) in the last third. Mazursky seems to need several things going on at once (as in that bathtub), and offhand, peripheral jokes, too. When Vlad and Lucia quarrel and the black friend goes to Alabama for a time, Mazursky doesn't have enough elements to juggle. Vlad trots around by himself and visits people, and a few scenes feel insecure, as if nothing's going on.

In terms of what this comedy offers, this, too, is minor. What counts is that it tackles a wonderful subject without preening, and brings it off unassertively—so unassertively that the movie is in danger of being overlooked. (*Variety* has already dismissed it as something "for a very limited audience.") We're getting to the point where the press assumes that movie audiences won't be willing to bring anything to a picture, and warns them off. This is a movie in which you are expected to understand the hero when he tries to explain the difference between being unhappy in New York and in his homeland. "In Russia," he says, "I did not love my life but I loved my misery, because it was mine." Those who respond to his words may, I think, love this picture as much as I do. Back in Russia, Vlad waited in line and bought two pairs of shoes (the wrong size but the only size) and gave one pair to the K.G.B.; in New York, he buys flashy red, yellow, and white shoes that look like part of a pimp's ensemble, and when Lucia objects to them he points out, "They were made in Italy." It's a one-world circus.

April 16, 1984

EXALTATION/ESCAPISM

ceman, the new Fred Schepisi film, begins with perhaps the greatest opening shot I've ever seen: a wide-screen image of Arctic ice and snow, with fluttering helicopters, and the small figures of men moving around a blue-white glacial cave. They carve out a block of ice that has a dark form inside, and the helicopter flies off, carrying the block dangling in a net. It's an eerie and enthralling sequence. Somehow,

Schepisi and his two longtime collaborators, the composer Bruce Smeaton and the cinematographer Ian Baker, achieve that special and overwhelming fusion of the arts which great visual moviemaking can give us. *Iceman* doesn't have a good enough script, but it has a marvellously suggestive idea for a movie, and it has scenes that affect us with something like the mystical power of primitive fairy tales. It also has the star presence of the Eurasian-American actor John Lone, who is awesome in the way he stirs our empathy with the film's hero, the prehistoric man who has been asleep inside that glacial ice for forty thousand years and hangs from a helicopter like Fellini's Christ statue in *La Dolce Vita.*

After being flown to an Arctic outpost—a research center run by the same mining and exploration company whose drillers found him—the Iceman is thawed out, in a sequence that is comparable in creepiness and fascination to the famous laboratory scene in James Whale's 1931 *Frankenstein*, in which the monster comes to life. But the tone here is altogether different: the water dripping from the icy casket suggests weeping. The creature's mouth is open, as if in a cry, and his arms are extended, as if he's asking for help, and when the rest of his body is revealed it recalls the rigid figure and pallid flesh tones of the Mantegna Christ.

The thirty-one-year-old John Lone lived at the monastic school attached to the Peking Opera in Hong Kong from the age of nine to eighteen, and was trained in the formal theatrical arts. His teachers there called him Little Dragon, and since the Chinese word for dragon sounds like "lone," he took that as his name when, after a brief career in Hong Kong kung-fu movies, he came to this country, where he worked first with the East West Players, in Los Angeles, and then, in New York, with the Public Theatre. As the powerfully built Iceman, Lone, whose name would be more appropriate for the character than Charlie, which his only new friend calls him, moves in a crouch that's a bit reminiscent of Toshiro Mifune's barbaric stance in *Rashomon*; his brow has been built out, and he wears jagged dentures that change the shape of his mouth. He makes scratchy, toneless sounds, yet they're expressive; everything about him is expressive. He's sociable and eager to communicate, and—this is John Lone's subtle achievement—he soon has an air of indefinable sadness. Uncouth as this Neanderthal may look, he has a full range of feeling in his eyes. He's unmistakably human, and he's confused about where he is; he's lost, he's alone.

As the head cryobiologist at the research center, Lindsay Crouse wears a no-nonsense short haircut and efficiency outfits; she sees the discovery of the Iceman as an opportunity for a medical breakthrough

—she hopes to find the cryoprotectant that has kept him alive. The eight or nine scientists she works with want to take the creature apart so they can find out how to extend people's lives by freezing them. But Timothy Hutton, as the scruffy, post-hippie anthropologist who is brought in, wants to get to know the Iceman, so he can learn more about our ancestors and how we evolved. The two competing learned doctors bicker, compromise, coöperate. She worries; he's benignly blank. And the Iceman is placed in a glass-domed vivarium—a simulation of the natural environment in a temperate zone—which is adjacent to the center. The scientists observe him and listen to his cries and moans, without his knowing they're there. I think that this vivarium was probably the filmmakers' worst mistake: it traps the movie along with the Iceman. The idea of the film almost demands that he come into contact with the modern world; instead, the film becomes constricted as he examines his prison and puzzles over artifacts, like a hose and a sprinkler. (They're magic objects to him.) And we're put off by plot developments, such as nobody's being on watch when the Iceman breaks out. This science fantasy is of such beauty and quality that we may be more put off than we are at a routine sci-fi picture, where we expect this sort of sloppiness, and even enjoy it.

The scriptwriters, Chip Proser and John Drimmer, don't develop the conflict between medical science and humanism which Crouse and Hutton represent. It falls by the wayside—which is probably for the best, because it's dull stuff. (There's also a stupefying scene in which one of the batch of scientists expresses doubts about whether mankind has advanced in the last forty thousand years; his nose should light up, and everyone on the screen should have a turn at punching it.) The Lindsay Crouse character is like a modern woman written to the specifications of a feminist magazine. And Timothy Hutton, whose slightly scared look suited his teen-age roles, has retained the look; it may be that he's frightened by the camera—he seems to hold back. In the scenes in which he enters the vivarium and makes friends with the Iceman, it isn't man to man; he's still a juvenile—his body doesn't seem lived in. The scientists take flesh and fluids out of the Iceman when he's unconscious, and he blames his diminishing strength on his anthropologist friend; Hutton should be able to summon up some rage at the vivisectionist experiments —something to match the Iceman's profound sorrow—but he doesn't quite have it in him. The Iceman has been crazily dislocated in history; he thinks he has been enchanted and that he's being punished. The anthropologist needs to feel disoriented too. The gleam of insanity in Lone's eyes is what Hutton lacks. Yet he isn't bad. He and Lone play off each other in a way that makes the film work, and this may be because of Hutton's slightly opaque, child-man quality.

The young anthropologist benefits from his contact with this primitive man; like the boy in *E.T.* and the hero in *Splash,* he needs to learn from the stranger. The anthropologist begins to see things through the Iceman's eyes, and so do we. When the Iceman breaks out and runs through the lab, we know that to him the rooms and passageways are a series of mythic challenges. Schepisi has been able to provide a modern interpretation of the events while making it possible for us to experience them as if we were primitive. The picture keeps us in an awestruck state, and at the end I felt that it fulfilled itself. The Iceman's visionary fervor takes hold; we can believe in his terrified worship of a trickster God in the sky, and in his triumph as he joins his God.

It's a very strange, elating movie, with the Iceman at its emotional center. It gives you the sensation that you're breathing pure air and that your senses have become more acute; you go out and look at the shops and streets as if you were a stranger. A real dramatist might have been able to provide dialogue and conflicts worthy of Lone's performance, and of the imagery and the music. But, working without a great script, Schepisi has still done something major: *Iceman* is like the flawed Herman Melville novels. It's full of passion and craft, along with parts that might be the work of a stumblebum. It's thrilling.

□

Romancing the Stone, a slapstick adventure comedy in the commercial genre of *Raiders of the Lost Ark,* is a simpler, more likable entertainment than *Raiders;* it doesn't leave you feeling exhausted. The picture's greatest asset is its taking-off place: a woman's wanting a more exciting life. Written by Diane Thomas, who got fed up with her jobs in advertising and studied to be an actress before sitting down to write this first script (while she supported herself as a waitress), the movie is about a timid, pleasantly slobby author of best-seller romances. Joan Wilder (Kathleen Turner) cries over the end of the novel she's typing, because she loves it so much. Padding around her Manhattan apartment, she sniffles happily—she left her heroine experiencing ecstasy—and feeds her cat, Romeo. Just after delivering the manuscript to her publisher, she receives a frantic telephone call from her sister, who is being held captive by smugglers in Cartagena, and in a few hours she's lost in the jungle in Colombia, ducking bullets. She's thrust into the kind of perils she has dreamed up for her books. The extravagant, self-mocking adventures that follow are kept on a human scale, because Kathleen Turner's Joan Wilder is always there reacting. Turner is particularly adept at letting herself be seen through. Her star performance is one long, infinitely varied double take, and it's exhilarating.

The picture has a bravura opening and a jolly kind of movement, but it becomes too slam-bang; the score is cheesy and loud, and there are a few too many unrealized gags. Still, the director, Robert Zemeckis, the Spielberg protégé who, with his sometime partner Bob Gale, wrote *1941* and made *I Wanna Hold Your Hand* (1978) and the juicy satire *Used Cars* (1980), sustains the carefree tone; and the wide-screen imagery, which is stunning at the start, is always good to look at—the cinematographer Dean Cundey and the production designer Lawrence G. Paull must love their work. The film also has a terrific suave and swinish villain: the Mexican actor Manuel Ojeda as Zolo the knifer, the head of the military police, who keeps following Joan and casually murdering people. In the single funniest scene, a crocodile chomps on Zolo's arm, and the bite has just the right amount of violence to release our laughter. Another Mexican actor, Alfonso Arau (of *El Topo* and *The Wild Bunch* and *Used Cars*), has an affable slapstick spaciness—he's all toothy smiles and bushy hair—as a drug-trade chieftain who's hooked on romance novels. And the scriptwriter has set up some explosively comic dilemmas, such as the scene in which the hero is torn between saving the loot (the gigantic emerald that everyone covets) and saving the girl (who, of course, having been romanced, is the real jewel).

But that hero, who has been given the phallic name Jack T. Colton, is played by the producer of the film, Michael Douglas, who isn't a comedian. The script was probably shaped so that Joan's fictional hero would materialize but he'd be tougher and more practical-minded than she expected, and she'd have to learn to take care of herself in order to keep up with him. With Douglas in the role, it isn't clear whether Jack is intended to be the fearless and dashing man of Joan's dreams or a parody of that swashbuckling cavalier. Douglas must know—or, at least, suspect—that he's wrong for the role. (It calls for a Harrison Ford, or perhaps a big, bland bruiser like Tom Selleck.) Douglas tries too hard. He talks in a low, hoarse voice and acts gruff; his face exaggerates everything and registers nothing. And no matter how fast he moves he seems to slow down whatever is going on around him. Some of the other casting is dubious, too. Mary Ellen Trainor seems all wrong as Joan's sister, and Danny DeVito, who plays a smuggler, is used for his cuteness, and as if our hearing him deliver commonplace expletives would knock us silly.

Luckily, Kathleen Turner is onscreen almost all the time, and the affection we develop for her in her early, dowdy scenes carries over to the action sequences. In the second half, when her hair is loose and she has become more conventionally sexy, this actress knows how to use her dimples amusingly and how to dance like a woman who didn't know she could. She and Zolo's stump of an arm help to give the movie some personality. Too bad that this cleverly worked-out woman's fantasy got muddied by the producer's fantasy that he could be the answer to a woman's steamy dreams.

April 30, 1984

SMALLER THAN LIFE

In *Swing Shift*, the director, Jonathan Demme, attempts to recapture the atmosphere of the "home front" during the Second World War. He has the kind of respect for working people's homes that James Agee had for the shacks of tenant farmers, and he shows you the details of lower-middle-class life without satire or condescension. Demme could be said to have a reverence for kitsch. His tenderness—his looking for poetry in the tacky—is a rare quality, but in *Swing Shift* it isn't backed up with much of anything else.

Demme's vision of the lives of the workers on the swing shift (4 P.M. to midnight) at an aircraft factory in Santa Monica has a glazed lyricism. Goldie Hawn is Kay, a cuddlebug housewife who married her blue-eyed Iowa high-school sweetheart (Ed Harris) and moved to California; he joins the Navy right after the Japanese attack on Pearl Harbor, and she becomes a riveter at the factory, where she meets a foreman (Kurt Russell) who's also a trumpet player. He develops a crush on her, and eventually they begin an affair. Christine Lahti is Hazel, who sings with a dance-hall band; she breaks up with her lover (Fred Ward), the dance-hall operator, and goes to work on the assembly line, and she and Kay —they both live in the same set of tiny garden-court bungalows—become pals. Most of these performers, along with others in the cast, seem too old for the parts they're playing. They look stuffed and posed, as if they were consciously trying to re-create themselves in the images of the shiny-faced teen-age servicemen and girls-next-door in the forties issues of *Life*. It's a case of talented, intelligent actors turning themselves into waxworks. The cramped, stage-set look of those bungalow interiors seems deliberate, and the way the workers are positioned at the factory makes you think the movie is about to turn into a musical, with candy-colored production numbers. For Demme, the film must have been an exercise in style, in the way that *New York, New York* was for Martin Scorsese, but Demme's style is softer, pastel, mild.

Kay and her husband hear the news about Pearl Harbor when they're spending their Sunday at an outdoor skating rink; we can't fail to observe the picturesqueness of the era. The people in this movie don't do anything that wouldn't have been done in forties movies, and the clichés of those movies are played here as daily life. Demme isn't debunking anything; on the contrary, he seems to insist that the images of innocence given to us by the magazines and the movies are accurate. And from the way he sees things it's as if movies never had a darker side. (In some ways, Demme's vision seems as privately enraptured—and as superficial—as that of his near namesake, the French director Jacques Demy, in his weaker films, such as his 1969 American production, *The Model Shop*.) The insubstantiality of *Swing Shift* may make us feel as if we were dozing. Or we may be tapping a toe, waiting for the heroine to lose her virtue—waiting for the public images of virtue to come into conflict with the characters' desires. But Demme doesn't appear to register that the audience has a problem; he sticks by this false innocence. And he keeps the camera gliding romantically, though its movements don't seem to relate to the situations that the characters are in.

Goldie Hawn dampens the picture. It's not that she gives a bad performance. Like *Private Benjamin*, this film was made by her own production company, and she certainly doesn't have the kind of cruddy role that she played in, say, *The Duchess and the Dirtwater Fox* (1976); she doesn't repeat herself, either, the way she has been doing in pictures such as the more recent *Seems Like Old Times*. The role of Kay is a stretch for her, all right, but Goldie Hawn as a subdued ingénue is not a stretch that does anything for the audience. A passive Goldie Hawn seems a violation of nature. We're used to her all turned on and infectiously funny, and for us not to feel let down by her performance in a straight role it would have to be a really good one. As Kay, she's trying to make herself simple and ordinary—she's playing a new stereotype: the child-woman who learns how to be a competent person. And there's very little she can do without calling up echoes of Jane Fonda in *Coming Home*. She has fallen into a very old acting trap: she wants us to identify with her character, and she thinks that she will become typical by flattening herself out. It's a stretch in reverse: she diminishes herself. At times, her mouth is set; she looks uncomfortable, repressed—not as the character but as an actress who's unhappy with what she's doing. (Maybe she senses that the picture is turning into a neutered version of *Private Benjamin*.)

Goldie Hawn and her moviemaking team have also made a basic mistake in strategy: they've given Christine Lahti's Hazel the wisecracks. Christine Lahti, who has dark hair, high cheekbones, and a long neck with great cords in it, is one of the marvellous new towering Venuses who are changing our image of women. Like Sigourney Weaver, Joanna Cassidy, Kathleen Turner, and, of course, Vanessa Redgrave, she's heroically feminine. She's also a ripsnorting comedienne, and she gives the picture whatever spark and intensity it has (which is mostly in the first half). Her role doesn't make much sense: she's a singer who never even hums after she takes the job in the factory, and she goes on for years carrying a torch for the man she broke up with (until he has an offscreen change of heart). But Lahti plays this role to the hilt, and the simple fact is that her height plus her tough manner and her few wisecracks make Goldie Hawn's Kay seem dim and shrimpy. (For one thing, there's more of Lahti for clothes to look great on, though she has become shockingly thin.) If Kay had been conceived as more hip and had swapped cracks with Hazel, Goldie Hawn might have had all her tickling charm to draw upon. But she's got both arms tied behind her back. And Lahti, a spangly goddess with her little forties hat propped on the side of her head, is smiling down at her.

At times, I got the feeling that everything in *Swing Shift* was muffled because the moviemakers were afraid of covering the same ground as Connie Field's documentary *The Life and Times of Rosie the Riveter* and also of overlapping with *New York, New York*. It's a wisp of a movie, with vague aspirations to be touching, and I got the impression that there had never been a very strong script. (The writing credit goes to the pseudonymous Rob Morton; the writers who were listed before and during production were initially Nancy Dowd, then Bo Goldman, then Ron Nyswaner, and there was last-minute, attempted-rescue work by Robert Towne.) The scenes rarely last more than twenty seconds. They don't quite come to anything; they abort—with a sometimes audible pop—and it's always before we can get a sense of what's going on with the characters. There are no high spots, no exciting moments. The picture just goes popping from one recessive, undeveloped scene to the next. *Swing Shift* was reëdited after Demme turned in his cut, and so it's difficult to gauge his plan for the movie, but it may be that he didn't want a stronger script. The charm in Demme's movies is in the small talk. He knows how Americans sound when they're relaxed, and Goldie Hawn and Kurt Russell have an easy, casual way with each other. But Demme isn't good at building scenes to move a story along, and this picture is never satisfying at more than a minute-to-minute level.

Last year, I sat all the way through *Romantic Comedy*—and that rather puzzled me, because I've walked out on a lot of much better movies. Then I realized that the reason I'd sat there was that the picture drained me of the strength needed to get up and leave. *Swing Shift* isn't stupid, like *Romantic Comedy*, but it, too, is draining. You sit there wondering what nothing is going to happen next. There's a feminist-fairy-tale aspect to Kay's story: she gets a job and proves her worth by saving a fellow-worker's life, she has her sexual fling, and then she goes back to her husband, and, in some screwy way, what she does seems meant to parallel and represent what happened to women in general. There's also something sickening about the way Hazel's lover turns up and apologizes for the way he treated her, and then turns up again, cringing, asking for forgiveness. Maybe part of what makes this movie seem so befuddled is that Demme's nostalgic fixation on the ambience of the war years excludes any real interest in the lives of women workers, and the feminist script sees the characters as precursors (with lessons to learn) rather than as people. The women's experiences in the "home front" are treated as a warmup, a rehearsal for the women's movement of the sixties and seventies. The point of this picture is that men laughed at the idea of women riveters and welders but that the women "showed them." It's as if the women were pampered darlings who went to work just to prove something to their husbands and to themselves. The fact is that many women needed to work before the war and had only been able to find low-paying jobs, and after the war they were pushed out and were once again trapped in domestic service, "women's" factory jobs, and department stores. The softening of economic facts devitalizes *Swing Shift*. You can't keep all that pie-eyed lyrical innocence without betraying the subject. The movie doesn't even put across the feeling that's so rousing in documentaries about the period: the sass and bounce of the women workers, earning good money for the first time, and strutting because they were doing what was considered "a man's job."

May 14, 1984

THE CANDIDATE

In 1924, on the train that is taking him to a tryout with the Chicago Cubs, young Roy Hobbs (Robert Redford), who feels he has it in him to be the greatest baseball player there ever was, makes the mistake of saying so. "I'm going to break every record in the book," he tells a beautiful brunette vamp. Convinced, she invites him to her hotel room, and shoots him in the abdomen at close range. (She may be a madwoman; she may be an agent of dark forces. Perhaps both.) It takes Roy until 1939 to make it back to the major leagues—this time, he is signed by a scout for the New York Knights. A rookie at thirty-six, he seems to be caught in a time warp. And so is the movie, *The Natural.* A platinum-blond temptress (Kim Basinger) goes to work on Roy; she's the pawn of crooked gamblers, and not above slipping him a poisoned bonbon. But a purehearted honey-blonde (Glenn Close) who was Roy's childhood sweetheart believes in him. And with these incarnations of evil and good contending for his soul, the movie asks: Will Roy be spiritually strong enough to triumph? In this era of inspirational time-warp hits such as the *Rocky* pictures and *Chariots of Fire* and *An Officer and a Gentleman* and *Flashdance* and *Staying Alive* and *Footloose,* there's no contest. Redford mimes innocence and hurt like a dreary master. He's the injured party, the blameless white Knight.

There isn't a whisper of surprise in the performance. It's guarded and dry; it's timid. Some movie stars are like political figures: they try to hang on to a constituency, and they approach their roles as if they were running for high office. If they've had their biggest successes as high-minded, shining-eyed Nice Guys, that's all they'll do. Watching *The Natural*, you get the feeling that Redford is making one of those political commercials that show you the candidate in "private" moments, playing with neighborhood kids. Redford doesn't take the camera by his acting; he takes it as a star—he's photographed looking like a wary, modest god, with enough back lighting and soft focus to make him incandescent even when he isn't doing a thing. The movie is a fantasy, and the director, Barry Levinson, must have wanted the picturesque, prose-poetry style that the cinematographer, Caleb Deschanel, supplies, but Redford is its principal beneficiary. Though part of the point of the movie is that the rookie hero is older than his teammates, we never see a well-lighted handsome young face; the other Knights are photographed as if they were made of putty. There may be a rule of thumb for gauging when a star has become so concerned with the politics of his image as a hero that he's afraid of acting: it's when he'll only play roles in which he's more sinned against than sinning. And the way that this picture has been designed, the myth of Robert Redford transcends the myths of baseball heroes.

Stars like Paul Newman and Jack Nicholson and Sean Connery are all there on the screen, but Redford (like Warren Beatty) is so hesitant to reveal himself emotionally that he seems distanced and distracted. He holds back. He presents his handsome face to the camera, but reluctantly; as an actor, he's hiding. Even Redford's smiles seem forced here; they're certainly rationed. (Heroism is such a burden.) In *Heaven Can Wait*, Beatty died and then reappeared; *The Natural* is Redford's *Heaven Can Wait*, but without Dyan Cannon. Roy Hobbs might almost have died before the picture started—Redford is ghostly, absent, a noble loner who doesn't interact with the other performers. He is no more than polite in his response to Kim Basinger's seductiveness—she's left to play her hot-number scenes in a vacuum. Glenn Close fares worse: Redford seems self-absorbed when he's with her, and the director keeps the camera staring at her reverently, as if she were a First Lady of the Stage who had deigned to drop in on his movie set. (She's being Meryl Streeped.) With nothing to play except the spirit of good-womanliness, she stares back. The love relationship is a disaster.

Part of the performers' problem is that the characters they play originated in a work with a completely different structure of meaning. The script, by Roger Towne (the younger brother of Robert Towne), with a credit also to Phil Dusenberry, who wrote an earlier version, is adapted from Bernard Malamud's first novel, published in 1952. The book is about a natural man who has it in him to be great but also has it in him to be weak. Malamud's Roy Hobbs succumbs to every temptation, and, given a miraculous second chance, he makes the same damn mistake he did the first time. He's human; he's a fool. What gives the novel its liveliness is Malamud's inspired mixture of an everyday American vernacular (it's reminiscent of Ring Lardner) with suggestions of the magical and the mythic. He tucked a lot into that mixture: the legends and scandals of baseball, a plot that was a variation on Joe E. Brown's 1933 hit movie *Elmer the Great* (which was based on a play by Lardner and George M. Cohan), and a sense of mystery—the kind that charms you and you don't need explained. And he makes it all seem easy. The novel is in the pink—it's fresh—but the movie feels dated, because the people who made it don't keep a balance between the everyday and the magical. Their version is all mythic; it's wrapped in metaphysical mothballs. The framing device—an early sequence and a final one in which fathers and sons are out in the wheat fields playing catch—is "Little House on the Prairie" mythic. Before the young Roy goes off to Chicago, he says goodbye to his sweetheart: they embrace, Glenn Close says, "I love you so much," Redford says, "I want you to marry me," unenthusiastically, and Randy Newman's tender, drippy, hymnlike music is heard. The conception of mythology here is old-movie make-believe; it's religioso-romantic sentiment and stale glamour. The hero is so pure he has no lust or greed in him; there is nothing to bring him down, and by the end of the picture the golden Redford has practically ascended to Heaven. Each time Roy is about to pitch or hit with supernatural help, he's glorified in slow motion, and the rhythm of the shots is unvarying. And we're supposed to sit there oohing and ahing over Robert Redford lifting his leg.

Except for the showiness of the photographic effects—the images are often very dark when evil characters lurk about—this is a film that Louis B. Mayer, in the mid-thirties, might have been proud to put his name to. *The Natural* has the message that Mayer used to send out to the world; it was also the credo of the heroine of *Flashdance*: Hold on to your dream. (In pop hits, people have only one dream, and it's unchanging.) This is an old-fashioned movie, but it lacks the dramatic precision and some of the payoffs that movies used to provide. When Roy's angel sweetheart first appears at a Knights game and stands up, with the sun giving her a halo, his luck changes, but we aren't shown the instant when he registers her presence and is transformed into a winner. Robert Duvall plays the part of a corrupt sports columnist; he sneers and grovels and acts parasitic—he climbs the rafters, to no appreciable purpose. Perhaps the role was trimmed in the editing—some gaps suggest that. One of them is sizable: although the columnist, who was on the train in 1924, spends most of his time trying to figure out where he remembers Roy from, we never get the recognition scene that we're set up for. And the moviemakers ought to have had enough pride not to stage the clumsy, postponed revelation about the angel's angelic offspring. It's primordial hokum.

There are a few performers who stand apart from the sludge of moral uplift. Barbara Hershey brings a hint of deviltry to the small, key role of the mystery woman who shoots the young athlete; she looks dangerously chic in her twenties clothes, and her veneered face says, Boy, do I have a surprise for you. As the Whammer (who's unmistakably Babe Ruth), Joe Don Baker manages to be mean and jovial at the same time; it's a big, hearty, malevolent caricature. And John Finnegan, who plays Sam, the old scout, in the opening scenes, carries the feeling of an earlier America. Other performances—such as Wilford Brimley's gruff, lovable Pop Fisher, the manager of the Knights, and Richard Farnsworth's decent, understanding coach—satisfy the archetypal demands of the roles but are of no particular interest.

Was *The Natural* made cynically? I don't think so. It probably wouldn't be so self-conscious and plodding (or so dark) if it had been made by wiseguys. This picture looks to be a case of intelligent people putting enormous care into a project that they have emasculated to the point of idiocy. And instead of editing the movie for greater speed toward the end, they let it run down. Its box-office success or failure probably depends on the equivalent of a laugh track: when Roy performs his feats on the baseball field the crowds in the stadium go crazy, and their shouting and cheering (and Newman's victory music) are so all-encompassingly loud that some of the people in theatres are bound to join in. If they do, they'll probably feel that they've seen a terrific picture. And the moviemakers may have the hit they wanted (more than anything else). Roy's team wins the pennant; he triumphs just the way Rocky did, and the way those two runners trying to escape the Vangelis fanfares did, and that hustler who was regenerated by military discipline, and the welder-ballerina, and the writhing chorus boy, and the kid who had to fight the town laws against dancing. Roy is a real baby-kissing politician's role. He makes a pal of the pudgy batboy who idolizes him, and when he's shown in a 1939 newsreel patting little boys' heads, he turns, sees a little girl, and has the foresight to include her in his constituency. And he gives the game of baseball everything he's got—

with blood seeping out of a wound and staining his uniform. At times, this movie is reminiscent of classic tearjerkers like *Madame X* and *Smilin' Through*, but with a male sufferer. Moviemakers can be calculating and shameless and still be perfectly solemnly serious. New movies reshape stories in terms of the prevailing box-office values of the era. But the people who do the shaping can feel that they're expressing what they believe (and, in some terrible way, they are).

□

Sixteen Candles is about suburban Chicago teen-agers, but it's less raucous in tone than most of the recent teen pictures; it's closer to the gentle English comedies of the forties and fifties. It doesn't amount to much, and it's certainly not to be confused with a work of art or a work of any depth, but the young writer-director John Hughes has a knack for making you like the high-school-age characters better each time you hear them talk. The picture has a good, simple premise: Samantha (Molly Ringwald), a high-school sophomore, is having the worst day of her life. It's her sixteenth birthday, and, in the midst of preparations for her older sister's wedding, the whole family has forgotten about it. And in the evening, when she goes to a school dance and longs to be noticed by the handsome senior (Michael Schoeffling) who's the man of her dreams, she's subjected to the humiliating attentions of a scrawny freshman (Anthony Michael Hall), who's known as Geek—a pesty, leering smartmouth with braces on his teeth. (His attempt at a sexy smile is pure weirdness.) Geek follows her wherever she goes, ogling her, and he tries to court her on the dance floor, circling around her like an impassioned whooping crane. He moves quickly, with his head down: he's not watching his feet—he's concentrating on the action of his body. He's turning himself on, and he feels masterful; he isn't aware of the effect he's having on Samantha until she runs off. Samantha gets so down on herself and the world that when the senior, who feels he's alone when he's with his prom-queen girlfriend, comes over to her she panics and bolts. The senior, misunderstanding, feels rejected.

Molly Ringwald, who played Miranda in Paul Mazursky's 1982 *Tempest* and was the young heroine of Lamont Johnson's 1983 *Spacehunter*, has an offbeat candor. Only fifteen when *Sixteen Candles* was shot, she plays a free-spoken modern cutie, and it's perfectly clear that Samantha's freedom is the result of a pleasant middle-class home and loving parents. There's nothing submissive about her, but she isn't rebellious, either. When Samantha is alone, she sometimes talks out loud, telling us what she thinks, and Molly Ringwald does it so artlessly it seems like a normal way of behaving. Her acting gives the picture a lyric quality. The tilt of Samantha's head suggests a guileless sort of yearning, and there's something lovely about the slight gaucheness of her restless, long arms. In one of the film's best scenes, she finds herself alone with Geek and discovers that she can actually talk to him about her troubles. She recognizes that the reason she hasn't liked him is that he's young, like her. He drops his brash, coming-on manner, and she tells him about its being her birthday that everyone forgot—as she puts it, her family "just sort of blew it off." He confesses that he has never "bagged a babe," and she tells him her deepest secret—that she is still "on hold," and that she has been saving herself for the handsome senior.

Geek treats that confidence very respectfully; he also loses his crush on her fast—he's not on the prowl for a maiden. During their conversation, he begins to look less Geeky and just unformed. He has pale eyelashes, and his fair hair sticks up on his head but is too downy to achieve the punk effect he hoped for; he has the soft features of a fledgling. Anthony Michael Hall is in fact no more than a year older than the freshman he's playing. His Geek is a computer-age teen version of the early Woody Allen character—the fast-talking genius nerd—but Hall moves like Steve Martin, and even more confidently. Geek, with his pitchman's hard sell, is a product of television (and his appearances are heralded by the theme music of TV shows). What's best about him is his self-awareness; he knows that he looks like a jerk, but he's not going to let that stop him from making out. He has nerve; he's an operator, and he knows how to put what he learns to use—he has a man-to-man talk with the senior which is a model of suave diplomacy. Part of what makes *Sixteen Candles* entertaining is that the senior—a confident-looking jock—has his own uncertainties and turns out to be as romantic at heart as Samantha, while Geek comes through as a stud.

This picture was John Hughes' début as a director (he wrote the scripts for a couple of National Lampoon films and for *Mr. Mom*), and he may have got in a little over his head. Samantha has a full complement of family: in addition to siblings (her younger brother is played by Justin Henry, of *Kramer vs. Kramer*, who's going through an odd phase—he looks like a little Stephen King), she has two parents, and her four grandparents have arrived at her house for the wedding. All these people are part of Hughes' farcical superstructure, and maybe there's too much of this apparatus. One set of grandparents (a huge man and a tiny woman) compete with each other, talking to Samantha at the same time; as dumb gags go, it's not bad, but Hughes shows no particular emotion about the people—nothing to make it more than a dumb gag. The four grandparents come off as sitcom characters, and so do the new in-laws and most of the people involved in the wedding. And somehow the relationship between Samantha and her sister (Blanche Baker), the bride, seems lost in a haze. It isn't clear what sort of girl this sister is meant to be, and though her scenes are skewed to be funny they don't quite get there.

The children in this family are a strange assortment—they couldn't look more unlike. But they sound like siblings. John Hughes has a feeling for verbal rhythms, and he knows how kids toss words around, especially the words that set them apart from their elders. What gives *Sixteen Candles* its peppiness is his affection for teen-agers' wacko slang—phrases carrying such strong positive and negative charges that they have a dizzy immediacy. And he's on to how kids use computerese, as in "By night's end, I predict that me and her will interface."

May 28, 1984

A BREEZE, A BAWD, A BOUNTY

T he great thing about a tall tale on the screen is that you can be shown the preposterous and the implausible. In *Indiana Jones and the Temple of Doom,* the director Steven Spielberg is like a magician whose tricks are so daring they make you laugh. He creates an atmosphere of happy disbelief: the more breathtaking and exhilarating the stunts are the funnier they are. Nobody has ever fused thrills and laughter in quite the way that he does here. He starts off at full charge in the opening sequence and just keeps going. There isn't a letdown anywhere in it. A friend of mine denounced the picture as "heartless"; another friend called it "overbearing." In a sense, they're right, but they're also off the beam. This kind of storytelling doesn't have to be heartfelt; it just has to hold your interest (and delight you). *Indiana Jones* is a series of whoppers—it depends on verve and imagination to concoct the next big fib. And it leaps from one visual exaggeration to another—overbearing-ness is part of its breakneck style. (If it were modest and unassuming, it would fall apart.)

Set in 1935, *Indiana Jones and the Temple of Doom* probably has to be called a pre-sequel, or prequel, to *Raiders of the Lost Ark,* which was set in 1936, but it isn't pulpy in the way that *Raiders* was. It doesn't have the serious undercurrents that *Raiders* had; it's less "sincere"— and that's what is so good about it. The two films have the same adven-turer-archeologist hero, Dr. Indiana Jones (Harrison Ford), who wears a brown fedora and carries specs and a bullwhip. Indy seems more assured now, and more formidable physically—he's a professor with the chest of a horse. The plot is minimal this time: the action starts in Shanghai, at the Obi Wan night club, where the lusty blond Willie (Kate Capshaw), in a spangled crimson gown, struts in front of a line of tap-dancing chorus girls and belts out the film's keynote song, "Any-thing Goes," in English and Chinese. After a scramble at the club that features a diamond, a dose of poison, a vial of antidote, a lazy Susan, a pack of Oriental gangsters, and a rickshaw, and turns into a full-blown masterpiece of cheerful slapstick, Willie and Indy and his tiny, daredevil sidekick, the Chinese orphan Short Round (Ke Huy Quan), make a fast getaway by plane and drop off (literally) in India. There they are greeted by an elderly tribal chieftain who believes they have come in response to his prayers to Siva. He takes them to his blighted village; the land is arid, and the starving villagers are in mourning. The sacred stone that they believe conferred blessings on them has been stolen, and their children have disappeared. The three agree to go on a mission to retrieve the stone and the children, and the chieftain provides them with ele-phants to ride, and guides. The quest takes the three to the sumptuous palace of an odious boy maharajah (where the gold-digger Willie breathes the atmosphere of wealth and is momentarily in ecstasy), and from there, by underground passageway, to the temple where the vil-lainous high priest Mola Ram (Amrish Puri), the leader of the Thugs, presides over human sacrifices to the goddess Kali. (The name Mola Ram is an anagram for Malomar; the Thugs—expert stranglers and sneaks —and the evil cult of Kali will be familiar to people who have seen the 1939 adventure comedy *Gunga Din.*)

The subject of a movie can be momentum. It has often been the true

—even if not fully acknowledged—subject of movies. In *Indiana Jones and the Temple of Doom,* it's not merely acknowledged, it's gloried in. The picture has an exuberant, hurtling-along spirit. Spielberg tried kinetic comic-strip routines in his *1941* and couldn't quite make them work; here comparable routines come off just about perfectly. Spielberg uses old wheezes like the lazy Susan and you're charmed by it, remembering how, as a kid, you were nuts about these spinning discs. *Indiana Jones* is the kind of comedy in which the hero, in the middle of terrifying circumstances, and with his foot smoking, yells for water, and a deluge comes at him. The film sets the comic-book context for the hyperbolic perils that the three central characters get into, and keeps us laughing at the very fact that they don't get a chance to catch their breath. The whole movie is designed as a shoot-the-chutes, and toward the end, when the heroic trio, having found the sacred stone and freed the stolen children from the maharajah's mines, are trying to escape in a tiny mine car, and a shift in camera angles places us with them on a literal roller-coaster ride, the audience laughs in recognition that that's what we've been on all along. Yet Spielberg seems relaxed, and he doesn't push things to frighten us. The movie relates to Americans' love of getting in the car and just taking off—it's a breeze.

Sometimes when a director gets a chance to do a sequel, he starts with the knowledge that he gained on the first film. Coppola and *The Godfather, Part II* are the classic example. In its own, very different way, *Indiana Jones* stands in relation to *Raiders of the Lost Ark* as *The Godfather, Part II* stands to *The Godfather.* Though the picture is a Lucasfilm production, and the story idea is by George Lucas (with a script by Willard Huyck and Gloria Katz), it doesn't resemble the *Star Wars* movies the way that *Raiders* did. It's more cohesive, and it's much more clearly and confidently a Spielberg movie, with parody links to *The Wizard of Oz* and *Gunga Din,* and also to Saturday-afternoon serials and the Hope-Crosby *Road* movies and more recent screen adventures such as the cliffhanger stunt in *Butch Cassidy and the Sundance Kid.* The jokiness about the Mysterious East has something of S. J. Perelman's waggery; to an American kid a man in a turban is automatically not to be trusted.

Spielberg and his team come up with sequences that have an elusive mixture of comedy and wonder. At night in the jungle, the three travellers pause on the way to the palace; Indy and Short Round sit on the ground playing cards, squabbling amicably, and ignoring Willie, who has thus far been nothing but a shrill, complaining nuisance to them. It's like a nostalgic American campfire scene or picnic on a *Saturday Evening*

Post cover, but Willie, in the background, is being attacked by vampire bats and menaced by baboons, iguanas, snakes, and even an owl. She rushes around shrieking; the man and the boy are oblivious. This gag may have seemed terrific even on paper, but the look of it—the American small-town-boys'-world images it recalls—is inspired. Kate Capshaw's Willie is the clown on the team; she has routines right out of burlesque. There's a classic cockeyed-comedy bit involving her and her elephant, who treats her as derisively as the others do—the elephant likes to come up behind her, nudge her, and spray her with water. Willie gets so fed up that she grabs at what she thinks is its trunk, and throws a python at Indy. (She's too exhausted to marvel at how she managed to detach it.) And there are sequences that are like what children dream up when they're having a gross-out and trying to top each other: the three hungry travellers sit down to a banquet, with the boy maharajah at the head of the huge table and the high-ranking members of his court in evening dress, and the servants bring platters of delicacies—slippery, squirming baby eels, baked beetles, eyeball soup, and, for dessert, chilled monkeys' brains to be scooped out of the skulls.

Later that night, Willie and Indy separate, but before he goes across the hall to his room she bets him that he'll miss her so much that in five minutes he'll be back at her door, and he bets her that she'll come to him. With each of them pacing, hoping for the other's arrival, this is the one relatively quiet interlude in the movie. Indy's pacing is interrupted by a gigantic Thug who's determined to strangle him. It's a long, terrifying fight, won only with Short Round's help. When it's all over with, Indy rushes to Willie's room to make sure she, too, hasn't been attacked, and she's triumphant. It feels like just five minutes.

Kate Capshaw had me laughing right from the start, but she—and her role—made me uncomfortable in the first half hour or so. You could see that she was trying to be funny—she squealed like Betty Hutton and she acted like a cross between Ginger Rogers and Bette Midler. She was playing a self-centered brat who was useless in emergencies; Willie's only response was to scream. And since Willie doesn't contribute much to the visual heroics, she could have used wittier lines—or at least a moment of intelligence—so that when she and Indy kiss there's a reason for it. (It seems as if they're getting together just because they're male and female.) But Kate Capshaw won me over: her low-comedy brazenness and the whole conception of Willie as uncouth give the picture an additional layer of parody. Instead of being a pallid little darling in distress, she's a broad in distress, and the situations gain from her noisy wholesomeness.

This entire flying-carpet movie, with its comic-strip frames, is a pastel tourist paradise, as if a kid had filled in the numbered spaces to show what colored pencils can do. The look of it is itself funny. (Older kids may think the picture is a demonstration of what mattes can do.) Part of the fun of moviegoing for children is in getting wise to what's fake and what isn't. There are so many degrees of "reality" and fakery involved here that it could almost have been designed to keep them guessing; the stunt work and the laboratory special effects seem inseparable, and at the close of the Shanghai night-club sequence there's a fall through several canopies which evokes the lineage of modern movie trickery—the Douglas Fairbanks, Sr., pictures, and the famous opera-house shot in *Citizen Kane*, and every cowboy movie in which the hero jumped from a building into a wagon or onto his horse. *Indiana Jones* plays with the whole idea of movie magic. This spirit of play (which I felt was present only intermittently in *Raiders*) makes possible some glimmering storybook effects that probably weren't planned at all and were achieved only half-consciously. When our three find their route from the palace to the temple, they go through a passageway carpeted with creepy, crawly things. But this isn't a gross-out. Our reaction is a mixture of horror and awe, because the shining, symmetrical insects look like crawling jewels. They're—perhaps inadvertently—beautiful. And when some of them fall from the walls and are tangled in Willie's frizzy reddish-gold hair they're like the precious gems she has always wanted. The picture has fun-house skeletons and a night scene with a shooting star (a Spielberg signature); it has startling twists and sometimes small poetic curves. When Short Round wants to get into the speeding, out-of-control little mine car that Willie is in and a huge villain is clinging to, he uses the man's body as a staircase and climbs right up. It's pure Buster Keaton; that's real magic.

The stunts are brought off with incredible precision. (The way the editor, Michael Kahn, clips shots, you can almost hear him chuckling.) But plot points are occasionally fuzzy. There's a bit of information planted early on: Willie tells Indy that her father made his living as a magician, and so when the three are hiding in the temple (they're posed so that the scene is an homage to a shot in *Gunga Din*) and they look down into the vast cave where Mola Ram is conducting the rituals of Kali-worship and plucking the heart out of a man's chest—and as the man is consigned to fire, his heart, held high in Mola Ram's hand, bursts into flame—everything is prepared for Willie to spot Mola Ram as a con man who had a heart up his sleeve. But that revelation never comes, and since Lucas's special-effects company, Industrial Light & Magic, has become virtuosic about simulating the look of flesh being torn into, the poetic flourish of the burning heart may be too "real" for some viewers. The movie is set in a make-believe world, with cross-references to both Lucas's and Spielberg's other films, but this sequence is said to frighten some people, and there has been talk on television and in the press of making the film's PG classification more restrictive.

It's my impression that almost invariably the media stir up a fuss about the wrong movies. If you take a child to Disney's *Dumbo*, this is what the child sees: Dumbo's mother—a circus elephant—is so angry at kids who taunt Dumbo and pull his ears that she attacks them, and as a result she is beaten and locked in a cage for mad elephants. Dumbo is left on his own, and the other elephants humiliate him constantly. He's made into an elephant clown, and during a routine he's left at the top of a fireman's ladder in a burning house, crying elephant tears, because the human clowns fail to rescue him. His only friend is another outcast —the mouse Timothy. Each sequence is brought up to its maximum psychological resonance, and when a child projects himself into this vat of bathos and moroseness it's agony: the situations on the screen have immediate correlations with his own terrors. But what correlatives could there be in *Indiana Jones and the Temple of Doom*? It doesn't take advantage of childhood traumas. With its *Road to Morocco* sensibility, it constantly makes fun of itself, and it's as remote from children's real-life fears as Sabu's escapades in *The Thief of Bagdad*. The emotional mechanism of *Dumbo* is to make what happens to the cartoon animals real to kids; the emotional mechanism in *Indiana Jones* is to make what happens to the human characters unreal. And the hero carries you through—you know Indy won't die. Grownups who are upset by the menu at the banquet must be forgetting how cheerfully kids have traditionally sung such macabre ditties as "The worms crawl in, The worms crawl out, The worms play pinochle on your snout, And one little worm, Who's not too shy, Climbs into your ear, And out your eye" and "Great green globs of greasy grimy gophers' guts, Mutilated monkeys' meat, Little birdies' dirty feet, Great green globs of greasy grimy gophers' guts, And I forgot my spoon, Aw shucks."

The fuss in the media may be caused simply by the fact that there's something slightly off in the tone and the timing of the cult-of-Kali sequence. All through the picture, the comedy dominates the thrills, but here, when, at Mola Ram's instigation, Willie is put inside a contraption that looks like a deep-fat fryer, lowered partway down toward a pit of red-hot molten lava, and raised and lowered several times, Spielberg's control seems to slacken. The sequence is tense but flat; Willie has no wisecracks to deliver, and even her shrieks (which we've learned to laugh at affectionately) aren't very funny.

Spielberg's work in this movie is being called mechanical, but there are machines and then there are Rube Goldberg machines. Just because the slapstick requires brilliant timing (and the director's genius for composition) doesn't mean it's cold or impersonal. Possibly some people have got that idea because Spielberg shies away from giving the audience full, clear satisfaction. When the rotten Mola Ram pours some horrible guck down Indy's throat, Indy fights it but is held down; the scene suggests a child's fear of a dose of medicine. The guck—a "potion"—puts Indy in Mola Ram's power; he's in a trance, and we wait to see what will get him to snap out of it, but Spielberg doesn't point up the instant of awakening (though it appears to be the result of Short Round's quick thinking). And although Ke Huy Quan's Short Round is a nifty conception—this grasshopper-size kid is smarter and more resourceful than Indy, and a good case could be made for his being the true (and invulnerable) hero of the adventure—his victory over the boy maharajah isn't given the rush of feeling that the moment seems to call for. The name Short Round is an homage to Samuel Fuller, who used that nickname for the Korean kid in his 1950 movie *The Steel Helmet*; for Fuller, action is everything—and that's the acknowledgment being given here—but Fuller also piles on moral sentiment. Spielberg doesn't, and although that's part of his elegance as a moviemaker, he slights the emotional resolution of the plot. Having made the visual point that after the children were stolen from their village the land became a desert where nothing grew, he almost owes us a drenching downpour and lush vegetation to signify the children's return. It isn't quite satisfying to see them united with their families on land that looks only a little greener. Spielberg's not providing a formal closure makes the film's structure seem weaker than it is. He polishes off routines like that five-minute gag perfectly, but he may be a little embarrassed about giving us the same kind of pleasure on the larger plot points. He just comes to the end of the story and stops. Still, this is the most sheerly pleasurable physical comedy I've seen in years. And I'm grateful that Spielberg doesn't give the audience a chance to revel in how noble Indy is.

The only thing that really bothered me about the movie was the John Williams score, which is always selling excitement; it's too heavy for the tone of the film, and it's set too loud. Although there isn't much talk, the film gives you such a lot to respond to that the nonstop music produces overload; you feel as if you'd been listening to a crowd roar for two hours. (And for almost the full time you are: the audience's enthusiasm is uncontainable.) Away from the discomfort of the sound, the movie plays even better, in memory. But that sound level isn't anything as simple as a miscalculation; it's more like a guarantee. There is still the question of why a director as skillful as Steven Spielberg should make a succession of "ultimate" roller-coaster movies. (He has indicated that he may do a third in the Indiana Jones series.) It can't just be that he wants the money. It must go deeper. What I think makes this movie so overwhelming that some people recoil from it is that there is an emotional drive in it. The picture's momentum may be congruent with Spielberg's own impetus. Having had the most meteoric rise of any young director in the history of movies, he may feel that he has to push on to ever more inventive fantasies. He has made the most successful movie of all time (*E.T.*) and three of the runners-up (*Jaws, Close Encounters of the Third Kind,* and *Raiders of the Lost Ark*). His own career is a roller coaster. How can he make a picture about "normal" life? He has only his childhood to draw upon. As an adult, he rides a fantasy wilder than anything in his movies.

□

E*réndira,* which was written by Gabriel García Márquez, seems like the work of someone faking Gabriel García Márquez. There's a stir in the audience each time one of his "touches" appears—a profusion of paper flowers in planters and hanging pots, paper birds and butterflies that fly. But the touches have no hallucinatory tingle here; they may fly, but they're not winged. The Brazilian director Ruy Guerra calmly and systematically puts them in place—*Eréndira* is like a museum exhibition of García Márquez artifacts. The only resonance these touches have is that they remind us of García Márquez's other writing. Though the material was apparently written first as a screenplay—and then (when no film seemed likely) summed up in a single paragraph in *One Hundred Years of Solitude,* and later turned into both a novella and a short story—it doesn't have the feeling of something freshly conceived. The original screenplay is said to have been lost, and García Márquez is supposed to have rewritten it from memory (and from his other versions). That, combined with Guerra's directing, may help to explain why this fantasy, which is about a mad old witch (Irene Papas) who forces her virginal fourteen-year-old granddaughter Eréndira (Claudia Ohana) to work for her as a whore, is in the author's surreal-picaresque mode yet has almost none of the shocking beauty of his writing. The movie suggests the work of a gray-bearded professor having his little tease.

The picture is a moderately amusing nothing; despite its attempts to be magical, it doesn't take hold of a viewer's imagination. But Papas is having a good time, and she's out to give us one, too. Papas isn't fake anything; she's an original, and in this role she has a tattoo on her back and she wears the ensembles of a regal ragpicker. She goes in for the layered look: quilts and tablecloths, and drapes—preferably black and purple—with ball fringe. She's carried in a sedan chair as she and Eréndira travel through the desert (the film was made in Mexico), setting up shop wherever they go. And before long the witch is festooned in gold ingots. Little Claudia Ohana is lovely, and the scene of Eréndira's sexual initiation—by rape—is affecting in a semi-prurient way; the actress is very convincingly just a budding young girl. But Eréndira's mechanism for dealing with her customers is to turn catatonic and feel nothing while they do what they want with her, so Ohana—who, to judge by this performance, isn't a very distinctive actress—doesn't need to do much but suffer blankly. She's Sleeping Beauty as a whore, and she's O.K. to watch, but it's Papas who puts on a show.

When the old bawd sits at her baby grand and sings in French, she sounds a bit like Jeanne Moreau in *Jules and Jim,* and there's a suggestion of better days in her past. And when she sits up in her bed at night, talking out all her life's dramas in her sleep, the power in her voice is scary. Her voice is more than an instrument—it's a club. You know why people do what she tells them to. She also laughs in her sleep—a laugh that can turn into a snore. (It's too bad that her nocturnal raving doesn't have anything to do with the events Eréndira is involved in; the moviemakers miss a chance to tie things together for us. They miss many a chance.) Papas is marvellous in the scene where she blows out the candles on her birthday cake in one quick, impatient gust, sinks her hand into the cake (which is full of rat poison), eats it gluttonously, and burps with pleasure. In the morning, she says she hasn't slept so well since she was fifteen. And when her hair starts falling out in tufts she cackles as she lifts it off. Roaring with laughter and giggling on top of it, the witch survives one attempt on her life after another; she may be the hardest-to-kill movie monster since Rasputin. I can't think of another actress whose merriment can be this gargantuan. Papas could play a female Falstaff. (This is not a suggestion.)

In *The Bounty*, the new version of the famous story of the mutiny aboard the British naval vessel in 1789, Captain Bligh (Anthony Hopkins) is not a sadistic despot; he is a disciplinarian who sticks to regulations, but he's a fair man. In this account, based on Richard Hough's 1972 book, *Captain Bligh and Mr. Christian*, Fletcher Christian (Mel Gibson), the second-in-command, who leads the men in taking over the ship, signed on because Bligh, his friend, wanted him to. The ship is to transport breadfruit trees from Tahiti to Jamaica, on the theory that the starchy fruit will provide cheap fodder for the slaves there. Christian, who comes from an aristocratic background, calls it "a greengrocery trip." Bligh, who comes from the middle class and whose rank is still lieutenant, hopes that the trip—he plans to go around Cape Horn and circumnavigate the world—will make his reputation, and get him a better command. (The Bounty is a small vessel—too small for the task ahead.)

Directed by Roger Donaldson, who made *Smash Palace*, this film originated with David Lean, who, with backing by Warner Brothers, commissioned Robert Bolt to write two scripts from the Hough material. After the replica of the Bounty had been built, Warners learned that the budget for the two films would be prohibitive; the project was sold to Dino De Laurentiis, who gave the go-ahead to Donaldson to make this twenty-five-million-dollar movie from a condensed version of the scripts. Donaldson has made a passable, tense action film out of something that needed to be bigger. This *Bounty* is shot very close in for dynamic power —you're thrust right in among the men on the crowded ship—and it's certainly not boring. But it doesn't work as an epic: it doesn't have the scope or the emotional surge of epic storytelling—or the clarity, either. Bligh narrates the film; presumably what we see is the account he gives at his court-martial. But the movie violates that point of view almost immediately, showing us events he didn't know about. And, probably because of the condensation, the story is misshapen.

We want more background and narrative detail to give meaning to the action, and we want more characterization; we need it, since the simple explanation that the earlier movies provided for the mutiny— Bligh's sadism—has been quashed. The reasons are now somewhat fuzzier: they seem to lie mostly in Fletcher Christian's and the other men's response to the sexual freedom of Tahiti. (The movie might be called

Blame It on Tahiti.) The story is now about the conflict of two cultures, and that's where the picture falls short. Donaldson doesn't seem to have much feeling for the period. We need to see at the start what the background of the sailors is—what kind of society they came out of. There's not much point in suggesting the class distinctions among the officers if we get no clue to where the men come from. We don't even know if they are conscripts or voluntary seamen. We also need to see what the basis of Bligh and Christian's friendship is, so we can understand what sort of men they are and why they react so differently to the people on the island. And if we are to experience what the hedonism of the Tahitians might mean to repressed, inhibited Englishmen of the eighteenth century we need something more than shots of giggling bare-breasted beauties with flowers in their hair coming out in canoes to meet the Bounty, and more than orgiastic dancing and sex, too. Donaldson doesn't provide the kind of sensuous imagery (and editing) that would have made us feel what it was like for Englishmen of that time to be among people who lived without backbreaking labor and threats and punishments.

We do get reasonably exciting shots of the men on the Bounty during a tempest, with lightning crackling and a seaman set on fire, but the sequence comes too early, before we're involved in how this event changes Bligh's plans and affects the crew's view of him. We also get a compelling, showoffy performance by Hopkins—especially during the five months in Tahiti, as he becomes more tormented and more isolated in his attempts to enforce discipline. There's a strong suggestion of sexual jealousy in Bligh's attitude toward Christian during this period, with Bligh almost hiding on the ship, as if to keep pleasure from corrupting him. He orders Christian to stop "mixing with the damned degenerate natives." When the trees are on board and the ship leaves Tahiti, it's apparent that some of the men are having a hard time readjusting to authority and to their cramped quarters. Bligh suddenly changes; he reacts to the men's hostility by becoming an angry, unforgiving martinet —he keeps complaining that "the ship is filthy." (Is he flipping because he didn't permit himself any sexual indulgence?) Hopkins wears his hair close-cropped, so his features look larger and pudgier, and he gives his vocal cords a workout. At times, he carries on a bit like Bette Davis; what he's doing in this part of the film doesn't make a lot of sense, but his obsessive busyness is magnetic. Mel Gibson's performance is considerably spottier. There doesn't seem to be any character written into the role of Christian, and Gibson is made faintly absurd when he's posed romanti-

185

cally against the wind in shots that look like inserts. He's playing the open-shirted man of impulse and instinct versus Hopkins' man of order and restraint, but beyond the indication of his upper-class background there are no clues to why he goes native so quickly or what he's giving up when he decides to spend the rest of his life with a lovely Tahitian princess (Tevaite Vernette). It really doesn't mean much to see a man go native if we don't know what he was before. And whether because of the condensing or cuts in the editing room or just plain miscalculation, in his big scene—his emotional outburst during the mutiny—he seems to be having a nervous breakdown.

With Bligh as no worse than ambitious, repressed, and somewhat harsh, and Christian as a moody flower child who's drugged on love, we have no particular interest in either. As I watched this film, which doesn't have much narrative pull, my mind kept drifting to what wasn't there, mainly because what *was* there seemed less vital to the story. We observe a prolonged fight belowdecks that's provoked by a powerfully built brute who beats up a much smaller man, but nothing follows from it. We don't find out what happened to the little guy, and though the big fellow is in many subsequent scenes, we never see anything in his character that links with the viciousness he displayed. There's a burial at sea, but we can't put a face to the dead man's name, so the melancholy music doesn't mean much to us. We get no more than glimpses of the Tahitians who go with the mutineers to Pitcairn Island, though the relations on the ship between the British and the Tahitians might give us some insight into what's going to happen to their new society.

The picture might be more pleasing without the hype of Vangelis's pulsing, important-movie music during the credits, and without the ominous boom-booms that he provides when Christian first touches the Tahitian princess's hair. Much of Gibson's screen time is given over to his going in the water with this girl to kiss and play and to his being ceremonially tattooed. In one scene, which could have been played as a sad love-sick joke, he gives her his only treasure: his gold watch. (What's she going to do with it—listen to it tick?) Meanwhile, back at the ship, Hopkins frets and worries. This *Bounty* isn't different enough from its predecessors; it's the same old breadfruit story.

June 11, 1984

THE POP JUNKPILE

When you look at the opening images of Joe Dante's *Gremlins*, you almost hear the words "Once upon a time, in a small-town movie . . ." Dante sets us down in Kingston Falls, a vaguely Middle American community that's based on dozens of other movie-created nice, sleepy towns—especially the ones that are familiar to us from Frank Capra's 1946 *It's a Wonderful Life* and from the 1956 *Invasion of the Body Snatchers*. The people who live in Kingston Falls have no more depth than comic-book characters; the town even has a meanie—a Wicked Witch–Scrooge, Mrs. Deagle (Polly Holliday), who gets a kick out of foreclosing mortgages, especially now, at Christmastime. She threatens to destroy the only creature in town who defies her—Barney, a little dog who yaps at her and tries to attack her. Barney is the pet of the hero, Billy (Zach Galligan); at twenty, Billy aspires to be a cartoonist and comic-strip artist but is stuck in his job as a bank teller, because he's supporting his parents. The only scenes that take place away from Kingston Falls are set in a Chinatown where Billy's father, Mr. Peltzer (Hoyt Axton), an impractical dreamer-inventor—he devises contraptions that backfire—wanders about, trying to obtain orders for his malfunctioning gizmos, and in a nameless city he goes to for an inventors' convention. It's in the Chinatown, in the basement curio shop of an ancient Chinese sage (Keye Luke, in a long gray beard and with a milk-white glass eye), that Mr. Peltzer hears the near-human sounds of a mogwai, a tiny creature with the big, round eyes of a Pekinese and four-digit paws, who nests in a box. Peltzer wants to buy the mogwai as a present for Billy and offers two hundred dollars (rather casually, I thought, considering that he's living off Billy's wages). The sage refuses, but his grandson—just a kid—follows Peltzer out, slips him the critter, takes the money, and gives him three instructions: don't get him wet, keep him away from bright light, and never, *never* feed him after midnight.

The movie is, of course, about what happens when these rules are inadvertently disobeyed. The mogwai—Billy calls it Giz, for Gizmo—multiplies, and those mogwai also multiply, and though Giz remains harmless its progeny turn into greedy, demonic little gargoyles: dwarf dragons, with the jaws and teeth of crocodiles. About two feet high, they're like the little devils of Hieronymus Bosch, but with a spark of drollery. They torment Giz the way, in the cartoons, Sylvester the cat tormented Tweety Pie. At times—when they play cards and carouse—they're like race-track touts or underworld hipsters. And in one triumphantly insane sequence they invade the bar-and-grill where Billy's girlfriend, Kate (Phoebe Cates), works nights, and, as she tries to keep up with their orders, they gorge themselves like a gang of happy juvenile delinquents, gloating over the size of their appetites. One of them flashes her, another wears leg warmers and does some break dancing, while yet another woozily sings the blues. When they get completely out of hand, Kate (in a takeoff of *Rear Window*) grabs her camera and shoots flashbulbs at them.

Good little Giz takes no part in their revels. Giz is an icky-sweet lap-dog sort of creature that sits in a box all day waiting to be picked up and cuddled; it doesn't seem even to be ambulatory—all it does is make gentle cooing sounds and bat its eyelids. But the scuzzy, malicious peewee dragons are everywhere; one of them hides among a pile of stuffed animals as E.T. did, and now there's a stuffed E.T. right next to the demon. What Dante appears to be up to is a demonstration that something charming, like E.T., can get multiplied beyond a moviemaker's control. He's also doing his own, black humorist's parody of Steven Spielberg's *E.T.*—a demonstration that the underside of E.T. is like the monster in Ridley Scott's *Alien.* Or, to put it more baldly, he's showing that E.T.'s id is Alien. Gizmo is a good child; the other mogwai are its aggressively vulgar, beer-guzzling brothers—children of the night. When one of them blows his snout on a drape, he's like Jean Renoir's Boudu expressing his contempt for bourgeois life by wiping his shoes on a bedspread. These demons are like bad pets making messes.

Dante has the sensibility of a freaked-out greeting-card poet. In *Gremlins,* even when he's at his weirdest the blandness is there underneath, and when he defiles his vision of the good American life it's Frank Capraland that he's defiling. Once again, as in his segment of *Twilight Zone* (the family terrorized by the ten-year-old TV addict), there are too many kinds of parody floating around, but this time there are also too many kinds of old-movie cloyingness. The incongruities are tantalizing, but they don't work to any larger effect, and the movie never turns into the malevolent fun it should be. For a good part of the time, Dante's tone is (perhaps deliberately) uncertain. Kate has told Billy that she doesn't like Christmas, and the explanation comes in a monologue she delivers about how she lost her father; it belongs to the theatre of the absurd, but Dante presents it in such an unresolved way that we don't know quite when to laugh. And what are we to make of the fact that the first casualty of the demons is the one black man in the movie, the high-school science teacher (Glynn Turman)? Is the movie using the old, standard ploy of disposing of black characters fast, or is this a parody of all those movies in which the good, kind black fellow is the first victim of whatever menace is at hand? The scene doesn't play like parody, but with Dante you often can't tell what's parody and what isn't.

The director builds suspense by postponing the audience's first view of the mogwai: we aren't allowed to see it when Mr. Peltzer buys it, and when he brings it home it's in a box tied up with ribbon. We don't see it until Billy first sees it, but this revelation has no sock to it, because the creature is such a wet-eyed blob—a kitten painted by Walter Keane, adorableness incarnate. Billy might be more likable if he were appalled by his father's assumption that he'd want this itty-bitty furball, and had to struggle to conceal his feelings. Billy is an autobiographical hero: as a boy, Joe Dante wanted to be a cartoonist (which, in a sense, he is: he never gets past cartoon characters with cartoon emotions). But Billy has been made out to be a considerate and responsible fellow—a personable dishrag. We can't tell if we're meant to see him as a younger version of his dreamer father or as a young man with the practical good sense that his father lacks. We don't even know if Zach Galligan and Phoebe Cates, who look alike in this movie (they have matching sets of teeth), are meant to be a charming pair or a spoof of dopey wholesomeness. (Where are *their* ids?) *Gremlins* doesn't play by the rules or by the anti-rules, either. And Joe Dante seems to be trying to put together a jigsaw puzzle with too many pieces. The young actor Judge Reinhold looks as if he enjoyed playing smarminess, and he's fine as a bastardly junior vice-president of the bank who brags about how quickly he's rising (and leaving Billy at the bottom), but the picture introduces him, sets him up, and then seems to forget about him. Billy is provided with the dog Barney, who then has to be shunted aside while Billy becomes attached to Giz. Why didn't the writer, Chris Columbus (an N.Y.U. film-school graduate), or Dante simply combine the plots and have Mrs. Deagle vent her anger on Giz, using that as the mechanism for setting Giz's id in motion? (That might have given the picture a little more coherence.)

Movies are Joe Dante's only frame of reference, and he slips in and out of movie conventions; I'm not sure that he himself knows when he means to be funny, since he seems to find the whole idea of making movies funny. But *Gremlins* isn't dull; there's always something going on. In one scene, we discover that Giz can reproduce musical tones; nothing comes of it. The picture is an unholy mixture—a whimsical pop shocker—and finally nothing comes of any of it. Dante can't pull his ideas together, and the movie has so little emotional impact that it might be called affectless. Yet it's obvious that Joe Dante is a genuine eccentric talent with a flair for malice, and it's certainly clear why Spielberg, whose production company made the film (and who glides through a shot at the inventors' convention, riding a little motorized cart), believes in him. There are some crack sequences. Upstairs in Billy's house, the first batch of Giz's progeny are in some gooey metamorphosing state while downstairs Billy's mother—very well played by Frances Lee McCain— is in the kitchen baking gingerbread men. And although we may wonder whom they're for—her husband and her twenty-year-old son?—they're metaphorically perfect. McCain's big scene comes just a minute later. Mrs. Peltzer, hearing strange noises upstairs, goes up to investigate. But she isn't one of those dreary fools who inhabit the usual horror movie—the ones who go up to be slaughtered. She takes a very sharp knife, and from the set of her chin we know she means business. When she encounters the repugnant little dragons, she goes at them systemati- cally, one after another, and when a couple of them make the mistake of invading her kitchen she traps one in the juicer (the only time her husband's gadgets come through for her) and the other in the microwave oven. Her efficiency is a thing of beauty. This tough and determined Mrs. Peltzer wouldn't be staying home playing housewife while her young son supported her (instead of having his own life); she'd be out making a living. But when a sequence is directed with the snap and freshness of this one, who cares?

The veteran horror-film actor Dick Miller (he looks like an older, more wizened Robin Williams) appears as Mr. Futterman, the town drunk, who accounts for his tractor's not starting by referring to the gremlins that were supposedly planted in machinery in the Second World War. Miller gets a chance to show what a likable low comic he is in the kind of part that Barry Fitzgerald used to play. When Mr. Futterman's TV goes on the fritz, he looks up at the antenna on his roof, which the demons have been using as a jungle gym; at that moment they come driving his tractor out of the garage and right through his living room. And Polly Holliday is a wonderfully astute and polished actress. She brings the Margaret Hamilton role a whiny, self-justifying undercurrent. You laugh at Mrs. Deagle because she's just so awful; she's someone you could love to hate. In her last moments on earth, Mrs. Deagle hears what she thinks are Christmas carollers, rushes to fill a pitcher of water so she can douse them, and opens the door to the fearless little devils (who should never be got wet).

For a movie that's a pop junkpile of movie references, *Gremlins* has a surprising number of good things in it. There's a marvellous effect when one of the mogwai falls into the swimming pool at the Y, and the whole body of water roils and smokes, like a Blakean vision of Hell, and from outside the building you can see the shadows of the demons who are taking shape. But the scenes that can make a claim to be inspired take place in the Kingston Falls movie theatre. It's an ingenious location, since the mogwai have to be in darkness, and they have multiplied so lavishly that they fill the seats. The theatre is packed with these lewd hipster dragons watching their gnomish counterparts on the screen in Disney's *Snow White and the Seven Dwarfs*; they pad up and down the aisles, eating, laughing, commenting on the action, and tearing up the place. And when the Seven Dwarfs on the screen start to sing "Heigh-Ho," the mogwai join in the singing. In their enthusiasm, they spin around on the projectors, and rip the screen to shreds. It's a delirious, kitschy travesty—a kiddie matinée in Hell. In some ways, Joe Dante makes these antic demons as disgustingly adorable as Giz. They're Katzenjammer Kids, and the action is all kiddie pranks in a cluttered comic strip.

It's typical of Dante's paranoid-cartoon approach that after this sequence Billy and Kate, who battle the demons in the theatre, must rush to do battle again in the town department store. The moviemakers have so many ideas that they lose track of their own central metaphor. The mogwai can't stand bright light—it kills them. The movie—and this ties in with Kate's monologue—is a Christmas Eve dream of something fearful coming down the chimney. When we see the mogwai at the debauch in the theatre, we may reasonably expect the sun to come up on Christmas morning and take care of them. The whole picture seems to point to that ending, because when the sun comes up movies end and our dreams are over. *Gremlins* just keeps going from one cartoon idea to another. There's a lovely last shot of Keye Luke in a Christmas-card landscape, but the picture has already self-destructed.

Gremlins is leaving something behind, though. Is Giz meant to be as mawkish as I found it? A little boy who visits the Peltzer house fusses over how cute it is; Giz makes a face and says something on the order of "Oh, that again." Joe Dante is certainly conscious of the creature's ickiness; Giz is designed to make everyone say "Aw," and the whole idea of the demons is based on Giz's repression of everything that isn't pure and sweet. But if Dante and his moviemaking team are aware of what a soft bundle of anthropomorphic ick this creature is, how can they be party to launching stuffed Gizmos into the toy stores of the world for children to covet and caress? It's one thing for a movie to lead to the manufacture of toys that delight the public because they delighted the moviemakers. But selling Gizmos is a horrible joke.

Periodically, a new comedy is acclaimed for all the things it wants to be but isn't. Last summer, *Trading Places*, with Eddie Murphy and Dan Aykroyd, was greeted as "an event" and "a film of real wit and imagination"; before that there were such pearls of wit and imagination as *Nine to Five* and *Foul Play*. The bummer that's getting the tributes this summer is *Ghostbusters*, which features Bill Murray, Dan Aykroyd, and Harold Ramis as parapsychologists. Thrown out of their cushy university research jobs, these three doctors set up a business: they advertise themselves as experts in trapping any ectoplasmic manifestations that may be bothering people. That's actually not a bad premise for a scare comedy, and the producer-director, Ivan Reitman, has assembled a good backup cast. What goes wrong? Well, the script (by Aykroyd and Ramis) provides Murray with funky lines, and he delivers them stunningly; he can make even the simplest statement seem a gambit or a fraud—his pores ooze untrustworthiness. Murray is the film's comic mechanism: the more supernatural the situation, the more jaded his reaction. But nobody else has much in the way of material, and since there's almost no give-and-take among the three men, Murray's lines fall on dead air. (Sometimes the niftier the line the bigger the thud.) Part of what goes wrong is in the script: Aykroyd and Ramis were too self-effacing—they didn't give themselves enough to do. A larger part, I think, is in Reitman's directing. He brought off the 1981 *Stripes*, which was a big jump up from his earlier comedy, the 1979 *Meatballs*, but this time his work is amateurish. He may have been overwhelmed by the scale of the production; at roughly thirty-two million, it's much more ambitious than anything he has attempted before. The sets and special effects include crowds watching as spirits come shooting out of the top of a Central Park West apartment building and skies go purplish—it's big, all right, but it isn't very funny. When the ghostbusters—the three have been joined by a fourth, a black actor (Ernie Hudson), in what seems like an afterthought—rush to save the city from spooks, they're in the converted ambulance they call an ectomobile, at the head of a procession of police cars, with an escort of police motorcycles; the scene is uncomfortably like the big convergence of vehicles in *The Blues Brothers*. I think Reitman also made a mistake in choosing Laszlo Kovacs as his cinematographer; the images have a heavy, overdeliberate look—they're too rigid for comedy. The actors look impaled in Kovacs' lighting.

The movie does have some things going for it: its logo, for one—a small, blobby ghost (like the Pillsbury doughboy or a member of the trio in *Casper, the Friendly Ghost*) who pops out of the "o" in *Ghostbusters*. (I came to associate this lump of dough with Aykroyd, who seemed rather unformed, and soft and sleepy.) Mainly, the movie has its performers. Playing opposite Bill Murray, Sigourney Weaver is a living zinger. She has a great set of bones and planes, and she's blazingly alive; she must be the least recessive beauty in movies. When she stands talking to Murray, she's eye to eye with him, and she looks indestructible. She throws herself into her role here, but her scenes don't go anywhere, and just when she's building up her "possessed" number, and seems ready to take off, the action cuts away. Annie Potts, who plays the ghostbusters' receptionist, uses her wonderful self-enclosed quality; she's wacked out in a petite, all-by-herself way. Rick Moranis, as a mild, nerdy accountant, takes the role so far that you can see the raging, bigger nerd at his core. And, of course, Bill Murray. His patent insincerity makes him the perfect emblematic hero for the stoned era. He has a genuine outré gift: he makes you feel that his characters are bums inside—unconcerned and indifferent—and he makes that seem like a kind of grace. (He's always an onlooker; he won't commit himself even to being in the movie.) What's surprising about him as a performer is the amount of alertness and energy he pours into being burned out and bleary and blasé. He turns burnout into a style. Murray does his damnedest in *Ghostbusters*, but he can't set the rhythms of his performance the way he has sometimes been able to on television, and the way he did in *Stripes* and in *Tootsie*; he's left with joke on his face. It's possible that the director's sluggish, kids-movie pacing is the reason Murray is getting a terrific response from people who had queasy reactions to him before; maybe he's so slowed down that they finally get his humor (and their laughter helps to fill the dead spots). To be more charitable, maybe audiences are roaring at him because he acts in a more outward and endearing way than usual: waiting near the fountain at Lincoln Center, he does a happy little hop, and after the majestic Sigourney has appeared and agreed to go out on a date with him he lifts his arms toward heaven and twirls.

June 25, 1984

SNEAKS, OGRES, AND THE D.T.S

In the Dutch thriller *The 4th Man*, the arrogant boozehound Gerard Reve, author of scandalous gothic tales, who has come to loathe the younger man he lives with, and is broke, as usual, prepares to go to the seacoast town of Flushing, where he is to pick up a fee for speaking at the local literary society. At the Amsterdam train station, he sees a muscular, boyish fellow, and every other thought is driven from his mind. He chases after the fellow but isn't fast enough, and, irritated, he boards his train. In Flushing, where the scene of his being introduced to the gathering recalls Joseph Cotten's literary lecture in *The Third Man*, Reve goes home with Christine, the blond widow who's the treasurer of the group. Reve has no particular interest in her—he just doesn't want to spend the night at the hotel. Without much enthusiasm, he allows her to mount him; the only thing he likes about her is the boyishness of her body. The next day, she tells him how rich and lonely she is, and propositions him to stay on and let her take care of him. He isn't interested until, nosing around her things, he spots a picture of a young man in swimming trunks: it's her longtime lover, Herman—the man he chased in the Amsterdam station.

The fun of *The 4th Man*, which was directed by Paul Verhoeven, is in Reve's caddishness and in the nasty comic skill that Jeroen Krabbé brings to the role. Krabbé played the second lead in Verhoeven's *Soldier of Orange*, but this part is much trickier—the film's comic tone depends on our being tickled by Reve's mean-spiritedness. The novel that the movie is based on is by the Dutch writer Gerard Reve, who endows the hero with his name and also with his reputation as a homosexual and his conversion to Roman Catholicism. Krabbé's Reve practically jumps for joy when he maneuvers Christine into inviting Herman for a visit; when Krabbé is sneaky he's reminiscent of James Mason in Kubrick's *Lolita*, courting Mrs. Haze while he can't wait to get his hands on her daughter. And, being a Catholic, Reve can be blasphemous: when he goes to church and stands in front of a sculptured figure of Christ on the Cross, he imagines that it's Herman hanging there, in his trunks, and, in ecstasy, he pulls them down. The author of the novel has also endowed the hero with his own methods as a writer. At the literary gathering, Reve explains that he takes incidents from life and lets his imagination embroider them—"I lie the truth," he says, clearly self-infatuated. All through the movie, we see glimpses, like the Herman-on-the-Cross scene, of Reve's embroideries; they're not conscious, they're involuntary imaginings—omens, forebodings, warnings. They prepare him for situations he finds himself in just a little while later. Some of these dream glimpses relate to Ingmar Bergman movies, some of them to Catholic symbolism, and some to the hero's phobia about women. In his visions, Christine is a deadly spider and castrater—a witch.

The dialogue in this movie is sharp and pungent. Verhoeven and his (usual) scenarist, Gerard Soeteman, are out to give us a shocking good time, and the picture doesn't waste words. Reve is brusque and slangy, and you can see him congratulating himself on his incredible rudeness. He enjoys his affectations, too: after he has told Christine that he'll stay on, he goes to a stationery store with her and takes a sensual delight in loading up with such items as a huge supply of penholders and nibs. He's the kind of articulate monster you can enjoy in a play or a movie but would detest in a room. What keeps *The 4th Man* from being anywhere near the class of *The Third Man* or of *Lolita* is that Christine isn't as entertaining as Reve is. She needs to be a teasingly ambiguous figure, who would have us puzzled about whether Reve is deluding himself that she's a killer witch who has already dispatched three husbands or whether his hyperactive imagination is alerting him to the truth. As the part is played by Renée Soutendijk (she was in Verhoeven's *Spetters* and was Eva Braun in the TV *Inside the Third Reich*), Christine is smooth and completely opaque. Her yellow hair is in a sleek pompadour, and she does indeed suggest a lithe, boyish strength, and no doubt her softly draped red dresses are meant to signify danger. But she's disappointingly placid. Verhoeven and the scenarist failed to work out a psychology for her; we never for a minute feel we understand Christine, and we don't get much kick out of watching her (apparently) luring men to their doom, because there doesn't seem to be any kick in it for her.

In a sense, the picture is locked inside Reve's phobia; there's no distance between his view of Christine and the movie's. When Christine stands naked before Reve and he blots out her breasts with his hands and tells her that she "looks like a beautiful boy," the scene has a campy frisson. The women in the audience can enjoy his pleasure in the naughtiness of his remark as much as the men can. It's funny to hear Reve express his homosexual preferences so languidly and, in his insolent way, so openly. But Christine has no reaction to what he says, so the movie comes across as no more than a tongue-in-cheek homoerotic fantasy. This is a tale of a woman Bluebeard, yet the moviemakers show no more curiosity about her than Reve does. The picture is locked inside Reve's I'm-a-bad-boy-but-I-love-the-Blessed-Madonna Catholicism, too. Verhoeven uses religious symbolism for sinister effects that have the tone of a put-on—they have no more emotional weight than such bitchy, semi-porno touches as Reve's imagining himself picking up a black bra, twisting it, and strangling his apartment-mate lover with it. But the structure of the story requires, finally, that we accept these effects as genuine religious experiences, and this gives the viewer a slightly soggy letdown at the finish.

Though the picture is amusing, there's nothing underneath its calm, pseudo-modernist surface—the *musique concrète* during the opening credits (while a spider devours its prey and crawls over the face of the crucified Christ), the frontal nudity, the creamy, intense color. *The Third Man* and *Lolita* have a dirty, glittering obsession underneath. But when *The 4th Man* is over it's really over. And if you think back on it at all the only life in it is in Jeroen Krabbé's performance. He really loves playing a worm, and he loves the scenes in which Reve exhibits his sleazy savoir faire. Herman turns out to be a plumbing contractor who's eager to hear about the sex lives of celebrities; he's a self-righteous bore, but he isn't boring to Reve, who sits back and skillfully dishes up the dirt.

With Leonard Nimoy as the director and a script by the producer, Harve Bennett, the Starship Enterprise keeps plugging away through space in *Star Trek III: The Search for Spock*. This one is really only for Trekkies; others are likely to find it tolerable but yawny, and to be worn down by the long mourning period for Spock. The crew can't get over his death: he gave his life to save theirs in *Star Trek II: The Wrath of Khan*, which ended with his casket's being sent to the newly created planet, the paradisiacal Genesis, where, the audience could assume, he would be reborn. But this new film seems to take a churlish attitude toward its lighthearted, delicately self-mocking predecessor; almost vindictively, the new film requires that Genesis disintegrate. Admiral Kirk (William Shatner) and his venerable crew must steal the now mothballed Enterprise and fly to the cracking-apart Genesis to rescue Spock—whatever form he's in—and take him home to Vulcan. Along the way, they have to fight off a bunch of ogres whose brains appear to be on the outside of their foreheads; these barbarians, who suggest Viking aeronauts, are called Klingons, and their Lord is the funky Christopher Lloyd (of the TV series "Taxi"), who manages to be droll despite the absolute nonexistence of comedy scenes in this movie. *Star Trek III* does have its share of eccentricities: the Klingons, who go in for droopy Mongol mustaches, lean their yucky foreheads close to each other and talk in hoarse, conspiratorial whispers even though they're out in space. (They hiss, like old cattle-rustling villains.) And every once in a while the music makes a pathetic stab at working up our emotions.

Directed by a Vulcan, the picture is achingly prosaic and so clumsily staged that when Kirk's young scientist son is killed it looks as if we're being fooled and he'll turn out to be fine. The stoic Kirk, preoccupied with regenerating Spock, shrugs off the loss, and the team moves on to Vulcan to try to unite Spock's body with his logical mind, which has somehow got "melded" with the sentimental thought processes of Bones McCoy (the likably silly DeForest Kelley). The mind-unmelding ceremony is conducted by a Vulcan priestess, played by Judith Anderson, now in her eighty-seventh year, and she gives the picture a sudden lift. For a minute or two, we listen to a voice that's so commandingly intense it's scary. (This is not the voice of someone you'd want for an enemy.) Anderson wears robes that might have been designed by Frank Lloyd Wright in his Incan Art Deco period, and she stands very still—an imperious, predatory bird of a woman. She brings a spot of high style to this movie; her huge, pointy ears only add to her grandeur. When the ceremony is over and Spock, his mind restored, is once more the glum Nimoy, it's not an occasion for dancing in the streets.

Nicholas Meyer, who directed *Star Trek II*, gave the longtime members of the crew of the Starship Enterprise a chance to loosen up and have some fun with their roles, and their performances had a little wit. They didn't come across as such bad actors. But Nimoy gets them back to a liturgical reading of their lines, and you can't help feeling that there's a special vacuity about this crew. At least part of the cause must be the collection of hairpieces they wear—each neatly and individually styled but with no organic relationship to the lined, thickening faces underneath. It can't be true, but it certainly looks to be true: empty is the head that wears a hairpiece. These actors have become puppet versions of themselves.

I have friends who swear by the greatness of Malcolm Lowry's *Under the Volcano*—by the density and expressiveness of its language. I don't know whether the lack is in me or in the novel—I've never been able to get through it. But in the case of the new film version, directed by John Huston from a script by Guy Gallo, I'm reasonably sure that the fault isn't mine. What we see on the screen is Albert Finney wrestling with a big role: the self-destructive Geoffrey Firmin, who was formerly the British Consul in Cuernavaca and is still a resident, as he lurches about the city for twenty-four hours, during the Day of the Dead festivities—it's November 2, 1938, which is also the last day of his life. There are two other main characters—Yvonne (Jacqueline Bisset), the actress wife, who left the drunken, impotent Firmin a year ago and divorced him but now returns, and his callow Marxist half brother Hugh (Anthony Andrews), a journalist whose affair with Yvonne precipitated the breakup of the marriage. But Finney is essentially alone on the screen —the other characters are just there for Firmin to talk to or to react to.

The novel, written by a drunk, is widely regarded as the best novel ever written about a drunk. That may be why it has attracted so many adapters and directors in the years since it was published, in 1947— more, it is generally agreed, than any other book. In 1957, Lowry, sotted and depressed, swallowed an overdose of Amytal and drowned in his own vomit. That is, essentially, what Firmin is doing throughout the movie. But Lowry had a mystique about alcohol: he somehow got himself to believe that this self-destruction (and only this self-destruction) would give him access to the states of mind necessary to set words on fire. To put it bluntly, his hero Firmin has come to Mexico to see into the heart of darkness and write an unwritable book. (Actually, Lowry proved that it wasn't unwritable—only, for some of us, unreadable.) Artists who take drugs have often claimed that they need the brilliance or the rush that drugs give them, but this sort of claim is less common among alcoholics, probably for the simple reason that an alcoholic pays a physical price almost immediately—he becomes hung over, smelly, and disgusting even to himself. But Lowry, with his mysticism, saw Firmin as a staggering drunk who was also a high priest. Lowry gave Firmin the status of a visionary. He's meant to be a dying giant—not just a man destroying himself but a genius with the courage to destroy himself so that he can transcend the limits of ordinary men and see things more intensely. The young literary critic Charles Baxter has speculated that arson was Lowry's metaphor for creativity—he wanted to capture the way things radiated just before they turned to ash. (The volcano in the title isn't only a reference to Popocatépetl, the Cuernavaca tourist attraction.)

It's not surprising that the adapters and directors who were attracted by the novel were defeated by it—and I include Huston and Guy Gallo. If there is a good way for a movie to suggest Lowry's conviction that art requires the alcoholic self-destruction of the artist, the team that worked on this production hasn't found it. For the story to mean anything resembling Malcolm Lowry's *Under the Volcano*, we would have to see something of what Firmin—with his psyched-up consciousness—perceives. Possibly, it would have had to be done by visual metaphors, or by techniques comparable to the hallucinatory intensifications of the landscapes in Werner Herzog's *Aguirre, the Wrath of God*. Mexico itself might have had to be visualized as a phantom country of the heightened senses—a now-you-see-it-now-you-don't country. The Mexico provided by Huston and the cinematographer, Gabriel Figueroa, and the production designer, Gunther Gerzso, has an unvarying visual texture—the images are statically composed, with a deep-toned flossy and "artistic" clarity. You could give these images high marks for neatness (and hollowness). They suggest the kind of perfectly detailed stage sets that make you not want to see the play, and when Firmin strays into a low dive—a cantina that's a hangout of thieves and Nazis—it has its quota of carefully positioned dwarfs and transvestites. All that the film does is take a literal approach to the novel, as if it were no more than an account of the final binge of a drunken former consul who becomes suicidally careless and gets himself killed. Since there's almost no attempt to find equivalents of Firmin's visions or of the excitement of Lowry's passages of incendiary prose, the film puts a terribly heavy burden on Albert Finney. The drama has to come from his performance, in a big yet virtually unwritten role.

It isn't what Firmin says in the novel that expresses his consciousness; the whole inchoate novel does it. Trying to suggest what isn't in the script, Finney can't help making us aware that he's giving the role more than his best shot—that he's pushing too hard (frequently in closeup)—right after his big, pushing performance in *The Dresser*. (This is two movies in a row in which everything is geared toward his death.) In some scenes here, he still has the actorishness that he built up for *The Dresser*: he overuses his facial muscles, the way he did in his parody of Donald Wolfit; even when he's not talking, his mouth is busier than anything else in the picture. And in a scene at a benefit for the Red Cross, where he takes the microphone and makes a crazed, incoherent speech, he still looks like Wolfit. (Sometimes, he can't help recalling Dudley Moore's drunks.) In *The Dresser*, Finney could at least use his humor and his flair for satire, but here, with the exception of a few bits and one scene involving a conversation between Firmin, who has passed out in the middle of the street, and a pip-pip Britisher (James Villiers) who stops to help, the movie is bereft of comedy. And the role doesn't take over Finney the way his role in *Shoot the Moon* did. There was no forcing in that; he was caught up in it—he and Diane Keaton were acting together. Here it's a long monologue of a performance, with too many stops pulled out. He looks right for the part: he has a massive head, and he's barrel-chested and thick-necked, like Lowry; bulky and bull-like, he's believable as a man with the constitution to drink night and day and to hold himself straight even when he's walking around in a stupor. Finney isn't bad—he keeps giving us emotional shifts and inflections. And when he's with Jacqueline Bisset he seems to be built on a different scale from her; on the bed with her, humiliated by his impotence, he suggests the bloated carcass of a beached whale. But there's nothing he can do to suggest what Lowry meant when he said, in the posthumously published *Dark As the Grave Wherein My Friend Is Laid*, that "not an hour, not a moment of my drunkenness, my continual death, was not worth it: there is no dross of even the worst of those hours, not a drop of mescal that I have not turned into pure gold, not a drink I have not made sing."

If we try to accept the movie not as an adaptation of *Under the Volcano* but simply as the story of a drunk, that doesn't work, either, because the movie is inept in a peculiarly literary way—the dialogue doesn't sound like living people talking. And the score, by Alex North, ages the material, gives it a terrible kind of pompous emotionalism. I retained some small hope that the picture might get going until Andrews (familiar to audiences from his starring role as Sebastian Flyte in the TV "Brideshead Revisited") appeared; then everything sank. He gives an arch, acting-by-the-manual performance; each flicker of expression signals an obvious meaning. Firmin couldn't be upset by his wife's adultery with this twit—it would have to be laughed off as a joke.

Thinking about this movie and about Lowry (who was the first to try to adapt the material to the screen) has made me feel ashamed of not finishing the book. The pages in my copy have yellowed; I mean to get back to it before it disintegrates.

July 9, 1984

ETHNICS

The *he Pope of Greenwich Village* is like a doughy plum cake with wonderful plums sticking out of it. The plums are the performers. The movie has colorful "ethnic" dialogue—Italian and Irish—by Vincent Patrick, whose script is based on his 1979 book, and the actors run with it. One of them, Geraldine Page, as a crooked cop's tough, caustic old mother, does more than that: she exults in it, and she gives an enthrallingly hammy performance, smoking, boozing, and picking horses. She seems to be from another picture, and the tension she brings to her two scenes is jolting. But viewers (me included) are delighted, because there have been scenes with no tension at all. The acting—and the overacting —gives *The Pope of Greenwich Village* its only vitality. Directed by Stuart Rosenberg, it's a moderately entertaining bad movie (and of considerably more interest than the novel).

Like Richard Price's *Bloodbrothers,* Vincent Patrick's book was influenced by the Martin Scorsese film *Mean Streets,* and Patrick's work, too, reads like a movie. But Patrick's talent is almost all in his ear, and the story is no more than a tabloid-style, broad-humored variation on Scorsese's subject: the ties among small-time Catholic hoods. The half-Italian, half-Irish Charlie (Mickey Rourke) and the Italian Paulie (Eric Roberts), distant cousins and pals from childhood, work for a living, but they expected to grow up into a world of unimaginable luxury and they're proud of knowing how to spend money. So they're always in debt, and caught up in chiselling and part-time thievery. Charlie is the more responsible of the two. He explains his fondness for Paulie in terms of tribal loyalty, and he's protective of Paulie, who at times seems so ignorant you could take him for retarded.

At first, Mickey Rourke seems in fine control of his character. He has a confidential, flirty softness in his voice and an angelic, secret smile; his lips dimple up at the corners—he seems to be smiling in his head. The discreet Charlie is the maître d' of a Village restaurant, and he enjoys being suave and professional, and puckering up to signal a kiss to the hat-check girl across the room. He's a smoothie with women—it's easy to see what has attracted Diane (Daryl Hannah), his Wasp girlfriend from Maine, who teaches aerobics. Eric Roberts' Paulie, who holds his job as a waiter because of Charlie but skims so much off his checks that he gets both of them fired, is a thin, nervous, jumpy mess, and the performance may seem irritatingly mannered. Besides, you can't help dreading the violent consequences of the stupid robbery that he involves Charlie in. But whether through the fault of the director, or the way Charlie's role is written, or Rourke himself, Charlie doesn't appear to have enough interior life to sustain audience interest. He's slightly withdrawn—maybe a little passive—and he lets the babbling, crazily extroverted Paulie talk him into things. Then, when he's disgusted with himself for having let Paulie louse up his plans, he bops Paulie, slapping him around in the manner of the Three Stooges. It's a tiresome, unpleasant reflex—a limited man's reflex—and he uses it repeatedly, without variations (which suggests that Rourke is a limited, repetitive actor). When Diane walks out on Charlie, he punches the wall in rage and dismay, and his readiness to explode seems no more than a convention of the genre. Rourke's light, soothing vocal range works against these explosions; when he goes into a rage, nothing ever snaps—there doesn't seem to be anything in him that *could* snap. His rages are polished. And we don't feel that he really has all that much pent-up energy—that he's keeping the lid on something. Rourke has humor (which counts for a lot), and he plays his scenes several shades cooler than they require—that's his style. But he isn't as daring here as he has been in smaller roles (the professional arsonist in *Body Heat*, Boogie the girl chaser in *Diner*), and he doesn't take himself a quarter of an inch further than he has gone before. He may be miscast: his Charlie seems too rational to put up with Paulie. Probably what we need to see is that although Charlie thinks he's hip and in control, in the back of his head he has the suspicion that maybe Paulie's demented ideas will work, and so he's the eternal patsy—something in him wants to be caught up in folly.

Paulie is childishly (and pitifully) dependent on Charlie, but it's clear that Paulie has a spark—that he's the leader (even if only in getting them in trouble). And Eric Roberts' weird, out-at-the-edge performance gives the picture whatever drive and point it has. Roberts dominates the film; what goes on between the two actors seems to parallel what goes on between the characters. Roberts is trying for something outré: he goes way past realism into a stylized, exaggerated clowning. It may be that Rourke's cool is what makes Roberts go so far; Roberts may be trying to shake Rourke up, so he'll have something to play against. His head covered with tight curls, he has an androgynous quality here, and in his tight, hot-shot clothes (no hip pockets, tan shoes) he looks like a Pre-Raphaelite pimp. His manner is often heady and nonchalant; his words seem to get tangled in his upper lip, but when they come out they're bitchy and persnickety. And there are scenes in which, despite Charlie and Paulie's tough-guy talk about women and their ritualized contempt for "fags," Paulie calls up echoes of Chris Sarandon's nakedly desperate candidate for a sex-change operation in *Dog Day Afternoon*. Roberts keeps us guessing: Are these overtones a deliberate choice, or is it that he was having fun with the cliché role, trying to make it work, and it went nelly on him? Two macho Italian fellows aren't likely to walk with their arms around each other in the Village—especially in the Village. Are we supposed to see Charlie and Paulie's arm-in-arm saunter as a put-on of some sort? Are the actors kidding buddy-buddy movies, or are Charlie and Paulie pretending to be so supremely confident of their masculinity that they can tease the world? Paulie's head is held high; he sniffs the air like a dowager. There's no way to be sure how we're meant to take this display.

Roberts succeeds in bringing off some wild effects, though. When Paulie gets scared, he has to urinate. With his bloodshot eyes and anxious expression, he's like a toy dog—a neurotic little poodle—that needs to go out all the time. He shifts from leg to leg, in the nervous rhythm that he has anyway—this is just another part of him that gets jazzed up. Roberts made me laugh in surprise several times, and I don't know of any other young actor who could give this role the final, impervious-to-reason charm that he does. I don't know of anyone else who goes so far from himself in a role. He's barely recognizable as the star of *King of the Gypsies* and *Raggedy Man* and *Star 80*; all I remember from *King of the Gypsies* is that he glowered proudly, but, whatever the range of his other roles, he has always been at its extreme end, reaching further into the character than seemed possible. In *Raggedy Man*, he went to an extreme openness—he went to the heart of openness. Here, as Paulie, he goes to the heart of gaga optimism. Roberts doesn't keep his feet firmly on the ground; that's what makes him initially hard to take. But he's probably the most imaginative high flyer of the younger actors. He has the audacity to risk going too far for the audience, and maybe even bewildering it. I've heard people say that he spoils this picture, but if he had given a less original performance the picture would be deadly.

Bad as the movie is, it's fun to watch these two—Rourke being fatherly and tolerant, Roberts spinning off into space. *The Pope* is like those old studio-factory melodramas, where you can't figure out what the director and the actors had in mind, or whether it was anything like the same thing. In one scene, Charlie, worried about Paulie's health, fixes him food and feeds him, and the scene goes on long enough to make you wonder if Stuart Rosenberg is trying to suggest a deep, loving attachment between the two or if he's just being clunky. Scene after scene makes you uneasy, because the director doesn't appear to take into account the meanings that are floating around. (Checking in the book is no help; you just get into a book-movie *Rashomon*.) The picture is by no means carelessly made; a great deal of planning has gone into the thriving Little Italy atmosphere, and the imagery (John Bailey was the cinematographer) has a shine, though the interiors may be a bit too elegantly dark and "rich." But *The Pope* is a pointlessly handsome production; it's a shallow movie that gives itself heavyweight airs. It's a candied *Mean Streets*, evenly and impersonally paced; it has no temperament—it doesn't even have any get-up-and-go.

That's what the performers help to compensate for. As the detestable lump of a Mafia boss Bedbug Eddie, Burt Young is better than he has been in years; sitting at a table in the back room of an Italian men's "social club," he leans forward to conduct an inquisition on Paulie, and his mad little porcine eyes are outposts of Hell on earth. As Geraldine Page's conniving cop son who has put in his twenty years on the force, Jack Kehoe has just the right kind of cagey, callow anonymity. Tony Musante, M. Emmet Walsh, Philip Bosco, and several other actors have big moments. Kenneth McMillan, who has slimmed down about fifty pounds, has been handed a role that's drenched in pathos: he's Barney, the old safecracker who needs to pull off one last job in order to provide for his retarded son. Honorable actor that he is, McMillan dries it out; it's a sly, astute performance—the ex-con Barney lets others speak first while he gauges how far he can trust them. The director, though, can't resist shooting the scenes so that you'll admire McMillan's demonstration of restraint. Stuart Rosenberg must really like actors who pour it on; when they have too much pride, he pours it on for them.

He doesn't do much for Daryl Hannah, though. She isn't given anything more to play than Diane, the aerobics teacher. That's the kind of occupation moviemakers select for a woman now, because it allows them to get some movement into her scenes; Diane is a blank—essentially, she's a physically stronger version of the sexy schoolmarm of earlier movies, and that makes Charlie and Diane a dull pair. Maybe the moviemakers think blankness *is* Diane's character—that could be how they think of a Wasp (without considering what goes on underneath). In the scheme of the movie, Diane stands for hypocritical Wasp preachiness. But shouldn't she at least have some qualities that make it apparent why the guy who is attached to Paulie is also attached to her? It would certainly be livelier if, say, Diane were as much of a nut case as Paulie but in a hidden way and in an opposite direction—if, maybe, she were as security-mad or as respectability-mad as Paulie is blithely unaware that there's a next week. (Teaching aerobics might be what a security-minded girl would feel safe in, on the theory that people will always need to be healthy.) Actually, Daryl Hannah does have a big scene, but it's not a display of her acting. Diane has a conversation with Charlie while she's standing in front of a mirror trying on clothes. That way, each time she's down to her undies the audience gets to see her fore and aft. When Charlie and Paulie fuss over their outfits, the scenes are about what clothes mean to the characters; the Daryl Hannah scene is about giving the audience an eyeful. The director's obvious manipulation has the quality of a joke being played on the actress, but the joke backfires, and part of the audience laughs—not at Daryl Hannah, who's so great-looking that she can take people's breath away, but at the lack of finesse of the director, who couldn't find a better way to show her off.

A pretty good case could be made that *The Pope of Greenwich Village* is really a consumer-oriented movie about food and clothing. It's full of scenes featuring people eating or talking about eating. Paulie the bum is an aesthete on the subject of cuisine; he's haughty and offended when he's expected to eat ordinary fare. And the film opens with Charlie putting on his sharpest duds to go to his job at the restaurant; the music that accompanies him is Frank Sinatra's record of "Summer Wind," with that Sinatra phrasing that sounds so sexy and easy. The connection is made for us: that's the way Charlie wants to feel—he wants that buoyant, graceful high. And that's how Paulie *does* feel when he's dressed in spiffy leather and eating fine food and sipping good cognac; everything else goes out of his head. These two hoodlum connoisseurs of food and fabrics are soft; they're infantile narcissists who steal so they can dress up. And with so much attention given to Charlie's and Paulie's coquettish wardrobes, there may be some potential comedy in the fact that Diane is in leotards most of the time. Part of what makes this a contemporary movie is that Charlie and Paulie care more about what they're wearing than the women do. Diane doesn't need to worry about clothes.

July 23, 1984

THE WOMAN QUESTION

When Henry James wrote *The Bostonians*, which was first serialized in *The Century Magazine* and then published in book form, in 1886, his sentences hadn't yet hit the grand stride of his later manner. His writing wasn't as imperturbably cadenced as it was to become in the maniacal, formal perfection of the novels he brought out after the turn of the century (*The Wings of the Dove* in 1902, *The Ambassadors* in 1903, *The Golden Bowl* in 1904). It's easier to recognize the greatness of those later novels: they are so circumspect and finespun they're almost abstract. You can get heady from the rarefied air. And even those of us who take an intense pleasure in their super-subtlety can recognize that there's a kind of battiness about them. It's James's battiness that we come to love, breathing to the roll of those arch, loony sentences—equilibristic feats that seem to constitute a world of their own. *The Bostonians* has a more earthly kind of greatness. Set in the period after the Civil War, among the abolitionists, who are now—it's 1875—turning their energies to the emancipation of women, it's a wonderful, teeming novel, with darting perceptions. It's perhaps the most American of James's novels—not just because it is set here but because all the characters are Americans, and because Boston, with its quacks and mystics, its moral seriousness and its dowdiness, is contrasted with New York's frivolous "society" and the South's conservatism. James had immersed himself in Hawthorne's work (he published his biography of him in 1879), and he may have been influenced by Hawthorne's novel about the Brook Farm socialists and idealists, *The Blithedale Romance.* He sees Boston as the capital city of the high-minded—the freethinkers, whom he views satirically, yet admiringly, too. The book is packed with rude (and detailed) psychological observations, and with ironies that aren't quite focussed—he's still in the process of discovering them when the story ends. It's the liveliest of his novels, maybe because it has sex right there at the center, and so it's crazier—riskier, less controlled, less gentlemanly—than his other books. He himself seems to be pulled about, identifying with some of the characters and then rejecting them for others. I think it is by far the best novel in English about what at that time was called "the woman question," and it must certainly be the best novel in the language about the cold anger that the issue of equal rights for women can stir in a man. I first read the book when I was in my early twenties, and it was like reading advance descriptions of battles I knew at first hand; rereading it, some forty years later, I found it a marvellous, anticipatory look at issues that are more out in the open now but still unresolved.

The mind-lock of the central male character, the tall, distinguished-looking, and intelligent young Mississippian Basil Ransom, is chilling. Ransom thought women "essentially inferior to men, and infinitely tiresome when they declined to accept the lot which men had made for them." Their rights "consisted in a standing claim to the generosity and tenderness of the stronger race." James is so sensitive to nuance that every time Ransom puts on his mask of chivalry and addresses a woman chaffingly, jocularly—gallantly—you just about feel your teeth grate. Impoverished by the war in which he fought, Ransom, who belongs to the aristocratic, plantation-owning class, has come to New York to be a lawyer and to try to repair the family fortunes. On a visit to Boston, to make the acquaintance of a distant relative, the wealthy, ascetic bluestocking Olive Chancellor, he accompanies her to a meeting at the home of a Miss Birdseye, an elderly leader of the suffragettes. The featured speaker is a lovely, flaming-red-haired young girl, Verena Tarrant, who is the daughter of a mesmerist faith healer and has a golden voice and a "gift" for inspirational oratory. Her father has to "start" her—he puts her in a semi-trance, but then she keeps going on her own. Verena has been brought up as a perfect hypnotist's subject: she has been trained to surrender her mind. Both Olive Chancellor and Ransom are drawn to her, and the novel becomes a tug-of-war between the repressed lesbian Olive, who takes Verena into her fine house on Charles Street and grooms her to be a spokeswoman for the emancipation movement, and Ransom, who likes women to be "private and passive." He thinks that the movement is a "modern pestilence," and he's only half joking when he blames the Civil War on women—the abolitionists, he says, were "principally females." He is offended by the idea of Verena's speaking in public—he wants her for himself alone.

The book has a whole gallery of women, with James's tone ranging from the affectionate (almost adoring) satire of the aged, selfless Miss Birdseye (based on Hawthorne's sister-in-law, the abolitionist Elizabeth Peabody), who is "in love . . . only with causes," to the caricature of Verena's mother, the inane, ever-hopeful-of-attaining-a-high-social-position Mrs. Tarrant. There is the diminutive Dr. Prance, a shorthaired, no-nonsense Boston physician with a friendly, dry manner of speech; she is absorbed in her work and has no inclination to listen to emotional feminist rhetoric. And there is Mrs. Burrage, the shrewd, rich New Yorker who arranges for Verena to speak at her home, because her son is in love with the girl and, besides, the movement is the latest fashion.

Virtually everyone in the novel loves Verena. She's a darling. She's one of James's incorruptible American innocents—the girls (Daisy Miller is the most obvious example) who are so often his trusting, ingenuous heroines. Ransom speaks for the author when he tells Verena, "You are outside and above all vulgarizing influences." And like James's other generous-hearted innocents—his fatally impressionable girls who fall in love with the wrong men—she wants to please. James shows us the mechanisms of the Southerner's manly will and certitude which would make him attractive to a soft and trusting girl. Poor pale Verena, who's only nineteen, is a conventional, perky, flirty girl. She's an asset to the movement just because she's agreeable and pretty rather than forceful. And it's because of her submissiveness—she can't say no—that she becomes the battlefield for the battle of wills between Ransom and Olive Chancellor, who, on meeting Verena, feels that she has found "what she had been looking for so long—a friend of her own sex with whom she might have a union of soul." Alone with Verena for the first time, Olive immediately asks, "Will you be my friend, my friend of friends, beyond everyone, everything, forever and forever?" Verena, the mesmerist's daughter, is, of course, willing. She's like an actress eager for a role. She has an appealing manner but no content; she's an exaggerated version of many men's (and women's) feminine ideal—she's an empty vessel. Ransom and Olive are at war over a vacuum. (At times, this book comes close to modern magic realism; it's no wonder it was a terrible flop when it came out.)

Olive takes on the task of educating Verena, and they study together—they study the history of "feminine anguish." James writes, "Olive had pored over it so long, so earnestly, that she was now in complete possession of the subject; it was the one thing in her life which she felt she had really mastered." And she wants revenge: she feels that men must pay. James is at his most devastating with the humorless Olive Chancellor. He writes that "the most sacred hope of her nature was that . . . she might be a martyr and die for something." And he shows us how Olive unconsciously coerces Verena while talking the rhetoric of freedom. Yet he comes to stare in wonder at Olive's quivering sensibility and her capacity for suffering. She says, of not having the vote, "I feel it as deep, unforgettable wrong. I feel it as one feels a stain that is on one's honour." She develops such neurotic exaltation that even her creator is impressed. In her intertwined folly and nobility, Olive, who has taken on protégée after protégée, and had each one desert her and the cause to which she has consecrated herself—always for a man—is the most heroic figure in the novel.

There's every reason in the world to read the book, and to do it before you see the movie (so that you don't let the movie images saturate what you read). The only good reason to see the film version is Vanessa Redgrave's performance as Olive Chancellor. Her voice shaking with emotion, she gives this woman who is "unmarried by every implication of her being" mythological size. Physically, she's so much stronger and riper than the tremulous fanatic of the book that she stands as proof of the absurdity of women's position in the society. With her powerful neck and broad shoulders, she's like a mature swan; she's gloriously neurasthenic. (And an actress who can be glorious in a role in which she never gets to laugh is a miracle worker.) She brushes off Ransom's flowery condescension as a minor indignity.

Vanessa Redgrave gives the film the force of repressed passion, and I don't know how she does it with so little help. (My companion suggested that she pulled the performance out of her skin.) *The Bostonians* was produced by Ismail Merchant, and directed by James Ivory, from a script by Ruth Prawer Jhabvala, and although it's not as limp as some of their other collaborations, they don't dramatize the great material they selected, and Ivory doesn't shape the performances. Christopher Reeve's handsome, mustachioed Ransom has too likable a presence; he's wholesomely romantic, and when he delivers the rigid-minded, contemptuous-of-women lines that James wrote, his crinkly smile and boyish affability take the sting out of them. He's more Rhett Butler than Basil Ransom. That makes him pleasant, dumb fun to watch, but the tensions that are necessary to the theme don't build. His Ransom isn't bitter; he isn't replaying the Civil War, determined that this time the South will win. And you just don't feel the irony of the bird-in-a-cage life he offers Verena. With Reeve as Ransom, that life seems rather jolly. I don't know what to make of Madeleine Potter's film début as Verena. Her plaintive, Trilby-like Verena is certainly not the fresh, sparkling ingénue that the material calls for; she's more odd than anything else, and she's overcontrolled. Her pallor is rather depressive. (I've seen Potter on the stage and have found her problematic there, too: she works hard, but it isn't acting, exactly—not yet, anyway; it's more like thoughtful pretending.)

Some of the other performers seem so right for their roles that you may want to yelp in pain at the way they're wasted. Jessica Tandy could do so much more with the angelic Miss Birdseye, and Linda Hunt is just a shade away from bringing out the full ironic possibilities in Dr. Prance. Nancy Marchand is luckier: as the New York society woman Mrs. Burrage, she gets to play a long scene (right from the book) in which the drama is allowed to develop—a conversation between Mrs. Burrage and Olive Chancellor, with Mrs. Burrage trying to strike a bargain, suggesting that Olive should encourage Verena to marry her son, as the lesser evil, and as a way of keeping her in the suffrage movement, which the Burrages will back with money and influence. Marchand's face perfectly expresses the "detestable wisdom" that, according to James, Olive sees in her; it's as if you'd looked into Mrs. Burrage's soul and a ravaged old panderer returned your gaze. The only other performer who makes an impression is, surprisingly, Wesley Addy, as Verena's ineffectual father, Dr. Tarrant, the mesmerist who doesn't have enough conviction or energy to be a real charlatan. Addy (who from some angles looks like a fuddled version of Jean Cocteau) brings just enough grotesquerie to his facial contortions—Tarrant seems always to be on the verge of saying something that no one will listen to. Other performances—such as Barbara Bryne's Mrs. Tarrant, John Van Ness Philip's young Burrage, Nancy New's Adeline (Olive's sister), and Wallace Shawn's newspaper reporter, Mr. Pardon—don't come through at all, or, as in the case of Pardon, come through awkwardly, as if the lines were being read from the script without ever entering the actor's consciousness.

The movie follows the book faithfully, except for an attempt at an upbeat ending—a story-conference type of ending—to reassure us that the movement will go on. (Is there some danger that we'll think it stopped?) Until then, the film's worst mistake is that it's full of short scenes in which nothing develops—glimpses of Ransom walking in the woods with Verena or standing on the shore with her at what's meant to be Cape Cod. These glimpses are simply intended to carry the narrative further—they're like those vacuous montages of couples cavorting in photogenic surroundings which were so common in sixties movies, persisted into the seventies, and then finally seemed to be consigned to commercials and MTV. They're filler in *The Bostonians*, and an embarrassment, because what is crucial to Henry James is that every scene have its exact emotional weight. In *The Bostonians*, he hadn't yet got to the point he reached in the later novels, where a single line of dialogue would explode and reverberate back over everything we'd read; *The Bostonians* has many explosions of meaning, and at the end there's a climactic one, in which you'd have to be a fool (or a saint, like Miss Birdseye) not to register that Basil Ransom isn't just expressing his devotion to Verena, he's also skewering Olive Chancellor. That has been part of his motivation from the start. He's sticking it to her.

Ivory's *The Bostonians* is the Henry James novel without the revelations. And the movie's upbeat ending deprives Olive of her tragic stature. But, in its own insignificant, washed-out way, it goes along fairly inoffensively until the last sequence, when we're given the impatient sounds of a large Boston audience that has come to hear Verena speak and is being kept waiting. The shouts and stomping noises from the audience are so unconvincing that the movie falls to pieces. The whole last section is nightmarishly mangled; it's as if the director had said, "Let's really foul this thing up."

Repo Man is set in a scuzzy sci-fi nowhere: it was shot in the L.A. you see when you're coming in from the airport—the squarish, pastel-colored buildings with industrial fences around them, though they don't look as if there could be much inside that needed to be protected. The action in the film takes place on the freeways and off ramps, and in the lots in back of these anonymous storefronts and warehouses that could be anything and could turn into something else overnight. It's a world inhabited by dazed sociopaths—soreheads, deadbeats, and rusted-out punkers. The young English writer-director Alex Cox keeps them all speeding around—always on the periphery. There's nothing at the center.

We're not asked to identify with the teen-age Otto (Emilio Estevez), the kid with a cross dangling from his ear who gets fired from his supermarket job, goes to work repossessing cars, loves the excitement, and takes off the cross, or with his clearly deranged mentor, the veteran repo man Bud (Harry Dean Stanton). L.A. is the perfect setting for a movie about men who take out their frustrations by confiscating other people's cars; there's a definite element of realism tucked into this low-budget nihilistic fantasy. It's a woozy comedy for people who will appreciate the idea of the mean, gaunt Stanton's being called Bud, and of his being anybody's mentor. (Or even just the idea of Harry Dean Stanton.) Bud teaches Otto the repo "code," and points out that "not many people got a code to live by anymore." That certainly looks to be the case. There's no civility or courtesy left—people kill for minor provocations and casually dispose of the corpses. And though there may still be police helicopters and clandestine government agencies, they don't seem to connect to anything. The attraction of the movie is its friendly, light tone, its affectlessness, and its total lack of humanity. Cox never once slips—he never lets it get sentimentalized or organized.

Repo Man is far from a brilliant movie, though it takes off from one —Godard's *Weekend*, the 1968 visionary satire that also dealt with cars as possessions and the hostility that drivers have toward one another. In some ways (especially at the beginning), *Repo Man* is an amateur's try at *Weekend*. Produced by Michael Nesmith, who was one of the Monkees, it's a little like something left over from the sixties that cheerfully moldered into the eighties. Cox may have picked up ideas from Robert Aldrich's *Kiss Me Deadly* (1955), and Zemeckis and Gale's *Used Cars* (1980), but the film's catatonic, shoofly humor is all its own. Cox has underhand ways of being funny, and the jokes don't often jump out at you—sometimes they barely peep out at all, because of the film's ramshackle ineptness. But the whole atmosphere of druggy burnout gets to you. The characters include a scientist from Los Alamos who has had a lobotomy and recommends it highly, a girl trying feverishly to locate the aliens deposited by a flying saucer "before they turn to moosh," and an acidhead philosopher in overalls (Tracey Walter, who makes everything he does seem loco and rather wonderful); he tends fires in garbage cans, and gets to deliver the film's only statement: "The more you drive, the less intelligent you are." Robby Müller's cinematography sustains the flat grunginess of the conception, the sense of stagnation; so does a song by the L.A. group called The Circle Jerks. The movie gives you the feeling that you've gone past alienation into the land of detachment. It takes place in a different dimension—a punkers' wasteland where you never really know where you are, and nobody cares to make things work, and everybody you see is part of the lunatic fringe. A movie like this, with nothing positive in it, can make you feel good.

August 6, 1984

THE CHARISMATIC HALF-AND-HALFS

'm disposed to like Prince, the twenty-six-year-old pansexual star of *Purple Rain*, because he is, as a friend of mine put it, "the fulfillment of everything that people like Jerry Falwell say rock 'n' roll will do to the youth of America." I like the teasing sexiness of some of his songs of a couple of years ago ("Little Red Corvette," especially, and "1999" and "Delirious"—they have a piquancy), and I like the brazenness that he shows at the end of this movie when, in a variation on Jimi Hendrix's guitar bashing, he puts on his impish smile as he holds up his own guitar and it ejaculates. But Prince the passionflower imp is only intermittently in evidence in *Purple Rain*, which his managers produced for him, and which in its opening week was the No. 1 attraction at the nation's theatres—at the same time that his *Purple Rain* album was at the top of the music charts. This custom-made movie, shot on location in Minneapolis, where he lives, features Prince the vulnerable loner. As a struggling musician known simply as the Kid, he's trying to break out of the bondage represented by his parents' violent love-hate marriage. His self-pitying black father beats his white mother, because he blames her for his failure to achieve success as a composer. The moody Kid is a tortured soul, who when he falls in love with Apollonia (played by the Hispanic American actress Patty Apollonia Kotero) begins to repeat the pattern. But, of course, the love that is the source of his torment is also the source of his redemption. The Kid learns to share with others, and conquers the brute in himself (but only after several reels of apocalyptic anguish). It's not difficult to see the attraction that the picture has for adolescents: Prince's songs are a cry for the free expression of sexual energy, and his suffering is a supercharged version of what made James Dean the idol of young moviegoers—this Kid is "hurting." And this picture knows no restraint.

In his live performances, when Prince mimics Little Richard or Mick Jagger, or whomever, he does it with a knowing, parodistic edge. And he retains this knowingness in his screen performance. But the moviemakers aren't skillful enough to use it; the movie is directed as if the maudlin story it tells were all there is to the Kid. Prince, though, uses his flair for outrageousness, and when you least expect it he will do something petulant or flirty. Alone with the overpoweringly sultry Apollonia, whom he presumably adores, he reacts to her light touch on his collarbone with an ingénue's high, breathless "Stop!" He's quite willing to pose as the little-boy wallflower at the rock 'n' roll orgy, but he doesn't seem willing to take seriously the plot devices that he had a hand in shaping. The poor, struggling Kid is dressed in the neo-Liberace finery of Prince, the star—the skintight pants, the ruffled shirts with high flounces at the throat, the spangled, embroidered vests, the white lace gloves, and the chains. He's lighted, by the cinematographer Donald Thorin, like a Josef von Sternberg heroine—a minx with sucked-in cheeks, pouting and making deeply religious doe-eyes at the camera from under a cluster of curls. When the Kid is supposed to be a failure as a performer at the Minneapolis club where he and his group, The Revolution, are an introductory act and are in danger of being fired for not giving the customers music they can respond to, Prince is not about to put on a closed-in, selfish performance just because the script calls for it. He whips those customers to a frenzy; he struts and preens himself with the same sexual bravado that he shows after the Kid has made his breakthrough.

This is a commissioned film: it was directed by Albert Magnoli (who also wrote the final script and was the co-editor), but Prince is in charge, and he knows how he wants to appear—like Dionysus crossed with a convent girl on her first bender. And his instinct is right: if he had performed the role more realistically, the picture would be really sodden. This way, his narcissistic, mock-shy pranks make the audience laugh, and his musical numbers keep lifting the movie's energy level. (The plot becomes a kind of shared joke between Prince and the audience.) Even the songs that are undistinguished have a good hot beat and a jangly plaintiveness and the punctuation of his falsetto shrieks and flourishes, and the lament "When Doves Cry" has something more (although it's presented as soundtrack music while the Kid thinks over his treatment of Apollonia and his hellish home life, and we have nothing to do but listen to the words, which are not its strong point). Prince's movements during his numbers are as provocative as he can make them, and near the end he finally gets around to some orgiastic—but perfectly precise —dancing. Maybe he doles it out so sparingly because he only has a few moves—but they're good ones. He's much more fluid than Mick Jagger (whom he often suggests); he's very fast without being at all spastic. He's a cutie when he dances.

Prince saves himself by his impudence, and the picture also introduces a full-fledged young comedian, Morris Day. The lead singer of the group The Time, he is cast as Morris the villain—the more conventional funk rocker, whom the Minneapolis audience responds to. Morris's music represents clowning and escapism; the Kid's music is meant to be a working through of his conflicts. (And that's part of what's the matter with Prince's lyrics; they're prosy, they explain what the Kid is suffering, they damn near have a program. "Maybe I'm just like my father, too bold/Maybe you're just like my mother, she's never satisfied/Why do we scream at each other/This is what it sounds like when doves cry.") Decked out in a glittering gold zoot suit and black-and-gold shoes, Morris Day does his vain, lecherous routines with the ease of the top vaudeville artists of decades past; he feasts his eyes on the mirror, giggling with joy at how he looks, all lighted up like a Christmas tree, or he hurls his magnificence into a waiting car—almost everything he does gets laughs. And when he and his handsome sidekick, Jerome Benton (who looks like a dark Douglas Fairbanks, Sr.), dance to The Time's music they have a loose, floppy grace. Morris Day suggests a Richard Pryor without the genius and the complications. Part of the pleasure of watching him is that his musical numbers are shaped; so is his performance—he uses distance and tension. This is certainly a contrast to Prince, who doesn't want us to react to a performance—he wants us to react to him, to his greatness. It's clear (and infinitely regrettable) that he sees himself as a sexual messiah, and wants to overwhelm us. He's trying to shortcut his way to artistic heights by a show of naked self-expression. (You see a lot of this in the work of the rock stars, such as Bruce Springsteen, that the rock press takes the most seriously.) Prince is trying so hard to show us sex as salvation that his musical numbers have no shape. (Even on the *Purple Rain* album, the songs don't take form or come to a satisfying finish; they maunder on.) The picture, being designed to show that the Kid's way is the right way and that The Time's way is a sellout, doesn't do much with the other characters. But as the Kid's frustrated-artist father, Clarence Williams III, who has a horrendous, completely unrelieved role, brings it off with conviction and earns the audience's respect. The women aren't so lucky. Most of them seem to be selected for how they'll look in hooker lingerie or hooker leather. (Couldn't Apollonia just once have put on civvies?)

As a movie, *Purple Rain* is a mawkish fictionalized bio—it's as if Lillian Roth (rather than Susan Hayward) had starred in *I'll Cry Tomorrow,* or Barbara Graham (rather than Hayward) had starred in *I Want to Live!* It's pretty terrible; the narrative hook is: will the damaged boy learn to love? There are no real scenes—just flashy, fractured rock-video moments. The Kid and Apollonia meet via the camera: it zings back and forth recording closeups as they look at each other, and that's all there is—it's like the way a cat and a dog meet in an animated cartoon. And this movie goes beyond jump cuts to plot leaps. (Morris talks to his crony Jerome about his designs on Apollonia before he has so much as seen her or heard of her.) The director isn't a man of subterfuges: when he wants you to share in the characters' steaming emotions he throws hot red mood lighting on them; when Prince, doing his act at the club, writhes on the stage floor in an ecstasy of longing and sings "I want you," the director cuts to Apollonia watching teary-eyed with empathy for his pain. Rock critics are being quoted in the picture's praise; one suggests that it's the *Citizen Kane* of rock movies, another ranks it with *A Hard Day's Night.* They've probably waited so long for a rock-movie classic that they were keyed up to see something inspiring and innovative in Prince's mere presence on the big screen. For several years, rock writers have been saying things like "Prince challenges listeners to examine their lives" and citing lyrics such as "Stand up everybody, this is your life/Let me take you to another world/Let me take you tonight /You don't need no money, you don't need no clothes/The second coming, anything goes/Sexuality is all you'll ever need/Sexuality, let your body be free." Prince may consider himself a revolutionary force because he (like his band) represents a fusion of the races and the sexes and because his music is his own, self-taught eclectic mix. But there's nothing revolutionary in Prince's wanting to be Susan Hayward and commissioning a film to enhance his star mystique.

Purple Rain is a landmark of sorts, though. It's the black crossover movie that many of us expected a decade ago, when Diana Ross appeared in *Lady Sings the Blues* and showed the kind of talent that made her seem a natural to attract both black and white audiences. (Although

Pryor has done it, that has been strictly in comedy.) But, as it turned out, Diana Ross wanted to be like the goddessy, self-glorifying white stars that moviegoers were fed up with; she appeared in *Mahogany* and *The Wiz* and lost the white audience. *Purple Rain* is Prince's bid for goddessy big-time stardom. In quality, it's about on a level with *Mahogany*. But a new generation has come along that isn't jaded about old movie-star self-absorbed emoting, and when Prince turns his life into a soap the audience loves it. The Kid's sequinned psychobabble goes over big. He learns to reach out and touch somebody's hand, and that frees him to be a star. And, yes, he does it his way.

A movie like this can make you wonder: Weren't all the people who learned to love better off before?

The *Adventures of Buckaroo Banzai* is a kind of fermented parody of *M*A*S*H*, *Star Wars*, *Raiders of the Lost Ark*, and the TV series "The A-Team," and it made me laugh a lot. It's about mankind learning to pass unharmed through solid matter—a nifty trick that requires the use of an Oscillation Overthruster. The half-American, half-Japanese hero, Dr. Buckaroo Banzai (Peter Weller), refuses to divulge the secret of its operation even after he has been captured by the mad genius Dr. Lizardo (John Lithgow), whose matted henna hair flies skyward off his high forehead. Dr. Lizardo commands his underlings to "take him to the Shock Tower," and when Buckaroo has been hooked up to a diabolic torture machine, its wires as tangled as the colored paper streamers at the end of a New Year's Eve party, Lizardo shrieks, "I want the missing circuit—now!" To his assistants, he cries, "More power to him." Weller has a tall frame, but as Buckaroo he has petite, angelic features, wide blue eyes that seem to be off on a secret faraway trip, and a quirky, private smile; he's like a male version of Mia Farrow—a jewel. The huge Lithgow, white-faced, with bloodshot eyes, dark, greenish teeth, and a wild foreign accent (Italian-Icelandic?), is a comic-strip mixture of Caligari, Eisenstein, Klaus Kinski, and a Wagnerian tenor.

The script, by Earl Mac Rauch, that W. D. (Rick) Richter, the highly successful young screenwriter (*Slither, Invasion of the Body Snatchers, Dracula, All Night Long, Brubaker*), has chosen for his directing début is a post-Altman jamboree, and he's a long way from being up to it. He has picked some terrific performers (Jeff Goldblum, Ellen Barkin, and Christopher Lloyd are among them), but he doesn't characterize them, and he doesn't bring out the baroque lunacy of the material. Richter's directing is almost nonexistent: the plot (which includes an inspired twist on Orson Welles' "War of the Worlds" broadcast) is laid down piece by piece, with nothing related to anything. Richter doesn't seem to know what to do with the hip dialogue—he has no follow-through. But though the characters don't develop and the laughs don't build or come together, the film's flat-footedness is somehow likable. I didn't find it hard to accept the uninflected, deadpan tone, and to enjoy *Buckaroo Banzai* for its inventiveness and the gags that bounce off other adventure movies, other comedies. The picture's sense of fun carried me along.

There's more than enough going on. Buckaroo is a laser-wielding neurosurgeon, a physicist, a jet-car racer (who goes right through a mountain), and the leader of a team of seven dapper, whizbang Renaissance men called the Team Banzai. He is also, for relaxation, the top man in a rock group formed by some of the members of the Team Banzai and called the Hong Kong Cavaliers. And there are so many different kinds of villains and humanoids and friendly and hostile aliens—some of them in the guise of Earthlings—that I'm not sure if we're meant to keep them straight or if part of the comedy is that we can't sort them out quickly enough to be sure what's going on. Some of the humor is in little doodles of plot that appear to be deliberately left dangling—the way Richter directs, you can't be sure. At times, the blandly presented inexplicable events are definitely satirical. In the middle of the Cavaliers' high-decibel performance at a New Jersey night spot, the hypersensitive Buckaroo catches the disturbed vibes of someone in the audience. It's a girl sobbing drunkenly, and he sings a song to comfort her. That's how the heroine, Penny Priddy (Barkin), is introduced. This is followed by a lovely detail, of the kind the movie features: alone at her table, Penny (not sufficiently comforted) takes out a gun to kill herself, but at the crucial moment her arm is accidentally jostled; at the sound of the (harmless) shot, everyone on the stage pulls out a gun.

The Team Banzai includes a platinum-haired fellow called Perfect Tommy (played by Lewis Smith); he never gets to demonstrate his perfection. And maybe it's enough of a joke that Jeff Goldblum, who's done up in full cowboy regalia (including the thickest chaps ever), is called New Jersey. From what we see, the seven knights belong to a peculiarly random interplanetary fantasy world. Mac Rauch and Rick Richter are Dartmouth men, who met some years after graduation—after Rauch, who was living in Texas, had published the novels *Dirty Pictures from the Prom* and *Arkansas Adios.* Richter persuaded him to move to L.A. and become a screenwriter (he wrote the script for *New York, New York,* which was only partly used, and that film's novelization), and they hatched the idea for *Buckaroo Banzai* almost a decade ago. (By the time they got to film it, the tall, cool men of the Hong Kong Cavaliers acquired New Wave hairstyles.)

The fantasy's origins are in a boy hipster's dreams of glory that are almost pre-sexual. (Buckaroo is the only one on the team who even has a girlfriend.) This may help to explain why the movie's cleverness isn't at all campy: it has no sexual innuendo, and when Penny is in a sleeping-beauty trance she is awakened not by a kiss but by an electrical buzz from Buckaroo's nose as he leans over her. The teammates aren't really integrated into the action, though. They're posed like a bunch of male models, and at the end, when Penny walks with them—chest held high, short, fringed shocking-pink dress swinging—we seem to be looking at a trailer for the team's next movie before we've figured out what's going on in this one. (Rauch's novelization is intellectualized pulp—sub–Thomas Pynchon.) Some of the other actors have a little more to do. Carl Lumbly is instantly likable as a friendly alien from Planet 10, who when he comes to Earth on a mission disguises himself as a Rastafarian with truly luxuriant dreadlocks; he's like a black Louis XIV. Matt Clark has some bright slapstick moments as everybody's straight man—the square Secretary of Defense, who keeps trying to persuade the President (Ronald Lacey, with a suggestion of Charles Foster Kane) that authority should not be invested in the Team Banzai. A tiptop sixties-style gag follows: there's a nuclear emergency, and the President is handed the papers to sign for a Declaration of War: The Short Form.

The picture went through a change of cinematographers (it was completed by Fred J. Koenekamp), but it has a consistent visual style, and that helps to compensate for the absence of directorial style. The young production designer J. Michael Riva (he's Marlene Dietrich's grandson) probably deserves some of the credit for the radiance that keeps you attentive to the images on the screen. Every once in a while, there's something awesomely whimsical up there, like shots of peaceable bug-eyed aliens hovering above Earth in a spacecraft; they sit on extremely high stools (the pedestals must be a full eight feet) at what might be tall bridge tables, and idle away the time while they wait to hear the results of Buckaroo's daring efforts to save the world. (Visually, they're magically right.) And if most of the action isn't clearly located in time or place, this, too, becomes a joke when Jeff Goldblum turns to Buckaroo and asks, "Where are we?" It's the perfect Jeff Goldblum line;

he finally got to deliver it—and in the right movie, because unrootedness is the picture's chief characteristic. If we can't quite figure out what Rauch and Richter's angle of vision is, that may be because they don't really have one. What they've got is an unmoored hipsterism—a wiseguy love of the ridiculous.

Mostly, I laughed at John Lithgow, who brings the movie the anchor it needs. It's a great relief to see him being a scurvy nut case after his god-awful sincerity in *Footloose.* He's amazing here. Having been locked away in a hospital for the criminally insane ever since his failed attempt to go through solid matter drove him into the eighth dimension, the homicidal Dr. Lizardo sits in his cruddy room—piled high with espionage novels and the debris of his calculations—and thinks over what he did wrong. Alone with his rage, he gives himself shocks on his tongue; that's how he reenergizes himself. (The shocks stir his memory, and there's a flashback to his crackpot effort to go through a wall and getting stuck midway.) Dr. Lizardo's gargantuan warped mind appears to have frazzled his hair, which is like a comic-strip artist's representation of electricity coming out of someone's head, and he looks as if he has been gnashing his teeth and gnawing on wormwood. When, having broken out, he delivers a speech to a batch of aliens, he's the Il Duce of the space age. He brushes aside Earthlings who don't believe in his genius with phrases like "Laugh while you can, monkey boy!" His scenes can make you crazy with happiness.

August 20, 1984

ROGER & EDWINA, SHEENA, AND UNCLE JEAN

Roger (Steve Martin), the hero of *All of Me,* loves jazz and has been moonlighting as a guitarist, but he doesn't quite have the guts to quit his squirrel-cage job as a lawyer and take his chances as a musician. On his thirty-eighth birthday, he comes to a decision—the wrong one. He'll give up his music, marry his fiancée—the boss's daughter—and buckle down to work. On this fateful day, the boss assigns him the task of going to the Beverly Hills mansion of the tyrannical rich invalid Edwina Cutwater (Lily Tomlin), who wants to revise her will. Born with a weak heart and bedridden from infancy, Edwina has been told by her doctors that she has only a few more days to live; she has used her immense wealth to research the situation and buy a new life, because she hasn't had any fun in this one. She has imported a Tibetan swami, Prahka Lasa (Richard Libertini), who will see to it that at the moment of her death her spiritual substance is astrally projected into another body. The curvy, long-legged frame she is scheduled to acquire belongs to the obliging blond Terry (Victoria Tennant), her English stableman's daughter, who has agreed to vacate it. Edwina instructs Roger to arrange for her entire estate to go to Terry, so that when she takes over Terry's luscious physique she'll finally be able to enjoy her millions.

Roger, with his new commitment to the grindstone, is in no mood to listen to Edwina's talk of fulfillment in another life. She squints in her foxy, spinsterish way and tells him bluntly that she can come back from the dead in a different body "because I'm rich." He thinks she's insane, and refuses to revise the will. She throws him out, and she and her entourage—Prahka Lasa, Terry, and all—drive to the law firm's downtown L.A. offices. There she talks to the boss, and he fires Roger and makes the changes she wants. Her rage at Roger and the expedition to the business district prove too much for her, though, and she expires right there in the office. The poor flustered swami captures her spiritual substance in his special bronze pot, but, caught off balance, he drops it out the window and it klonks Roger, who's leaving the premises, on the noggin. Edwina can't take full possession of his body, because he's still in it; she enters into joint occupancy with him—she controls the right side of his body, he the left—and though she talks to him all the time, she's visible only when he looks in the mirror. *All of Me* is a romantic comedy about how these two antagonists in the same body fall in love and find happiness.

This nifty premise, taken from an unpublished novel, *Me Two*, by Ed Davis, is given classic American-comedy contours in the script, by Phil Alden Robinson. It isn't an elegantly written script; at times it's rather rudimentary and just sketches things in. But Robinson juggles a whole raft of major and minor characters and variations in the manner of movies such as the Cary Grant–Constance Bennett–Roland Young

Topper, or the Cary Grant–Irene Dunne *The Awful Truth* and *My Favorite Wife,* or the more recent *Tootsie.* If the movie doesn't quite have the snappiness of those pictures—and it certainly lacks the high spirits and dazzlement of a comedy such as *The Lady Eve*—the reasons aren't in the structure. They're mostly in the casting of a couple of key roles, and in the directing, by Carl Reiner.

He isn't a terrible director; he has an intuitive rapport with his funny performers—with Steve Martin and Lily Tomlin and Richard Libertini, and with Jason Bernard, who plays Tyrone, Roger's black musician pal, and with Madolyn Smith, the talented and stunning brunette (she was the sophisticated lech in *Urban Cowboy*) who plays Roger's nasty and extremely self-possessed fiancée. But Reiner doesn't have the instincts of a movie director. The gags just don't seem to be thought out visually in terms of the locations, and so we don't take an aesthetic pleasure in them, the way we do in, say, the gags of the most visual of all comedy artists, Buster Keaton. We don't even get the crackle of excitement that we get in the work of a director like Sydney Pollack. The camera doesn't seem to enter into Reiner's thinking; he uses it as if it were simply a recording device. The only time he uses it expressively is in the film's last —and best—moments. Reiner's *The Man with Two Brains* had more visual vitality—maybe because the cinematographer was Michael Chapman, who brings some directorial instincts to his framing. This time, Reiner is working with Richard Kline, who's often a virtuoso cinematographer but who probably, like most cinematographers, expects the director to tell him exactly what he wants. Reiner, however, is thinking only of what he wants from the performers. The camera setups here are klunky, especially in the scenes at the mansion, and the film often has the bland ugliness of sitcoms.

All of Me has charm, though, because of that yummy premise, and because Steve Martin and Lily Tomlin—who would have guessed it?— are a perfect match. Tomlin packs a personality and a whole language of movement into her early scenes; she's a distinctive enough caricature for us to intuit her presence when Martin simulates her being inside him. And we can respond to the gradual thawing out of that caricature as Roger begins to have tender feelings for this all but invisible woman. (In most of the movie, except for her brief appearances in mirrors Tomlin has to win us over with her voice.) Martin keeps her vivid for us. Right after the astral potty lands on him, Edwina jerks him around, and at first he recalls Roland Young's Topper being yanked about by invisible hands. But Martin's peculiar wizardry is that he evokes Edwina so accurately that he makes you feel it's she who's doing the yanking. He makes you feel that he has two conflicting spirits in him, and then, by the changes in his movements, makes you understand the developing harmony of those spirits. And he does some showier stunts, too. In a courtroom sequence, the exhausted Roger has fallen asleep, and Edwina takes over his legal duties for him, trying to speak and gesture like a man. So we get Steve Martin acting as Lily Tomlin acting as a gruff Steve Martin. Though Martin is on the screen most of the time, there's less of him than you may want, because he gives himself over to Edwina's spirit so thoroughly that she seems to dominate the picture. (In the courtroom scene, you're thinking of her while you're watching him.)

When Roger begins to understand how deprived Edwina has been and how much she wants to live, they start to empathize with each other —they've both been repressed, they both need a new life—and soon they're a loving couple inside him. The scriptwriter has come up with just the right bit of invention for what softens her: Roger hires his pals in a Dixieland band to escort her remains to the burial site. She loves the music, and she's touched by his wanting to give her cadaver a real sendoff. When he borrows Terry's compact and looks in the tiny mirror, he sees Edwina sniffling. Tomlin makes you know that Edwina really digs being inside Roger's body with him. And, in one flash of mad inspiration, Roger, who's trying to carry out Edwina's original plan and put her spirit where it was supposed to go (into Terry), crashes a party by disguising himself as one of the musicians; in dark glasses and a tuxedo, and with his gray hair, he somehow turns into Cary Grant. It's only for a second; when he takes off the dark glasses the illusion evaporates.

All of Me doesn't spill over in your mind the way some comedies do —maybe because, despite the originality of the premise, the situation (the heiress heroine, the hero's slightly antique commitment to the jazz of an earlier era) feels a little dated, a little too "nice." Besides, every scene that doesn't click takes a toll of a comedy. Dana Elcar, who plays the boss, isn't a character—he's just smooth pink padding—and the bedroom-farce subplot that he's involved in is halfhearted and undeveloped. The film also suffers a dip in energy after Roger succeeds in having Edwina's spirit projected into Victoria Tennant's Terry. Victoria Tennant is a perfectly beautiful woman, but she doesn't seem to have a funny bone in her body. She doesn't have much crispness or enthusiasm, either. And when Edwina's spirit moves into Terry's vacated body Edwina disappears, because Tennant isn't any different with Edwina inside her; she's still a droop. There's probably an idea behind Terry's equability in the early scenes, but Victoria Tennant doesn't put it across, and it's depressing when she fails to suggest that Edwina has taken over her chassis. This mild, minimalist actress seems born to be on television. (Too bad that Madolyn Smith, who knows how to make guile and bitchery funny, and who has a comic charge comparable to Lily Tomlin's, didn't get a crack at the role.)

I wish *All of Me* were better, because it's so likable—parts of it give viewers the kind of giddy pleasure that is often what we most want from the movies. I loved watching Richard Libertini in his swami helmet (with horns), which is always a little tipsy on his head. As the totally disoriented Tibetan, he steals scenes without your ever catching him asserting himself; it's as if he were helplessly funny. He has a real Libertini moment when Tyrone and Prahka Lasa make music together: Tyrone toots "All of Me" on his sax, and the swami plunks a piano key at regular intervals. And Steve Martin and Lily Tomlin are great unclassifiables. The romance here is in the partnership of two performers who are both uninhibited physical comics. They tune in to each other's timing the way lovers do in life, only more so. They're unified in their love of comedy, and in the last sequence—it's set in a mirror—they dance together and generate an explosive joy.

Sheena features some of the best animal actors ever to grace a movie—an elephant, a rhino, chimps, lions, leopards. They're dream animals, and they form a peaceable kingdom around Sheena (Tanya Roberts) in this lighthearted adventure film—a takeoff of the late-thirties comic-strip heroine who was featured in a mid-fifties syndicated television series. Sheena, a girl Tarzan, whose white parents were killed in an avalanche in "Zambuli territory" in Africa, is raised by a hyper-cultured black woman shaman, played by Elizabeth of Toro, the Cambridge-educated lawyer princess who was Uganda's Minister of Foreign Affairs before she had differences with Idi Amin and went into exile in Kenya (where the movie was shot). The majestically beautiful Elizabeth of Toro puts Tanya Roberts, late of "Charlie's Angels," in the shade, and Roberts is too tense anyway; she takes her role a trace earnestly—she seems afraid to loosen up and come to life. But she has the face of a ballerina, a prodigious slim, muscular form, and a staring, comic-book opaqueness. She gazes into space with eyes as exquisitely blank as if they'd been put on with pale-blue chalk. She's a walking, talking icon, and she's fun to watch.

Trained by the ultra-chic shaman, Sheena can communicate tele-pathically with animals and creatures of the sea and sky by pressing two fingers on the center of her forehead and thinking hard. Legions of waterbucks turn their heads at her unspoken command; tall birds unfurl their necks and fly—swarms of them wheel about and do her bidding. When she draws a magic circle on the ground in the jungle—as she does to protect Vic, the American TV-sports-producer hero (Ted Wass), and his cameraman (Donovan Scott)—even the mosquitoes stay out. Her zebra-striped horse is an amusing design element; it's like the horse of another color in the land of Oz. It's an honorary zebra, and she rides bareback, her blond hair blowin' in the wind. But best of all are her guardians, padding around her like household pets: the amiable lion who pokes his gigantic head into the jeep that the cameraman is in and nuzzles him, the big chimp and little chimp who trot around holding hands, the rhino who's always barging into scenes and backing out, the enormous, stately elephant who, as the shaman prepares for death, sadly digs a grave with its trunk (and not in a cutaway but in the same frame with the shaman). Sheena's pets, who are said to have constituted the largest shipment of animals ever sent *to* Africa, were trained by Hubert Wells, the head of an outfit called Animal Actors of Hollywood, and he is clearly the real hero of this project.

Written by David Newman (of *Bonnie and Clyde* and the *Superman* films) and Lorenzo Semple, Jr. (*Pretty Poison, King Kong, Flash Gordon*), the script has a central reversal-of-sex-roles joke—Sheena has the skills to survive in the environment, while the city-boy hero is almost helpless. Most of the time, Vic stands around lovestruck while Sheena does everything; it's a role that could wipe out an actor, but Ted Wass treats it lightly and pleasantly. (He has his best line early on, when he looks at Sheena and says, "Who is that girl?" It sounds just like "Who is that masked man?") The script also plays with the conventions of the white-goddess, queen-of-the-jungle genre, and it contrasts the Western-ized style of the corrupt Prince Otwani (Trevor Thomas), who plays pro football in the States, with the Zambuli tribal values represented by the dignified shaman. (When Otwani, in his orange satin Cougars jacket, bounds into the government offices, a secretary addresses him deferen-tially as "Your Highness," and he responds with "Hi, baby." He greets Vic at the airport with "Hey my man, what's happenin'?") The plot gets going when Otwani murders his brother the king, who has been protect-ing the Zambulis' land, and tries to grab it.

The director, John Guillermin, shows you Sheena's troops doing battle—elephants pushing boulders at Otwani's invading mercenaries, the rhino charging a tank, the chimps doing whatever damage they can. Guillermin also has his pensive moments: he spends time at the edge of a lake just looking at the water birds, and there are lovely shots of the dusty plains and the African cities with their flowering plants. The cinematographer, the celebrated Pasqualino De Santis (he shot Zeffirelli's *Romeo and Juliet*, Visconti's *Death in Venice*, and Francesco Rosi's *Three Brothers* and his new *Carmen*), never starves the eye. (When the animals are up close, De Santis finds surprising, rich colors in them—purple and yellow and silver swirling around each other the way they do in an oil slick.)

Sheena is stilted, and on some level it isn't quite awake. It needs some big climactic scenes; moments that could be emotionally powerful are muffled (despite the use of fiery effects). But the picture never forgets its own silliness. When Vic, hiding from Otwani's mercenaries, sneezes, a chimp in clear view of the soldiers covers for him with a perfect matching *atchoo*. Children should love the animals and like the movie—there's a dizzy slapstick sequence of Sheena's guardian elephant knocking down a prison (Otwani has made the mistake of locking up the shaman), and there are magical images, such as the child Sheena sleeping peacefully in the custody of a giant snake who is coiled around her. The little Sheena has a jungleful of playmates, and when the lovely shaman calls her "my daughter" it's like a title. For the riffraff among us, there are throwaways such as Sheena's asking Vic to "tell me more about the places you'll show me where the jackals eat—'21'?" And there are gags such as having the villains toss the TV men's camera high in the air and use it for skeet shooting. The friends I saw the picture with stayed in a good mood; when Sheena was summoning the Zambuli warriors and all the creatures of the jungle to fight against Otwani, one of them called out, "Send in the tsetse flies!"

□

"Kids today are scum," says Uncle Jean, the dotty, broken-down filmmaker played by Jean-Luc Godard in his latest movie, *First Name: Carmen*. When his young niece, Carmen (Maruschka Detmers), who is mixed up with a gang of terrorist robbers, comes to see him in his hospital room and tries to entice him to make another film (so that the gang can use it as a cover for a kidnapping), he says, "We should close our eyes, not open them." Godard plays a dishevelled, grumpy old dear

226

with stubble on his chin; he's the film's comic relief, muttering spacy epigrams, whacking himself in the face, and generously giving his niece whatever she asks for. She wants to use his apartment at the seashore; he tells her it's empty but, yes, she can use it. Adapted by Godard and/or his collaborator, Anne-Marie Miéville, from Prosper Mérimée's brief novel that became famous when Bizet used it for his opera, this *Carmen* is scored to Beethoven string quartets, with only a teasing echo of Bizet —passersby are heard whistling bits of the "Habanera."

The conception of woman as a (helplessly) destructive, amoral force is retained in the film, but it's presented in a French modernist way— as a given. We're not meant to question it, or even think about it. Carmen meets her red-haired, long-jawed Joseph (Jacques Bonaffé) while she and her confederates are robbing a bank where he works as a security guard; smitten, he joins up with her then and there, and very soon (lifting a line from *Carmen Jones*) she tells him, "If I love you, that's the end of you." (He agrees, without so much as a "Huh?" or "What are you talking about?") She's completely explicit: "What do I want in life? To show the world what a woman does to a man." In this movie, either a man's passion is frustrated or it's partly fulfilled, and then, when he's more deeply aroused, he's crushed. Joseph has to kill the proud and defiant Carmen because she has rendered him incapable of doing anything else. The movie is about fate and impotence. Joseph tries to rape Carmen but can't get an erection; Uncle Jean used to make movies, but his fire is banked—it may not have gone out completely, but it doesn't flare up, either. A man's passion—whether for a woman or for movies—is what destroys him. In the film's terms, it's Godard's—it's man's—fate to be frustrated. (The picture carries the epigraph "In memoriam small movies.")

Uncle Jean, the madman artist who can say anything (and have it come out sounding witty and apropos), is a bemused self-parody. He's a crank who knows he's a crank; at the same time, he's meant to be the only voice of sanity. You can see that Godard enjoys playing his slapstick role—he brings something like a twinkle to his cynical, scatological utterances. Besides, he's the only performer in the movie who has a clear-cut idea of what's wanted of him, and Uncle Jean is the only character I could feel any connection to. The others (Carmen included) are like actors seen walking through a rehearsal. They don't even make much of a visual impression, because Godard as director doesn't have the emotional bonds with them that he had with the performers in his movies during the period from *Breathless* to *Weekend*—1959 to 1967. We were entranced with Anna Karina and Jean-Paul Belmondo and Jean-Pierre

Léaud and Marina Vlady and many others because he was; the camera seemed to look right into their essence. In *First Name: Carmen,* the camera looks at the performers with the eyes of an apathetic stranger.

Godard uses a number of alienation devices. The crime scenes aren't led up to: we're suddenly thrust into the scramble of the bank heist, which is staged like a brawl in a Western; it's a theatre-of-the-absurd heist that negates any element of suspense or excitement. Or Godard will give us voice-overs of people who are at a distance, and they'll be delivering tangential remarks that relate to the director's past concerns —remarks that are like family jokes. Or he'll interrupt the dialogue track and leave us watching Carmen and Joseph moving their lips while we hear the sound of the sea. Right after the bank holdup, he sends Carmen and Joseph (tied together at the wrist) to a men's washroom and keeps the image of Carmen sitting on the urinal totally sanitized, except that a slob of a man is standing at the washbasins eating something like jelly out of a container with his fingers—slurping it greedily, disgustingly. But we don't need to be alienated from this movie—Godard (as he works now) can't help alienating us. We need to be drawn in.

His dissociation techniques here may be similar to the ones in his earlier movies, but they're not used to wake you up. They're his way of brushing the narrative aside. (It's no more than a few familiar signposts of the femme-fatale genre anyway.) From the way this movie is put together, we can guess that though Godard is resigned to having to tell some sort of story, he feels it's an imposition on him—an irritation, or worse. And he displaces the sensuality that people expect from a Carmen movie onto images that have no specific relation to her story. Part of the picture is set in the seaside town of Trouville, where Carmen and Joseph use Uncle Jean's empty apartment (in a lackadaisical reminder of *Last Tango in Paris*), and, throughout the film, shots of the waves breaking against the rocks are intercut with Carmen and Joseph's travails; there are also intercut images of the Paris traffic at dusk and of two Métro trains crossing over a canal at night, and frequent views of the string quartet that is practicing and (sometimes) performing the Beethoven we hear on the soundtrack. (Actually, we're hearing recordings by several different groups, and a ringer—the actress Myriem Roussel, who has a small part—is put among the musicians to give the music a whimsical tie to the story.) The movement of the sea and the flow of traffic have a sense of mystery, and the musicians are photographed glowingly, serenely. These cutaways are where the feelings are, and the scenes that we might expect to be voluptuous and hot are perfunctory, and sometimes depressive, sometimes coy. Initially, at least, a viewer may be charmed by the mournful, unkempt Uncle Jean (who fumbles with his slide rule the way Godard in public appearances sometimes fools around with his pocket calculator), but we never get to know Carmen or Joseph, and their nudity has an impersonal chill, a vapid "frankness." When Carmen stands, wearing only a red T-shirt, next to the seated Joseph, his eyes are on a direct level with her pubic area—and so are the eyes of the audience. Godard may be playing a few games here, but the point of the scene is that Carmen is so contemptuously indifferent to Joseph that she doesn't care if she tortures him or not. This is what makes the poor lug impotent: he's alone with a half-naked girl who treats him as if he were part of the furniture. And the director treats both of them as part of the furniture. Godard might almost be taking a weird sort of revenge on the supple, pretty girl with a puffy lower lip and free, tangled hair. He might be saying, "I'm not entranced by you. You don't drive me crazy."

The women in his sixties movies did drive him crazy—that's part of what gives those movies their lyrical zing. The 1965 *Pierrot le Fou*—which was his real *Carmen*—had such a poisonous masochistic charge that the hero wrapped dynamite around his head and blew himself sky high. And that, metaphorically, must be what Godard felt his relationship to moviemaking was. From the way this new film is made, it appears that Godard feels hurt on some deep level and he thinks the movies did it to him—and he's not going to let himself get hurt again. He won't throw himself into this project. He gives the story a flat, dry treatment and entertains himself with Beethoven and the rolling surf and with a limited palette—soft, somber tones and subdued golden ones—that suggests the classics (but not of movies).

The surf has too close a relationship to the ineluctable-fate aphorisms: it's used meaningfully (the pull of the sea, the power of woman), and so there's a redundancy here, and—if I may be forgiven—an old-wave banality. (After dunking us in the wet over and over, the film actually has Joseph explain his passion for Carmen to the girl who's playing viola in the string quartet by telling her that he is driven toward Carmen by a force "like the tide.") In this context, even simple shots of ships passing each other are banalized. Some of the images, though, are redemptively beautiful: the nocturnal views of cars gliding out of Paris, the moving white line of the surf at night—an abstraction with no sentiments attached. And Godard keeps all his sets of images in motion: he's the rare case of an artist whose command of his medium becomes more assured as his interests dry up. Working with Raoul Coutard as cinematographer, he gives you the feeling that he can do almost anything and you'll keep watching it, mesmerized by the rhythms of sound and image. But you may not feel very good afterward.

Godard's movies have always been self-referential, and this one has links to his whole body of work (particularly to *Pierrot le Fou*, in which he used Sam Fuller the way he now uses Uncle Jean, and to the 1975 *Numéro Deux*), but it doesn't have the fresh, exploratory quality of the sixties movies—the excitement of going back over earlier themes and seeing new possibilities in them. The references—such as the use of a Tom Waits song that recalls Coppola's *One from the Heart*—seem empty. The picture is Godardian in a way that is sometimes amusing but makes us condescend to it, fondly—and, after a while, not so fondly. Despite Coutard's ravishing lighting, it feels drained. I began to long for the jazzy primary colors that gave Godard's sixties movies their Pop clarity, and for the contemporaneity that kept a viewer's mind leaping —and did it impudently, joyously. When you see a highly praised new work by the man who is the greatest innovative artist of modern movies —the man who reënergized movies—it's a letdown to see something as thin and precious as *First Name: Carmen*. If there are some not-bad jokes and some neat little tricks (such as a slapstick bit of dissociation: the musicians are playing on camera while seagulls screech on the soundtrack), there are also metaphysical quizzes, like Joseph's "Why do women exist?" and Carmen's "Why do men exist?," and garbled profundities—"The police are to society what dreams are to the individual." And there's indifference.

Uncle Jean has lost his interest in youth, in Pop culture, and—if he is to be believed—in movies. And he makes the mistake that many other artists who have lost their strength make: he condemns the public. ("Kids today are scum.") The picture isn't as rancidly self-pitying as Godard's 1979 *Every Man for Himself*, but it's more shallow, more withdrawn. He's contemplating the eternal; he's also wryly (and ambivalently, of course) celebrating being out of it. The basic feel of *Carmen* is "What's the use?" Godard can hardly bring himself to throw up his hands. He gives the impression that maybe he'd rather sit around listening to Beethoven's late quartets than make movies. (Uncle Jean the comedian wanders through the action turning away from whatever he sees and muttering comments like "I won't work under these conditions.") At the start of *Carmen*, Uncle Jean doesn't want to leave the seclusion of his hospital room; he wants to stay inside. And by the end of this movie you may agree that he should—that he's in need of healing.

September 17, 1984

230

TIGHT LITTLE THRILLER

Dreamscape starts with Eddie Albert as the President of the United States, who is tan and fit-looking in his bed in the Western White House but is racked by nightmares of nuclear war; seeking peace for himself as well as for the world, he decides to make a disarmament deal with the Russians, and arranges for a conference in Geneva. Max von Sydow is a research scientist who, with Kate Capshaw as his assistant, has a small experimental project in one wing of a Los Angeles college hospital; there especially gifted psychics attempt to enter the dream world of the tortured patients whose disorders have been resistant to other treatment, locate their unconscious fears, and help the patients conquer them. Dennis Quaid is Alex, a young psychic who has been having a fine time hanging out at the race track picking winners and making out with girls; when von Sydow sends for him, Alex discovers that he doesn't have any choice in the matter—government agents come for him. Von Sydow is a decent enough fellow, but his project has been financed by the government, and it's under the aegis of Christopher Plummer, the head of covert intelligence, who will do anything to prevent what he regards as the weakening of our defense system. He is so sleekly entrenched in power that even the President dare not touch him, and he is a man known for his patriotism and his rectitude. When he suggests that the President spend a night at the hospital to see if he can be helped, the President assents. Plummer doesn't believe in taking chances: in addition to controlling the project, he has a special relation to one of the resident psychics—David Patrick Kelly—who knows exactly what Plummer wants him to do and has no compunction about doing it. Meanwhile, Alex is honing his skills, working with von Sydow and Capshaw's psychiatric patients by entering the funniest, most audacious dream sequences I've seen on the screen since the 1962 *The Manchurian Candidate*—which was also a fantasy thriller about a political assassination (and was also, as I recall, dismissed by most of the press).

The young director Joseph Ruben made his first feature, *The Sister-in-Law*, in 1973, not long after finishing his film courses at the University of Michigan. (He was twenty-three.) That was followed by *The Pom-Pom Girls* and two more pictures about teen-agers—*Joyride*, and *Our Winning Season*, which also starred Dennis Quaid. In *Dream-scape*, Ruben takes you out on little flights of parody and imagination, and then snaps you back—everything fits into place. He's an entertainer-director; he starts off with a cocky swagger, and he can sustain it, because he has the bedrock of a script, by David Loughery, Chuck Russell, and himself, that has real development and structure. This sharp-witted script (with its echo of an early passage in *Gravity's Rainbow*) makes it possible for him to use the dream sequences as separate extravaganzas, suspense stories, and jokes. Though we enter these dreams with Alex, each of them belongs to a different dreamer—with whom Alex then interacts—and each dream is in a different, easily identifiable style. A boy patient who's terrified of going to sleep because "the snakeman" is out to get him dreams in the Joe Dante manner of *The Howling* and the Dante cartoon episode of *Twilight Zone*. When Alex, who hasn't been able to break through Kate Capshaw's professional aplomb, catches her napping in her office and sneaks into her dream, it's in the languorous soft-core-porn style of *Emmanuelle*—Alex joins her in her train compartment, she tears off his shirt, and they make gauzy, passionate love. (When she awakes, she glowers at him.) The President's dream is in the manner of John Carpenter's *Escape from New York* and George Romero's *Night of the Living Dead*. And it seems perfectly natural for the dreams to be in these movie styles, because, of course, people's dreams do take off from the movies. (Would the President be likely to have seen Carpenter and Romero pictures? It's hard to tell, but President Reagan sometimes whiles away his mornings at Camp David watching movies.) The dream sequences are designed slyly, artfully—the snakeman dream has a great, twisty staircase (a stark-mad staircase that might have come out of Dr. Caligari's fertile mind). Each dream advances the plot while having an enjoyable sophomoric bounce of its own. As the movie proceeds, we may notice that its atmosphere has become more nocturnal. By the time Alex is being chased by Plummer's men, who are shooting at him, his reality has become as crazily dark as the horror dreams.

Dreamscape really moves, and its movie jokes (such as a quick display of martial arts out of *Enter the Dragon* and a visual allusion to *The Pom-Pom Girls*) don't slow it down. They're part of the texture—part of the characters' consciousness. The actors seem to be eager and on their toes; they seem to enjoy thinking well of themselves, and the director must be in on it. The whole movie has a playful cockiness working along with the suspense. (This extends even to the dream décor: the tilt of that staircase to no paradise makes you gasp and laugh.) The main characters are all smart and, in varying degrees, highly intuitive —in the case of Quaid's Alex and David Patrick Kelly's Tommy Ray Glatman, preternaturally so. Quaid plays smart here as convincingly as he played dumb in *All Night Long,* and he does it without the element of moral ambivalence that he used as Gordo Cooper in *The Right Stuff.* Quaid combines braininess with a physical ease; he's completely unapologetic about playing a smart character, and he manages to suggest that Alex is capable of putting his brains to use. Quaid plays intelligence and intuition as a sexy advantage, and his slightly mocking free-and-easy manner makes it possible for him to hold his own against Kelly, whose cunningly evil Tommy Ray might otherwise have walked away with the picture. As Kelly demonstrated in a smaller part in *The Warriors,* he has a gift for giggly psychopathology of the kind that movies thrive on; his performance here is in the tradition of Richard Widmark's tittering Tommy Udo in *Kiss of Death.* Kelly never lays it on that flamboyantly, yet his thin-lipped, calculating sadism gives the assassination plot the primal terror it needs. Small and compact—as if the better to slither in and out of the walls—Tommy Ray enters a woman's dream and shocks her into a massive coronary, just for practice. He's pleased at his prowess; he gives himself an A. When von Sydow first tells Alex about the research he wants him to engage in, the two actors seem to enjoy their interplay—they appear to be charming each other. When Christopher Plummer, the arch-patriot, talks to Tommy Ray, the killer, there's another kind of interplay: Plummer is such a past master at suggesting that there's something tainted about his characters that when he addresses Tommy Ray as "son," the little psycho psychic does seem to be his offspring—a devil child.

Plummer's trying to use psychics for secret political purposes may suggest the John Cassavetes role in De Palma's *The Fury,* but it's only a superficial resemblance. This movie doesn't have obsessive, hallucinatory moments of greatness, like *The Fury*—it's an efficient, clever thriller in happy control. I suppose some people might call it a B picture, because it doesn't aspire to be anything more than a clever thriller. But it's awfully good for what it is. Joseph Ruben lays things out simply and clearly; the narrative is easy to respond to, yet none of the actors wear labels and you never get the feeling that they're trying to act up to some big conception. Everybody in the movie seems distinctive and perfectly comprehensible, and that goes even for the sharpers at the track who are furious at Alex for not letting them in on which horses are going to win, and the thugs who do Plummer's bidding. Kate Capshaw plays in a comedy style that's completely different from the shrillness she affected in *Indiana Jones and the Temple of Doom.* She's funny in a much softer way; she has reddish light-brown hair and an intimate, small voice that's full of comic modulations, and, sitting in that train compartment, she somehow sexualizes every inch of herself. Ruben's light touch brings out a form of acting magic: the actors here respond to each other so intuitively that their leaping into each other's heads seems just one more step. It seems to be just what intuitive people ought to be able to do.

□

With some movie stars, the more successful they become the less interesting they are. In *Country,* the opening-night presentation of the New York Film Festival, Jessica Lange doesn't have a single scene in which she shows anything like the giddy sensuousness she brought to *King Kong,* or the heat she brought to *The Postman Always Rings Twice,* or the tension in her *Frances,* or even the cuddle-me dreaminess she had in *Tootsie.* She's doing a performance that's all interior, and she isn't playing a character—she's playing a set of virtues that she associates with her idea of an "ordinary" luminous Midwestern woman, a contemporary Ma Joad. When the tornado hits and Ma's teen-age son is buried head down in a truckload of grain, she's the first one to realize what has happened and to dig for him. And when the Farmers Home Administration moves to foreclose on the hundred-and-eighty-acre farm that has been in her family for over a hundred years, and the men fall apart, she's firm in her resolve and she holds on to that land. *Country,* which Lange conceived and had a hand in producing, is, like some of Jane Fonda's productions, an attempt to raise the audience's consciousness. With Richard Pearce as director and with a script by William D. Witliff, it's trying to be a feminist *The Grapes of Wrath,* and doesn't succeed at all—awful as that would be. The picture is reverential about showing you the outside of the house where Ma and the family live; the camera moves toward the building over hallowed ground. The people here are good 'cause they work the land. (Watching them, you may find yourself muttering "granola, granola.")

Country is set in the eighties, but when Dad (Sam Shepard) goes into the bank to borrow money on the farm he's crushed by the discovery that loans are now made on the basis of an economic evaluation of the farm's prospects rather than on a judgment of "the man"—of his moral fibre. (What mythical era did this fellow grow up in?) Early on, there's a tenderly observed scene of the little girl in the family—she's about nine —amusing herself while taking care of her baby sister by putting Ma's lipstick on the baby's soft mouth. Later, that scene has a nagging irony, because Ma Jessica never wears any lipstick. With her wide, noble brow, strong jaw, clear eyes, tousled honey-blond hair, and the light from within, she doesn't need artificial aids—makeup would soil her image. This is the kind of eighties-farm-life movie in which the characters show you that they're into deep, eternal values by wearing plain print dresses as faded and shapeless as if they'd been in and out of the washtub since the thirties. Jessica Lange looks great in them, of course, and is quite chic in her well-worn plaids—roughing-it classics. This family has a TV —on Sunday, after church, Dad watches football with Ma's father (Wilford Brimley)—and the boy has a Walkman, but they're not culturally polluted. At a local shindig, Ma and Dad dance together in the courtly way country folk in the movies have been doing for decades, and you don't see any kids trying out break-dance moves. There's some sweet, nostalgic stuff about Ma's getting all worked up over the discovery that her son has a condom hidden in his room; nobody has ever heard of drugs or dope.

These people are made virtuous by being turned into old *Saturday Evening Post* covers. When the threats of foreclosure start, with a long list of families to be evicted, it never seems to occur to anybody to talk to a lawyer; the people in this movie have been made too dumb and too passive to go to court and fight for their rights. You wonder how they've survived as long as they have. When a neighboring family with a beloved brain-damaged son is under the pressure of having its livestock confiscated, the boy, seeing the animals being prodded, becomes upset, grabs one of the prods, hits a deputy sheriff with it, and is arrested. (In movies, only bad guys prod animals.) There are no visible efforts to get the poor kid out of jail; the father in his hopelessness and grief shoots himself.

There was considerable television coverage of the farm liquidations and foreclosures that took place in 1982, and the farmers weren't taking it lying down. They were lively and angry; they had personalities, and they were using all their resources to fight back. In the movie, Sam Shepard looks whipped at the first hint of trouble and takes to the bottle, and Gramps, or Pops, or whatever Wilford Brimley is called this time, complains bitterly, mumbles about how things used to be, and shrivels into decrepitude. (It's never explained why the land, which was in Lange's family, isn't still in her father's name—Pops is treated as if he were a family retainer.) The other farmers are caving in, too. Everybody is pooped but our Ma. Hauling the plump baby on her shoulder, she goes from farm to farm asking the people to come to the auction at her place, and when they do she starts a chant of "No sale! No sale!" that spreads and drives the auctioneers off. And since the entire foreclosure policy is attributed to the push of one inhumane bureaucrat who's trying to clean up his books, there's an easy happy ending.

Richard Pearce's background is primarily in documentary (his only other theatrical features are *Heartland* and *Threshold*), and the lack of dramatic impetus in his work is probably at least partly responsible for his reputation—he seems to be doing something higher. After the opening scenes, in which Dad is revealed as the family humorist, and there's some cozy old barnyard humor, Pearce gives us standard hokey melodrama (brain damage as moral force), but he doles it out as if it were full of integrity. (Although *Country* doesn't contain nearly enough factual observation, it's staged like an acted-out documentary.) The movie's sensitive observations, such as Dad's feeling emasculated when he faces the loss of the farm, are usually stale. And since the trained actors are reaching for the common—the universal—and coming up with a kind of non-acting acting, the only members of the cast who have anything fresh to give us are the children. They aren't trying to be types; they're responding to the situations they've been placed in, and Levi L. Knebel, who plays the teen-ager, gives an affecting performance. The stars in this movie have nothing to give us but their self-celebratory look: in his narrow-cut jeans, Sam Shepard is the man with the Gary Cooper legs; Jessica Lange could be posing for a new Statue of Liberty.

I know there are people who will applaud *Country* for the worthiness of its subject and the seriousness of its tone. But *Country* isn't a serious treatment of its subject. It's a morally uplifting treatment of its subject: every frame is planned to be a work of American art, and we're meant to be proud of these farmers and their heritage. This is a movie about Jessica Lange's spirit-of-the-prairie face. This ordinary woman brushes mere mortal men aside and does what needs to be done. Lange the star presents herself as totally self-sufficient, which is a big mistake —it means that as an actress she doesn't relate to anyone. (Lange doesn't seem to have a clue to why people enjoy watching her.) Here, she's the people, she's the land, and she will endure. The director has too much taste to end with a closeup of his star superimposed on the American flag, but that's the general idea.

The teen-age boy raises the only practical issue in the movie. When Dad is going in to town, the kid reminds him that they're low on feed for the sheep. Since Dad is ashamed to ask for more credit, he doesn't do anything about it. Days pass, and the boy informs him that there's no feed left; the father ignores him. It gets to the point where the boy is announcing that the sheep are starving. By then, the father is boozed up and in a funk. At the end of the picture, the family faces a bright, heroic future, but the sheep still haven't been fed.

□

olker Schlöndorff's *Swann in Love* doesn't even have the force of real desecration; it's easy to forget you've seen these stiff arrangements of people in ornate, cheerlessly lighted rooms that every instinct tells you they never lived in. As Swann, Jeremy Irons doesn't suggest intelligence or feeling; he's a stick, a dried-out Wasp, with dead eyes. (He couldn't be more miscast; he's out of Poe, not Proust.) You expect something from him and he gives you nothing—not even his voice, which has been expressive in other roles. Here, speaking French, he has to use it *très* carefully. Ornella Muti is a wily, plausible Odette. She's made up to look appropriately sallow and Botticellian, and she does manage to suggest that she could torment a man without half trying. (She squirms beautifully, and her luscious, smiling underlip turns sullen very quickly.) As Swann's friend the eminent pederast the Baron de Charlus, Alain Delon (with a little thumbprint of hair under his mouth) looks game enough to handle at least the lighter side of the role, but he only gets to come on for a few turns—he's like a painted vaudevillian who ogles the boys or twinkles knowingly. Of all the imaginable material for the screen, Proust's writing requires the most subtle feeling for rhythms—the meaning is in his rhythms—and neither the director nor the scriptwriters (Peter Brook, Jean-Claude Carrière, Marie-Hélène Estienne) seem to do anything to draw us in. It's an empty shell of a movie. Schlöndorff doesn't achieve an emotional tone even in what is (arguably) the most emotionally devastating passage in all of *Remembrance of Things Past*: the Duc and Duchesse de Guermantes's rushing off to a dinner party and not wanting to be bothered when their old friend Swann tells them he's dying.

ightrope has been the No. 1 box-office attraction in the country for several weeks. Why? Clearly, people don't go to see Clint Eastwood films for a demonstration of congeniality or charm. (The movies in which he has tried to be a likable guy—such as the quaint *Bronco Billy* and the lachrymose *Honkytonk Man*—have been relative commercial failures.) People do go to the conventionally structured movies in which he's a man of action; when he's a big-city cop he doesn't talk—he punches and shoots. Charles Bronson only draws crowds overseas; John Wayne is gone; Burt Reynolds is a joke. Eastwood is the only one left who makes these movies about how tough it is to be a man. They are worked out in such primitive terms that there aren't even any crosscurrents or subplots—you just watch Eastwood as he marches from scene to scene blasting his enemies with an auto-mag or, as in *Tightrope*, handcuffing women to bedposts.

Written and directed by Richard Tuggle, *Tightrope* is a seamy, gaudy melodrama, in which Eastwood is Homicide Inspector Wes Block, of the New Orleans Police Department, and the devoted father of two young girls—his wife left them behind when she took off. Wes is investigating a series of murders: young prostitutes are being tortured, raped, and strangled. The gimmick is that the killer is Wes Block's doppelgänger. Wes is good and the killer is evil, but Wes's anger at his ex-wife has knotted his insides and he has developed a taste for bondage; he likes to handcuff the prostitutes he has sex with, and the killer knows it. He dogs Wes's steps through the French Quarter, and if Wes talks to a girl in the course of his investigation and has sadistic fantasies about her, the killer—sometimes masked, sometimes just hidden in the shadows—carries them through. Once a few of the girls have been murdered immediately after Wes has been with them, you'd think it might occur to him that he's the real target, but he just goes along providing the man in running shoes, who is right behind him, with more candidates for extinction.

Tuggle keeps whomping us on the skull with the good-evil symbolism, and the laudatory reviews suggest that there is real daring and soul-searching in Eastwood's playing a man struggling with dark, sexist impulses. But the movie has no more depth than the usual exploitation film in which pretty girls are knocked off. The victims aren't given the kind of introduction that would make us have some rapport with them; the affectless way they're presented, you get the feeling that they're tough cookies selling sex and they deserve to be tortured and killed—

they're asking for it. Their naked corpses are photographed more tenderly than their live bodies. And the movie has a queasy (unexplored) aspect: Eastwood's own twelve-year-old daughter, Alison, who looks like him and acts like him, plays Wes's daughter Amanda, whom the doppelgänger means to rape.

In order to keep the symbolic apparatus going until Eastwood finally rips off the killer's mask (and it's a long, long movie), Tuggle makes Wes Block the most inept police investigator of all time. He has to be paralyzed by his own sense of complicity, so that the corpses can keep piling up; there's a scene in which the doppelgänger literally presents him with a male prostitute, and Wes innocently sends the fellow off to be murdered, as if it had never occurred to him that that might happen. Tuggle never uses the possibilities in the doppelgänger idea: Wes ought to be able to outwit and trap the killer by reading his own mind. Instead, he keeps chasing the man who's following him, and Tuggle keeps them both running through colorful New Orleans locations, with plenty of masked figures (it's Mardi Gras, of course) and a warehouse with grotesque big papier-mâché celebrities, including Reagan—a touch that can mean anything you want it to. This is a crudely commercial movie that offers a tour of flesh-peddling establishments and a psychobabble seriousness. A black woman psychologist (Janet MacLachlan) explains to Wes how we're all on this tightrope between good and evil, and he is given a girlfriend (Geneviève Bujold) who runs a rape crisis center; she's handily qualified to help him exorcise his sexism.

Tightrope is the opposite of sophisticated moviemaking. There's no progression in the plot—it's just one body after another. And there's no point in ripping off the killer's mask—we don't know him anyway; the mask is just there to serve the movie's schematism. (At one point, this killer, shrouded in a ski mask with tiny eye holes, is being chased around a railroad yard, and you do wonder why he doesn't take it off so he can see better. The symbolism makes no narrative sense.) The scenes that show Wes as a gentle father are dismally bland, and there are traditional gags, such as Wes's always having one dog or another in bed with him (his daughters take in strays); like John Wayne, Eastwood keeps the audience comfortable. A sadistic fantasy may sneak in—he's human, and the audience likes that. But there won't be any art or style, or even much emotion. Audiences appear to like him undemonstrative, or, to put it bluntly, wooden.

Wes, like Eastwood's San Francisco cop, Dirty Harry Callahan, is a gritty realist, with no ideals. That's probably what makes Eastwood's cops accessible to a huge audience. Eastwood takes account of disgust in a way that few other trash filmmakers do. He has a real *New York Post* side to him: in his cop movies, the world is set up as a jungle, and you're one of the beasts in it, and so is he. Beatty and Redford play idealists, but Eastwood found what disgusts him in hippies (*Dirty Harry*), in homos (*The Enforcer*), in lesbos (*Sudden Impact*), and now, as Wes Block, he sees that the source of what disgusts him is partly in himself. That *could* make *Tightrope* effective—he's wrestling with self-disgust. And that may be what the *New York Post* junkies among the movie reviewers are responding to. When they find something deep and austere in the good-evil gimmickry, that may be their way of feeling low-down and honest.

If there's anything new going on in Eastwood's performance, it's that he seems almost to be punishing himself for wanting to act. At times, he seems to be trying to blast through his own lack of courage as an actor. But the picture just grinds along, and it's like an emanation of Eastwood's dullness. He seems to want to be fiery, but he doesn't have it in him—there's no charge in his self-disgust. *Tightrope* isn't exciting, because there's no vigor or puritan grandeur in Wes Block's character and there's nothing in the psycho doppelgänger—he's just a bogeyman. Without flamboyance of his own, Eastwood needs a director who can set some flamboyance swirling around him—Sergio Leone did it in the spaghetti Westerns, and Don Siegel did it in *Dirty Harry*. But *Tightrope* is no more than a sombre, pedestrian *Halloween*. It's *Halloween* taking itself seriously.

October 1, 1984

MIRRORS

Geoff Murphy, the director of the New Zealand film *Utu*, has an instinct for popular entertainment. He also has a deracinated kind of hip lyricism. And they fuse quite miraculously in this epic about the relations between the Maori, the dark-skinned Polynesians who started migrating to the volcanic islands that form New Zealand around a thousand years ago, and the British, who began to migrate there in large numbers in the eighteen-thirties. By 1870, the year in which the movie is set, the British were the government (and within the next few decades confiscated millions of acres of Maori land—much of it as "punishment for rebellion"). Murphy uses the conventions of John Ford's cavalry-and-Indians Westerns, but he uses them as a form of international shorthand —to break the ice and get going, and for allusions and contrasts. His primary interest isn't in the narrative; it's in how the characters think and what they feel. By 1870, the Maori, trained and educated in mission schools, speak English and are imbued with Englishness. And they certainly know how to mock the English—playing off the Englishmen's expectations that they will behave like ignorant savages.

Te Wheke (Anzac Wallace), the troublemaker at the center of the story, is a literate, Europeanized Maori with a taste for Shakespeare. He's a uniformed scout with the British colonial forces who returns to his tribal settlement—a village friendly to the British—and finds that the huts are still smoking: the cavalry rode in and set them ablaze after casually slaughtering everyone there, leaving the bodies where they fell. In grief and rage at the death of his people, he feels the need to exact *utu*—the Maori word that means honor and includes ritualized revenge. Te Wheke's honor requires that he achieve balance through reciprocal acts—*utu* can be attained only by the shedding of blood.

By the thirteenth century, the Maori in New Zealand were having disputes over land, and warrior-cannibal tribes built fortified villages and ate or enslaved the enemies they defeated. Since the justification for the raids and killings was the need for *utu*, the members of the tribe that had been attacked would then have the same need, and the warfare was continuous—it was the normal way of life. Because of this tradition, the Maori weren't united even in resisting European encroachment on their land. Some were with the British troops, some tried to remain neutral, and by 1870 the hostile Maori were so demoralized by defeat and slaughter that they couldn't manage much more than occasional guerrilla raids. As more and more land-hungry British settlers arrived, the wars between the Maori and the British became wars of atrocities (on both sides).

Te Wheke prepares for his return to the barbaric, mystical heritage of the warrior tribes by having his face carved to symbolize his new purpose. In the Maori variant of tattooing, deep lines are cut, so that the

241

skin in between stands out in ridges; Te Wheke, with curves and spirals covering his face, has a new aura. He's like a living version of the totemic figures exhibited in the Maori show at the Metropolitan Museum of Art. With his long, thick black hair and his mustache and elated eyes adding to the symmetrical pattern, he suggests the posters for the Broadway show *Cats*. He's a commanding presence—a Maori Che Guevara. He's also engaged in a form of make-believe—he's a travesty of an ancient warrior. When he's dressed for *utu* in his red British Army jacket, and with a military cap perched on his matted hair, it's as if all the contradictions in the society were popping out of his skin—as if he couldn't contain them anymore. He formally announces his *utu* in a rural Christian church after chopping the pastor's head off. He challenges the bewildered white and Maori parishioners by assuming the openmouthed pose of the totems and jiggling his protruding tongue at them.

Joined by a band of guerrilla recruits, Te Wheke sets out on his rampage. The code that governs *utu* does not require that the specific perpetrators of the offense be killed; any members of their tribe will do —so all Europeans are fair game. When the guerrillas attack the idyllic farmhouse of the Williamsons—Bruno Lawrence (of *Smash Palace*) and the fine actress Ilona Rodgers—they assault the two and proceed to desecrate everything European; they shoot up Mrs. Williamson's china, loot the place, and dance to the pounding of her grand piano before shoving it out the window. Picking up a volume of Shakespeare, Te Wheke entertains himself by reading a passage from *Macbeth* before setting fire to the house. It's an insane vandalization, and he knows it, but he's committed to this mad course of action because the history of his country appears to have left him with no other recourse.

At times, when you're looking at Maori, with their beautiful broad, relaxed faces, you can't tell which side they're on; then you realize that this confusion is part of the subject. They're on both sides: almost everyone in the movie wavers in his allegiance from time to time—even the young Lieutenant Scott (played with a likable mixture of callowness and élan by Kelly Johnson), who has been posted here by the British War Office, because he has been with the Boers putting down the natives in skirmishes in South Africa and has learned new, experimental counter-insurgency tactics. He turns out to be a flop, because he was born in New Zealand and becomes attached to a lovely, fleshy Maori girl; he can't give his work the wholehearted, career enthusiasm he had in South Africa. And the girl (played by an eighteen-year-old Maori student, Tania Bristowe), who is tied in with Te Wheke's band, acts the part of dusky enticer to Scott but feels closer to him than she does to her Maori friends; she gets to the point where she's marked for execution by both sides. As for Te Wheke, he runs his army as a parody of the white man's army. He and his guerrillas deck themselves out in a ragtag assortment of parts of British military uniforms and scraps of Victorian clothing they've picked up in raids on farms, and have hatchets and knives and guns tucked into their belts and boots. They have turned themselves into the Europeans' images of them as butchers and buffoons. (They're like American blacks playing Jungle Bunny.) If that's what the Europeans think they are, that's what they'll be. That's all that's left for them to be. In murdering the British, they're murdering themselves anyway. In a trancelike sequence, Te Wheke's guerrillas take over a wagon full of supplies for the militia and use it to ride in for a surprise night attack; along the road, one of the men rips open a sack of flour, plunks his face down in it, and says, "I've only been one of them for a minute, and already I hate you Maori." As the wagon rolls on, his white face is almost phosphorescent in the moonlight—he's like a phantom.

Mimicry goes on at so many levels in this horror comedy of colonialism that the viewer may be laughing, exhilarated by constant discovery, yet be a little discombobulated and scared. Murphy throws you at the start—he may want to disorient you, as Te Wheke disorients people—and he keeps you in a state of suspension. A few scenes go by before it's clear that the movie is cutting back and forth between the trial of the captured pattern-faced Te Wheke and the events that led the smooth-faced man to transform himself. At the trial, when Wiremu (Wi Kuki Kaa), a smart, fair-minded Maori who's a mercenary with the British forces, explains what has been going on to the officers, Te Wheke yawns. Wiremu, who plays chess with the racist colonel and puts a crimp in his theory of Maori inferiority by winning, has noble twin arches in his upper lip (like V. S. Naipaul)—he's smiling even when he isn't smiling. (He has some of Naipaul's gravity, too.) I doubt if any other director has treated the conventions of this colonial-epic form with Murphy's offhand audacity. He turns the form into a mirror of racism.

Murphy uses an abrupt, lurch-ahead editing that works well (except at the beginning), and there are real streaks of madness in the pursuit story. This isn't an impassioned lament, like the great Australian film *The Chant of Jimmie Blacksmith*; the lamenting quality is implicit in the material. And *Utu* doesn't have a strong protagonist; there are a whole string of leading characters—Lieutenant Scott, the young Maori girl, and others—who take over for a sequence or two and then recede, but may return. Left for dead, Bruno Lawrence's bald, bearded Williamson gets on Te Wheke's trail with the obsessiveness of a man who has lost his wife and seen the destruction of everything he has worked for. He's in the same position as Te Wheke, and has only one desire: to kill him. Slogging through the countryside carrying a quadruple-barrelled shotgun that he has put together (it's the size of a baby cannon), going for days and nights without sleep, and speaking in a dry rasp of a voice that gets lower and lower, Williamson is the only other character with the intensity of Te Wheke, who keeps firing at him but can't seem to kill him. Williamson has the same trouble killing Te Wheke. One with too much hair, the other with hair in the wrong place, they're like the pairs of adversaries in Sergio Leone's *Once Upon a Time in the West*, and we expect them to meet in a final shootout. But Murphy and his co-writer, Keith Aberdein, skewer your expectations, and you think, Of course, it's richer this way. Murphy throws you curves all through the picture: Te Wheke will suddenly be singing "Old MacDonald Had a Farm," or the soundtrack will make a satirical comment on the action, using "Marching Through Georgia," or Lieutenant Scott will casually survive being shot a few times, or Te Wheke's grimaces will remind you of Toshiro Mifune's Macbeth in *Throne of Blood*. (Anzac Wallace's performance as Te Wheke—his first acting—may owe something to his own experiences as a wild, sociopathic thief; he spent fourteen years in prison before becoming reconciled to living with other people, leading an industrial strike, and becoming a union organizer.) There are other reminders of Kurosawa, and of *Macbeth*, too, when Te Wheke stages his own version of moving Birnam wood to Dunsinane.

Te Wheke's Shakespearean flourish in the Williamsons' vandalized home may be somewhat fancy and more than somewhat trite, but Geoff Murphy has the popular touch to bring it off. This fellow, who in the late sixties was a scat singer and trumpet player in Bruno Lawrence's rock group and travelling road show, and also its visual-effects man, seems to be directing with a grin on his face. (After years of working in film, Murphy had a big hit—relative to a country of only three million people —in 1980, with *Goodbye Pork Pie*, which played around the world; that's probably what enabled him to get hold of the three million dollars it took to make *Utu*.) The score, written by John Charles, who was also with the road show, and recorded by a traditional Maori flautist and the New Zealand Symphony Orchestra, takes risks, and most of the time the risks come off gloriously. The film has sweep, yet it's singularly unpretentious —irony is turned into slapstick.

As the militia ride out to go after Te Wheke, young Lieutenant Scott asks Wiremu, "Whose side are you on?" Wiremu answers, "Same side as you, sir. I was born here, too." The fatalistic, pragmatic Wiremu knows there's no side to be on; there's no justice. It's obvious that the British will win, and just as obvious that Te Wheke is a folk hero. He's a hero even when he has become so cruel that he is more like a bug than a man, and his own followers are disgusted by him. No doubt Murphy was conscious of taking a balanced, nonjudgmental position, but you feel that the material itself—and his own instincts—dictated it. He couldn't have made this movie any other way, because it's a comedy about the characters' racial expectations of each other, which come out of the tragedy of their history—a history too grotesque for tears. In one sequence, the soldiers are tracking the guerrillas, and Te Wheke, catching their scent, sniffs the air; his dogs, also sniffing, turn their heads this way and that. Murphy's absurdism is a matter of temperament—it's part of the texture of the movie, which appears to be a reasonably accurate version of a totally crazy birth of a nation.

Probably what Murphy does that makes a viewer respond so freely is that he distances us—very slightly—and makes comedy out of the distancing. (He's a joshing, razzing director.) And because we're not asked to respond in the banal ways that action-adventure movies usually impose on us—there's no one we could conceivably root for—we're free to respond to much more. We're turned loose inside this epic, and the freedom is strange and pleasurable. Some of it has to do with the Maori, who have the placid features of Gauguin's Polynesians but appear to be completely expressive, and have such a fluent, unaffected wit that they seem to be plugged into the cosmos in a different way from the British. (In a scene out in a remote woodland area, Lieutenant Scott, talking companionably to a Maori soldier, says that Maori laugh at things that aren't funny. He gives as an example a horrible prank that some Maori played on the British—adding human meat to a barrel of pickled pork. When he finishes the story, the Maori laughs.) And some of the pleasure has to do with the quality of the light and the uncanny splendor of the New Zealand landscapes. There's a vista of an army encampment—small white tents dotting the pale-green hills—that's like a child's dream of outdoor living. Much of the film was shot in high country in wet weather, and the cinematographer, Graeme Cowley, lets us see the mountains and forests and mist-covered farms as if we just happened to look up and there they were. In New Zealand, no one is ever more than seventy miles from the sea, and maybe that helps to account for the feeling of exaltation and spirituality that hovers over this film. We know this basic story of colonialism from books and movies about other countries, but the ferocity of these skirmishes and raids is played off against an Arcadian beauty that makes your head swim.

The smooth meticulousness of *Places in the Heart*—what some might call its craftsmanship—drives me a little crazy. And since I have an aversion to movies in which people say grace at the dinner table (not to the practice but to how movies use it to establish the moral strength of a household), the opening montage of Sunday-night supper in one home after another in Waxahachie, Texas, in 1935—a whole community saying grace—made me expect the worst. The movie's major accomplishment is that it never goes over the brink into utter corny shamelessness—that's where the pristine, courteous style of the writer-director Robert Benton comes in. This is another movie, like *Tender Mercies* and *Terms of Endearment* and *On Golden Pond*, that has a positive human message; a lot of people are calling it a masterpiece, and it's likely to be around for a while and rack up a few Academy Awards. (God knows it's got heart, but it doesn't need that slopes-of-Parnassus title. What places? A ventricle? An atrium? It turns out that the places are where we lived as children—where our roots are. But those places may not be in our hearts.) Sally Field is Edna Spalding, a homebody in the town, thirty miles south of Dallas, who has been married for fifteen years and has been busy taking care of her sheriff husband and raising two kids; widowed suddenly, by a stray bullet, and left without enough money to meet the next mortgage payment, she holds her family together and hangs on to her house and forty acres by, of course, grit and total determination. The film isn't just about Edna, though; it's about the lives of Edna's family and friends, and about the community. And more than that it's about America, and about Christian love, and about forgiveness of those who fail to live up to it. It's about decency.

The story, I'm afraid, centers on a cotton-pickin' contest. Gallant little Edna goes after the money to save the farm by trying to win the hundred-dollar prize that goes to the one who brings in the earliest harvest of the season. (This may be the first time the movies have given us white folks pickin' cotton, sweatin' in the sun, and havin' their hands torn, right alongside black folks.) Edna has the help of two men who become part of her household: Moze (Danny Glover), an itinerant black laborer, whose efforts on her behalf get him in trouble with the local branch of the Ku Klux Klan, and Mr. Will (John Malkovich), a blind First World War veteran, whom she takes in as a boarder. Floating around the edges of Edna's life are her sister (Lindsay Crouse), who runs a small beauty parlor, and the sister's weakling husband (Ed Harris). He has been having an affair with his best friend's wife, an elementary-school teacher—played by Amy Madigan, who gives the most persuasive performance in the film. She has a passionate delicacy, and her guilt takes the form of making her recoil just a trace from all human contact—she looks as if she were withdrawing into herself. It's a small role, but Amy Madigan, with her precisely modelled, tiny features and dark, wavy hair, suggests a major presence. Except maybe for pink, shiny-faced Bert Remsen, who turns up as a hymn-swinging musician at the local dances (he lip-syncs "Cotton-Eyed Joe" to a Doc Watson record), she was the only person in the movie I wanted to see more of, though there are two other impressive performances. Danny Glover has greater vitality than anyone else onscreen and gives the all too endearing role of Moze a humorous, eccentric force, and Malkovich is certainly attention-getting as Mr. Will.

Whenever Malkovich is on, he creates a stillness—a hush—and Benton clears other things out of the way so we can admire his great acting. He has a soft, rather high voice and a large, rounded forehead with a slightly receding hairline, and as Mr. Will he holds his lips small and puckered, and, with his almost expressionless face and empty gaze, he's so touching he's creepy—he's spectral. Malkovich succeeds in conveying the impression that blindness has made him unsure of things, and that his mind is always teeming with incompletely developed ideas. He's affecting, but Mr. Will's hush doesn't vary—it's as if there were a brief patch of blank film before and after his appearances, and it gets to be dead space. And he's too sensitive. Benton has conceived Mr. Will as if blindness purified him and drove out ordinary faults; blackness does the same for Moze.

As for Edna, who's based on Benton's great-grandmother (her sheriff husband was shot in 1882), she's a good Christian woman, firm in her faith from the word go. The movie is a tribute to what Edna represents, and Sally Field seems to have got the Jane Fonda bug—she's being earnest and archetypal (and she doesn't seem to enjoy acting, the way she used to). She gives us her all, but that doesn't include much depth or subtext. She's a one-emotion-at-a-time actress, and her face is always floodlit with whichever one it is. Fortunately, when Sally Field, our leading exemplar of gumption, holds the thought "careworn and anxious" she's likely to look plain rattled. She doesn't really have a star presence here, and so she isn't a pain. She has a saving kind of giddiness: she's playing the equivalent of the role that Gregory Peck had in *To Kill a Mockingbird*, but she's not a Lincolnesque lawyer—she's more like a sweet, light-headed woman working in a small-town five-and-dime or stationery store. It's easy to forget about her. And the kids are just standard-issue movie kids.

Places in the Heart is a series of set pieces of the utmost conventionality; it's like a remake of a prestigious movie of the forties about "the home front" and what we're fighting for. There is even the scene that was popular in twenties and thirties films—the one where the blind man asks the heroine "What do you look like?" and the audience always gulped. Here the music gulps for us, swelling with emotion as Edna describes herself for Mr. Will (though, oddly, she doesn't say what color her hair is, which you might expect would come first). Mr. Will listens wistfully. That's the closest Edna ever gets to a love scene. The quotes in the ads say *Places* is about growing up American, but it's about growing up at American movies. Benton seems to have put together family stories he remembered from childhood and scenes from naïve, prettied-up movies, and blended them into a mythological view of the American past, scrubbing them (in this movie the Ku Klux Klansmen wear the crispest, whitest sheets you've ever seen) and shaping them into an expression of the very highest innocuous values. Humility comes easy to Sally Field; that must help to explain the casting. And she can stand for land and church and family without putting an audience off.

When Benton plays with characters and ideas, as he did in the script of *Bonnie and Clyde* and in *The Late Show* (which he wrote and directed), there's more of him at work than in the projects, like *Kramer vs. Kramer* and this one, where he's "sincere." The sincere Benton falls back on hollow craft and tastefulness and restraint. They serve as a neutralizing force, a form of protection. It's quite a mean town, Benton's Waxahachie. Except for Edna Spalding and, to a lesser degree, her sister, and Mr. Will and Moze, and possibly the other black people, there isn't a true Christian around. The bank manager uses a form of blackmail to dump Mr. Will (who's his brother-in-law) on the destitute widow. Nobody gives her a helping hand. The merchants and traders try to cheat her, and when Moze prevents it they get into their KKK robes and go after him, and when Mr. Will rushes to his aid they're not above threatening a blind man. These people aren't above anything: a mob of white men lynch a black teen-ager. But somehow Benton's gentle presentation muffles all this. His craftsmanship is like an armor built up around his refusal to outrage or offend anyone; it's an encrusted gentility. A friend of mine says that Benton knows how to swim. There may be something to that: he goes with the currents. In the sixties, he (and David Newman) wrote *Bonnie and Clyde* and other scripts with an impudent countercultural tone. In the seventies, he wrote and directed *Kramer vs. Kramer*, a primer for sensitive men in the "Me" decade. And now he's out there with this subdued, inspirational vision of a righteous America, healed by love and decency. (All it lacks is Lassie.) He's the same Robert Benton who (with Harvey Schmidt) wrote that guide to staying *au courant The In and Out Book*. I don't mean to suggest any conscious deception; I'm sure he believes in what he's doing. But he has exquisite feelers.

October 15, 1984

MOZART AND BIZET

The story of a genius who isn't appreciated and dies in poverty has the same basic appeal whether its subject is Stephen Foster or Wolfgang Amadeus Mozart. That's not the kind of story the director Miloš Forman and the writer Peter Shaffer set out to tell in *Amadeus*, but it's essentially what they wound up with, and that appeal is probably what saves the movie from being a disaster. *Amadeus* has a very complicated surface—there's a steady stream of rhetoric about high-flown things. But after a while the rhetoric cancels itself out, and what we see is the unworldly Mozart (Tom Hulce) caught in a web of intrigue by his enemy, the unctuous Hapsburg court composer Salieri (F. Murray Abraham), and worked to death, in 1791, at the age of thirty-five. The story is told to a priest (and to us) many years later, by the mad, suicidal old Salieri, and there is the suggestion that what we're seeing is his delusion, but the weight of the production, which is reminiscent of big biographical movies such as *The Life of Emile Zola* and *A Song to Remember*, asserts its own kind of authority.

Peter Shaffer writes eloquent confrontations between two adversarial figures: in *The Royal Hunt of the Sun*, Pizarro and the Inca king; in *Equus*, the sterile psychiatrist Dr. Dysart and the teen-age patient with his psychotic head full of Dionysian ecstasies and mysteries; and, here, the minor composer Salieri and the incomparable Mozart. This conflict was formulated in the brief, ironic play *Mozart and Salieri* that Pushkin wrote in 1830 (which Rimsky-Korsakov used as the basis for an opera); the play takes only ten pages in the D. M. Thomas translation in *The Bronze Horseman*. Pushkin has Salieri soliloquize:

> I will say it
> To myself—I am envious. I
> Envy. O heaven! where is justice,
> When the sacred gift, when immortal
> Genius, is sent not to reward
> Self-sacrifice, burning love, toil,
> Ardour, supplications, but illumines
> The head of a madcap, an idle rake?
> O Mozart, Mozart!

And when Mozart comes to see him, Salieri cries out, "My God, Mozart, you are not worthy of yourself." He poisons Mozart's wine, and Mozart, offering the toast "Let's drink to the true bond linking us two sons of harmony," swigs it down. Shaffer elaborated on this small conceit in his stage play *Amadeus*—probably choosing this name because it can be construed to mean "beloved of God"—and he has further elaborated on it in the screenplay he wrote in consultation with Forman. Peter Shaffer can give clichés a glitter, and the polarities that are his specialty may sound convincingly clever at the beginning of his plays, but when he starts to add elements the polarities are contradicted, and the conflicts become highly abstruse and drift off into the murk. (He is the twin of the playwright Anthony *Sleuth* Shaffer—which isn't really parenthetical.)

What is *Amadeus* about? Salieri, who has worked hard at his music, been a servile courtier, and achieved fame and high position, is envious of Mozart's incredible talent. You might expect him to ask himself whether he'd want Mozart's talent if Mozart's money troubles went with it, but this movie isn't about such mundane matters. Shaffer has Salieri declaring war on Heaven for gypping him, and determined to ruin Mozart because God's voice is speaking through him. Shaffer turns Pushkin's metaphor into a whole megillah. At first, it's quite funny when the slimy-smooth Salieri complains that his exertions—his always doing the proper thing, studying, going to church—haven't been rewarded. He's the least humble of Christians—he seems to expect God to give him exact value for every prayer he has ever delivered. (He's like a kid saying to Mommy, "I was always a good boy and ate my spinach and did my homework, but you love my brother more than you love me—and he uses dirty words and chases girls.") Salieri thinks that because he suffers so much he should be a genius.

The movie, though, by showing you Mozart as a rubber-faced grinning buffoon with a randy turn of mind, as if that were all there was to him, begins to lend credence to Salieri's mad notion that Mozart doesn't have to do a thing—that his music is a no-strings-attached, pure gift from God. The tone of many of the incidents and details is quite opaque. Are Mozart's bushy white wigs (and the sometimes faintly pinkish ones) a shaky attempt at historical fidelity, or is it Shaffer's or Forman's thought that the young audience will identify with Mozart if he's made to look like Harpo Marx as a rock star? (The effect was also used in the stage version.) Many of the scenes appear to support Salieri in his belief that Mozart's prankish obscenities and his boastfulness are proof that he's unworthy of his artistic gift. Ribald cloacal jokes were an accepted part of ordinary people's conversation in the Vienna of the day, but in the movie Mozart is the only person who seems to enjoy talking dirty. And the movie doesn't make it apparent that his scatological games and his carousing were quick vacations from his work, or that when he gleefully tells the emperor that he shaped a duet into a trio, and the trio into a quartet, and so on, it's not boastful one-upmanship. It's because of his delight in shaping playful structures—the delight that is at the heart of his music.

There's nothing but confusion at the heart of the movie: it's a semi-realistic musical biography of Mozart built on a madman's justification for envy. Forman has something working for him here, though: this aspect of the film ties in with the very old popular beliefs that artists are bawdy and undisciplined, and that genius comes from God—that it's just handed to some people. And later on, when Hulce finally gets out of his fright wigs, and Mozart, ill and desperate, stays up nights working with total concentration on his music, Forman switches to that other popular mode—the dedicated artist who lives only for his art, and, sweating feverishly, dies for it. (Mozart's suffering redeems him.) The corniness in *Amadeus* is that the view of artistic accomplishment which Salieri spouts—that if art comes without plodding it must be a gift from above

—is at least half shared by the writer and the director. They don't appear to register that the whole notion of dictation from God is an insult to Mozart.

Forman's insensitivity to what Mozart might have been like is so flagrant that for the first hour or so you almost think you're being kidded —"Wolfie" Mozart and his wife, Constanze (Elizabeth Berridge), are like teen-agers in some mid-American Dogpatch. And the use of Mozart's music to illustrate snippets of his life and to provide the film with comic (and gothic) punctuation is offensive. (Composing the overture to *The Magic Flute*, Wolfie dances a clumsy jig and thumbs his nose at the framed portrait of his stern, disapproving father on the wall.) Each time you hear the music, it invalidates the movie's bumpkin Mozart, with his hideous, high-pitched whinny-giggle. And if you've read Mozart's letters you know this twerp couldn't have written them. But Forman's crudeness is a form of showmanship—not one I respect but one I'm forced to acknowledge. He trudges through the movie as if every step were a major contribution to art, and he keeps the audience hooked the same way people were hooked by Hollywood's big, obvious, biographical epics. Some members of the audience (and of the press) seem to be awed as well.

There are some real aberrations in this movie, such as a shot of Salieri in a cuckoo's nest where the passageways are lined with bare-chested loonies chained to the walls who seem to be giving a performance of *Marat/Sade*. There's also a long deathbed sequence—the muzziest part of the movie—with Mozart, who looks as if he'd been painted light green, innocently and pathetically dictating his *Requiem* to Salieri, who's plotting to steal the music. And it's definitely one plot too many. The episode totally fuddles the fratricidal issues; Salieri seems about to echo the boy's cry to his God in *Equus*—"Make us one person." This whole section appears to have leaped out of the end of Ken Russell's film on Delius, where it made more sense, since Delius was blind.

Despite the uses to which Mozart's music is put, the musical passages are the best thing about the movie, and that's allied with Twyla Tharp's staging of the dances and the opera excerpts. Most of the picture —especially the scenes in Mozart's chambers and at the court of Emperor Joseph II—is static, in the manner of opulent costume epics of the past. And the court scenes are harshly bright—probably Forman and the cinematographer, Miroslav Ondříček, want us to see the pomp coldly and realistically. So each time there's a musical sequence it's like a reprieve —Twyla Tharp brings the picture some lightness and wit. Her staging of the operas (with sets by Josef Svoboda) shows her great flair for theatrical artifice, and she also stages a parody-pastiche of *Don Giovanni* that Mozart attends (and loves). It's a featherweight low jinks by Bosch—a whirling tableau, with actors playing puppets, a horse that comes riding through paper walls, a soprano who comes crashing through the set, and a dove that flies out of a paper horse's rear end.

As written for the screen, the big, showy role of Salieri seems to be an impossible one (he has too many schemes), and, the way the material is laid out, F. Murray Abraham doesn't get to shape his performance. It never comes together. But Abraham's intensity has a theatrical charge to it in the glances that tell us what's going on under Salieri's polite smiles. And some of the scenes he's in are just about irresistible— arriving at the court in Vienna, Mozart thoughtlessly improves on the march that Salieri has composed to welcome him, and Salieri listens, his face falling apart. Abraham is a wizard at eager, manic, full-of-life roles, and he gives Salieri a cartoon animal's obsession with Mozart—he's Wile E. Coyote. He's also (in his later scenes) a reptile, with an obscene vitality in his crazy eyes. Tom Hulce's Mozart is jarring in the first half—I found it hard even to look at him. He was less unbearable toward the end— possibly because he was confined to bed and couldn't toddle around anymore. Forman probably got the performance he wanted: he seems to like amateurish, telegraphic acting, just as he likes to load the aged Salieri with too much froggy, rotting-old-man makeup. (Abraham's triumph is that a vile kind of humanity gleams through.) A word should also be said for Jeffrey Jones, who plays Emperor Joseph II: maybe because of his imperial rank, he's the only member of the cast who gets to shine by giving a restrained performance. (He does amusingly polished, vapid line readings—the emperor is a boob.) And John Tomlinson, who sings the role of the Commendatore in *Don Giovanni*, has such power he can give you chills. Downtown Prague does just fine as eighteenth-century Vienna. It was fine as Dresden in *Slaughterhouse-Five* and as Hanover in *Saraband* and in many other roles, but I can't remember its ever being cast in a good movie.

□

The composer Georges Bizet, a child prodigy who never knew success as an adult, worked at hack jobs—as an audition pianist, a chorus master, a teacher, an arranger—and died at thirty-six in 1875, a few months after the (dismal) opening of his opera *Carmen*, adapted from Prosper Mérimée's short novel by the librettists Henri Meilhac and Ludovic Halévy. (Ludovic's cousin, Geneviève Halévy, was Bizet's wife; several years after his death, she married the wealthy lawyer Émile Straus, and her salon was frequented by Marcel Proust, who used her as one of his models for Mme. Verdurin, as well as the Duchesse de Guermantes. Somehow, this movie season seems to tie together.) The opera entered the public domain in 1980, and producers, directors, and assorted artists of several countries converged on it. Francesco Rosi, a great moviemaker who is open enough to admit to interviewers that this economic fact was what set his project in motion, has made a version—*Bizet's Carmen*—that has a clean, raw vivacity and is supremely romantic.

Rosi selected 1875 for the period and filmed entirely on locations in Andalusia, using Ronda and Carmona and Seville itself to simulate the Seville of that era. But the natural settings are never merely naturalistic; they have an extra, formal dimension. They're both theatrical and austere, and the striking perspectives provide something that filmed opera needs: the recognition that the singers are not ordinary people performing ordinary tasks—they're part of a ritualized performance (in this case, in four acts, with interludes). The subdued colors are toned differently in each sequence, and the screen is often intersected by diagonals—the ramp of the hilltop fort where Corporal Don José (Plácido Domingo) is stationed, the narrow, crooked street where he walks with shining-eyed Micaëla (Faith Esham), the young girl from Navarre who loves him, and whom he thinks he loves. With its whitewashed houses and stone walls, the film has the lustre of nineteenth-century painting with the near-abstract clarity of twentieth-century art.

The images are never mawkish or Zeffirelli-ish, and the scenes aren't overemotional. Rosi lets the music carry the passion. What he supplies is ideal conditions for the viewer to experience the opera as a totality. Working with his longtime collaborator, the cinematographer Pasqualino De Santis, and with Enrico Job supervising the sets and costumes, he achieves lighting so beautiful (and so evocative) that the images seem serenely right—just what the arias call for. When Carmen (Julia Migenes-Johnson) taunts the priggish Don José, they're out on the dusty beige streets, under gray-blue skies. But when he is sent to investigate a disturbance at the cigar factory, he enters the dim labyrinthine building where she and five hundred other girls work half naked. In the gypsies' camp at night, small campfires tint the darkness, and Carmen, though she's temporarily in love with Don José, keeps in practice by charming the torero Escamillo (Ruggero Raimondi). The locations look as if they had been created by a master scenic artist—a God with a pastel vision. And when Carmen has lured Don José into the life of a smuggler, and all four of the leading singers are up in a mountain pass just before dawn, the mountains, too, and the faint orange glow suggest a magnificent stage set. The images may call up Corot or Goya, but Rosi acknowledges Gustave Doré's illustrations for Baron Charles Davillier's *Spain* (which was published in serial form in 1873) as his principal source; he believes that Bizet, who was never in Spain, was guided by these engravings, and he has shot scenes in some of the exact places that Doré drew.

Julia Migenes-Johnson's freckled, gamine Carmen is the chief glory of the production; she revitalizes the story—if we have come to regard it as banal, she makes us rethink it. The proper Don José, who comes from northern Spain, is afraid of Carmen—he's repelled by her. Her strutting, her dark, messy, frizzy hair—her sexual availability—attract him and drive him crazy. Carmen, who's true to her instincts, represents everything he tries to repress. This tiny Carmen has something of a tough street urchin about her, and she has a marvellous combative stance. Migenes-Johnson, an American singer who has been appearing in musical comedy, on television, and in opera since childhood, moves quickly and impudently; she's very flexible—vocally as well as physically. She often sings quietly—seductively—and then has sudden, witty shifts of timbre; her singing always has a sense of dramatic rhythm. And she's an uninhibited carnal comedienne. Her Carmen enjoys tantalizing Corporal Don José—she tempts him mercilessly, and when she's disgusted with him her voice has the crack of a whip. (There's the possible suggestion that she teases men to show her erotic power because it's the only power she has.) When she wants Don José to join her in a smuggling job, and he wants to respond to the bugle sounding roll call, she razzes him as a little tin soldier.

In these scenes, Migenes-Johnson, with her childlike naughtiness and her twitching thighs, has a restless eroticism that makes you laugh at poor Don José—he can't hold out against her. But after he has deserted the Army and lost the respectability that meant everything to him, he thinks she owes him lifelong devotion. As Don José sees it, she's nothing more than a whore (she's perfectly willing to be a harlot-decoy for her smuggler friends), yet he's having trouble hanging on to her. By then, Carmen sees him for what he is: a suffering middle-class clod. Sick of his ordering her around and his moping over what he gave up for her, she's ready to fall in love with the handsome torero.

It was Don José's stuffy middle-classness—his being a big fool— that amused Carmen in the first place; he was a challenge. Her mistake was in thinking she could take him as a lover on her own terms. The film's romantic motor is Carmen's trying to assert her sexual freedom, and Plácido Domingo's Don José looms very large as an implacable lump blocking her path. Domingo's Don José has a self-centered sameness about him—he has no light side, even vocally. He has no brutal side, either. Domingo has beautiful modulations, yet his musicianship seems to homogenize emotion: his voice is majestically bland. But his tenor is perhaps peerless for storytelling: narrative arias roll out of him with superb ease. And his squareness here has its own operatic quality. He has the sturdy oppressiveness of a man who thinks to persuade a woman to stay with him by saying that he'll be anything she wants. Domingo plays the clod to perfection.

The movie has many felicities. Initially, Faith Esham's Micaëla has a lovely squinty smile that's like a good-luck charm; she has something of a minx about her. After she has lost Don José, the smile is gone, and when she's alone in the mountains singing the soprano aria that may be the finest song in the opera, her voice has the plangency of a young woman who sees no end to her aloneness. The resplendent basso Raimondi is a tall, elegant Escamillo—a man who has been a popular idol for so long that he's like a natural aristocrat. Riding through the mountains on his white steed, he cuts a great profile. You feel he appreciates Carmen for her gaiety, her fearlessness—for her not being the middle-class woman that Don José wants to turn her into. The straightforward screen adaptation that Rosi (and Tonino Guerra) worked out stays with Bizet's original version, which used spoken dialogue. (The infernal recitatives were a later "refinement.") With choreographic help from Antonio Gades, Rosi deploys the choruses to better effect than I can recall ever seeing before in opera on the stage or on the screen—his handling suggests the most fluently stylized movie musicals. There's a wonderful courtly old man (Enrique El Cojo), short and heavy-set—a man bowed down by the weight of the years—who partners Carmen in a dance in the square outside the factory. Rosi takes the time to fit in moments like this which round out the movie.

Much of the pleasure of the film is in its satisfying structure. At the opening, the matador Escamillo is seen in the bullring. He's in closeup and the bloodied bull is in closeup. Escamillo comes in for the kill, and the tragic black beast sinks down, as the overture begins. The crowd cheers, and the bull's carcass is dragged out on the sand while the bullfighter is carried around the ring on the shoulders of his admirers. Then another ritual is seen: a religious procession, with figures in black carrying tall candles around a statue of the Blessed Virgin. In the fourth act, Escamillo is once more in the ring, and once more we see a closeup of the bull's head—the deathly blackness filling the screen. These scenes are as stylized and ritualistic as the rest of the movie, but in a more intense way. At the end, just outside the bullring where Escamillo is being cheered Don José and Carmen have their final fracas. He's in a black suit, and Carmen, for the first time, is dressed in a ladylike outfit —a deep-rose tailored dress with a bolero top that suggests a toreador's jacket, and a black lace mantilla. The conventional clothes—she's wearing them to please Escamillo, who bought them—seem to diminish her. And her defiance of Don José and the brute force he incarnates is all the more poignant because of this dress-up dress. She's a gypsy urchin defying the male-dominated, Church-dominated social system. She dies in what is probably the only expensive dress she ever had, and it's all wrong on her.

October 29, 1984

FAKED OUT, COOLED OUT, BUMMED OUT

At the start of *The Little Drummer Girl,* Diane Keaton is jittery and off-putting. As Charlie, an American actress working in a small, third-rate repertory company in England, she comes on strong and talks faster than anybody else. She's like someone on speed or on a caffeine jag: she responds to what people say before they've finished saying it. Then she's dissatisfied with what she hears herself rattling off, and before the words are out of her throat she half wants to take them back. The conception of Charlie is a modern cliché, a piece of psychobabble: she's an actress—i.e., a woman without a center, a flighty woman who feels empty and is looking for a role to play that will make her feel "real." But Keaton takes this conception so far that she gives it a painful, shrill validity. She doesn't do anything to make you like Charlie.

257

Rather, she shows you this woman's avid attempts to be lovable, and she plays the part without creamy makeup; her dark, smudgy eyeliner and the pile of curls covering her forehead make her look flirtatious and anxious. It took me a while to comprehend that Diane Keaton was being off-putting because she was totally in character. Charlie is emotionally hungry. Smart and brazenly attractive, she's so miserably starved there's something wolfish about her. At the same time, she's trying to be tough—she's trying not to let herself be kidded. She's a jangled, poignant mess.

This George Roy Hill version of John le Carré's *The Little Drummer Girl*, adapted by Loring Mandel, suffers from a dramatic flaw that is built into the material. The movie is set in 1981, during a rash of Palestinian terrorist bombings of Israeli institutions around the world. Charlie, a left-wing pro-Palestinian, has taken part in demonstrations in Trafalgar Square and shown her enthusiasm at a meeting addressed by a terrorist. Kurtz (Klaus Kinski), the head of an Israeli intelligence unit that is engaged in counterterrorist activities, perceives that this actress, eager for a cause, and already associated with the pro-Palestinian left, could be used as a shill to trap the chief Palestinian terrorist. He turns her thinking around, and recruits her to infiltrate the Palestinian guerrillas and serve as a double agent. The flaw is that as the movie is presented the two sides are tarred with the same brush: decent, intelligent, disciplined people in both camps commit unspeakable, barbarous acts. But this pseudo objectivity seems to cancel everything out. The film is proudly noncommittal, while the audience is waiting for something (or someone) to commit itself to.

The tragedy of these two peoples, killing each other because each has just claims to the same plot of ground, is presented with efficient, impersonal evenhandedness, so that we care about neither of them. "We weren't making a political film," Hill told an interviewer from the *Times* last month. What, then, were they making? According to Hill, "a suspense story that happened to have a political background." That may sound perfectly reasonable, but there's a lunacy about using an ongoing tragedy as a plot convenience. (And Hill must know it, because in the next breath he expressed his pride in having treated the Palestinians as he believes they were treated in the book—"in a human light.") The movie was shot on locations in West Germany, England, Greece, and Israel, with intricately staged realistic bombings and tortures and a Palestine Liberation Organization training camp, and with characters of many nationalities played by actors of an even larger number of nationalities. Hill has the willingness to take on a project with these huge logistical problems, and he's able to lay out the plot lucidly, profession-ally. What he doesn't have is the ability to create the texture of a conflict where no justice is possible or to give you any feeling for the spirit or the individuality of either camp. He proceeds in a detached, businesslike way, showing us cruelty now on one side, now on the other—he balances the books.

And when it becomes apparent that Kurtz's manipulation of Charlie's need for involvement and approval is the emotional center of the movie it isn't enough. When Charlie's activities become more danger-ous and she begins to respond to the intelligence unit as a family cheer-ing her on to greater deeds, the narrative develops a viselike effect, and we experience some of the tension of what she has been drawn into. Yet the atmosphere is a blank, and the movie is too big to be a suspense story about the effects of violence on Charlie. There's a disproportion here. We see too many Israelis and Palestinians murdered for us to zero in on whether this wreck of a woman is emotionally destroyed or finds love— or both, which is what the ending suggests.

Clearly, Diane Keaton's Charlie digs being center stage, but in the glimpses of her as Shaw's Saint Joan and as Rosalind in *As You Like It* she's peculiarly offhand and unemotional. Even an actress who's los-ing her youth and knows that she's not getting anywhere could have a little more showmanship; Charlie seems too flaccid a performer. As Keaton plays her, she's much more vivid and emotionally naked offstage. Klaus Kinski's Kurtz maneuvers her like a master puppeteer, and she responds gratefully. (Kinski still has his purring, Peter Lorre accent, but he cuts down on his eye-popping shenanigans and does a respectable enough piece of work; he brings a plausible streak of impatience to the rather conventional role of the longtime agent who doesn't fool himself with the niceties of idealism and gets the dirty job done.) Although Keaton works hard at it, there's no electricity between Charlie and the stolid, manly Israeli agent Joseph (played by the Greek actor Yorgo Voyagis), whom she is supposed to fall in love with; Charlie doesn't seem to be the sort of woman to respond to a man who's like an oak tree with yearning, cow eyes. There's a lot more spark in the air when she's with Sami Frey, who plays Khalil, the star Palestinian terrorist—the man she is sent to ensnare. Frey, in black leather, gives the movie it's only bravura. He has a small role (in terms of screen time), but when Khalil realizes that Charlie has set him up for slaughter his twisted smile at his own gullibility makes you feel what's missing from the role of Charlie. As Khalil, Frey makes direct contact with the audience in a way that Keaton doesn't until well into the second hour.

A woman without a clear sense of identity is highly problematic as the protagonist-victim of a journalistic spy melodrama. Diane Keaton has, of course, played women with identity problems before; that was Annie Hall's trouble—she kept putting herself down, apologetically, and Keaton made a light art out of indecision, exasperated sighs, eyes rolling upward. Charlie, though, isn't comic. She has all of Annie Hall's self-consciousness and self-doubt, and, yes, she's distrustful yet overeager. But it isn't charming flakiness; it's desperate flakiness—you can read the panic in her flickering expressions. And the character of Charlie, who, wanting to be a heroine, gets into a world of horrors beyond her imagining, is maybe *too* flaky to give the shallow picture substance and resonance.

Keaton's performance starts clicking when Charlie is in the Palestinian camp and has to condemn an Israeli boy to death, and it snaps together in a shocking scene toward the end, when Khalil asks Charlie what she is, and she howls out what she feels is the truth about herself. Keaton takes you right into the core of Charlie's neurosis; she galvanizes the audience, and for an instant the movie seems to work. But the tense, abrasive Charlie doesn't have anything of the conventional heroine about her, and she's at odds with Hill's logical methods of storytelling. (If she were more conventional, she might fit into the movie better, but we'd forget the whole thing immediately.) Keaton leaps right over likability and crowd-pleasing—she's out there all alone doing something daring. Sometimes the performances we remember the most are the ones that threw us off initially; I wasn't prepared for Keaton's passionate immersion in her role. Her Charlie is a compulsive liar who keeps trying on styles and discarding them, looking for one that will convey sincerity; she winds up a compulsive truthteller. It's maddening that this performance can't carry the dead weight put on it.

□

Jim Jarmusch's *Stranger Than Paradise*, which was honored at Cannes this year and received an enthusiastic press at the recent New York Film Festival, is an easy film to like. Jarmusch, a young American writer-director, uses a minimalist aesthetic for low-key comic effects. The film is in black-and-white, and each scene is a single take followed by a blackout. So each bit of action (or, as is mostly the case, stagnation) is separate, discrete, and the three anomic principal characters—deadpan deadbeats—live in dead space. They're like druggies, but without drugs; they're drugged on their own apathy. They're also—and this is what makes the film a popular novelty item on the order of the 1959 *Pull My Daisy*—rather sweet.

The first section is set in the bare Lower East Side apartment of Willie (John Lurie), who is forced to take in Eva (Eszter Balint), his sixteen-year-old cousin from Budapest, for ten days. The joke here is the basic joke of the whole movie. It's in what Willie doesn't do: he doesn't offer her food or drink, or ask her any questions about life in Hungary or her trip; he doesn't offer to show her the city, or even supply her with sheets for her bed. And it's in Eva's not expecting any civility. Willie is tall and skinny and glum, with broad lips and a long, squashed nose, and even when he's sitting at home in his suspenders watching TV he wears a little, narrow-brimmed felt hat on top of his sad horseface. Willie has a lumpen, melancholic look, and you'd think there wasn't another person in the world like him. Then Eddie (Richard Edson), who hangs out with him, comes in, and he's like Willie's long-nosed twin, even to the dumb little hat, except he's not as tall. Eddie is more sociable than Willie but even further down on the lumpen scale. Willie bets on the horses; Eddie bets on dog races. These two go out into the cold streets to loaf around, and in this movie—with virtually nothing going on—we fixate on Eddie's regretful look. He thinks they should take Eva along—she's rather pretty, and, with her toneless way of talking (on the rare occasions when she speaks), she seems to fit right in. But Willie vetoes the idea. He doesn't show any cordiality to her until shortly before her ten days are up, when she brings home some groceries and cigarettes she has snitched; then he shakes her hand and tells her she's all right—he means she's scroungy and marginal, like him.

The movie is a punk picaresque. Eva, who never gets to see more of New York than the drab, anonymous-looking area where Willie lives, goes off to Cleveland to stay with Aunt Lotte and work at a hot-dog stand. And when, a year later, Willie and Eddie take their winnings from cheating at poker, borrow a car, and go to Cleveland to see her, all they see is an icy wasteland—slums and desolation—and Eddie says, "You know, it's funny. You come to someplace new, and everything looks just the same." When the men decide to go to Florida, and they take Eva with them, they stop at a crummy motel on a bleak stretch of windswept coast, and, yeah, once again everything looks just the same. But only in this movie—though I swear I heard someone quoting Eddie's line appreciatively, as if it weren't part of a gag, as if there were something deep to it. *Stranger Than Paradise* is a nothing-ever-happens movie; it has something of the same bombed-out listlessness as Paul Morrissey's 1970 *Trash*—it's *Trash* without sex or transvestism. Jarmusch pays more attention to the film frame, though, and to keeping the movie formal and cool.

The images, like the characters' lives, are so emptied out that Jarmusch makes you notice every tiny, grungy detail. And those blackouts have something of the effect of Beckett's pauses: they make us look more intently, as Beckett makes us listen more intently—because we know we're in an artist's control. But Jarmusch's world of lowlifers in a wintry stupor is comic-strip Beckett. There's no terror under or around what we see—the desolation is a gag. And the three characters' unexpressed affection for each other gives the film a pulpiness. These three are some kind of cross between what punk used to mean and what punk has come to mean. (Their affectlessness seems both pre-civilized and post-civilized.) Tough, forlorn Eva, listening to the woozy rhythms of the Screamin' Jay Hawkins record "I Put a Spell on You," really just wants a little sunshine and companionship, and the men would like to give it to her, but they don't know how. The film draws you in by its use of an absurdist style to show you people who walk through their lives expecting almost nothing. Then it holds you by their efforts to get closer to each other. Punk cool plus glimmers of warmth, and a too cute downer ending—that doesn't add up to an aesthetic crime, but it's not a big deal, either.

Stranger Than Paradise has an odd, nonchalant charm; it's fun. But it's softhearted fun—shaggy-dog minimalism—and it doesn't have enough ideas (or laughs) for its ninety-minute length. It has its own look —which is a genuine accomplishment—but it isn't as entertaining as the messier *Repo Man.* Jarmusch (who raised the $120,000 to make the film) and his cinematographer, Tom DiCillo, clearly know what they're doing, and the idea of single-take scenes to convey comic anomie is a very astute one, but the format wears thin. When the two bozos head out for Cleveland and we see them during their dismal, wet drive, there's no variety—no relief from the gloom. It's just a long, boring trip. At times all you can admire Jarmusch for is his relentlessness in holding to the dejected, empty look. At his best, he has the kind of irrational, instinctive timing that can catch you off guard and make you laugh out loud—as I did at the scene where Willie and Eddie are playing cards with decrepit old Aunt Lotte (Cecillia Stark), and she loudly announces, "I am the veener." But to think *Stranger Than Paradise* was a knockout of a movie you'd have to tune in to its minimalism so passively that you lowered your expectations. The film is so hemmed in that it has the feel of a mousy Eastern European comedy; it's like a comedy of sensory deprivation.

☐

If Brian De Palma were a new young director, *Body Double* would probably be enough to establish him as a talented fellow. In its own terms, this murder mystery set in L.A., in the overlapping worlds of "serious" acting and performing in porno films, is stupid yet moderately entertaining, and it has a tickling performance by Melanie Griffith as Holly Body, a porno star with a punk-vamp haircut and a sprig of holly tattooed on her rump. But, coming from De Palma, *Body Double* is an awful disappointment: the voyeuristic themes and the scare sequences are so similar to elements of his earlier movies that you keep waiting for the thrills—the moments when he'll top himself. And he doesn't. He doesn't equal himself, either. He stages the big scenes mechanically, without the zest that used to send them off to horror-comedy heaven. He has grown past this material, and he must know it. (According to his statements in the press, he took on the directing end of this project, which he had been scheduled to produce, only after repeated failures to raise money for projects he had prepared—one on the Yablonski murders, with a script he wrote with Scott Spencer, and one on a rock star like Jim Morrison, with John Travolta in the part.)

The central role here is played by Craig Wasson, which is the worst piece of casting in a De Palma movie since Cliff Robertson stared at the camera and drifted through *Obsession*. Wasson may, in a sense, seem right for the part—a clean-cut, not too bright young L.A. actor who easily slips into voyeurism and fetishism—but what makes him seem right for it is what makes him too bland to play it. He looks like the kind of guy who as a kid had an old man's face and was always praised for being mature. Whatever Wasson does, he's dead earnest about it, and his conscientious acting is a drag on the movie. Dennis Franz plays the horror-film director who fires Wasson from his job as the vampire in *Vampire's Kiss* for the very good reason that the claustrophobic Wasson is paralyzed with fear if he's put in a tomb. Franz does his scuzzo number: the guy who's so blatantly uncouth he's funny—only this time he isn't. The movie has no center, and it's a washout until Holly Body arrives, close to the midway point; we were waiting for something, and she turns out to be it.

Double-entendres in the movies used to be labored; here it's as if the atmosphere around Holly—where she works, what she does—were so porny that she couldn't talk except in double-entendres. She's like a dirty-minded teen-age seductress, and what she says has an element of surprise even for her; her talk is so sexy it gives her ideas and drives her eyebrows up. De Palma's affection for funkiness makes Melanie Griffith's performance possible, and in scenes such as Holly's barging into the middle of traffic trying to hail a taxi De Palma gets a fresh visual quality, too. Most of the film's best moments have to do with actors and actors' lives; there's a sisters-under-the-skin moment when Holly Body meets a "serious" actress who's looking for a job, and tries to be helpful, neither of them realizing that they're not in the same line of work. (It's like the wonderful fluke encounters in early De Palma films, such as *Hi, Mom!*)

But the big, showy scenes recall *Vertigo* and *Rear Window* so obviously that the movie is like an assault on the people who have put De Palma down for being derivative. This time, he's just about spiting himself and giving them reasons not to like him. And these big scenes have no special point, other than their resemblance to Hitchcock's work. Crude, real fears were addressed in De Palma's earlier films. *Phantom of the Paradise* made everything you'd heard about the rock industry as a gigantic casting couch come true, *Carrie* was about the dread of menstruation, *Dressed to Kill* was about your qualms that sexual pleasure would get you into trouble, *Blow Out* was about your apprehensions that you were a coward and would fail those who counted on you, and so on. But *Body Double* has no subject other than the plot contraption that De Palma and his co-writer, Robert J. Avrech, thought up—unless there are a lot of claustrophobes in the audience. The only thing that's new here in terms of getting at deeper fears is the dirt flung onto (living) people in graves, and that isn't particularly well worked out.

Body Double is not, to put it mildly, a spirited piece of moviemaking. It features (on a character called "the Indian") the worst makeup job of recent times. And the score (by Pino Donaggio) seems to have been ladled over the images. (The thought of what some of the scenes might have been like without it is a little frightening.) There's a key difference between this picture and good De Palma. In *Carrie*, when the camera moves languorously around teen-age girls in a high-school locker room there's a buzz between the camera and what it's filming. But here De Palma and his cinematographer, Stephen H. Burum, get away from the out-of-work actors' low-rent apartments and the litter of pizza rinds very quickly. De Palma saves the languorous camera for the sleek, expensive settings, such as the Beverly Hills shopping mall called the Rodeo Collection, and there's not only no comic buzz—the camera seems wowed, impressed. The voyeuristic sequences, with Wasson peeping through a telescope, aren't particularly erotic; De Palma shows more sexual feeling for the swank buildings and real estate.

November 12, 1984

THREE CHEERS

Stop Making Sense makes wonderful sense. A concert film by the New York new-wave rock band Talking Heads, it was shot during three performances at the Hollywood Pantages Theatre in December, 1983, and the footage has been put together without interviews and with very few cutaways. The director, Jonathan Demme, offers us a continuous rock experience that keeps building, becoming ever more intense and euphoric. This has not been a year when American movies overflowed with happiness; there was some in *Splash*, and there's quite a lot in *All of Me*—especially in its last, dancing minutes. *Stop Making Sense* is the only current movie that's a dose of happiness from beginning to end. The lead singer, David Byrne, designed the stage lighting and the elegantly plain performance-art environments (three screens used for back-lit slide projections); there's no glitter, no sleaze. The musicians aren't trying to show us how hot they are; the women in the group aren't there to show us some skin. Seeing the movie is like going to an austere orgy—which turns out to be just what you wanted.

Clean-shaven, with short hair slicked back, and wearing white sneakers and a light-colored suit, with his shirt buttoned right up to his Adam's apple, the gaunt David Byrne, who founded the group, comes on alone (with his acoustic guitar and a tape player) for the first number,

"Psycho Killer." He's so white he's almost mock-white, and so are his jerky, long-necked, mechanical-man movements. He seems fleshless, bloodless; he might almost be a black man's parody of how a clean-cut white man moves. But Byrne himself is the parodist, and he commands the stage by his hollow-eyed, frosty verve. Byrne's voice isn't a singer's voice—it doesn't have the resonance. It's more like a shouter's or chanter's voice, with an emotional carryover—a faintly metallic wail—and you might expect it to get strained or tired. But his voice never seems to crack or weaken, and he's always in motion—jiggling, aerobic walking, jumping, dancing. (They shade into each other.) Byrne has a withdrawn, disembodied, sci-fi quality, and though there's something unknowable and almost autistic about him, he makes autism fun. He gives the group its modernism—the undertone of repressed hysteria, which he somehow blends with freshness and adventurousness and a driving beat. When he comes on wearing a boxlike "big suit"—his body lost inside this form that sticks out around him like the costumes in Noh plays, or like Beuys' large suit of felt that hangs off a wall—it's a perfect psychological fit. He's a handsome, freaky golem. When he dances, it isn't as if he were moving the suit—the suit seems to move him. And this big box that encloses him is only an exaggeration of his regular nerd-dandy clothes. Byrne may not be human (he rejects ordinary, show-biz forms of ingratiation, such as smiling), but he's a stupefying performer —he even bobs his head like a chicken, in time to the music.

After Byrne's solo, the eight other members of the group come on gradually, by ones and twos, in the order in which they originally joined up with him, so you see the band take form. Tina Weymouth, the bass player, who also sings, comes on next; a sunny, radiant woman with long blond hair, she's smiling and relaxed. (She couldn't be more unlike Byrne —he's bones, she's flesh.) Watching her, you feel she's doing what she wants to do. And that's how it is with the drummer, Chris Frantz, and the keyboard man, Jerry Harrison, and the others in the sexually integrated, racially integrated group. The seven musicians and the two women who provide vocal backing interact without making a point of it; you feel that they like working together, and that if they're sweating they're sweating for themselves, for their pleasure in keeping the music going. They're not suffering for us; they're sharing their good times with us. This band is different from the rock groups that go in for charismatic lighting and sing of love and/or sex. David Byrne dances in the guise of a revved-up catatonic; he's an idea man, an aesthetician who works in the modernist mode of scary, catatonic irony. That's what he emanates. Yet when the other Talking Heads are up there with him for a

song such as "Once in a Lifetime" the tension and interplay are warm
—they're even beatific. The group encompasses Byrne's art-rock solitari-
ness and the dissociation effects in the spare—somewhat Godardian—
staging. The others don't come together with Byrne, but the music
comes together. And there's more vitality and fervor and rhythmic dance
on the stage than there is with the groups that whip themselves through
the motions of sexual arousal and frenzy, and try to set the theatre
ablaze.

It's slightly puzzling that this band's music absorbs many influences
—notably African tribal music and gospel (the climactic number here is
"Take Me to the River")—yet doesn't have much variety. The insistent
beat (it stays much the same) works to the movie's advantage, though.
The pulse of the music gives the film a thrilling kind of unity. And
Demme, by barely indicating the visual presence of the audience until
the end, intensifies the closed-off, hermetic feeling. His decision to keep
the camerawork steady (the cinematographer, Jordan Cronenweth, used
six mounted cameras, one hand-held, and one Panaglide) and to avoid
hotsy-totsy, MTV-style editing concentrates our attention on the performers and the music. The only letdown in energy, I thought, was in
Byrne's one bow to variety—when he left the stage for the Tom Tom
Club number. It's a likable number on its own, but it breaks the musical
flow. (It's also the only number with a cluttered background, and it has
a few seconds of banal strobe visuals.) One image in the film also stuck
in my craw: a shot of a little boy in the audience holding up his white
stuffed unicorn. It's just too wholesome a comment on the music. But
these are piddling flaws. The movie was made on money ($800,000) that
was raised by the group itself, and its form was set by aesthetic considerations rather than a series of marketing decisions. (This is not merely a
rock concert without show-biz glitz; it's also a rock-concert movie that
doesn't try for visual glitz.) Many different choices could have been made
in the shooting and the editing, and maybe some of them might have
given the individual numbers (there are sixteen) more modulation, but
in its own terms *Stop Making Sense* is close to perfection.

The sound engineering is superb. The sound seems better than live
sound; it *is* better—it has been filtered and mixed and fussed over, so
that it achieves ideal clarity. (The soundtrack-album versions of some of
the songs that are also on the Heads' 1983 album *Speaking in Tongues*
are more up, more joyous.) The nine Talking Heads give the best kind
of controlled performance—the kind in which everyone is loose. At the
end of the concert, they're still in control, but they're also carried away.
And Jonathan Demme appears to have worked in exactly the same spirit.

Alan Bird (Bill Paterson), the hero of *Comfort and Joy*, is a prim, innocuous fellow in his late thirties. When we first see him, he's tailing a beautiful red-haired kleptomaniac as she rampages through a Glasgow department store at Christmastime, grabbing everything in sight. He follows anxiously a few steps behind, and we take him for a store detective who's just about to seize her. But when they're both outside he says, "You'll be the death of me, Maddy." She kisses him lightly on the ear, and he looks at her adoringly; he's in paradise, and the two of them head home, set up their Christmas tree, and make love. A little later, Maddy (Eleanor David), who has been living with Alan for four years, starts throwing things into boxes. When he asks what she's doing, she replies, "I'm leaving," and she packs up the mountains of bric-a-brac she has accumulated, strips the house—since the contents are hers, in the sense that she shoplifted them herself—and goes off in the van with the movers she has arranged for. Alan now has nothing but a bed without sheets or blankets, and, outside, the snappy little red B.M.W. Cabriolet that he dotes on. We don't have to be told why the sexy, mad Maddy leaves. We can see Alan's pride of possession in the sparkling clean car and the complacent blankness in his face.

This latest comedy by the Scottish writer-director Bill Forsyth has a character rather than a story. It's about a romance between a man and his job. (At least, that's what gives the film much of its charm.) Alan, the disc-jockey host of the local early-morning radio show, is known to the listeners as Dickey Bird, and this ordinary, rather fussy fellow undergoes a magical transformation when he's in his glass booth, helping his listeners get through the blur of sleep and into the new day by playing records (Scottish favorites), reading commercials, supplying tips about the weather and the traffic, and improvising cheerful chatter. He's a real smoothie, changing expressions to brighten his voice, signalling to the engineer in another glass enclosure, waving to greet other members of the staff as they arrive. (The booths are much like the glass-partitioned offices that the hero of Forsyth's *Local Hero* was trapped in; Forsyth uses glass reflections in the way Altman did in *Nashville* and *The Long Goodbye*—you see an image and you see through it at the same time.) Dickey Bird turns the arriving workers into characters for his listeners, creating a daily sitcom out of the trivia of what mood they're in, the tasks they perform, and so on. He's professionally genial, and with no cynicism underneath; he has a glow of pride in his clear enunciation and his mastery of the job. It's his show—"The Dickey Bird Early Worm Show." And though there are many other characters—all of them likable in unexpected ways—we meet them because of their connections with him. He's the one we hang out with.

The movie, which was shot on locations in Glasgow (Forsyth's native city), is set in the few days before Christmas, as Alan takes to cruising around the city thinking about how empty his life is. A stunning girl, Charlotte (Claire Grogan), in a passing Mr. Bunny ice-cream van grins at him, but they're both encased in glass. Wanting to meet her, he impulsively follows the van, and sees it deliberately banged up, with much shattering of glass, by a couple of thugs. (One of them spots him and demands his autograph.) The movie is about what Alan gets into when he attempts to mediate the wrangling over turf and price between the Mr. Bunny venders and the Mr. McCool venders, two factions of an Italian family who have started roughing each other up. In short, it's about a shallow man trying to fight off loneliness and depression by changing his life, and very soon Alan's job is endangered and his car is a pathetic battered heap. "I'm a serious person, with serious friends," he tells the stunned station manager, in explanation of why he suddenly sees himself as an investigative journalist digging into the city's hidden crime (the ice-cream wars he has stumbled on).

In scenes like this, Bill Paterson plays Alan's fatuousness with just the right tone—so that you like him for it. "You wouldn't believe the things going on in this city," Alan says to the boss. He's really talking about his own state of mind; he's trying to break out of "Dickey Bird." He drives around and is lost in the new subdivisions, which are like glass enclosures, and he's wide-eyed with fascination watching grown men— the venders—in a miniature power struggle over who's going to get a choice treat, a kunzle cake. Alan has caught a glimpse of naked passion, in all its looniness. (Sweets and junk-food snacking are a motif in the film, and, of course, a principal item in the commercials on "The Dickey Bird Early Worm Show." And Alan's closest friend sums up Maddy as "choc-olate mousse.") Those who saw Forsyth's *Local Hero* or his earlier films, *Gregory's Girl* and *That Sinking Feeling,* will be familiar with the movie's swerving, unaccountable humor. In a scene at the Mr. Bunny factory, workers are welding and hammering—putting the busted vans back in shape—and re-recording the rinky-dink tinkle tune that the vans play. People in the audience laugh at different times during *Comfort and Joy,* and I think that sometimes they may be laughing simultane-ously at different jokes. (You catch on to Forsyth's jokes at your own speed, and there are always some piled up at the back of your head.)

The movie is somewhat misshapen, though; there's a deeper comedy here in vestigial form. Forsyth was trying to treat the subject of depression because he wanted to get down under his comic tone; he wanted to crack the surface—to penetrate the image of Scottish reserve and make contact with the dimness behind it. He might have been trying to do something like *McCabe & Mrs. Miller*. But he didn't, and the movie has more visual depth than he quite knows what to do with. Its visual scheme is warm and cool—amber and fluorescent blue—and it's stark raving gorgeous. The cinematographer, Chris Menges, who also shot *Local Hero* (and *The Killing Fields*), sustains this scheme with colors that are rich yet seem newly revealed. Much of the movie takes place at twilight or at night or in the pre-dawn. (Menges is amazing at catching the quality of light when you first wake up.) Forsyth was trying for a contrast between the Italians, with their emotions right out in the open, and the Scots, in their grim industrial city—a place of partitions, and of walled-in feelings that they keep way down in themselves.

Maddy walks out on Alan, and the Italians appear. They probably embody Forsyth's restlessness, his desire to break out of his comedy shell, to take risks—to take himself seriously as an artist. He wants to show that there's more irrationality in the Scottish psyche than has been assumed—Glasgow in the movie is the Scottish psyche with an Italian war going on in it. But he backs off from giving the venders any fullness as characters and uses them as petty buffoons, in some rather pinched ethnic humor. The actual ice-cream wars among the Italians in Glasgow caused five deaths last year, shortly after the film was shot, but Forsyth presents the wars (lamely) as screwball farce. And that's what throws the movie off. He outwits his own basic impulse; he sets up the conflicts, then drops them, leaving only remnants of his plan. When, for example, Alan goes to negotiate between the Italians, the meeting is outside Glasgow, in a parking lot with countryside behind it—it's freedom, it's release—and this is probably the only scene shot in straight sunlight. And when Alan stumbles upon the recipe that will resolve the dispute it's ice-cream fritters—fried ice cream, the unification of hot and cold—and he has the secret ingredient, the agent to bring them together.

But as this material has been treated it seems to be just a stupid mechanical plot that doesn't relate to Alan Bird's life falling apart. He seems to become involved in the wars simply because of Charlotte's ravishing grin, and there's no follow-through: he never even lands a date with her. We appear to be expected to share in Alan's satisfaction with the shrewd business deal he makes for thirty per cent of the profits from the fritters—a deal that includes the Italians' fixing up his car. But money wasn't his problem, and though it's apparent that his self-image has suffered the bruises inflicted on the car, we're not eager to see him back in his immaculate glass pod. The end of the movie—Christmas Day, with Alan doing a virtuoso job on the air, creating the illusion that the studio is filled with merrymakers having a Yuletide shindig—is a marvellous capper to Bill Paterson's performance, but it doesn't necessarily sit well with the viewer. It's a kind of finger-snapping end. Alan Bird's personality comes out when he's on the show, and that's a delight, but we're invited to see him as a little man, as no more than "Dickey Bird," and there's an element of betrayal in this—and of self-betrayal, too. Forsyth seems to be laughing at himself because he feels that's what we expect of him.

Comfort and Joy is much less than Forsyth must have hoped for, yet even the failed plot doesn't wreck it. Forsyth works against the usual expectations that things will get bigger; he makes things small. That may be what he wanted to fight this time (by getting under it), but it still works for him. And so does the dreamy surface. What's best is the hero's daily routines—Alan has a session recording a radio commercial which is a pure comic triumph. Everyday life is an idyll in *Comfort and Joy*. And the frothy Maddy has an idiosyncratic burr—it sounds fluted—that you want to listen to forever. It was a pity to lose her so soon in the movie. (She turns up again, but only in Alan's dreams.) I would have been happy to see her raid a few more department stores, but Forsyth never milks a joke. Nothing is forced; something is raised, and then it's up to you. That's what puts him in a class by himself.

□

I rather dreaded going to see *A Soldier's Story*, the film version of Charles Fuller's *A Soldier's Play*, because I expected it to be one of those overexplicit socially conscious plays transferred to the screen with all the characters making speeches to the camera. Well, it is and it isn't. The speeches are there, all right, but the director, Norman Jewison, who made the crack 1967 comedy-mystery *In the Heat of the Night*, can sometimes summon up a highly entertaining kind of craftsmanship. *A Soldier's Story*, which has an atmosphere that recalls the 1967 film, has a beautiful sense of pace, and Jewison brings out all the humor he can find. The movie is set on and around an Army base in Louisiana in 1944. A black drillmaster, Sergeant Waters (Adolph Caesar), has been murdered, and a black lawyer, Captain Davenport (Howard E. Rollins, Jr.)—the first black commissioned officer ever to be seen in this part of the country—has been sent down from Washington, D.C., to investigate the killing. As he interrogates the black troops and white officers at the base, we see, in flashback, what led up to the murder. The flashback structure is handled very artfully—and this artfulness saves the picture, I think. Sergeant Waters is a stage villain, and Adolph Caesar plays him as a skinny bantam with a strained, angry, low rasp of a voice and such lip-twisting nastiness that he would have been intolerable in the present. (The skillful interweaving of the flashbacks provides distancing.)

Fuller (who did the screen adaptation of his play) uses the structure of a whodunit for an inquiry into the psychological dynamics of racism. And the truth is that even those of us who dread an excess of virtue on the screen may have a secret hunger for this kind of trumped-up powerful situation, in which the actors can be bigger than life. The light-skinned Sergeant Waters, as we gradually come to learn, was a Regular Army man and veteran of the First World War who tried to be whiter than the whites—trim, perfectly creased, always snapping to attention, a martinet. He suffered from an inverted form of racism: he hated the ignorant Southern blacks who he believed confirmed the whites in their bigotry. A black Hitler—on a small scale—he wanted to purge the Negro race of its lazy, shuffling clowns. It's a sickness that also afflicts people of other races and ethnic backgrounds—quiet, tasteful Jews tend to loathe "pushy" ones, and so on—but Sergeant Waters had it in a virulent, sadistic form, and he was in a position to make life hell for the black recruits. As Captain Davenport gathers the horrifying evidence of how Sergeant Waters treated the men in his platoon, he soon recognizes that the blacks had more reason to kill him than any of the whites had. And we get a parade of confrontation scenes between Davenport and the white officers, who are stunned to see a black officer and don't know how to deal with the embarrassment it causes them, and between Davenport and the black soldiers, as he pokes into what they're concealing.

The result is a tense, wholehearted combination of melodrama and psychodrama, and, as most of the time Davenport is one-on-one with the people he questions, a number of actors get to dominate the screen for a scene or two, and they do solid, lightning-fast characterizations. The standout is Denzel Washington (of the TV series "St. Elsewhere"); as Peterson, the best educated of the group, he never overacts, yet we always know what he's thinking, and he draws us into his detestation of the scummy sergeant. There are also finely detailed performances by

Art Evans, Larry Riley, David Alan Grier, Robert Townsend, and David Harris. And there are several good serio-comic performances in the white officers' roles—most notably by Dennis Lipscomb, as Captain Taylor, a Bob Newhart type who's trying to be decent to Captain Davenport but doesn't quite know how. If the black actors come through stronger in this movie, it's partly the way their roles are conceived, but also, and maybe in larger share, a result of Jewison's care and feeling, and of the loving treatment afforded the black actors by the cinematographer, Russell Boyd. The Caucasians are pasty and pink; the black actors' skins seem iridescent. And Rollins, who is perhaps the darkest of them, is the most gleaming, and is photographed so that he has a heroic, sculptural presence. He's the visual star of the movie, yet he's still rather rigid as an actor; he doesn't have much give and take, and even when he uses his aloofness in terms of the Davenport character he lacks excitement. It may be that we want too much from him, because he's in the role that Sidney Poitier used to play with a power and a grace that brought you right inside his emotions and knocked you silly. Rollins has too much properness in his acting, but he eases up after a while and becomes more likable.

It's a funny thing about the movie—it almost clicks, except at its core. There's some daring in Fuller's perception that in a racist society the temptation toward self-hatred is part of being black, and that Captain Davenport and Sergeant Waters' killer suffer from it, as Waters did. Yet the moviemakers themselves—the black Fuller, the white Protestant Jewison—don't want to show us the kind of lewd or loutish or plumb ignorant black who might really make other blacks feel disgraced. The particular target that the barking-seal Sergeant Waters singles out for his abuse—Larry Riley's C.J., a guitar-playing, blues-singing Mississippi farm boy who is also the star of the black baseball team—doesn't ring any psychological bells. (The easygoing, slow-moving C.J. has his own dignity; he doesn't represent what Waters hates and fears in himself.) The movie seems to be a black version of *Billy Budd*, with Sergeant Waters as Claggart, but the attraction-repulsion between him and C.J. is missing. Fuller's conception is totally asexual; that may be what gives the film a hollowness right at its center.

What's surprising about *A Soldier's Story* is how enjoyable it is despite its limitations, and how well shot it is. Even the scenes that open out the play—such as the beginning, at an off-base café, where Patti LaBelle sings for the black servicemen, and a blacks-versus-whites baseball game, and the going-to-war ending (which is different from the play's)—are effective. The people who complain "They don't make movies the way they used to" ought to take a look at this one. The ones who don't complain might take a look, too.

November 26, 1984

UNREAL

The Killing Fields, which is based on Sydney Schanberg's 1980 *Times Magazine* article "The Death and Life of Dith Pran," is by no means a negligible movie. It shows us the Khmer Rouge transforming Cambodia into a nationwide gulag, and the scenes of this genocidal revolution have the breadth and terror of something deeply imagined. The picture is at its most powerful when nobody is saying a word. When the director, Roland Joffé, and his cinematographer, Chris Menges, are looking at the wind from the choppers buffeting the American evacuees or at roads packed with masses of confused, displaced people or at purplish, hothouse landscapes, each widescreen image seems to make a complete statement. These images suggest paintings, because the horror and the exotic colors are "unreal." We see what Dith Pran meant in the article when he said that "in the water wells, the bodies were like soup bones in broth, and you could always tell the killing grounds because the grass grew taller and greener." The landscapes appear to absorb the cruelty and the corpses and remain pristine—paradisal. The imagery suggests a documentary made by a macabre lyric poet. It's the shallow foreground story that keeps letting us down.

In the article, Schanberg, who was the *Times'* correspondent in Cambodia from 1972 to 1975, recalls his friendship with Pran, his interpreter and assistant, who stayed on with him in Phnom Penh after the Americans were evacuated, because Schanberg was determined to cover the story and Pran knew that Schanberg would be helpless without him. The fast-thinking, multilingual Pran was able to save Schanberg—and

Jon Swain, the correspondent of the London *Sunday Times*, and Al Rockoff, an American free-lance photographer—from slaughter by the Khmer Rouge soldiers, but his Caucasian friends weren't allowed to keep him with them, and he had to slip off into the countryside. The article was a record of Schanberg's subsequent efforts to locate Pran, and the remorse and general anguish that he experienced until the wily, resourceful Pran, after four years of slave labor and hiding and pretending to have been an illiterate cabdriver, made his way into Thailand, late in 1979, and got word to him. Schanberg's account may have seemed like first-rate screen material: a story of the friendship of an Asian and an American, against the canvas of a brutal revolution.

But as it comes across in this British film, Pran, played by Haing S. Ngor, who was a physician in Cambodia and now lives in Los Angeles, is selflessly good, and Sam Waterston's bearded Schanberg is an idealistic journalist driven to pursue the truth, but he's also a manipulative fellow who's morbidly sensitive, stuck-up, and humorless. In Cambodia, the film's Schanberg seems to be in chronic pain from the weight of his determination to get the story: he paces irritably and glowers with importance; he stands as if he were doing his best to relax while on the rack. Back home, he mopes and looks distressed, and the hoarseness in his stagey voice equals moral agony. The way the movie is constructed, Schanberg's consciousness is the battlefield, the theatre: we're supposed to be watching what Cambodia makes him feel, and if he'd forgotten about Dith Pran the movie would have ended. It's almost as if Cambodia only existed to make Waterston's Schanberg suffer and soliloquize, endlessly asking, "Did I do what was right?"

Joffé is making his début as a movie director, but he has had a great deal of experience in the theatre, on television, and in documentary. He and the scriptwriter, Bruce Robinson, must have known what our reaction to Waterston's Schanberg would be: he's always bawling people out, and the only emotions he offers us are his dry angst and his guilt. The moviemakers may have intended us to perceive some sort of equivalency between Schanberg's irresponsible treatment of Pran and the United States' irresponsible actions in Cambodia: the bombing that Nixon kept secret, and the invasion, and the support of the corrupt, unpopular Lon Nol government—all of which contributed to the demoralization that made it possible for the Khmer Rouge, under the crude (some say psychotic) Communist theoretician Pol Pot, to take power in 1975. By 1979, when the rule of the Khmer Rouge was overturned by a Vietnamese invading force, an estimated forty per cent of the Cambodians (three million out of seven) had been massacred or had died of starvation or disease. The movie quite explicitly (and cavalierly) lays the blame for this on Nixon and Kissinger—on us. It says that the American government talked high ideals while lousing things up and then waltzed away, just as Schanberg did.

Joffé is saddled with the mechanics of crosscutting between Pran's experience of the atrocities in Cambodia and Schanberg's worry and remorse in various settings in San Francisco and New York. The Schanberg-in-the-U.S. scenes have no substance; they're just filler, and some of them are worse than filler—they're designed to rub Schanberg's nose in the dirt. In one nastily pointed scene, at a plushy New York gathering at which Schanberg is honored as the 1976 "Journalist of the Year" for his dispatches from Cambodia, he goes into the men's room and runs into Al Rockoff (John Malkovich), who sneeringly accuses him of having let Pran sacrifice himself so he could pick up his big award. (It stands in for the Pulitzer Prize, which the actual Schanberg did in fact win, and the film punches up the accusation by cutting directly from Pran wading among human skeletons in the flooded rice paddies to Schanberg being applauded as he goes up to the dais to speak.)

Striving for prizes and pursuing the truth get all mixed up in this movie, and there's an unintended consequence of the emphasis on Schanberg's motives. Waterston's Schanberg, who uses the *Times* as his shield and his glory (it's what the flag is to the American Ambassador in Phnom Penh), is so cut off from other people that Pran's loyalty to him makes a viewer uncomfortable. If the "friendship" isn't a true one, if Schanberg is a self-promoter with a gnawing conscience—and that's how the movie presents him—then the small, smiling Pran is too close to the patronizing cliché of the trusting, childlike native. And his devotion to the master-race American seems flat and—well, puppy-doggy. When we see Pran in a Khmer Rouge prison labor camp undergoing forced reëducation, the light has gone out of his face. It comes back when we hear him on the soundtrack whispering his thoughts to Sydney. (It's an indication of the movie's shaping of the relationship that Pran, who in Schanberg's accounts calls him Syd, is more formal in the movie.) We don't hear Pran whispering to his wife or children—only to Sydney. And it feels fraudulent and sticky—a colonial version of "Come back to the raft ag'in, Huck honey!" Perhaps the stickiest moment in the movie is the one in which Pran, explaining to Schanberg why he has decided to stay with him, says that he's "a newspaperman, too." The pathos in this scene is naked and a bit pushy; the moviemakers show us Pran as a naïve man, duping himself. The scene also makes Schanberg more culpable, but they may not have intended that. They may simply have been trying to make us find Pran more touching and lovable—more of a victim—so that the movie would be involving.

The Killing Fields is an ambitious movie made with an inept, sometimes sly, and very often equivocal script; it's written like a TV docudrama, but you can't always tell what the scenes are getting at. A major early sequence, set in 1973, deals with the accidental bombing of a Cambodian town by an American B-52, but we don't find out what our B-52 was doing there—were the bombs intended for another country or for a different spot in Cambodia? The incident seems included so that we'll see how Schanberg and Pran work together to get the facts, despite the attempted coverup by an American diplomatic officer (Craig T. Nelson), and to introduce a suggestion of American business interests in Cambodia—Schanberg and Pran spend some time holed up in a Coca-Cola bottling plant. The questions about the B-52 are simply left dangling. Some of the episodes covering Pran's four years of slavery and escape attempts and beatings and his being tied to a tree and left for dead are almost as phonied up as the men's-room scene; there are fictional episodes in which Pran, entrusted with the child of a disaffected Khmer Rouge official, tenderly carries the little boy in his arms over dangerous mountain passes, and the glossy piousness affects even the cinematography—it becomes blandly pictorial. (The film was shot in Thailand.) Yet the power of the images of urban death squads and the mass exodus from Phnom Penh stays with you. The great scenes are so impressive that the weak ones don't cancel out your emotions. And there are some first-rate dramatic vignettes: Bill Paterson plays a harried doctor at a hospital packed full of bleeding, mangled children who were caught in the fighting between the Lon Nol government troops and the Khmer Rouge; a day or so later, he has nothing to do but tinkle the piano keys in the French Embassy and talk to another doctor (Athol Fugard) —their patients have been forced out of the hospitals and onto the roads. And there are tense moments at the French Embassy when Malkovich's Al Rockoff, in his hippie headband, and Julian Sands' Jon Swain (who's like a blond, British Edward Albert) hatch a plan to save Pran with a forged passport, and Rockoff tries to develop a passport photo of Pran, though he doesn't have the necessary chemicals. Paterson and Fugard give colorful, accomplished performances, and Malkovich does more: the function of his touchy loner character is to recede into the background, and Malkovich somehow creates a drawling, sloppy pothead who would naturally do just that. (The only sour note in the performance is the unplayable men's-room confrontation.)

It's likely that the producer, David Puttnam, undervalues the full emotional expressiveness of Joffé's vision of Cambodia under siege. Sometimes, just when we are holding our breath at what we're seeing, music, by Mike Oldfield, is poured on top of the images to pump up our emotions. During the evacuation scenes at the American Embassy, there's loud chanting. When the central characters have been taken prisoner, and they watch other prisoners being killed and expect to be killed themselves, there's music—it suggests that Oldfield was weaned on Tangerine Dream—to make the panic and hysteria more heart-poundingly intense. The executions are so convincing that I would have thought the audience had all the emotions it could handle—there are fresh corpses all over. But the music insists on hyping death. It gets between the imagery and our responses; it tries to mythologize the scenes, and it deprives us, I think, of honest feelings. When we see the dull-eyed young-boy soldiers of the Khmer Rouge forcing the entire population of Phnom Penh onto the roads out of the city—masses of people, lost children, the wounded, the aged—the soundtrack cries of the people are turned down and we get loud Oldfield. And when Schanberg is back at home he looks at TV footage of Nixon explaining his decision to bomb Cambodia and why it had to be secret, and then presses the fast-forward on his video, and we get speeded up images of atrocities at the same time that the hi-fi is on at full volume—Franco Corelli, backed by a symphony orchestra, singing the "Nessun dorma" aria from Puccini's *Turandot*. The only bit of appropriate music—or, rather, music that through some cross-cultural mystery seems appropriate—is heard under the final credits, and it's balm to the ear.

Puttnam was also the producer of *Chariots of Fire*, and in a recent interview he said, "When you're in post-production, the composer becomes vastly important. I've seen *Chariots of Fire* without a score and can speak with great authority: I don't think it would have won the Academy Award or very much else without Vangelis." I belive him, and if *The Killing Fields* had been made by the director of *Chariots of Fire* it, too, might have needed souping up. But the music is an insult to Joffé and to Menges—even if they don't know it. In the same interview, Puttnam, referring to *The Killing Fields*, explained that "over the years, I've wanted to try and make a film that could be described as 'operatic realism,'" and said, "I always wanted to try and combine the toughness of *The Battle of Algiers* with a story that was a bit more accessible and mix in some of the operatic quality, if you like, of *Apocalypse Now.*" This is a case of a producer pinning down his own aesthetic crime. It's highly doubtful that Sydney Schanberg let Dith Pran stay on with him in Phnom Penh because—as the film's innuendo has it—he was looking ahead to a Pulitzer. But it's a cold cinch that David Puttnam is hoping that the kind of musical inflation which won the Best Picture Award for *Chariots of Fire* will do the same for *The Killing Fields*. As for the friendship between Pran and Schanberg which is supposed to make the movie "a bit more accessible," it's what is most ambiguous. Among the film's lesser aesthetic crimes, there's a tiny, glaring one: Accepting his award, Schanberg makes a speech in which he refers to the American officials who made the decision to secretly bomb and invade Cambodia, and says that he and Dith Pran tried to make a record of the concrete results of those decisions. And we get a cut to a baldish man in the audience bobbing his head appreciatively. The director may not have been able to do anything about Puttnam, but surely this guy's head could have been cut off.*

Can a vacuum love another vacuum? That's the question posed by *Falling in Love*, a piece of big-star-packaging in which Robert De Niro and Meryl Streep look, respectively, handsome and pretty as Frank, an architectural engineer, and Molly, a free-lance commercial artist— two prosperous Westchester commuters, each married to someone else, in marriages that have become (who'd have thought it?) empty. We don't get a clue to what might make their own union any different, because there's nothing to draw them together. They don't share any tastes; they don't enthuse over anything; they don't argue over a book, a movie, a painting, a building, or even TV. They have nothing to say; each stares past the other into a separate space. The most compelling thing about them is the beauty-spot wart on De Niro's cheekbone: it has three dimensions—one more than anything else in the movie.

Peter Suschitzky's cinematography has a vibrancy that makes you feel hopeful, and Michael Kahn's editing has an elating precision, but after a while the pleasures of technical proficiency shrivel. Frank and Molly are too nice—too decent and loyal and conscience-stricken—to be adulterous, but they think about each other longingly, and the camera watches them think. The screenwriter, Michael Cristofer, is the gent who made terminal cancer romantic (in the play and TV film *The Shadow*

*I may have gone too far in this review in exculpating Roland Joffé: in a letter, he states that he made his own choices, and that David Puttnam is "a good, thoughtful, supportive producer."

Box); this time, he's trying to make not having sex romantic. Frank finally kisses Molly, after racing through Grand Central to find her, but maybe he's out of breath, because when he says, "I love you, I do love you," it sounds blah—it's remote, like a dubbed voice-over.

The picture has been called a new *Brief Encounter*, but it's interminable, and in some ways it's more like an East Coast *Tender Mercies*—it's about two anomics who inch their way to spiritual rebirth. Frank and Molly are so full of misgivings that when they try to go to bed together they seem to be crucifying each other; her unhappy eyes are misty and red-ringed. They can't go through with it, of course. (They can't bring themselves to do much of anything—even put a sentence together.) But they're honest people, and they have to tell their respective spouses the truth about their feelings—those gossamer feelings that the camera can't catch. (We don't actually see Molly tell her husband about Frank, but we assume she does, because the husband suddenly knows about him; this seems like a glitch, and it's jarring—it suggests that these characters have a life offscreen.) And so Frank and Molly suffer and earn their right to happiness. Their spouses conveniently reveal moral flaws: Frank's tense, distraught wife (Jane Kaczmarek, who has been the liveliest person in the movie up to this point) slaps him, and doesn't want to go on with him anyway, and Molly's husband (David Clennon) is untrustworthy—he tells a lie. (This movie takes you back to the moral bookkeeping of the Production Code days; the issue of Frank's kids is neatly squared—his wife doesn't want them, so he gets to keep them.)

Cristofer and the director, Ulu Grosbard, must believe that the patterning of old romantic movies—in which the hero and the heroine each have one best friend to confide in, and the cutting goes back and forth between parallel incidents in their lives—has some kind of formal magic to it. De Niro and Streep are made up and lighted to look creamy perfect. And New York City itself has been turned into a miracle of serenity. The commuter trains are shiny and spotless and run smoothly; there's no litter or noise or abrasiveness in Grand Central, or in any of the other locations. When Molly visits her father in the hospital, his room is large and cheerful, and if Frank and Molly go into a restaurant there's sure to be at least ten feet of clear air around their table, and the waiters and busboys and the other customers all speak in hushed tones. (If Grosbard wanted to make a Toronto movie, why didn't he just go to Toronto?) Grosbard deliberately transforms New York into a setting for a romantic fable, but since the movie has no core (no romance, no fable), this city is just a benign, brightly colored playpen for two people who are bored silly with themselves. The ultra-mediocre music, by Dave Grusin, confirms the cuddliness of the make-believe New York.

Falling in Love is too genteel and refined to be a howl. And, except for Streep's rather charming revamp of an old comic pantomime—as Molly prepares for a date with Frank, she disgustedly changes from one outfit to another and another and another, because she doesn't like the way she looks in anything—it doesn't even rise to the status of a piffle. De Niro appears to be alert and ready to do something, but the inanity seems to be worse on him than on Streep, who stays fine-tuned, as if she really thought she was in a movie; he turns numb. It's pleasant to see these two in a picture where they're not carrying all the sins of mankind on their shoulders, but they've gone too far in the opposite direction—they're not carrying anything. The purpose of the techniques of natural-istic acting that they have been trained in is for the inner emotions to be expressed in the external gestures; what they're doing here is a parody of naturalistic acting—it's all externals. The stars didn't need to be called Frank and Molly; they could have addressed each other as Nada and Nada.

The small, coy role of Streep's confidante in *Falling in Love* is played by Dianne Wiest. I just recently had the chance to catch her in a major performance, in *Independence Day*, the film by Robert Mandel, from a script by the novelist Alice Hoffman, which opened in January, 1983, and disappeared almost immediately but has now turned up on HBO. It's a very fine movie about the small-town youth of a woman artist. Kathleen Quinlan plays the part with a cool, wire-taut intensity —the heroine challenges herself to become what she's *almost* sure she could be. Her desperation takes the form of affectations and pretensions that are a little like those of the young Katharine Hepburn in *Alice Adams* and the young Margaret Sullavan in *The Shop Around the Corner*, but the Quinlan character has her talent driving her on past all that. Wiest plays a battered wife, clammy with fear, who revenges herself on her husband in the grand manner. It's a funny thing about her performance—you keep expecting it to turn into something trite, but pretty soon you're forced to admit you've never seen anything like it. Part of the credit for this goes to Alice Hoffman's writing and to Robert Mandel, who keeps the whole cast interacting quietly and satisfyingly, but most of it has to go to Wiest, who has hold of an original character and plays her to the scary hilt. Maybe *Independence Day* is the kind of small movie that seems better on television than it does in a theatre, but it has a marvellous look (it was designed by Stewart Campbell and shot by Charles Rosher), and I'd love to see it on a big screen that would give the actresses the scale they deserve.

December 10, 1984

DAVID AND GOLIATH

he David is David Lynch, who made *Eraserhead* and *The Elephant Man* and is a painter-director of feelings and moods, of dreams, hallucinations, textures. He's entranced by the interactions between the organic and the mechanical—by corrosion and rot. He likes to have strange things growing—things like polyps. Lynch is awestruck by what is generally considered disgusting; he's hypnotized by it. He shows you what he sees, and you find yourself looking at things that you normally couldn't bear and tuning in to his hypnotic state. You're caught not just by images but by silences and discombobulating sounds and editing rhythms that give you the dreamy willies. The Goliath is *Dune*, Frank Herbert's ecological sci-fi fantasy, with its own galactic system, hordes of characters parcelled out over four planets, and a Messiah— Paul Atreides, who is pre-ordained to lead the righteous in a holy war and deliver this make-believe universe from darkness and evil. The stories that make up the first *Dune* book were written on the West Coast, printed in installments in the magazine *analog*, starting in 1963, and then put in hardcover in 1965, and the book and its sequels have together sold something like fifteen million copies and are now going stronger than ever. Those are intimidating figures, and the book's reputation as a sci-fi masterpiece is intimidating, too.

Herbert fantasized about man's changes in consciousness, and about the battle over consciousness-altering drugs. The conspiracies and power struggles of the ruling families of the four planets are centered on the narcotic spice that is mined on the arid planet Arrakis, which means "dune" in the language of the natives—the Fremen. The spice gives people special powers—it raises consciousness, turns the whites of the Fremen's eyes blue, makes space travel possible, and prolongs life—but it's also addictive, and if it's used to excess it causes mutations. It holds this universe together, and Lynch brings on the giant man-eating sandworms that live beneath the desert on Dune and grow to be more than a thousand feet long. "The worm is the spice," we are told, "and the spice is the worm"—they are the same creature in different stages of its life. Undulating under the sand, these killer worms—they're as long as skyscrapers are tall—thrash up reddish and ochre dust, and when they come near the surface they zap the air with streaks of static electricity. They put on quite a show, though they're not as squishy as you might hope they'd be in a David Lynch movie.

It doesn't take long to realize that basically this isn't a David Lynch movie—it's *Dune*. Lynch doesn't bring a fresh conception to the material; he doesn't make the story his own. Rather, he tries to apply his talents to Herbert's conception. He doesn't conquer this Goliath—he submits to it, as if he thought there was something to be learned from it. He's being a good boy, a diligent director. And though Herbert's prose can prostrate a reader—it's dry, with gusts of stale poetry—Lynch treats the book so respectfully that he comes out with a solemn big-budget version of *Up in Smoke*.

The movie opens in the year 10,191, and the first half hour is practically an orientation course. Lynch has so much to do laying out the basic elements of Herbert's vision and setting the interplanetary treachery in motion that he doesn't get around to clarifying what the narcotic means to this galaxy, or to gripping the audience, either. The exposition doesn't seem to point the way to anything; the story isn't dramatized—it's merely acted out (and hurried through), in a series of scenes that are like illustrations. And several of the principal actors—those playing the Atreides family, especially—are like walking, talking pictures in a book of legends. Luckily, others (mostly in minor roles) are blissfully warped, so that we do a double take at our first sight of them, and even if they're knocked off disappointingly fast—in some cases they go right from an introduction scene to a death scene—they make their presence felt. Herbert's grandiose vision plays into only a few of Lynch's strengths, yet it's these strengths (rather than the fidelity to Herbert) that keep giving you something to look forward to. And, surprisingly, Lynch's best work here is almost all in comedy.

Lynch is at his neo-Dickensian ease when he presents the addicts: the fat and fey, red-haired Baron Harkonnen (Kenneth McMillan) and his red-haired nephews (Sting, of the rock trio The Police, and Paul L. Smith, who was Bluto in *Popeye* and the brutal chief guard in *Midnight Express*). The Harkonnen family, rulers of Giedi Prime—an ugly planet of oil and factories and industrialization (and one that seems to be devoid of women)—have been in charge of spice production on Dune, and perhaps they have overindulged. They seem to be mutating into something like overgrown Katzenjammer Kids. They're manic and giggly and mean. Kenneth McMillan's wild, grinning Baron is so spiced up that he normally floats in the air about eighteen inches off the floor. When he's excited, he goes much higher. (Padded out to weigh maybe four hundred and fifty pounds, and with a belly like a beer keg, he's the biggest Peter Pan ever.) McMillan's slobby Baron is certainly the villain of the year: his face is a mass of festering, suppurating boils, which his doctor (Leonardo Cimino), who's as mad as he is, treats with such adoring care that you're not really sure if he's lancing them or tending them like a gardener and trying to make them blossom. The Baron's sadistic pleasures and games can be guessed at when you catch glimpses of his retainers—their mouths and ears are stitched closed. You don't have to guess when you see him go gleefully high up in the air and then plunk down on a young boy. You don't recoil, though. Everything to do with the Baron is a marvel; that includes the plugs in his body, and his garments—he's trussed up in straps that look like gigantic soiled Band-Aids. And he always seems to be having an uproarious good time. His nephews love him for the spectacle: he's obscenely funny—a comic-strip Nero. (And Nero didn't levitate.)

You don't recoil, either, when Lynch presents you with a spice-produced mutant—a Third-Stage Guild Navigator, it's called—that some generations back was human. It looks like an enlarged brain, with a fish mouth and elephant eyes; it's all pinkish innards, and it floats in a tank of spice gas like an octopus in an aquarium. This huge tank is carried into the gold throne room of the Emperor of the Galaxy (José Ferrer), whose home world is the planet Kaitain. The tank is set down on the green jade floor, and the monster talks to the Emperor. It does more than that: speaking for its Guild, it gives the Emperor orders. And the power-broker Emperor, who appreciates his dignified golden splendor—he's even blessed with a lovely golden-haired daughter (Virginia Madsen)—

and is dependent on the Guild, which controls all interplanetary travel, is happy to oblige.

These orders set the plot in creaky motion. The Guild, which has secret plans to rule the universe, wants Paul Atreides killed. The Emperor sets a trap for Paul's father, who is Duke Leto Atreides (Jürgen Prochnow), the ruler of Caladan, and lives high up in a wood-panelled castle on his Earthlike planet of forests and water. In order to separate the Atreides family from its loyal subjects, the Emperor offers the Duke the biggest plum he can: the Duke is to move his family and staff to Dune and take control of the spice mining. As soon as the Duke arrives on Dune and is isolated and helpless, the red Baron attacks, slaughters him, and sends the Duke's concubine, the Lady Jessica (Francesca Annis), and their fifteen-year-old son, Paul (Kyle MacLachlan), out to die in the desert as worm fodder. And it's there in the desert that Paul grows into a mystical warrior-leader. Of course, in this feudal future all these rulers have their entourages of associates, attendants, spies, and betrayers, and there's much planet-hopping between the Emperor's gold throne room on Kaitain, the wooden Atreides castle on Caladan, the repulsive home site of the slob Baron on Giedi Prime (with its strident, psychedelic green walls, it's like an industrial prison or a public urinal), and the fortress cut into the rock which is the seat of the repressive government of Dune.

Lynch and his designing crew have done a fairly amazing job of simulating the different ecologies of the planets—their building materials and architectural styles and furnishings. And the cinematographer, Freddie Francis, lights the various sets and locations to bring out the different color values and, in some scenes, the quality of the air. The visual textures are glorious, and the golds and greens work on you. Nothing looks new, or right from the manufacturer; Lynch likes things aged, weathered—he likes decay. (And he likes dissolves—which are a metaphor of decay.) The people are dressed in styles that echo many different old cultures—among them Renaissance Venetian, Victorian, and (for the Harkonnens) punk—and this could be witty if only there were a hint of tackiness about the clothes. But they're so elegant that there's nothing to laugh at. Tackiness, though—and the wrong kind— is always present in the insistent, droning score, by Toto, with contributions by Marty Paich, Brian Eno, and others. And, despite the care that has gone into the staging, the editing rhythms are limp and choppy, and the narrative loiters on dull scenes and then rushes past the climactic ones.

The script, which Lynch wrote, has the kind of functional dialogue that pulls an epic movie down; you feel a thud when the teen-age Paul, still in his happy castle life on Caladan, reflects out loud, "Things have been so serious here lately." And at the time the handsome, resolute Paul and his beautiful, stiff-backed mother were first dumped on the desert, there were moments when I longed for the sight of a dreaded worm. Lynch seems lacking in vulgar show-biz talents; he doesn't ever get his heroic characters to lighten up. Francesca Annis's Lady Jessica is alarmingly stately, and even the miraculously gifted Sian Phillips—who, with her head shaved and almost no eyebrows, plays a sorcererlike Reverend Mother—seems a shade monotonous here.

If you ask what makes the bland Paul more fit to lead the native tribes of Dune in their rebellion against Harkonnen rule than the robust native leader (Everett McGill), the only possible answer is that the prophecy stipulated that it was to be Paul. He has less personality than anyone else in the movie—except, maybe, his father, the Duke, and his true love, Chani (Sean Young). He's just a polite, indomitable storybook hero. And when Sting, as the most agile of the Harkonnens, comes out of a steam bath stretching like a cat and just stands there half naked, displaying himself—all arrogance and spiky aplomb—he's spellbinding in a way that makes you wish David Lynch could cut *Dune* loose from its "ordained" plot. Trying to be faithful to Frank Herbert's woozy mythology, Lynch presents a singularly ambiguous and unappetizing Messiah story. I don't know how we're supposed to take this hero-savior Paul, who speaks the word of God but is also very quick to make a virtue of expediency when he decides to marry the Emperor's blond daughter and keep his true love as a concubine. And I don't know how we're supposed to react to his leading the Fremen warriors, with their blue, blue eyes, to domination of the whole Empire. The cry of these highly disciplined troops is "Long live the fighters!" There's nothing in the tone of the film to suggest an attitude toward any of this.

Lynch himself appears in a straight-arrow role as the engineer at the controls in the spice mine. Too bad that he's also such a straight arrow as a director here. The movie is most otherworldly when he does something Lynchlike—something marginal or unexplained. It's otherworldly, too, when the creepy, precocious eight-year-old Alicia Roanne Witt, as Paul's little sister Alia—a miniature sorcererlike Reverend Mother—pricks the swollen, leering Baron with a poisoned needle and pulls a plug in his chest, and he hits the ceiling. Or when Brad Dourif (he's the Harkonnens' human computer) smiles to himself like a new Dwight Frye eager to pop a spider in his mouth. Or when Linda Hunt, who's the housekeeper of the fortress on Dune—and the most imposing housekeeper since Cloris Leachman in Mel Brooks' *Young Franken-stein*—speaks, in her firm you-will-hear-what-I'm-saying tones. What a voice she has, and what a sense of comic authority! If she declared herself the rightful heir to the Emperor's throne, the audience would go wild cheering for her.

In *48 Hrs.*, Eddie Murphy played a thief, and the joke was in his sleekness and suavity, in contrast to the uncouthness of the profane white cop played by Nick Nolte. With Nolte on the receiving end, Murphy was a hipster delivering nonstop zingers. In the new *Beverly Hills Cop*, Murphy is on his own, yelling and fast-talking, and hotfooting the picture to keep it going. He has no zingers—he just rattles off pitifully undistinguished profanity—but we're cued to react to every stupid four-letter word as riotous. The whole picture is edited and scored as if it were a lollapalooza of laughs. And, with Murphy busting his sides guffawing in self-congratulation, and the camera jammed into his tonsils, damned if the audience doesn't whoop and carry on as if yes, this is a wow of a comedy.

The movie is about a Detroit cop who takes a vacation to go to Beverly Hills and hunt down the men who killed his best friend. But the plot is slipshod and insignificant even by TV cop-show standards, and we're not so much as given a scene in which to develop some feeling for the friend. The plot is just a peg for little set pieces in which the street-smart Murphy, in his worn-out sweatshirts, saunters through swank Beverly Hills locations, tells whopping lies, and outsmarts the white dumbos. This isn't a movie about an underdog—he's Mr. Top Dog, Mr. Cool. He goes to an expensive, full-up hotel, without a reservation, and pulls an elaborate whitey-baiting number in order to get a room; he's so intimidating he's given a suite, and the audience seems to love it, even though the script, by Daniel Petrie, Jr., hasn't provided any pretext for why he goes to this hotel. (The reason is simply to get laughs for baiting whitey.) Murphy bounces around town outsmarting the hotel clerks, the restaurant staffs, the crooks, the flunkies, and, especially, the police officers. The Beverly Hills cops can't drive anywhere without smashing into each other, and there's no plot point to the car pile-ups—it's just to give you a laugh at what jerks they are. The picture starts off with a big, pointless car chase in Detroit—just in case you were feeling nostalgic for your TV. And there's no rationale for the mayhem at the end, in which everybody in the cast seems to be running around with a submachine gun blasting.

The director, Martin Brest, handles a few of the minor characters well. Judge Reinhold, a young man with an old man's name, has some soothing low-key comedy moments as a credulous, velvet-voiced cop. Stephen Elliott uses his deep, lordly tones effectively as the police chief. And Bronson Pinchot does a sweetheart of a comedy turn as the amiable swishy Serge, who works in an art gallery and speaks in an unidentifiable accent. Pinchot sets his own comedy rhythms, and he steals a couple of scenes from Murphy—a relief, because Murphy's aggressive oneupmanship through most of the film kills your interest in him as a performer. Your reaction to these other actors reminds you of what unforced laughter feels like.

According to this movie, street wisdom means: You talk dirty and you lie. And if you're a cop you're contemptuous of the law. What the picture is about is merchandising: in its first weekend, Eddie Murphy alone did bigger business than Clint Eastwood and Burt Reynolds rolled together in *City Heat*. Murphy is half their age and twice their gross.

□

The love roundelay *Choose Me*, written and directed by Alan Rudolph, on a budget of $835,000, is pleasantly bananas. The characters, who wander in and out of a bar called Eve's Lounge, are lighted as if Edward Hopper lived across the street and Reginald Marsh prowled the alley; they're all vaguely amnesiac, and their dialogue is overintellectualized in a hammy-hilarious way. The songs are performed by Teddy Pendergrass, and he's just right—he does what Tom Waits is supposed to do. The entire movie has a lilting, loose, choreographic flow to it. Rudolph and his cinematographer, Jan Kieser, have developed a swoony camera style befitting the romanticism of a movie in which everyone is obsessively looking for love. A friend once wrote me that ten minutes into Rudolph's first film, *Welcome to L.A.*, he had the urge to walk out and find somebody doing something: running a jackhammer, fixing a tire, cutting hair—anything routinely useful. This movie may give him the same urge, but it's fun in something like the way that Jacques Demy's 1961 *Lola* was fun. *Lola* was about a girl whose faith in her illusions was vindicated; *Choose Me* is about a group of lovers whose madnesses and illusions interlock. It's giddy in a magical, pseudo-sultry way—it seems to be set in a poet's dream of a red-light district. And though you can't always tell the intentional humor from the unintentional, this low-budget comedy-fantasy has some of the most entertaining (and best-sustained) performances I've seen all year.

Eve is played by Lesley Ann Warren, who has a rare kind of off-and-on beauty. She has acres of eyelids in a face that can seem young and fresh or agelessly old. At moments she's Garboesque, but in the next breath she may remind you of someone as contemporary as Susan Sarandon or Margot Kidder. Her acting isn't as steady as that of the other key performers, but she brings her pivotal role the mystery that is essential to the film. (In some odd way that I won't attempt to explain, her beauty authenticates Rudolph's vision.) Geneviève Bujold has the dippiest and funniest role: she dispenses sex-therapy advice on a radio show, and when she's feeling hot she gets listeners hot. Over the years, Bujold has developed a marvellously close rapport with moviegoers; she can make us feel we're reading her mind. And here she has us entering into every twist of her character's nuthead frigidity and nymphomania; after a while, we giggle happily at sight of her, anticipating that she'll do something naughty, and she doesn't let us down. Rae Dawn Chong is the film's biggest surprise. As the part-black wife of a European racketeer, she puts a sophisticated, comic spin on her line readings, and she's ripely sensual and dirty-minded. The movie has elements of interracial fantasy: the hookers in the street outside Eve's place pair up and triple up with their johns in racially mixed combos—they meet and go off together like dancers, in rhythm with the music. Rae Dawn Chong's amours are more intense, and much more fleshly. She's presented like the occasional exotic black woman in French movies—her husband calls her *"mon petit chocolat"*—but her wit is strictly American. The only big flaw in Rudolph's sex-farce construction is that she's left stranded about half an hour before the close of the picture, and the romanticism loses some of its lift when she isn't around.

The central male role—the starring role—is played by Keith Carradine, who may never have been this impressive before, even in his performances for Robert Altman. He's playing a perhaps crazy stud, who comes to Eve's bar straight from the mental ward. It's a literary conceit of a role—the kind that almost invariably makes an actor look like an idiot. He has to suggest that he's a lunatic who's saner than anyone else, and yet emanate danger and untrustworthiness. Carradine carries it off, while boyishly hopping into all three of the women's beds. He's not callow anymore. The years have given him a handsome, sculptural presence, and he manages to validate every bad idea Alan Rudolph throws at him. Other directors aren't this lucky.

December 24, 1984

FEVER DREAM/ECHO CHAMBER

M*rs. Soffel* gets into a great subject: repressed, often well-educated women who fall in love with prisoners—men in cages. In our day, we read news accounts of a woman lawyer helping her client escape from prison, or a woman professor abetting a jailbreak, or a business or professional woman reading about a prisoner, visiting him, marrying him. *Mrs. Soffel* is based on an actual case that goes back to 1902, when the wife of the warden of the Allegheny County Jail in Pittsburgh helped two prisoners—the Biddle brothers—escape from Murderers' Row, and ran off with them. As the movie tells it, Kate Soffel (Diane Keaton) isn't radicalized in any ideological sense, and Ed Biddle (Mel Gibson) and his brother Jack (Matthew Modine) aren't political, or even big-time. They're just holdup artists who have been condemned to be hanged because someone got killed when they robbed a grocery store. But they're young and handsome, the fiery-eyed Ed swears that they're innocent of murder, and they've developed a considerable following among the impressionable women of Pittsburgh. Teen-age girls bring flowers to the prison, and the next-to-oldest of Kate's four children—the naïve twelve-year-old Margaret (Jennie Dundas)—is staunch in her belief that though the Biddles have committed ninety robberies, they're laboring-class rebels who have never hurt anyone; she pastes newspaper clippings in a scrapbook so she'll have a record of all the injustices done to them. Their case becomes political.

Working from a script by Ron Nyswaner, the young Australian

director Gillian Armstrong doesn't lay out the reasons for what happens; she evokes them partially, suggestively, inviting you to feel your way into Kate Soffel's disappointment with her marriage. We can see the torment and dissatisfaction in Kate's face, and the neurasthenia that has kept her in bed for three months, and keeps her from sharing a bedroom with the husband she married eighteen years ago, when she was seventeen. (At first, we see that she's sick and that she's married to Edward Herrmann; soon we suspect that she's sick because she's married to Edward Herrmann.) The family lives in the warden's quarters, which are built right into the jailhouse structure, and the ornately furnished rooms seem airless and confining. Surrounded by husband, children, and servants, the imprisoned Kate sits in her tightly bound clothes; under the curls on her forehead, her eyes are full of misery. As the warden's gracious, devout wife, she makes her own rounds, taking Bibles to the inmates and offering words of moral guidance. But there's something about her that makes you uneasy; she's telling the prisoners that faith will do something for them that it has obviously failed to do for her.

What's daring in the way Gillian Armstrong presents this love story is that we don't quite trust the emotions of either Kate Soffel or Ed Biddle. She's sickly, frustrated, unstable; he's an opportunist, with only one opportunity—to make her love him so madly that she'll bring him and Jack the saws they need to get out. From behind bars, he works on her, quoting the Bible in a ringing, romantic voice, challenging her by telling her he's not a believer. He asks her to read to him—that keeps her close. He writes her a poem; he touches her, grabs her, kisses her. (And Jack, in the cell next to Ed's, grins.) But Kate isn't a fool, and she's twelve years older than Ed; she's aware of how he's trying to use her. At the same time, she's sexually aroused by him—he's like a trapped animal reaching out to her, pulling her up against his cell.

Mel Gibson, who miscast can seem a lightweight, is superb here. Much wirier than in his earlier roles, he's convincingly passionate, shrewd, relentless. There's concentrated emotionality in this performance—an all-out romanticism that you don't expect from an actor who's only twenty-eight. As Ed, he's like the young Henry Fonda, but with a streak of something darker, more volatile, and more instinctively knowing. Ed comes on so strong that we don't know quite how to read him —especially since much of the time he's behind bars and we see only part of his face. He puts the squeeze on Mrs. Soffel, and it makes her feel alive; it takes a while before we realize that she does the same for him. Diane Keaton has trouble with the period role: her fast, distraught manner of speaking, the words she emphasizes, the ones she throws away—it's all very specifically modern. So is her conception of neurosis, and so, I think, is the tender, easy manner Kate has with her children. (Shouldn't she be more erratic, taking out some of her suffering on them, or, at least, be negligent and indifferent?) But she has a moment here that's freakishly inspired: Ed has been holding her against the bars and she has been speaking like a moral exemplar when suddenly, in mid-sentence, she lets out a dirty little giggle. We know then that Kate is living in a fever dream and doesn't want to wake up. And the post-hippie diction and the other surface flaws in Keaton's performance fade into relative insignificance, because the things that come from inside are so startlingly right. Kate has a broad, lewd smile when she holds out her Bible to Ed—with the saws in it; then she reads the Good Book out loud to the brothers, keeping watch for them as they saw away.

The movie is set in winter, in the grime and fumes of an industrial city at its worst, and then in snow-covered farmland as the three try to escape to Canada. There isn't a single image that looks ordinary or stale; Armstrong and her cinematographer, Russell Boyd, give us a completely fresh vision of the American past, and the whites glisten in Boyd's deep-toned shots. But Armstrong may have overdone the ominousness and gloom of the early scenes—the murk indoors and the sootiness outdoors may make the movie hard for viewers to get into. Even if you know that Pittsburgh used to need its street lights on in the middle of the day, the darkness may seem affected. If you give the movie a chance, though, it justifies the early dreamlike funereal underlay. Each of Armstrong's three features has been amazingly different from the others. As a piece of filmmaking, the first, the feminist princess fantasy *My Brilliant Career* (which she made in 1978, when she was only twenty-seven), was careful, pictorial, leisurely. The second, the pop musical *Starstruck*, set in modern Sydney and starring the blithe new-wave singer Jo Kennedy, was visually jangly and all over the place, but exuberant and likable. Clearly, Armstrong adapts herself to her subjects, and this time her style has an edginess: the scenes have unexpected tempos, the perspectives on the richly furnished Soffel household are always slightly unsettling, and we never know when we'll hear the clanging of the iron gates and doors. The prison is a major presence—it's the prison from which the actual Mrs. Soffel and the Biddles fled into the night. Designed by Henry Hobson Richardson to resemble a fortified church and built in the eighteen-eighties, it's oppressive yet in its way exalted—an architectural marvel that is still in use, housing five hundred inmates. With its majestic cell-block atrium, and the warden's quarters as part of the structure, it's a perfect setting for a Gothic romance.

This stone-and-iron monster is so solid that you may get the feeling that at first Kate Soffel could enjoy the titillating danger that Ed Biddle represented because she felt cloistered and secure—she could go anywhere in the prison, but he was safely behind bars. She could go to him, but he couldn't come to her. One thing that makes their love story different from the familiar ones is that they finally come clean with each other. She abandons her protected status; he abandons the public poses that turned her little daughter into a groupie. (And Gibson has a rare kind of delicacy when Ed offers Kate proof of his love.) There are some surprising elements in this movie—such as the confusion of the prison break, the shock of seeing Ed and Jack in the warden's quarters, the hostility that Ed and Jack's friends feel toward Kate, and the brotherly bond between the Biddles that we're aware of throughout. They match up well physically, but that's only a small part of it; Modine enables you to see how Jack takes his cues from Ed, and why Ed feels responsible for him.

Mrs. Soffel lacks humor, and its themes don't fully emerge. (The fault may be in the screenplay—that it just doesn't go far enough.) But the movie builds an excitement that has something to do with the fact that the flight of the Biddles with Kate in tow is deranged. They're killing each other by staying together, yet you can see that staying together is all that matters to them. When the three of them are out in the snow, rushing toward the border, the hurrying about makes Kate flush, and her eyes and teeth shine—she seems elated and glamorous. She's experiencing freedom, and the feelings that were buried in her are released. When a stranger says something grossly insensitive in her presence, and she slaps him, all her senses seem to be whirring. She's a Victorian madwoman heroine.

□

If a whiz-kid director from the three-minute-rock-video field tries his hand at a Jazz Age gangster musical, the result might be *The Cotton Club*. Francis Coppola, who co-wrote and directed it, seems to have skimmed the top off every twenties-thirties picture he has seen, added seltzer, stirred it up with a swizzlestick, and called it a movie. The shots don't look as if he were framing for the movie camera; they're framed for video excitement. His only goal seems to be to keep the imagery rushing by—for dazzle, for spectacle. The thinking (or the emotional state) behind his conception appears to be that it's all been done before, and that what remains is to feed your senses. He just wants to look at pretty lights, movement, color. He's watching his brain cells twinkle.

The action is centered on the famous Harlem late-night supper club that from 1923 to 1936 was situated upstairs over a theatre on the corner of 142nd Street and Lenox Avenue—a speakeasy with a great floor show, in which "colored" headliners and the "tall, tan, and terrific" Cotton Club Girls (who were required to be "high yaller," under twenty-one when hired, and at least five feet six) performed for a white clientele. The club was a showcase for the "primitive" joyousness and sensuality of the black singers and dancers, and the revues, which were produced by whites and ran for an hour and a half or two hours, with the last of the three nightly shows starting at 2 A.M., had motifs in keeping with the club's advertising itself as a "window on the jungle . . . a cabin in the cotton." (The jungle predominated, and the club itself was decorated jungle style.) Seven hundred socialites, celebrities, Broadway stars, bootleggers, and assorted mobsters could be seated at the tiny tables, arranged in a horseshoe around the dance floor; among them might be Mayor Jimmy Walker, Fred Astaire, Irving Berlin, Fanny Brice, Charlie Chaplin, and such underworld figures as Legs Diamond, Dutch Schultz, and Lucky Luciano. Starting in 1927, the house bandleader was Duke Ellington, and he soon began broadcasting a nightly radio show live from the stage; when the show went national, on a weekly basis, the whole country heard of the Cotton Club and listened to its music. And people went on listening after Ellington left for other commitments and Cab Calloway, who at first had just filled in, replaced him. The entertainers, who were the highest paid in Harlem, included Bessie Smith, Josephine Baker, Lena Horne, Ethel Waters, Bill Robinson, and, later, Buck and Bubbles, and the Nicholas Brothers. Financed by a syndicate of white mobsters, the club had a slightly flexible Jim Crow policy: twelve seats could be filled by Negro dignitaries, racketeers, and the families and friends of the performers, and a few more if the applicants were well groomed and very light-complexioned. (This exclusionary policy was somewhat further eased under pressure from Ellington, though people of color were likely to be seated at the back, near the kitchen.)

The movie has its own racial problems: white moviegoers will rarely attend pictures on black themes or with black stars, and so Richard Gere was signed up to play the leading role—on a contract in which he stipulated that he was to appear as a cornet player—before there was anything resembling a role or a script. After a few attempts at scripts failed,

Coppola was brought in; he had trouble, too, and enlisted a collaborator, the novelist (and former film critic) William Kennedy. Together, they hatched some thirty to forty versions—an insane number. But how do you make a movie about the Cotton Club starring a white cornet player when there were no white musicians at the Cotton Club?

In diagrammatic terms, the intricate plot that Coppola and Kennedy devised isn't bad. They introduced another famous Harlem nightspot— the Bamville Club—where Gere could go to blow his horn in jam sessions, and then they worked out a gimmicky scene in which Gere, a smiling-eyed young Irishman, saves Dutch Schultz (James Remar) from a stick of dynamite planted by assassins. In gratitude, Dutch puts him on the payroll, and hires his loutish brother (Nicolas Cage), too. This still doesn't give Gere much connection to the Cotton Club, except that he sometimes goes there with Schultz, a married man, who uses Gere as escort to his teen-age mistress (Diane Lane). Having compounded the initial lunacy of the white-cornettist hero, Coppola and Kennedy created a parallel set of black brothers (Gregory and Maurice Hines)—tap dancers who get their big chance at the Cotton Club. These parallel plots don't converge; there's no more than an occasional "Hi" as Gere and Gregory Hines go past each other on the street or at the club until close to the end, when Dutch Schultz, enraged, wants to kill Gere, and Hines, with his dancer's speed and agility, kicks the gun out of Schultz's hand. But the two sets of brothers give the movie an illusion of symmetry: both sets have families and fights, and Gere's troubles with the tough, tarty Diane Lane are matched by Gregory Hines' troubles with a light-skinned showgirl and singer, played by Lonette McKee. By then the movie is packed with characters and complications and incidents that it doesn't have time for; it's so overloaded with plot that it might just as well have no plot at all. And I haven't even mentioned that the black crooks who control the Harlem numbers racket are being challenged by the Irish and Jewish mobsters, and then the Italians—led by Lucky Luciano (Joe Dallesandro)—move in. Maybe because of the need to work around that horn-player hero, Coppola and Kennedy kept adding elements until the plot became a composite of the old Warners musicals and gangster pictures. Coppola apparently believes this pastiche to be an authentic, epic view of the Jazz Age. Describing it to an interviewer from *Film Comment*, he said, "It's a story of the times: it tells the story of the blacks, of the white gangster, about entertainers, everything of those times, like Dos Passos, and the lives all thread through with 'Minnie the Moocher' and 'Mood Indigo.' "

Actually, it's an echo chamber of a movie. When Warners made those pictures that were snatched from the headlines, the crude, simplified characters had a tabloid immediacy. Reproduced here in composite form, they have no inner life and no emotional force. *The Cotton Club* is so dense about so little. It's a movie made by a director who has lost his sense of character. The joke of the long effort to concoct a script around the star Gere is that there are no stars in any of Coppola's recent movies (*One from the Heart, The Outsiders, Rumble Fish*); stars may be signed on, but when the movies come out there's just a bunch of bewildered performers wondering why they don't make a stronger impression.

If there's something more upsetting about this movie than there is about other failed epics, it's that a great time in the history of black people has been screwed over. Yes, the Cotton Club was a racist institution, but it was something more, too: it was part of a liberating social upheaval—not the most creative part but the most conspicuous part. And if some of those white swells were slumming when they went up to Harlem to watch "the colored" they put on their evening clothes to do it. There was joy in those black entertainers, and there was heat. That was what the white audience recognized; that was what the radio listeners responded to. It's what the Jazz Age was about: the emergence of black music—hot jazz—and the thrill that white artists and white audiences felt as black artists began to enter the cultural mainstream, moving from Harlem to Broadway and across the country. In the thirties, when I was a kid in San Francisco, I thought I would die from pure pleasure when I saw Buck and Bubbles perform in the stage show that came on before the movie at the Golden Gate Theatre; I'd sit through the picture over and over so I could watch John W. Bubbles glide through his tap numbers, smiling crookedly, his eyes hooded, as if he knew that kids like me had never seen anything so slinky sexy. I thought he was evil, but I loved it.

Coppola, with his staccato imagery fragmenting the songs and dances, knocks the life out of the performers. The tall, sinuous Lonette McKee, with her long, expressive arms upraised, actually gets to complete a number (the torchy "Ill Wind"), but she has none of the impudent energy she showed in the 1976 *Sparkle*. And the Hines brothers' dancing is fast and proficient yet uninspired. If you look at a clip of the Nicholas Brothers, say, in the 1942 *Orchestra Wives*, where they dance to "I've Got a Gal in Kalamazoo," you just about go crazy from the sheer aesthetic excitement of what they're doing—they're flying. The way Coppola shoots dance, nobody flies. In a sequence at the all-male Hoofers Club, Honi Coles and the other great tappers are just starting to limber up and go into their moves when they're chopped into dancing feet without bodies and wiggling bodies without feet. Coppola doesn't seem to know that it's criminal not to let these artists do their thing. The movie is all his thing—he keeps the images scrambling ahead. It's a self-defeating technique: he's so antsy that he doesn't stop to let us look at what we've come to see. The picture opens with the dancing bodies of the Cotton Club Girls in smoky color. Their dancing—intercut with black-and-white titles and angled spotlights that establish the film's visual style—is routine and impersonal. It never becomes anything more, and during the whole movie we never get close enough to these girls to see their faces, their spirit. We never get to see what we might expect to be at the heart of the movie: how the black performers and the white customers (and bosses and floor-show staff) feel about each other.

The movie certainly has a visual style: Art Deco with *film noir* lighting, and montages that skitter through the years, signifying what's happening to the country and the principal characters. But this dark, lacquered style doesn't come out of the material; it's a fashionable style that's imposed, like the visual formats of videos. Coppola doesn't build a dance through editing, as Busby Berkeley did; the jazz singers and dancers are in the background to be broken into. They're used to give the movie contrasts and sheen—to give it more of a spin. When Diane Lane and Richard Gere have their big sex scene, burnished rainbows fill the room, and then the shadow of the curtains makes lace patterns on her bare body; these effects are what we get instead of the emotion that the moment might be expected to call up. Coppola gives us all this design and he doesn't seem aware of what's missing. He's not taking old techniques and applying them; he's just taking them.

Musicals of the past rarely had fully written characters, but they didn't need them, because the actors' personalities filled out the roles. Here most of the actors are hardly allowed to show they're alive. It's a toss-up whether Nicolas Cage or Diane Lane has the worst part. Cage easily passes as Gere's younger brother, but he is made such a crude dope that there isn't a single scene in which we're happy he's around. Diane Lane was eighteen when she played her role, and that's roughly the age of Dutch's moll, but she's encased in makeup and wigs. And though most of the dialogue in the movie is reasonably pungent, her lines express a callous, moronic cynicism. Statements such as "Money's the only thing that ever saves you" don't do a lot for an actress, and her performance is equally blunt. (In the kissing scenes, she and Gere chew each other's lips so hungrily that something besides passion seems implied, but what?) Gregory Hines doesn't come off as badly, but his role is miserably misconceived. When he's smitten at first sight of Lonette McKee, the audience can share his emotion, but you expect him to be hip and to court her with his talent. When, instead, he chases after her, calf-eyed and stupidly sincere, and gets into backstage squabbles, he becomes embarrassing—you don't want to look at him. As for Gere (whose role is based partly on George Raft), with his hair brushed back flat and brilliantined, and a natty little mustache, he flashes a pretty smile and is more agreeable than usual. But there's nothing to draw us into his simp-sheik character. (In his brief appearance as Luciano, Joe Dallesandro, who's reminiscent of De Niro in *The Godfather, Part II*, has a much more romantic presence.)

A few of the actors seem to be invincible. Lighted from below, Julian Beck, of the Living Theatre, who plays Sol, a corrupt-to-the-bone hit man, looks like an Old Testament vulture. He takes his time and delivers his world-weary remarks in amusingly ghostly, sinister tones—he could be the John Carradine of the avant-garde. And Bob Hoskins, as Owney Madden, the cunning gangster who operates the club, and Fred Gwynne, as his henchman, Big Frenchy DeMange, who welcomes the guests, are like a vaudeville comedy team. Big Frenchy, as gloomy as a basset hound and always formal, walks a step behind the little bulldog Owney and stands behind him when he's seated; he seems to be Owney's butler and bodyguard, and his partner, too. When they finally have a full scene together, after Big Frenchy has been kidnapped and Owney has ransomed him, they one-up each other belligerently, but in rhythm, and with undercurrents of so much affection that it's the most touching moment in the movie—even though it doesn't make a lot of sense.

This Hoskins-Gwynne scene stands out because it doesn't just refer to old-movie scenes about friendship; you actually experience the emotion. In most of the movie, you don't get the feelings that made old-movie scenes memorable—you just watch people referring to those old scenes. (An example: the break between the Hines brothers causes us no pain, and their reunion has no exhilaration.) That's why the movie's plot doesn't give you the pleasures of a plot. Coppola uses the plot pro forma —he doesn't invest it with meaning. The movie is Felliniesque (especially in its last section, which cuts between Grand Central Station and a Grand Central set on the Cotton Club stage), and Coppola, like Fellini, assumes the role of the master of ceremonies, the eye of the hurricane. But his expansiveness has become strictly formal. Emotionally, he seems to have shrunk. The way he directs the cast here, people exist to reflect light.

January 7, 1985

UNLOOS'D DREAMS

The title of E. M. Forster's *A Passage to India* is an homage to one of the loveliest sections in Whitman's *Leaves of Grass*, and, unlike Forster's other, more neatly constructed novels, this one has an all-embracing, polymorphous quality, an openness. Forster had lived in India before and after the First World War, and in story terms the novel, published in 1924, is about the tragicomedy of British colonial rule. The liberal, agnostic author projects himself into the Indian characters—into the humiliation they feel at being governed by people who have no affection for them, who don't like them. In its larger intentions, the novel is about the Indians' spirituality, their kindness, their mysticism. The novel's flowing, accepting manner is related to Eastern philosophy. It embodies that philosophy, yet when Forster attempts to explain it—when he tries for mystery and depth—the writing seems thin, fuzzy, inflated. (When his exaltation goes flat, it's like flat Whitman; it's like hearing someone dither on about oneness with the universe.) I don't think the novel is great—it's near-great, or not-so-great, maybe because mysticism doesn't come naturally to an ironist, and in *A Passage to India* it seems more willed than felt. But the novel is suggestive and dazzlingly empathic. Forster never falls into mere sympathetic under-standing of the Indians; he's right inside the central Indian character—the young Muslim Dr. Aziz. He embraces Aziz, all right; it's the British he pulls away from.

The movie version, adapted, directed, and edited by David Lean, is an admirable piece of work. Lean doesn't get in over his head by trying for the full range of the book's mysticism, but Forster got to him. In its first half, the film (it lasts two hours forty-three minutes) has a virtuoso steadiness as the story moves along and we see the process by which the British officials and their wives, who arrive in the fictitious provincial city of Chandrapore with idealistic hopes of friendship with the Indians, are gradually desensitized to the shame experienced by the natives, and become imperviously cruel. The movie shows us the virtual impossibility of communication between the subject people and the master-race British, and between the Muslims and the Hindus, at the same time that we observe the efforts of two Englishwomen to bridge the gulfs—to get to know the Indians socially.

Mrs. Moore (Peggy Ashcroft), an elderly woman, whose son Ronny (Nigel Havers) has been in India for a year as city magistrate in Chandrapore, comes to visit him, accompanied, at his suggestion, by Adela Quested (Judy Davis), whom he expects to marry. Mrs. Moore is displeased to see her son turning into a dull sahib, and the young, inexperienced Miss Quested, who has never been out of England before, is shocked by Ronny's new callousness and the smugness of the people he emulates. Mrs. Moore, who has little patience with her son and his warnings about the dangers of mingling with the natives, strikes up an immediate, instinctive rapport with Dr. Aziz (Victor Banerjee), a glistening-eyed, eager doctor-poet, whom she meets by chance in a mosque. And later the two women have tea with Fielding (James Fox), the principal of the local Government College, who, to help them socialize, invites two Indian guests—Aziz and a Hindu scholar, Professor Godbole (Alec Guinness). Dr. Aziz, a bit heady with the joys of this social intercourse with English women who treat him as an equal, and unable to invite the group to his squalid one-room cottage, proposes an excursion—a picnic at the distant Marabar Caves.

And that's where, despite Aziz's careful, elaborate planning, everything comes to grief. Hearing the echo in a cave, Mrs. Moore is overcome by heat and fatigue, premonitions of death, and the feeling of a void where God should be. While Mrs. Moore rests, Miss Quested goes on alone with Dr. Aziz and a guide, and soon comes rushing from a cave suffering, perhaps, from what Whitman called "unloos'd dreams"—she is hysterical, and is convinced that Dr. Aziz has attempted to rape her. He is arrested, and the British, with their surface unflappability and their underlying paranoia about the Indians, react as if they were under siege. The British colony closes ranks, except for Fielding, who asserts his belief in the doctor's innocence, and the now irritable and distressed Mrs. Moore, who, without waiting to testify on the doctor's behalf, starts the journey home. For the others, the supposed attack on Miss Quested is further proof of the racial inferiority of the Indians. Besides, as the Superintendent of Police explains at the trial, it's a matter of scientific knowledge that the darker races are attracted to the fairer, but not vice versa.

Forster's plot is a very elaborate shell game: in the book, just when you think the nugget of truth about Miss Quested's accusation has been located Forster evades you again. He's very lordly, in his way; it's a cosmic comedy—each group of players has its own God. (The inscrutable Hindus, with their policy of self-removal, are wittier than the British Christians, with their disdain. The Muslims are anxious.) Lean isn't as playful, but he has his own form of lordliness. He knows how to do pomp and the moral hideousness of empire better than practically anybody else around. He enlarges the scale of Forster's irony, and the characters live in more sumptuous settings than we might have expected. But they do live. Lean knows how to give the smallest inflections an overpowering psychological weight. The actors don't sink under it.

Lean's control—a kind of benign precision—is very satisfying here, because of the performers (and the bright-colored, fairy-tale vividness of the surroundings). By the time he gets to the trial, everything has been prepared, and, in a departure from Forster's mode, he delivers suspense, drama, excitement. The courtroom scenes are far more climactic than in the novel, but Lean has necessarily shaped the material to his own strengths. This isn't the *Passage to India* that Satyajit Ray hoped to make—though he, too, wanted Victor Banerjee to play Dr. Aziz (and he had met with Peggy Ashcroft). And perhaps Ray might have been able to convey the spiritual grace that Forster was reaching for. But Lean's picture is intelligent and enjoyable, and if his technique is to simplify and to spell everything out in block letters, this kind of clarity has its own formal strength. It may not be the highest praise to say that a movie is orderly and dignified or that it's like a well-cared-for, beautifully oiled machine, but of its kind this *Passage to India* is awfully good, until the last half hour or so. Having built up to the courtroom drama, Lean isn't able to regain a narrative flow when it's over. The emotional focus is gone, the tension has snapped, and the picture disintegrates. The concluding scenes, in which he follows the general plan of the book, wobble all over the place. But by then we're pretty well satisfied anyway, and we don't mind staying a little longer with these actors, even though they seem lost.

The cast is just about irreproachable, with the exception of Guinness, who's simply in the wrong movie. The presence of Victor Banerjee makes you feel embarrassed for Guinness. It's dangerous for an actor to try that Peter Sellers–Indian routine when he's next to the real thing. (You keep expecting Guinness to break into a soft-shoe or do something silly with his turban.) As Dr. Aziz, the slim, compact Banerjee, with his handsome, delicately modelled face (the round eyes, the cupid's-bow mouth), belongs to this society—he's like a piece of erotic sculpture, a sensual cherub. When he gets ready to go out, he puts a black line under his eyes with a swift, practiced motion; he makes the most of his beauty. This soft-voiced Bengali actor is more fluid emotionally than anyone else in the cast; Dr. Aziz's feelings of generosity, servility, hurt, and rage slide into each other, and we get the impression that this is what trying to please the British has done to the man. He's too easily hurt; he's all exposed nerves and excitability. He's the most "human" of the characters, because he's so far from being like the English—and the more he tries to be like them, the farther away he is.

As Miss Quested, Judy Davis has none of the bloom that she had in *My Brilliant Career*; she's pale and a trace remote—repression has given her a slightly slugged quality about the eyes. But she's still very attractive in Western terms. Her broad-brimmed hats and virginal, straight-cut dresses are simple and uncoquettish. You like watching her —she has an unusual physical quiet, and her mouth is very expressive (despite the brick-colored lipstick she wears throughout). And it's clear that India represents her first chance to live. She longs for adventure, though she's frightened of it. And she's drawn to Dr. Aziz, though she doesn't know how to get closer to him. So it isn't until the trial that we register that to the Indians she looks tall, flat-chested, and sexually undesirable. To them the charge of attempted rape is something of an insult to Dr. Aziz's taste. All along, there's a lascivious fear that runs through the proper behavior of the British—a fear of India's voluptuous erotic traditions. And Lean has interpolated a sequence that makes this unmistakable: alone on a bicycle ride, Miss Quested chances upon an overgrown park with a temple covered with statuary—coupling bodies. She's fascinated, and as she walks about looking at what the statues are doing she seems transformed—awakened and beautiful. But the statues are suddenly swarming—a bunch of chattering, screeching monkeys come down to the bottom of the temple and onto the statues. They're like little demons blending with the lovers, and they charge at Miss Quested, terrifying her, and chase her as she dashes away on her bike. This dramatization of Miss Quested's fear of sex is very effective. (It's actually more effective than the major episode of Marabar.) But we can feel its function: it's to cue us for her hysteria at the caves, and that's not how Forster's material works. (Lean gives us a pointed reminder of the temple scene when Miss Quested is on her way to the courthouse and a man in a monkey suit jumps on the running board. This is a real blunder; for a second, it throws us out of the movie.) But Judy Davis's performance is close to perfection; her last scene (in England) is a little skewed, but that's no more than a flyspeck. Despite her moment of hysteria, this Miss Quested is a heroically honest figure who, in testifying as she does at the trial, escapes being raped of her soul by Ronny and the British colonial community.

As Mrs. Moore, Peggy Ashcroft comes through with a piece of transcendent acting. She has to, because Mrs. Moore is meant to be a saint, a sage, a woman in tune with the secrets of eternity. Forster never devised anything for her to do; in the novel, she simply *is* a sacred being —she's an enigma, like Professor Godbole. It may have been in an attempt to convey her wisdom that Lean gave her what is probably the worst line in the script: "India forces one to come face to face with oneself. It can be rather disturbing." (Substitute "Transylvania," and that's a line for Dracula to speak.) Except for Mrs. Moore's brief rapport with Aziz, who tells her she has the kindest face he has ever seen on an English lady, she's simply a weary, practical-minded woman who's very sure of things. She's not much of a mother—she's quite out of sympathy with her son Ronny—and she has no particular feeling for Miss Quested. She's a cantankerous old lady, yet Peggy Ashcroft breathes so much good sense into the role that Mrs. Moore acquires a radiance, a spiritual glow. It makes us like her. Fielding, the character who behaves most courageously, doesn't seem to have stirred Forster's imagination much; Forster was probably too much like Fielding for Fielding to interest him. The character is always on the verge of being too decent, but James Fox (he was the weakling master turned slavey in *The Servant*) gives the part a doggedness that saves it.

The novel wants to be about unresolvability; the movie doesn't, and isn't. What's remarkable about the film is how two such different temperaments as Forster's and Lean's could come together. There's a tie that binds them, though: Lean certainly hasn't softened Forster's condemnation of the British officials' poisonous thick-skinned detachment. Like the book, the movie is a lament for British sins; the big difference is in tone. The movie is informed by a spirit of magisterial self-hatred. That's its oddity: Lean's grand "objective" manner—he never touches anything without defining it and putting it in its place—seems to have developed out of the values he attacks. It's an imperial bookkeeper's style—no loose ends. It's also the style that impressed the Indians, and shamed them because they couldn't live up to it. It's the style of the conqueror —who is here the guilt-ridden conqueror but the conqueror nevertheless. Lean has an appetite for grandeur. That may explain why, at the start, he puts the Viceroy on the ship with the two women (and why, the caves in India not being imposing enough, he dynamited and made his own). But his appetite for grandeur also accounts for such memorable images as the red uniforms and headgear on the Indian band mangling Western music in the brilliant sunshine at the whites-only club, and the ancient painted elephant that lurches along from the train to the caves with Dr. Aziz, Mrs. Moore, and Miss Quested on its back.

January 14, 1985

LOVERS AND FOOLS

Micki & Maude is a small screwball farce, a tame and trivial contraption, and it would probably seem insipid to people who hoped for something substantial, but there's a special delight about the timing of actors who make fools of themselves as personably and airily as Dudley Moore and Amy Irving do here. Moore looks better than he has in his recent films: he's lighter on his feet and more relaxed, and his changes of expression seem faster than the speed of thought, yet they're easy to follow. He plays a TV reporter—he does the human-interest stories for a local station in L.A.—who becomes a bigamist through his tender regard for two pregnant women's feelings. He doesn't want to hurt either his wife, Micki (the blazing Ann Reinking), a lawyer who has just been appointed to the California Supreme Court, or Maude (the pearly Amy Irving), a cellist he got involved with when his wife was too busy to have time for him. And he's perfectly convincing. You can see why the two women fall in love with him. He's romantic in the silken, self-effacing manner of Cary Grant. It isn't difficult to imagine Grant in the role, or possibly Steve Martin or Robin Williams, but I can't think of anyone else who could do it with the delicacy and the knockabout athleticism and the faint air of pleading that Moore brings to it. This TV reporter is an ideal playmate, because he has nothing else on his mind; all his energies are devoted to making the woman he's with happy, whichever one it is.

304

Micki, the judge, is supposed to be a dynamo; still, Ann Reinking, with her white skin and raven hair, is a bit too resplendent—she seems somewhat more turned on than necessary (in a slightly vacuous way), and too physically charged to play opposite Moore. When she's stretched out on her bed, her thighs are like a powerful pair of scissors—you almost fear for him. When Amy Irving's Maude is onscreen, the movie is in better balance, because Irving attunes herself to Moore's energy level. Her acting here is a form of heavenly flirtation: her eyes widen and shine, her voice drips honey. Everything about her is soft and willowy and funny. Her words seem to be wafted to us on a warm breeze. Amy Irving is the best partner Moore has had, except for John Gielgud in *Arthur*, and Peter Cook a number of years earlier, and she brings out something ethereal in him. He's peaceful with her—he's half in a dream —and during the courtship their conversations are cadenced and giddy. They make verbal music together, like Shakespearean clowns.

Working from a script by the young playwright Jonathan Reynolds, the director Blake Edwards has got clear of the rancid angry streak that smudged his recent comedies, and of the dry mold that formed over his last picture, in 1983—*The Man Who Loved Women*. The story here is flimsy, and by the time Moore is taking care of his two infants all we can think of is: How are the moviemakers going to find an ending? (The way the plot is set up, there's no way to resolve it, and they don't—they just sort of bug off.) The story also wastes the lovely Maude character for the sake of the comic symmetry of two career-centered mothers. But Edwards' directing has some of the love of free-for-all lunacy he showed in his Peter Sellers pictures, such as *The Pink Panther* and *The Party*. There are a couple of extended slapstick sequences that suggest reworkings of the earliest screen comedies: in one, the women have simultaneous appointments with their obstetricians, who have adjoining offices; in the other, the women are in labor at the same time. Edwards keeps Moore in constant, darting motion in these scenes, and the gags proliferate, but there isn't an instant when you say to yourself, "Oh, I've seen this before." You haven't—the timing makes it all new. And these set pieces click into place because they develop out of the reporter's character, with a boomerang effect. He's an urbane, reasonable fellow whose penchant for pampering women turns him into a comic projectile hurtling into walls.

Reynolds' dialogue has a fresh wit, and, whether through his skill or Edwards', it's tied in with sight gags. The lines spark Dudley Moore. He often laughs as he speaks, and he'll speak to himself (like Sellers) while going into a piece of physical comedy. Sometimes it's the counterpoint of his words and his tumbles which makes you respond to him. It's puzzling that a director with Edwards' mastery of sight gags (he's great on bits like Moore bumping into a tree) would come up with a picture as visually undistinguished as this one is, especially at the beginning. (It looks like an in-flight movie.) And a couple of the plot elements have no payoff: Micki, with all her vim, starts a catalogue business during her pregnancy, and then almost nothing more is heard of it; and the reporter has a nibble from CBS, and nothing comes of that, either. (Surprisingly, neither of the pregnant women watches her husband on TV to keep track of him.) But there's just one really jarring episode: Maude gives her husband a green sweater, and he wears it for some time, until Micki, who doesn't like it, and thinks he bought it for himself, takes it back to the store. The scene would make perfectly good sense if Micki gave the sweater away, but her returning it after he has been wearing it steadily gives you pause. It makes her seem like a tightfisted villainess, yet that doesn't appear to be the point at all. It's as if no one on the set had thought out the overtones of what she was doing. But apart from this, and Edwards' taking too long to wind things up, and Moore's having to go through too many assorted miseries near the end, the movie keeps its agility.

Edwards directs Moore here to bring out the character's living-in-the-moment hopefulness. This bigamist is convinced that everything will come out all right, because he doesn't feel he has done anything wrong. And the audience is put in the position of experiencing unqualified empathy with him—we share his loony optimism. That's the essence of the picture, and, of course, anyone who gets fussed over its sexual politics probably won't be able to enjoy it. (But if you start worrying about real-life morality you can drain the fun out of almost any bedroom comedy, and what do you gain?) This small farce has a genuinely frivolous nature. That's not something to sniff at.

In *Starman,* the director John Carpenter tries to bring a romantic-comedy spirit to sci-fi. Although he acknowledges that he was trying for something like Capra's *It Happened One Night,* the film's tone is more like that of Capra's *It's a Wonderful Life* and *Meet John Doe.* With Karen Allen as a young, childless widow with sad, glazed eyes and Jeff Bridges as a gentle alien who takes the form of the husband she mourns, *Starman* has a melancholy gooeyness. The story line is simple: The starman has come to Earth from a distant planet because of the greetings that the United States sent into space on Voyager 2 in 1977; in over fifty languages, we sent a welcome to anyone out there. But when this alien arrives—in the form of a white light—his spacecraft is shot down over Wisconsin by our early-warning air-defense system. The heartless, scared creeps who run the government's Search for Extraterrestrial Intelligence Department track him to the widow's cabin on a bay, and soon they prepare an autopsy table with leather straps—they mean to vivisect the starman. But he has fled, forcing the woman, who's in shock, to drive him, because if he doesn't make it to a designated spot in Arizona in three days, to be picked up by his mother ship, he will die. The widow and this exact likeness of her dead husband set out for Arizona in her souped-up 1977 Mustang. En route, her fear of him changes to love, and he experiences some of the pleasures and pangs of being human, male, and American.

Bridges tilts his face upward and moves his head like a bird scenting things out, and he walks with his body tilted forward—he's like an automaton without joints. It's mildly amusing—he's oddly unhuman (and he has been given a Paleolithic haircut). But he doesn't have enough else to do. In *It Happened One Night,* it was the interaction of Gable and Colbert with the all-American eccentrics they met along their way that made them appreciate each other. Carpenter seems afraid of losing his hold on poignancy; he's a one-note director. He was single-minded in the way he went for scare effects in *Halloween,* and he goes for tenderness here in the unabashed manner of a Frank Borzage romance such as the 1927 *Seventh Heaven.* But Borzage made you feel that he believed in it. Carpenter just pours it on, and the film slides around in it. The script, by Bruce A. Evans and Raynold Gideon (rewritten by the uncredited Dean Riesner), may have been a little peppier than the way it comes across. The picture is full of opportunities for humor: the starman is like a super-serious Soviet youth who has come to study our ways —he mimics the slang he hears and the rude gestures he sees, he mimics Sinatra singing on the car radio. But the scenes are deliberately muted, and most of the gag lines are softened. We keep going back to the plaintive widow, murmuring her reminiscences of her honeymoon. Karen Allen is terribly emotional, in a skimpy way. So there's no one for Bridges to play against—there's no friction between them, no tartness or impudence. He falls in love with her ickiness, and she with his. When the two are in a roadside restaurant, he asks her to define "love," and she tries helplessly, wet-eyed, thinking of her dead husband, while a synthesized heavenly choir in the distance makes wistful, whimpering sounds.

As soon as we see a dead deer slung across a hunter's car, we know that the starman will restore it to life. (We've seen the same movies Carpenter has.) But when the deer bounds away, Carpenter can't seem to work up even the tiniest bit of thrill. The scene is enervated and snoozy until we get the sudden bam-pow violence of the hunter and his pals attacking the starman. It's preachy violence—we're supposed to see that the starman is better than we are; he shows us what we've lost and what our potential is. Watching him through ever-widening eyes, the widow begins to look like a diligent starlet trying out for the Passion Play. Soon we get the beautiful-sex rite: we see their heads in silhouette —first hers on top, then his on top. This is bleeding-hearts sci-fi, and it isn't long before a dozen or so helicopters are chasing the two lovers around the slope of a crater in Arizona. (In contemporary movies, helicopters are embodiments of evil.) In this victimization fantasy, it's all sweet innocence between the starman and the widow because everything else has been displaced onto the hunters and the government.

The persecution of these two flower children by the macho hunters and the government is ritualistic pop hype. The film has something of the sentimental paranoia of *Easy Rider*, transposed to the eighties; it even has a similar draggy holiness. When the starman and the widow have their kissy parting, her eyes shine with new hope: he has given her the child she wanted. Wasn't there a *National Enquirer* headline—"I HAD A MARTIAN'S BABY AND THE GOVERNMENT TRIED TO TAKE IT AWAY"?

The Flamingo Kid is about the summer that Jeffrey Willis (Matt Dillon) grows up. It's the summer of 1963, and Jeffrey, an eighteen-year-old Brooklyn boy whose father (Hector Elizondo) is a plumber, gets a job parking cars at El Flamingo, a beach club on Long Island. The tips are good, and so are the boy's winnings at gin rummy; he plans to go to Columbia in the fall, and he's able to put away a chunk of dough for his college expenses. But when he's taken up by the club's gin-rummy champ, Phil Brody (Richard Crenna), a foreign-car dealer who wears silk shirts and sports a sapphire on his pinkie, he begins to think college would be a waste of time. His head is turned by the gaudiness of the unfamiliar milieu and the money, the sun and water, the semi-naked girls, the sex. At the center of it all is Brody, the big shot, the type of salesman who's proud of having made it to the top without book learning—of having got into the big money on his own moxie. Brody enjoys playing man of the world to the kid, and the kid is temporarily blinded by Brody's flash. He rejects his family's solid values, and his father's belief in the importance of education; he decides he just wants to make money and live it up, like Brody. Of course, by the end of Labor Day weekend he has got himself straightened out: he sees through Brody, the father figure he has idealized, and learns to appreciate the fact that his own father is an honest man—a hardworking plumber who gives value for money.

The movie is a crude, convivial sitcom about disillusionment as a rite of passage. The director, Garry Marshall, is known as the "creator"— one of the executive producers—of several TV series ("Happy Days," "Mork and Mindy," "Laverne and Shirley"), and he has a particular kind of TV wizardry. His flair for comedy is mixed with a special, trained reflex—he goes for the audience like a carny pitchman. Television watchers and moviegoers are his mark. Marshall pushes you around, but in an amiable way, and he gets his laughs, though nothing carries over and the gags turn into a blur. *The Flamingo Kid* is a slapped-together comedy in the genre of the more eloquent *Breaking Away* and *Diner*. It's anti-crass in a crass style; watching it, I began to feel that Phil Brody had directed it. That's not all bad: part of what's enjoyable in the movie is its junkiness—Marshall knows how to stage Fiesta Night at the club, and he knows how to call attention to the jaunty little butt on Brody's golden-girl niece Carla (Janet Jones), a Southern California hottentot who doesn't mind Jeffrey's being a few years younger than she is. (When this pair are in silhouette, it's just his head on top.) A beach in the sunset can get to a director, so Marshall's one outbreak of calendar art can be forgiven. And a dull sequence at the race track in Yonkers, and another one when Jeffrey quarrels with his father, who has just bailed him out of jail, can be shrugged aside. What can't be is the way Marshall squeezes the good plumber's scenes so that they show "humanity." He's a sanctimonious pitchman—he sets up the movie so that it has a moral. He flattens everything out so the audience will understand it, yet there's still some vitality in the material that glimmers through. (Elizondo, for example, shows his skill whenever the plumber father makes an ass of himself.)

The summer of 1963 was part of a forward-looking time, and I imagine that the original writer, Neal Marshall (he's not related to the director), wanted Jeffrey Willis to stand for youth in the days just before

Vietnam and the assassinations and the drugs. (Neal Marshall's screenplay was first optioned in 1972; he later revised it, and then it was rewritten by Bo Goldman, who had his name removed after the director reworked it.) In the finished film, nostalgia and realism are packaged together, and the director presents his version of 1963 as more "real" than the way things are now. There's a kind of cultural fundamentalism at work in this movie. Garry Marshall is telling us that the complications of the last two decades are unimportant. He's saying that what matters is: Listen to your honest old man and don't sell out. And, so that everything will be cartoon-simple, Brody isn't merely a blowhard—he's a cheat. That way, he and the kid's honorable, square father can be in perfect opposition. And, to make the moral package even tidier, Jeffrey doesn't merely reject Brody—he punishes him. The director has been trusting his TV instincts for so long that maybe he doesn't see the ugliness in this.

There were great pop songs in 1963, and many of them are on the soundtrack, but they're not used in a way that sticks with you. When a new song starts, you may perk up for a second or two, but Garry Marshall doesn't bring out anything of what was energizing in the songs. He makes them overfamiliar—he uses them to evoke the period, to blend in and disappear (like the gags). What Marshall creates is a ruckus for a synthetic community (which is what a TV audience is).

The movie might be said to be for a synthetic community and about one, too. Matt Dillon has a charming, easy, corny naturalism here. (It's a relief after seeing him straining so hard to act in *Rumble Fish*.) He's almost too open-faced and graceful—he's so ingratiating he's like an Irish Robby Benson, though he doesn't seem meant to be Irish. His family looks vaguely Italian (and his father says grace over *breakfast*), but nobody in this movie—except maybe Irving Metzman as hairy, itchy Big Sid at the gin-rummy table—is meant to have a definite background. The moviemakers must have wanted to take advantage of the ripe possibilities in a Long Island Jewish club (the crowded pink stucco El Flamingo is based on the old El Patio, where Neal Marshall worked as a kid), but they didn't want to limit their "universal" theme. Though the Brodys and most of the other people at the club are Jewish caricatures circa Larry Peerce's *Goodbye, Columbus*, some of the younger generation, such as the golden-hind Carla, are almost ostentatiously gentile. In this movie, people's names don't provide much clue to their backgrounds. (Garry Marshall, who is Italian, must like the name Brody: it was the heroine's name in his only previous movie as a director, the 1982 *Young Doctors in Love*.) As Brody's brassy, bored wife, Jessica Walter is so overtly snobbish it's like a form of innocence, and she's rather winning. But Richard Crenna's crooked, soft-in-the-gut Brody is the film's one major character. Brody's flesh seems to be expanding because he wants to fill a larger space. This man who feels alive only when he's selling himself—who blooms with a little worship—is probably the best screen role Crenna has ever had, and in scenes such as his encounter with Jeffrey's trim little father he's smooth in a seasoned, scummy way that makes you laugh. Garry Marshall has an affection for this scoundrel. He ought to. A director who can give us ethnic humor without ethnics has certainly learned how to cut a few corners.

January 28, 1985

SCHOOLBOYS

John Schlesinger's hour-long 1983 TV film *An Englishman Abroad*, starring Alan Bates as Guy Burgess in Moscow, is probably the best hour of television I've ever seen. (It was first shown here late in 1984.) Though it was clear that what made it memorable was the script, by Alan Bennett, and Bates' entering into the squirmy soul of a traitor who's in exile from everything he cares about, Schlesinger directed it so simply that I was really cranked up for his new movie, *The Falcon and the Snowman*, which is another tale of traitors—ours this time. The story of Christopher Boyce and Daulton Lee seemed a natural anyway; when it was reported in the press, it had everything—bravado, black humor, and a kind of all-American kinkiness. Boyce and Lee, parochial-school pupils in one of the best-heeled communities in Southern California—Palos Verdes Peninsula, on Santa Monica Bay—were altar boys together; they became close friends on the high-school football squad, and developed a common interest in falconry. The intelligent Boyce, who couldn't get along with his father (an F.B.I. man turned security specialist in the aerospace industry), idealized earlier centuries and thought he would like to go back about five hundred years. He entered a seminary to prepare for the priesthood, and then, questioning his faith, left, and went to a secular college. Lee, the adopted son of a Second World War hero who became a doctor, dealt in pot in high school and, after graduation, began to push cocaine and heroin; by the time—July, 1974—that Boyce decided to knock off college for a year or so and took a clerical job that his father arranged for him in a company under contract to the C.I.A., Lee (who had stopped growing in the fifth grade, when he was five feet two) was on probation, with legal problems hanging over him —and a junkie.

Clean-cut and quiet, Chris Boyce did well in his job, and after a few months he was (at the age of twenty-one) given top-secret clearance and sent to work in the Black Vault, a communications center for surveillance satellites that the C.I.A. denied the existence of. He was shocked to discover the extent of C.I.A. manipulations of the internal affairs of allies, like Australia (where the Agency was maneuvering to discredit the Labour Prime Minister). And, for a mixture of motives, including revenge on the C.I.A. for its crimes, he decided to sell some of this information to the Soviet Union. It was like a secret (and lucrative) form of protest. He saved key documents that were supposed to be shredded, and in April, 1975, his coked-up buddy Lee, acting as courier, presented himself at the Soviet Embassy in Mexico City and established relations with the K.G.B. Out on bail, still dealing dope, and with all kinds of charges against him, Lee kept slipping back and forth over the border. These two casual, sloppy spies delivered documents to the Russians for two years, until January of 1977, when the Mexican police arrested Lee for causing a disturbance outside the Soviet Embassy. Boyce, who had quit his job and gone back to college with plans to become a lawyer, was picked up ten days later. (The code name that he used in his espionage activities was Falcon.)

The story of Boyce, who when he was out with his falcons dreamt that he was a Renaissance prince, and of the wastrel Lee, who had a genuine talent for cabinetwork but was discouraged by the Palos Verdes teachers from doing anything that smacked of manual labor, is a gorgeous sick comedy. (And it didn't end when the two were sent to maximum-security prisons—Boyce for forty years, Lee for life. Boyce escaped and robbed a few banks, and he might have stayed free if he hadn't started to fly falcons again.) At first, I gave the Schlesinger movie the benefit of the doubt, and kept waiting for it to get to the good stuff. He does get to some of it, but only glancingly; he pretty much throws the story away. We don't see the boys' weekends together flying falcons, and we don't get a sense of their relationship. (Schlesinger may think that if he shows a thing once—such as Boyce greeting Lee warmly—he has done his duty and established what we need to know.) And maybe because the movie is based on a factual account (Robert Lindsey's *The Falcon and the Snowman*), Schlesinger doesn't bother to make it credible that the coolheaded Boyce would be in partnership with the strung-out, hysterical Lee. The director seems hardly interested in the absurdist aspects of the case, such as Lee's living high, giving parties in his parents' house, and boasting of his exploits as a spy. The script, by Steven Zaillian, is disjointed; it never takes hold of anything, and Schlesinger doesn't, either.

The sumptuousness of Schlesinger's style is impressive. A falcon vaults across the sky onto its prey; the shot has a perfect cruel zing to it. There's something lordly (and a little bored) in this director's command of the medium. While he gives you the feeling that he knows what he's doing, he has no staying power. He doesn't develop the idea of the élitist parents, with their rigid, out-of-date thinking and their lackadaisical permissiveness—he falls back on such staples as closeups of Boyce's mother (Joyce Van Patten) that suggest she's some sort of inept, piggy monster, an emblem of America's grotesque shallowness. He tosses in spy complications that you can't quite follow. He lays on shot after shot of jetting falcons without ever indicating what this (rather horrible) chivalric sport means to the two deeply reactionary kids.

"It's not so much *what* they did as *why* that interests me," Schlesinger says in the publicity material. "Without condoning their actions, we explore what was going on in their heads—and in the world around them—in the early seventies." But if we don't get a clear idea of what happened how can we perceive the why of it? Schlesinger seems to think he's exploring the boys' thoughts when he flashes reminders of the Vietnam era: Martin Luther King, Nixon, Agnew, the Kennedys, John Lennon—the whole bloody mess. He's busy making a countercultural statement and a work of art when if he had just told the story straight it might have really been those things—it might have meant something. Maybe the more deeply Schlesinger understands the material he's working with, the simpler he is. (Hence the lucidity of *An Englishman Abroad*.) And when the material is alien to him he goes for art and political thunder. So in *The Falcon and the Snowman* he explicitly makes the point that Chris Boyce's actions weren't the traitorous ones—the C.I.A.'s were. The movie isn't really interested in either the what or the why of the Boyce and Lee case—Schlesinger wants to shock the hell out of us by justifying Boyce's actions. But we've had so many movie directors shooting off at us that all the flash and denunciation have lost their impact. (They've become modern conventions.) We keep trying to get into the boys' characters, and neither the writer nor the director gives us much help. All they supply of Boyce's motives is a multiple-choice test. We're to take our pick of (a) loss of faith in God, (b) not getting along with Dad, (c) the cynical, circus atmosphere in the Black Vault, and so on.

In the early scenes, Timothy Hutton brings some excitement to the underwritten role of Chris Boyce. The conscientiousness and the physical timidity of Hutton's earlier performances seem to have been burned out of him. At twenty-three, he's no longer the sensitive stripling of *Ordinary People*; he has a new physical stature—he's turning into a strikingly good-looking man, with a sexual presence, like a young Warren Beatty. This young actor is ready to take off into uncharted realms, and he makes you respond to the secret Chris Boyce, the freak hidden inside the proper manners, the good clothes, the young prince. (As an innocent-faced altar boy, Chris had a sly little trick: he dragged his feet on the carpeting and worked up enough electricity to administer shocks on the chin from the platter as people received the host.) But by the time Boyce is making speeches about how the C.I.A. preys on weaker governments, you've almost forgotten the foxy intensity he had in the first half, and how furtive and gleaming his eyes were when he talked to his father and his father's friends who were his bosses at work. In those scenes, Hutton's Chris Boyce takes the center of the picture, because he's too smart and too cagey and dishonest to show those people what he thinks. He plays along with them while doing tiny double takes with his eyes for the amusement of another side of himself. Schlesinger probably has no idea why the boys did it, but Hutton does have an idea, and the flickers of subversive life inside his clean-cut, regular-featured handsomeness suggest possibilities that we want to see explored. This Boyce is secretly out for kicks, and then some. (Boyce named his favorite falcon "Fawkes" —for Guy Fawkes, who tried to blow up the Houses of Parliament.) That's what we expect the movie to be about—that's where the drama is. But it isn't developed. And the last part of the picture—which is when it really goes bad—has Schlesinger doing his ritual song and dance: showing us how we are really the guilty ones. At the very end, we get the sanctimony of David Bowie singing "This Is Not America."

Sean Penn's whiny Daulton Lee, with a thick head of hair that's like a homemade wig, and dark glasses and a measly, pencil-line mustache, is like Rupert Pupkin's little brother. It's an embarrassment—the kind of fanatic actor's performance that's obvious and empty in a way that's bound to be compared admiringly to De Niro's run of bum work. Sean Penn earned the praise he received for *Fast Times ct Ridgemont High* and *Bad Boys* and *Racing with the Moon*, but he's a self-conscious catastrophe here, complete right down to the choked voice—he sounds as if his lungs had collapsed. Daulton Lee is supposed to be a braggart and a hustler, but all Penn's energy goes into the impersonation—he has nothing left for his big scenes, and they're lifeless. (You get the impression that Penn thinks the only part of character creation that's authentic is the groping; he abdicates half the actor's job—the projecting and shaping. A good actor takes on a different character—he doesn't dissolve into it. Here, you feel as if the artist had disappeared, and you were left watching a twerp playing a twerp.) Partly because of the blubbering and flailing about that Sean Penn does, the two principal K.G.B. men—Alex (David Suchet), who is Lee's regular contact, and the senior official (Boris Leskin)—seem to be the only ones who know what they're doing, the only sane and responsible people in the movie. (They're far from this levelheaded in Lindsey's account.) Suchet, who spent ten years with the Royal Shakespeare Company and is appearing now as Freud in a BBC series on cable, has wide, dark eyes and the suavity of an actor who never wastes a motion; he modulates his soft-edged voice ever so slightly to suggest Alex's bafflement in his dealings with the strutting, shouting Lee, who at one point tries to talk the Russians into a heroin deal. And Dorian Harewood, as one of Boyce's co-workers in the Black Vault, livens up the scenes he's in. The goddessy young Lori Singer is cast as Boyce's girlfriend, but has nothing to do except get in bed with him; she appears to be in the picture for the sole purpose of letting us know that the boys aren't homosexual.

Schlesinger is no slouch when it comes to directing actors. He casts Pat Hingle as Chris Boyce's father, who's still an F.B.I. man at heart. It's a role Hingle has played dozens of times—he's a pop-culture joke in this role—but I doubt if he has ever done it as well. And Schlesinger always has some dynamic activity going (even if it's off-key or confusing or there's something missing and things don't add up right). He has many of the attributes of a first-rate director. There's one he's missing. If you think back to his calamities, such as *The Day of the Locust* and *Marathon Man*, you can see that they fail for the same reason *The Falcon and the Snowman* does. It's his failure to be involved on the simplest level. It's his detachment from the events and the people, from the plain facts of a story.

friend of mine said that she liked the book *Birdy*, by William Wharton (a pseudonym), which was published in the late seventies, because Birdy "wasn't a metaphor for anything—he was simply a kid who wanted to fly like a bird," and I can see how someone might take the novel literally, because of all the terrific bird lore in it. But the movie version, directed by Alan Parker, and updated from the Depression and the Second World War to the sixties and Vietnam by the adapters, Sandy Kroopf and Jack Behr, is all metaphor. Part satire, part Christ myth, it's like *The Little Prince* rewritten by Kurt Vonnegut. The central characters are two boys from the drab working-class suburbs of Philadelphia. Al (Nicolas Cage), a high-school athlete, has come back from Vietnam a sergeant with battle stripes on his uniform, a steel jaw, and a mutilated face wrapped in bandages. He has been summoned to the psychiatric section of a military hospital to see if he can help his friend Birdy (Matthew Modine), who was wounded and missing in action, and now squats naked on the floor. Crumpled like a broken bird, and with his head slightly twisted, Modine peers up at the window high in his cell, as if he wanted to fly up and away, but it's crossbarred and covered with wire. The cell seems as tall as a Gothic cathedral, and the light streaming from the window comes down from the sign of the cross onto the mute, suffering boy—he's a deformed Christ figure in a cloister-cage.

Al, bandaged and in pain, continues to visit Birdy, who doesn't acknowledge his presence, and in flashbacks, through the two boys' thoughts and fantasies, we see them in their high-school days, when they caught and raised pigeons together and then, after Al's interest in birds had waned and he was concentrating on sports and girls, Birdy kept canaries in his room. In those days, birds were Birdy's hobby and passion. He could watch them fly, build winged contraptions, and create an aviary-world of his own—a world without the meanness of the corrupt society. In his bird world, he could escape the heartlessness of his crazy mother, the despondency of his school-janitor father, and the taunting of the neighborhood kids, who called him Weirdo. The two boys stayed close, because Al didn't laugh at Birdy's dreams; they needed each other. With Cage playing flesh to Modine's spirit, the movie is made in a process that's like simultaneous translation. Everything that happens instantly converts itself into vaguely abstract terms. The movie is about the purity of madness, about male bonding, sadism, violation, and so on. And, with the war-ravaged Al sitting on the hospital floor in that stream of light, holding the catatonic Birdy in his arms, it's one Pietà after another.

The movie takes itself inordinately seriously as a moral fable expressing eternal truths, and everything you're supposed to react to is laid out for you. When the adolescent Birdy puts on wings he has made and attempts to soar over a garbage dump, the bluntness of the metaphor is deadening. At times, every shot seems metaphoric. We have no sooner seen Birdy's rhapsodic love of a golden-yellow canary, whose feathers glow brighter than anything else in the movie, than we see a cat sneaking upstairs to his room. The incidents we are shown and the ones we hear about all relate to victimization: Birdy's mother kills the two boys' pigeons; Al's father sells the '53 Ford the boys have put together; the boys get a job with a dogcatcher who grabs animals off the streets and rushes them straight to the slaughterhouse; and then there's Vietnam.

Fooling around with the novel's time frame produces some odd results. Though the physical details of the boys' lives in the sixties seem accurate enough, what's missing—the pop culture of the sixties—makes their adventures seem still to be happening in the quieter Depression years. And the omnipresence of choppers in the boys' Vietnam recollections may make you wonder why Birdy didn't graduate from wanting to fly to wanting to be a flyer, and why he expresses no interest in planes or gliders. (He's in ecstasy when he's up in the shoot-the-chutes at the beach, so his lack of expression when he's up in a helicopter seems a glitch.) Most of all, the change in the period encourages the moviemakers in their sense of mission. The movie has the tone of a requiem for the two maimed boys, for Vietnam, for the human condition.

Alan Parker gives you surface realism, but he keeps you aware of his accomplishment. He makes a great show of serving the material. He keeps you standing back, watching him bring off emotional numbers full of torment and pathos. His work here—with an elegant Peter Gabriel score mated to it—has a high-tech industrial finish, an impersonal sheen. He achieves some fairly amazing swooping, flying-over-the-neighborhood shots when we see things from Birdy's fantasy perspective. But if ever there was a sequence that called for silence this dream of flying is it. Gabriel's synthesized drum music is far too clever for Birdy's flight —it outclasses Birdy, with his awe of wings and his sexual immaturity. And Parker's assured approach gives the material a slickness that finally locks a viewer out. (It may even be that Parker and his regular team— the cinematographer Michael Seresin, and the camera operator, the editor, the designer, and the production people—have become too smooth a unit.) I found myself watching the actors as actors—not as Al and

Birdy—and the visual effects as visual effects. I don't know that anyone could have brought this material off. (Robert Altman stumbled with his bird-boy story, the 1970 *Brewster McCloud*.) It's material that should be magical—straightforward yet elusive. It probably needed a director who found the story lulling, tantalizing, its meanings hidden—a director who would risk making us laugh at what he was doing. Parker's technological sophistication nails everything down. John Schlesinger wasn't interested in boys who use birds to create their own worlds, and neither is Parker. The movie feels morose and unrelieved, despite the efforts of the two actors, who make everything they can of the humorous rapport between the adolescent boys.

Matthew Modine puts his whole body into character; he doesn't hold anything back, and he has a clean style, unencumbered with actors' tricks. When he grins (in the flashback scenes), his Huck Finn goofiness helps to cauterize the pure-boy, Little Prince aspect of the role; he's as "natural" as anybody could be who's posed as a contorted Christ figure. Modine has remarkable control, and he's still young enough to be convincing as a sixteen- or seventeen-year-old Catholic angel. His is the showier role—an actor playing a catatonic is almost certain to be intense and riveting. Al is probably the more difficult role. He has to be muscular and earthbound; he has to be a kid who's treated brutally by his vicious old man (Sandy Baron, in a convincingly dark performance). And he also has to spend a lot of time with his face half obscured by bandages while he grieves over Birdy's silence. Al is supposed to be ordinary, except for his friendship with Birdy, and ordinariness is one of those bad, literary ideas that can destroy an actor. Nicolas Cage has some of the dopey soulfulness that was so charming in his appearance as the Hollywood High boy in Martha Coolidge's 1983 *Valley Girl*, but he can't infringe on Modine's terrain—he has to be raw and girl-crazy and scared of his father. He's fine in the flashback scenes, when he and Birdy are just kids doing reckless teen-age things; the two boys have matching smiles, the way best friends with shared secrets often do. They move together, as if they were both hearing the same signals, the same music. Cage doesn't quite sustain his hospital scenes, but he's at a terrible disadvantage in them—he's the noisy supplicant, begging Birdy for a sign of intelligent life.

Near the end, Al gets his sign, in a scene so misconceived that I can hardly believe that it actually made it to the film's final cut. Talking to the unresponsive Birdy, Al suddenly delivers an impassioned anti-war statement. It's totally out of character, and you're groaning at the moviemakers' intruding in this way when damned if Birdy doesn't react against it, too. But he doesn't blame the writers or the director for it; he blames Al, and, rousing himself from his stupor, he says, laughing, "Al, sometimes you're so full of shit." This flip scene invalidates the two hours of movie that preceded it. After all of Birdy's Christ-like, broken-bird posturing, how can he suddenly turn up his nose at something phony? It's not as if Birdy had come to his senses; it's as if Matthew Modine had waked up, seen through the role he'd been straining to play, and walked off the set.

February 11, 1985

PLAIN AND SIMPLE

In the new Peter Weir movie, *Witness*, an eight-year-old Amish boy (Lukas Haas), on his first trip to a city, sees a murder taking place in the men's room of Philadelphia's Thirtieth Street train station. In order to protect the boy and his mother, Rachel, a widow (Kelly McGillis), from the killers, John Book (Harrison Ford), the police captain who's in charge of the investigation, tries to hide their identities, and, with a bullet wound in his side, drives them back to their farm in Lancaster County before he collapses. At that point, the film has already built up the contrast between the devout, gentle Amish and the greedy, brutal Philadelphians—seen through the eyes of the child, who takes in everything. In the days of silent pictures, the distinction between rural virtue and big-city vice was a standard theme. The girl on the farm was steadfast; she represented true, undying love. The city girl was fast and spoiled and selfish. This split between good farmers and bad urban dwellers takes an extreme form in *Witness*. Last year's rural trilogy (*Country, Places in the Heart,* and *The River*) prepared the way: moviegoers have been softened to accept the idea that people who work the land are uplifted by their labor. And *Witness* goes the trilogy one better by having its farming people part of a pacifist religious community that retains an eighteenth-century way of life and stresses "plainness." (The Amish reject *buttons* as decorative.) Also, in the past twenty years we have been battered by so much evidence of crime in the cities that moviegoers may be ready to believe that city people are, of necessity, depraved. *Witness* seems to take its view of the Amish from a quaint dreamland, a Brigadoon of tall golden wheat and shiny-clean faces, and to take its squalid, hyped-up view of life in Philadelphia from prolonged exposure to TV cop shows. Murder is treated as if it were a modern, sin-city invention.

Though you can feel in your bones that a solemn cross-cultural romance is coming, the first section of the story moves along at an even clip until John Book's collapse. There's even a bit of visual comedy in the train station, when the little boy, in his black suit and broad black hat, thinks he sees another member of the sect: he walks over to an elderly Orthodox Jew, and the two look at each other in wordless rejection. But the narrative is becalmed during Book's recuperation at Rachel's farm, because the screenwriters (Earl W. Wallace and William Kelley) haven't provided him with any plan of action. When he rushes Rachel and the boy back to safety among the Amish, it's because he has learned that the killers are his superiors in the police department, who are involved in a twenty-million-dollar narcotics deal. But once he knows that, his mind seems to go dead. During his stay among the Amish, he gets out to a nearby town and phones the only cop he can trust—his partner—who wonders if they should go to a reporter or to the F.B.I. The suggestion seems to fall into a void, and Book just waits for the killers to track him down and show up at the farm. Maybe the movie is trying to tell us that the whole American system is so rotten that Book has no recourse —that there's no agency that isn't contaminated. Whatever the moviemakers had in mind, the way the story is set up there's nothing for us to look forward to but the arrival of the bad guys and the final fit of violence.

While we wait, *Witness* is a compendium of scenes I had hoped never to see again. There's the city person stranded in the sticks and learning to milk a cow, and—oh, yes—having to get up at 4:30 A.M. to do it. There's the scene with this city person sheepishly wearing clothes that are too short and look funny on him, so that the countrywoman can't restrain herself from giggling. There's the barn-raising (out of *Seven Brides for Seven Brothers*) and all the hearty fellowship that goes with it. There's the natural woman who stands bare-breasted and proud; in earlier American movies, the film frame used to cut her off at the bare shoulders, but you got the idea. *Witness* also takes first prize in the saying-grace department: a whole community of people bow their heads over their vittles. It's like watching the Rockettes kick. We can't have prayers in the public schools, but movies are making up for it.

Weir, an Australian filming in this country for the first time (*Witness* was shot in Pennsylvania), has succumbed to blandness. Book's stay at the farm is like a vacation from the real world; the rural images have a seductive lyricism that's linked to the little boy's dark, serious eyes. He's a subdued child—boyish only in his quiet curiosity and low-key playfulness. Lukas Haas is a good little actor—his shyness is lovely —but the moviemakers' conception of the boy is so idealized it's as if they'd never been driven nuts by the antics of a real, live child. This kid never develops beyond our first view of him. He doesn't argue with his mother, he doesn't complain, he doesn't make any noise. He's a miracle of politeness and obedience—a walking ad for fundamentalist orthodoxy. But Lukas Haas at least stays in his perfect character. As his mother, Kelly McGillis is like a model in a TV commercial that reproduces a seventeenth-century painting of a woman with a pitcher of water or milk. She shifts uneasily between the heroic naturalness of Liv Ullmann and the dimpled simpering of the young Esther Williams. She's so dimply sweet that when she's happy she's like a wholesome, strapping version of a Disney Mouseketeer.

The moviemakers try to balance things by introducing the suggestion that the sect is narrow-minded; Rachel is warned that her interest in John Book is causing talk among the Amish and could result in her being "shunned." But the whole meaning of the movie is that her life and her child's life are far better than anything the two could experience in the outside world. And, of course, John Book comes to love Rachel and her bonnet too much to want to expose her to the ugliness outside. (The spoiled city woman is represented here by Patti LuPone, who plays Book's divorcée sister—a tense urban type to the ultimate degree.) It's suggested that the women in the community don't take part in the decision-making, but never that there's anything basically repressive or stultifying about living in this authoritarian society without music* or dance, without phones or electricity, without the possibility of making friends in the outside world. The picture isn't interested in what life in such a closed-in community might actually be like for a woman or a child. The farm country is used as a fantasyland for the audience to visit; it has its allure, but you're ready to leave when Book goes—you wouldn't want

*When I wrote this, I forgot that the sect permitted some vocal music—the men sing after the barn-raising.

to live there and get up at 4:30 A.M. and work like a plow horse. *Witness* uses the Amish simply as a way to refurbish an old plot. And as soon as you see Rachel's galumphing Amish suitor (Alexander Godunov), with his dear, mischievous grin, you know that the film is going to avoid any real collision of cultures, and the risk of giving offense. The suitor is there so that John Book can make the right, noble decision. He makes the decision for both himself and Rachel. The implication is that, coming from the world of violence and being a man who uses a gun—i.e., a sinner—he knows that there's no possibility of true happiness out there.

The picture is like something dug up from the earliest days of movies: it starts off, during the titles, with the wind blowing through the wheat, and the actors often looked posed. Weir seems less interested in the story than in giving the images a spiritual glow. (It's easy to imagine this picture being a favorite at the White House.) It must be said that Harrison Ford gives a fine, workmanlike performance, tempered with humor. The role doesn't allow him any chances for the kind of eerie intensity he showed in his small part as a burned-out Vietnam veteran in the 1977 *Heroes,* and he doesn't have the aura that he has as Han Solo and as Indiana Jones, but he burrows into the role and gives it as much honesty as it can hold. He's not an actor with a lot of depth, but he has an unusual rapport with the audience—he brings us right inside John Book's thoughts and emotions. Granting him all that, I must also admit that the only time I really warmed to him here was when he suddenly broke out of character and, his face lighting up demoniacally, parodied a TV commercial as he cried out, "Honey, that's *great* coffee!" (It's a free-floating joke, like Jack Nicholson's "Here's Johnny" in *The Shining.*) It's a measure of how sedate the movie is that you feel a twinge (as if you were being naughty) when you laugh.

But my instincts tell me that this idyllic sedateness could be the film's ticket to success. In its romanticism and its obviousness, *Witness* has got just about everything to be a *Lost Horizon* for the mid-eighties. There's the charming, obedient child, and there's the widow whose eyes flash as she challenges John Book to look at her nakedness. (And—I swear I didn't make this up—a storm is raging on the night she flashes him. It's the same storm that used to rage for Garbo when her passions rose.) There's the implicit argument that a religious community produces a higher order of human being than a secular society. There's something for just about everyone in this movie—even the holistic-medicine people. John Book's bullet wound is healed by folk remedies: Rachel gives him herbal teas and applies poultices to the affected area. (I'm disposed to have some trust in the efficacy of these methods, but I still wish that just once somebody in a movie who was treated with humble ancient remedies would kick off.) Scenes like the one in which some showoff kids try to provoke the Amish to fight can be discussed by editorial writers and in schools. All those dug-up scenes are probably just what is going to sell the movie. There's a little paradox here: *Witness* exalts people who aren't allowed to see movies—it says that they're morally superior to moviegoers. It's so virtuous it's condemning itself.

Blood Simple has no sense of what we normally think of as "reality," and it has no connections with "experience." It's not a great exercise in style, either. It derives from pop sources—from movies such as *Diabolique* and grubby B pictures and hardboiled steamy fiction such as that of James M. Cain. It's so derivative that it isn't a thriller—it's a crude, ghoulish comedy on thriller themes. The director, Joel Coen, who wrote the screenplay with his brother Ethan, who was the producer, is inventive and amusing when it comes to highly composed camera setups or burying someone alive. But he doesn't seem to know what to do with the actors; they give their words too much deliberation and weight, and they always look primed for the camera. So they come across as amateurs.

The movie is set in a familiar, cartoon version of Texas, where Julian Marty (Dan Hedaya), a swarthy middle-aged Easterner with a wrestler's crouch, owns a roadhouse, the Neon Boot, and thinks he owns his young wife, Abby (Frances McDormand). When she leaves him and goes off with one of the bartenders—tall, well-built Ray (John Getz)—Marty hires Visser (M. Emmet Walsh), a sweaty, good-ol'-boy private detective, to follow the pair, and after Visser, grinning with malign satisfaction, shows him pictures of the two cuckolding him in a series of positions (it's like a porny slide show) he makes a deal with Visser to kill them. The plot is about how the detective takes Marty's money and double-crosses him. The one real novelty in the conception is that the audience has a God's-eye view of who is doing what to whom, while the characters have a blinkered view and, misinterpreting what they see, sometimes take totally inexpedient action. *Blood Simple* gets almost all its limited charge from sticking to this device, which gives the movie the pattern of farce—it works best when someone misinterprets who the enemy is but has the right response anyway. (It's like a bedroom farce, except that the people sneaking into each other's homes have vicious rather than amorous intentions.)

Early in the movie, Marty and his only friend, a German shepherd named Opal, who's like his shadow, sneak into Ray's apartment, and Marty makes a grab for Abby. She breaks free by kicking him hard in the groin, and we know at once that *Blood Simple* is an art movie, because Marty moves front—to the camera—to throw up. It's a splatter-movie art movie. Marty throws up again and again, and he's a mighty good bleeder, too. One liquid or another is always splashing out of him. And there are *film noir* in-jokes: there's a whirring, growling ceiling fan in just about every room in the movie. At one point, Coen cuts from Marty, in his office at the roadhouse, looking up at his fan to Abby, at Ray's place, looking up at *his* fan. The cut should come across as funnier than it does—these moviemakers don't always have their comedy timing worked out. And often you can't tell if something is a gag or just a goof. When Abby, practically overnight, turns out to be living in a magnificent loft with huge arched windows, you may do a double take—she didn't seem to be that chic a girl. Is it a gag when bullets are fired into a wall of her loft and the holes might have been made by cannonballs? I don't know, and it doesn't seem to matter. *Blood Simple* isn't much of a movie; it's thin—a rain-on-the-windshield picture that doesn't develop enough suspense until about the last ten minutes, when the action is so grisly that it has a kick.

At moments, the awkwardness of the line readings is reminiscent of George Romero's *Night of the Living Dead*, but *Blood Simple* doesn't have the genuine creepiness of the Romero film. And though the dialogue is much sharper and smarter than Romero's dialogue, the actors talk so slowly it's as if the script were written in cement on Hollywood Boulevard. The picture is overcalculated—pulpy yet art-conscious. It has the look of *film noir,* but it lacks the hypnotic feel, the heat and the dreaminess of effective *noir.* Even when the material leads us to anticipate something nasty, it often doesn't pay off. When Ray goes to see Marty and tries to collect the two weeks' pay that's due him, they talk together while we look out the window that's between them: there's a huge, blazing incinerator behind the Neon Boot, and a couple of people are tossing large objects into it. In a movie as uninhabited as this one, if a gigantic prop like the incinerator isn't going to be used for body disposal, surely whatever it *is* used for has to be comic? Coen sets up an inferno and then, except for a bloody jacket being thrown into it, nothing comes of it, one way or the other. Nothing comes of Opal, the

German shepherd, either; she disappears, and nobody seems to notice—not even Marty. (This happened in *Rocky* and *Silkwood*, too. Sometimes I get the feeling that *The New Yorker*'s Current Cinema is turning into The Lost Dogs Department.)

Joel Coen may flub the point of some of the scenes, and toss in inane closeups of a bludgeoning weapon to show us that it's a piggy bank, but he knows how to place the characters and the props in the film frame in a way that makes the audience feel knowing and in on the joke. The film's technique is spelled out for the audience to recognize. Coen's style is deadpan and klutzy, and he uses the klutziness as his trump card. It's how he gets his laughs. The audience responds (as it did at *Halloween*) to the crudeness of the hyperbole, and enjoys not having to take things seriously. The cinematographer, Barry Sonnenfeld, works in ghouls' colors—thick, dirty greens, magentas, and sulfurous yellows. The film looks grimy and lurid; it seems to take its visual cues from the neon signs in the bar and a string of fish putrefying in Marty's office. What's at work here is a visually sophisticated form of gross-out humor.

Dan Hedaya's performance as Marty the gusher is almost wrecked by too much lip curling between words, but Hedaya develops a funny presence—he's like a primate version of Michel Piccoli—and his acting seems to get better when Marty is twitchy and writhing and only semi-conscious. As Visser, the cackling obscenity, M. Emmet Walsh is the only colorful performer. He lays on the loathsomeness, but he gives it a little twirl—a sportiness. The Coens wrote the role with him in mind (they didn't have anything in mind when they wrote Abby and Ray), and when Walsh is onscreen in his straw cattleman's hat and his bulging yellow suit the muggy atmosphere is like congealed sweat. Visser drives a VW bug; he *is* a bug, a rotting one—he draws flies. Most of what's framed by the camera is of no interest—it's barely animate, except for Walsh. His broad buffoonery helps to ground the picture, to keep it jaundiced and low-down. (At one point, when Abby and Ray are in bed together and Visser takes a flashbulb snap of them, the director apparently can't resist having the screen turn white, as if they'd been nuked. The effect nukes the tawdry genre Coen is working in.)

Film students looking at old movies seem to find it exciting when a cheap B thriller or an exploitation picture has art qualities, and they often make draggy, empty short films that aren't interested in anything but imitating those pictures and their "great shots." (The student directors of those shorts never know what to do with the actors—there's nothing for them to express.) *Blood Simple* is that kind of student film on a larger scale. It isn't really about anything except making a commercial narrative movie outside the industry. The Coens, who live in New York (Joel graduated from N.Y.U. film school), raised their million-and-a-half budget from private investors, most of them in Minneapolis, where the boys grew up. In interviews, the brothers (Joel was twenty-nine when he made the film and Ethan only twenty-six) are quick and bright; they sound as if they'd popped out of a Tom Stoppard play. But I don't quite understand the press's enthusiasm for these two young, well-educated Americans, the sons of college-professor parents, who want to make the most commercial kind of Hollywood movies but to do it more economically and with more freedom outside the industry. What's the glory of making films outside the industry if they're Hollywood films at heart, or, worse than that—Hollywood by-product? Joel and Ethan Coen may be entrepreneurial heroes, but they're not moviemaker heroes. *Blood Simple* has no openness—it doesn't breathe.

The reviewers who hail the film as a great début and rank the Coens with Welles, Spielberg, Hitchcock, and Sergio Leone may be transported by seeing so many tricks and flourishes from sources they're familiar with. But the reason the camera whoop-de-do is so noticeable is that there's nothing else going on. The movie doesn't even seem meant to have any rhythmic flow; the Coens just want us to respond to a bunch of "touches" on routine themes. (These art touches are their jokes.) *Blood Simple* comes on as self-mocking, but it has no self to mock. Nobody in the moviemaking team or in the audience is committed to anything; nothing is being risked except the million and a half.

February 25, 1985

GOLDEN KIMONOS

A friend of mine says that when you go to a Kon Ichikawa film "you laugh at things, and you know that Ichikawa is sophisticated

enough to make you laugh, but you don't know why you're laughing."
I agree. I've just seen Ichikawa's 1983 *The Makioka Sisters*, which
opened in New York for a week's run and will open nationally in April,
and although I can't quite account for my response, I think it's the most
pleasurable movie I've seen in several months—probably since *Stop
Making Sense*, back in November. The last hour (the picture runs two
hours and twenty minutes) is particularly elating—it gives you a vitaliz-
ing mix of emotions. It's like the work of a painter who has perfect
control of what color he gives you. At almost seventy, Ichikawa—his
more than seventy movies include *The Key (Odd Obsession), Fires on
the Plain, An Actor's Revenge, Tokyo Olympiad*—is a deadpan sophis-
ticate, with a film technique so masterly that he pulls you into the worlds
he creates. There doesn't seem to be a narrative in *The Makioka Sisters*,
yet you don't feel as if anything is missing. At first, you're like an
eavesdropper on a fascinating world that you're ignorant about. But
then you find that you're not just watching this film—you're coasting on
its rhythms, and gliding past the precipitous spots. Ichikawa celebrates
the delicate beauty of the Makioka sisters, and at the same time makes
you feel that there's something amusingly perverse in their poise and
their politesse. And he plays near-subliminal tricks. You catch things out
of the corner of your eye and you're not quite sure how to take them.

The Junichiro Tanizaki novel on which the film is based was written
during the Second World War and published in 1948, under the title *A
Light Snowfall* (and it has been filmed twice before under this title—
in 1950, by Yutaka Abe, and in 1959, by Koji Shima), but it has become
known here as *The Makioka Sisters.* The women are the four heiresses
of an aristocratic Osaka family. Their mother died long ago, and their
father, who was one of the big three of Japan's shipbuilders, followed.
Tsuruko (Keiko Kishi), the eldest of the sisters, lives in the family's
large, ancestral home in Osaka and controls the shrinking fortunes of
the two unmarried younger girls. The film is set in 1938, and the traditions in which these women were raised are slipping away, along with
their money. Tsuruko and the next oldest, Sachiko (Yoshiko Sakuma),
have married men who took the Makioka name, but its prestige has been
tarnished by the behavior of the youngest of the sisters, Taeko (Yuko
Kotegawa), who caused a scandal five years earlier, when she ran off
with a jeweller's son and tried to get married, though the Makioka
family's strict code of behavior required that Yukiko (Sayuri Yo-
shinaga), the next to youngest, had to be married first. The scandal was
augmented, because the newspaper got things wrong—wrote that
Yukiko had eloped, and then, when Tsuruko's husband complained about

the error, mucked things up more in correcting the mistake. Taeko still lives in Sachiko's home, along with Yukiko, but she's trying to achieve independence through a career. She wants to start a business, but Tsuruko won't give her her inheritance until she's married, and she isn't allowed to marry. It's Catch-22. She's flailing around, and waiting for the demure Yukiko to say yes to one of her suitors.

Each suitor is brought to a formal ceremony—a *miai*—where the prospective bride sits across a table from the prospective groom, with members of their families and go-betweens seated around them. At thirty, Yukiko is a veteran of these gatherings, but she has still not found a man to her liking. During the year that the movie spans, there are several of these *miai*—each a small slapstick comedy of manners. The last, when Yukiko finally meets what she has been waiting for (and the camera travels up the suitor's full height), has a special tickle for the audience, because you can see exactly why Yukiko said no to the others and why she says yes to this one.

These *miai* are just about the only formal, structured events; in between them, Taeko gets into highly unstructured emotional entanglements—falling in love with a photographer who becomes ill and dies, taking up next with a bartender, becoming pregnant, sampling a few lower depths, and planning to go to work, which means another scandal. While Taeko wears Western clothes and goes off on her own, the exquisite, subdued Yukiko stays in her sister's house. (The two married women's houses are like theatres-in-the-round, with the four sisters and the servants as each other's audience.) Is Yukiko the priss that her Southern-belle curls and her old-fashioned-girl manner suggest? Not by what you catch in glimpses. Yukiko, who clings to the hierarchic family values of the past, with all the bowing and the arch turning away of the head and the eyes cast down, is inscrutable, like Carole Laure in Blier's *Get Out Your Handkerchiefs*. But we see the come-on in her modesty. That's what's enchanting in the older sisters, too. Taeko, the animated modern girl, the one asserting her sexual freedom, is the least teasing, the least suggestive, but when she's with the others and in a kimono she's lovely. They're beauties, all four of them, with peerless skin tones, and they move as if always conscious that they must be visual poetry. (And they are, they are.)

Yukiko appears to be the most submissive, but she's strong-willed, and she has a sly streak. Living in Sachiko's house, she dresses with the door open to the hall Sachiko's husband passes through. And when she sees him looking at her bare thigh, she covers herself slowly, seductively. Sachiko, who observes what's going on, gets so fussed she starts tripping on her kimono and bumping into things. When she sees her husband kissing Yukiko, she crushes a piece of fruit in her fist and shoves it into her mouth to keep from crying out. And she renews her efforts to find Yukiko a suitable husband.

Ichikawa has said, in an interview, that he took his cue from the book's original title, *A Light Snowfall.* He said that light snow, which melts away instantly, "expresses something both fleeting and beautiful," and that he looked at the sisters in these terms. And that may help to explain why it's so difficult to pin down the pleasure the film gives. It's like a succession of evanescent revelations—the images are stylized and formal, yet the quick cutting melts them away. It's not as if he were trying to catch a moment—rather, he's trying to catch traces of its passing. When the four stroll among the cherry blossoms in Kyoto, the whole image becomes cherry-toned and they disappear.

Ichikawa's temperament brings something more furtive and glinting to the material than Tanizaki gave it in the novel. (In its spirit, the movie actually seems more closely related to other Tanizaki novels, such as *The Key,* than it does to this one.) The film builds to its last hour; what's distinctive about the buildup is that the darts of humor don't allow you a full release. Taeko's first bid for independence involves becoming an artist, and her sisters speak of her work in perfectly level, admiring tones. Sachiko even pays for a show at a gallery. Taeko's art is the creation of dolls—exact, lifelike small reproductions of girls in heavy makeup and elaborate gowns, and with eyes that open and close. They could be little Makioka sisters. This is sneak-attack humor, played absolutely straight—Ichikawa is satirizing the material from within. And when this kind of suppressed joke plays right next to sequences such as a display of shimmering golden kimonos that the Makioka girls' father had bought for Yukiko's wedding presents, with one after another placed center screen—a glorious celebration of textures and color—an unusual kind of tension and excitement builds in the viewer.

I don't know enough about the Osaka culture to interpret the film as social criticism or as an elegy to a vanishing form of feminine grace. (Ichikawa himself comes from the Osaka area.) But the actresses are perfectly believable as the works of art that women like the Makioka sisters were trained to be. And it's easy to be entranced with the world that the film creates. (The industrialization of Japan is kept on the periphery.) When the banking company that Tsuruko's husband works for transfers him to Tokyo, and Tsuruko doesn't want to leave the Makioka home—a cool palace of polished wood that seems built on an intimate scale—you don't want to leave it, either. The rich colors, the darkness, the low-key lighting—they're intoxicating. When Tsuruko decides to make the move, and her husband falls to his knees to thank her, it has the emotional effect of a great love scene. But the film's finest moment comes at the very end. It's a variation of Joel McCrea's death scene in Peckinpah's *Ride the High Country*, when the old marshal falls out of the film frame. Yukiko is going off to be married; she boards the train in soft vanishing snow, and we realize that she meant far more to Sachiko's husband than a casual flirtation. We see him alone, getting drunk, and he looks terrible—he's all broken up. Then images of the four sisters among the cherry blossoms are held on the screen in slow motion that's like a succession of stills. At last there's only Yukiko's head in the center of the screen, and the head of her disconsolate brother-in-law passes across the screen behind her and out of her life.

The horrible thing about Peckinpah's recent death was that he was the most unfulfilled of great directors. Like Peckinpah, Ichikawa has had more than his share of trouble with production executives, but he has weathered it, and there's a triumphant simplicity about his work here. This venerable director is doing what so many younger directors have claimed to be doing: he's making visual music. The themes are worked out in shades of pearl and ivory for the interiors and bursts of color outside—cherry and maple and red-veined burgundy. He's making a movie that we understand musically, and he's doing it without turning the actors into zombies, and without losing his sense of how corruption and beauty and humor are all rolled up together.

Alan Bridges' film version of Rebecca West's first novel, *The Return of the Soldier*, which she began writing in the winter of 1915–16 and published in 1918, when she was twenty-five, creates a special literary universe. It gives you the feeling that you sometimes get when you read an "advanced" novel of the twenties, with a "daring," "modern" way of looking at things, and are touched and charmed by its streamlined Victorianism. Set in 1916, the movie is like a piece of intellectual history. It re-creates an era when Freudianism was new, and when an author might apply it to characters' lives in a spirit of heroic revelation. The conflict is: Should the shell-shocked, amnesiac Captain Chris Baldry (Alan Bates), who has forgotten the last twenty years of his life, be allowed to remain in his boyish state of happiness, or should he be forced to confront the truth? (It's the same theme that O'Neill wrestled with in *The Iceman Cometh*: Are people strong enough to live with "the truth"?) Chris was unconsciously discontented, the Freudian-minded doctor from London suggests, and that is why he has blotted out all knowledge of the years of his maturity and his marriage to the beautiful Kitty (Julie Christie). He has regressed to the time of his greatest joy, when he was young and in love with Margaret (Glenda Jackson), an innkeeper's daughter.

Although it takes a few minutes to yield to this movie—to enter this past and to enjoy the psychological and sexual dilemmas that Rebecca West posed—Julie Christie brings you into it, by making you laugh. Kitty sits in her elegantly decorated manor house, in its immaculate grounds, and when the drab, middle-aged Margaret, in an ugly, practical raincoat, comes to tell her that Chris is in a hospital, Kitty won't believe her. She is so offended that this grubby creature could presume to bring her news of her husband that she rings for a servant to throw the woman out. Kitty's vanity and self-centeredness are outrageous and uncon- cealed, and her snobbery is so mean-spirited that she's funny. And she's so possessive that her husband's having forgotten her existence seems like crazy justice. Julie Christie is wonderful to watch; she's a ravishing camera subject who knows how to turn her beauty against herself. With her body caressed by soft silks, she still manages to divorce Kitty's beauty from sexuality. She makes you feel that Kitty is ornamental through and through, that there's no passion in her, or generosity, either. Kitty uses her beauty as a blindfold. She's petulant and ineduca- ble, and so her inability to understand how Chris can prefer the dowdy creature whom she finds physically nauseating is a source of comedy. Kitty has lived up to her understanding of what a wife should be, and she wants this messy inconvenience of her husband's amnesia cleared away.

As the shabby, gentle Margaret, Glenda Jackson has a marvellous leanness to her acting. She's completely in character, though it's the sort of simple, good-woman role that, reading the book, one might think unplayable—and she might be the last actress to come to mind. When she and Chris walk together, you can feel the bond between them, and when she sits on the ground watching him stretched out next to her, you feel she has given him the gift of untroubled sleep. Miscast, Jackson can scratch on one's nerves; she can even seem to be scratching on her own nerves. But she takes Rebecca West's literary conception of an instinc- tual, loving woman and gets right down to the nub of the character, and she does it with an ease that's fairly astounding. (Her leanness is particularly fine in her scenes with Frank Finlay, who plays Margaret's puttering-in-the-garden husband.) Hugh Whitemore, who adapted the novel, has written other roles Glenda Jackson has scored in (the play and film *Stevie*, the six-part "Elizabeth R" on television); here, he takes much of the dialogue from the novel, and the novelist's dialogue is essential, because of the film's literary ambience. The novel has a narrator—Chris's cousin and childhood playmate Jenny. Whitemore uses Jenny (Ann-Margret) merely as the mediator between Kitty and Margaret. It's a colorless, thankless role—the unselfish Jenny adores Chris, but knows that the contest is between the two other women. At one point, Kitty, moving across a room, kicks a little dog out of her way; a moment later, Jenny leans over and pets it. That's her function all the way through—she soothes ruffled feelings. What Ann-Margret is doing here as an English spinster is a little puzzling (it has to do with the mysteries of getting a film financed), but her bone structure has an aristocratic quality and she acquits herself with likable dignity.

Alan Bates has a gift for letting us see that the character he plays is being acted upon. As Chris, he has to carry the burden of being loved by Kitty and Jenny, and he carries it rather heavily—which makes it work. When Chris comes home from the hospital, he tells Kitty and Jenny, "If I do not see Margaret Allington, I shall die." That's a period-novel line, and Bates wouldn't get away with statements like this if it weren't for the weight he gives them and a piteousness that you don't laugh off. Amnesiac war heroes have been a subject for parody for several decades (the 1942 *Random Harvest* was the last straw), but Bates has an aura of middle-aged bewilderment that saves him. He's not playing simply a shell-shocked man of the First World War era—he's giving an authentic performance as a shell-shocked romantic hero of that era. And when Kitty, under duress, permits Chris to see Margaret —certain that he'll be appalled at the sight of her frumpiness—Bates brings off the scene in which Chris runs to Margaret and embraces her and doesn't even notice that she looks sallow and ordinary; they walk together with immediate intimacy and understanding.

In the novel, Jenny goes out in the woods to find Chris and Margaret and sees them "englobed in peace as in a crystal sphere." That's how they are in the movie, too. And the phrase might describe the whole movie. Alan Bridges' storytelling methods aren't much more than a thoughtful application of television technique, but the feeling of enclosure in time and space is just what this story needs. As Rebecca West conceived it—and she was writing during the First World War—it is partly about women's attitudes toward the fighting. The title refers not just to Chris's return to the manor but to what Margaret and Jenny fear —that if his memory is restored he will have to return to the trenches. (This possibility doesn't faze Kitty in the slightest.)

The middle-aged Chris, who's in love in a young man's way, is, in effect, experiencing a second childhood. As Bates plays him, he might seem perfectly happy if it weren't for the blankness in his gray eyes. His eyes tell us that he's lost—that he's not fully there. And Jenny and Margaret recognize that he can't be fully a man without his memories of pain. (In the novel, part of that pain was his slaving in business all those—now forgotten—years to pay for Kitty's tastes, her redecoration of the house, and the upkeep on the grounds; in the movie, he seems to have done nothing, except go to board meetings and ride horses and play golf—perhaps so that the film can score a point against his class.)

The movie's simplified psychology is amusingly fragrant, and melo-dramatic. Ian Holm is on hand, as the lively, gnomish London doctor who parcels out the meaning and significance of Chris's shell shock. The film (it was made in 1982, but is showing in New York for the first time) is a "civilized entertainment"—a curiosity. It's neither great nor exciting, and much of what makes it enjoyable is what we usually think of as peripheral: the *moderne* décor in the manor house which the production designer, Luciana Arrighi, has come up with; the jewels and clinging silks that the costume designer, Shirley Russell, has put on Julie Chris-tie; the toylike automobiles; Kitty having her thick dark-blond hair brushed, or piling it up in wonderful loose, Pre-Raphaelite coils; even an outré witch's hat that Ann-Margret wears—it's black, with spidery red embroidery running around the crown. And the contrast between the details of Baldry Court and the little row house where Margaret lives is like a visual essay on class determination of taste. But the acting saves the conception from preciousness. (The acting is so good that Bridges and Whitemore might have dispensed with the flashbacks to Chris and Margaret's youthful ardor; seeing them together now tells us about their past, and it's more stirring.) The movie isn't essentially different from the Masterpiece Theatre adaptations of famous novels, but it doesn't have all that drawn-out tiresomeness, and since it's based on a little-known and minor novel, it has some freshness to it. And the novel's dated modernity may give us pause. It has only been a few decades since Freud and Victoria walked arm in arm: in this material, Chris's return to reality doesn't mean learning what his repressed feelings are and freeing himself from a dead marriage—it means going back to being a proper husband and a good soldier.

he Mean Season starts out huffing and puffing about oppor-
tunistic journalism. There are sizable indications that it's going to be
about the press's responsibility for building up people like Son of Sam,
for giving killers the notoriety that can impel them to commit a series
of atrocities. So when it turns out to be nothing more than an inept
thriller about a Miami reporter (Kurt Russell) who gets hot tips from a
serial murderer about where to look for fresh corpses, the audience can't
help laughing contemptuously. Besides, the picture has a bottomless
source of hilarity: the reporter's schoolteacher girlfriend, who screams
helplessly in emergencies, is played by the six-footer Mariel Hemingway, who could just haul off and whack whoever was terrorizing her.
When she isn't screaming, she's lecturing the reporter, trying to get him
to quit in the middle of the case; when the murderer phones, she proceeds
to lecture *him.* No wonder he decides to go after her; the surprise is that
the reporter doesn't encourage him. This girl has a serious case of
preposterousness, plus she is a large pain.

The director, Phillip Borsos, and the cinematographer, Frank Tidy,
sustain a lively, stormy gothic atmosphere. And there's nothing the
matter with most of the cast that a good script wouldn't cure. The script
that Borsos is working with is based on John Katzenbach's *In the Heat
of the Summer,* and is credited to Leon Piedmont, a pseudonym for a
couple of fellows (and some helpers on the set). Using a pseudonym may
be the smartest thing these writers did. At the beginning, when the
reporter's account of the murder of a teen-age girl comes out, the killer
calls and tells him that it's only the first—that before he's done he's
going to kill three women and two men, and "You're going to be my
conduit to the public." The reaction of the reporter's Mephistopheles, his
editor (Richard Masur), is "This is the one you've been waiting for.
Fabulous." And a little later he says insidiously, "Our illustrious publisher thinks you may be entering Pulitzer territory." That's the level of
the melodrama here. Those are high points, compared with what follows.
Audience morale sinks audibly when the reporter and the schoolteacher
start playing scare pranks on each other while the Lalo Schifrin score
works on us so our hearts will pound when the reporter approaches his
girl in her shower, or when she hides in the back seat of his car and puts
a hand the size of Bigfoot's print on his shoulder.

The only real point of interest in the movie is Richard Jordan, who
has often been the only real point of interest in his movies, but is more

spectacularly so this time, in the role of a sociopathic killer. Jordan has put on some heft, and it takes him out of the romantic-juvenile class. The fleshiness makes his smoothly handsome baby face more imposing, and with the pampered quality he has, and the big, deep voice, he has finally become *weird*. Jordan has a Brando-like look about him now. And it's entertaining to see an actor who likes hamming it up, who enjoys the flash of playing an insanely clever villain. (Kurt Russell plays his role professionally and acts in a believable manner, but it's a fake-serious part that might have been helped by a little ham and histrionics.)

In movies of the early thirties, reporter heroes used to talk about quitting and writing a novel. The audience understood why: they all wanted to be Mariel's grandpa. Now, when the reporter hero talks of being burned out and of wanting to quit and go to work on a small-town paper in Colorado, he just seems to be mouthing the words of a phony screenwriter who's trying to put over the notion that a small-town paper means purity and moral regeneration. You can see the reason for it: if the reporter said he was quitting to write a script or to go to work for *Time* or *People*, there'd be whistles and catcalls. It's getting very hard for an American hero to tell us how he's going to renew himself. Heroines have their troubles, too. Though it's great to have collarbones and shoulders like Mariel's, it's not so great if you're in a role that obliges you to shrink and cower. The screenwriters ought to be photographed saying her lines and doing the screaming and trying to hide behind Kurt Russell.

March 11, 1985

CHARMER

Mia Farrow seems just naturally stylized. Weightlessly beautiful, and with a considerable acting technique that she draws upon without the slightest show of effort, she might have been created for the camera. She's both real and unreal—she has a preternatural glowing sweetness. In *The Purple Rose of Cairo*, which Woody Allen wrote for her and directed, she is Cecilia, who lives in a small town in New Jersey. It's 1935, and her husband is unemployed; he fritters away his days with his buddies and his evenings with womenfriends, and she's lonely. She works in a diner and finds solace in the pictures that come to the Jewel Theater. But Cecilia can't hold a job for long, because she can't keep her mind on it; her thoughts wander away to the glamorous worlds she sees on the screen, and the Hollywood lives she reads about in fan magazines. It's the dreamy-souled Cecilia who's the jewel in this movie. She has been fired, and is watching the week's attraction at the theatre—*The Purple Rose of Cairo*—for the third day, when one of the characters, the young explorer Tom Baxter (Jeff Daniels), in his safari suit and pith helmet, suddenly talks directly to her. He tells her that he has been aware of her seeing the picture over and over, and then he bounds down from the black-and-white image and into color, and takes her out of the theatre with him. We're not startled by the confusion of realms—by a screen character entering Cecilia's life—because Cecilia and her Depression town are not quite real, either. And we're eager to see how Woody Allen is going to work things out. Though he doesn't appear in this picture, he doesn't need to: his spirit informs every tickling nuance. And there may be an advantage to his not being physically present: maybe the actor has been holding the director back.

The thirteenth film he has directed, *The Purple Rose of Cairo* is, I think, the most purely charming of the bunch. And though it doesn't have the sexual friskiness and roughhousing of some of his other comedies, and doesn't speak to the audience with the journalistic immediacy of his movies in contemporary settings, it may be the fullest expression yet of his style of humor. The movie is a gentle, complex variation of "The Kugelmass Episode," which he published in *The New Yorker* in 1977—the story in which a City College professor entered *Madame Bovary* a few pages after Léon's departure and just before Rodolphe's arrival, and had an ecstatic affair with Emma, which ended after he brought her to the Plaza Hotel for a weekend and had trouble getting her back into the book. The movie also bears a relationship to the glorious two paragraphs that Allen published in the *Times Book Review* last year, in answer to the question which character from a book he'd most like to be. His reply began: "Gigi. I want more than anything to be Gigi. To meander, feather-light, down the boulevards of *belle époque* Paris in a little blue sailor dress, my sweet face framed by a flat, disk-shaped hat with two ribbons dangling mischievously past my bangs." Woody Allen's parodies and fantasies are inseparable; their unstable union is his comic subject.

In *The Purple Rose of Cairo*, the paradoxical crossovers from one level of unreality to another are played deadpan straight, as they were in Buster Keaton's 1924 *Sherlock Jr.*, where the projectionist hero dreamed that he became involved with the characters on the screen (and as they were in the 1981 Steve Martin–Bernadette Peters *Pennies from Heaven*). Cecilia, like Keaton as that projectionist, isn't very vivid. (If she were, she wouldn't need to make these crossings.) In her neatly buttoned brown coat, she's a little brown mouse. But she's also self-possessed. In the early scenes, she and her sister (played by Mia's sister Stephanie Farrow) work side by side at the diner, and they talk together in soft, confiding voices; they have a sisterly conversational rhythm, and a trust in each other. When Cecilia is fired, Sis threatens to quit, but Cecilia is practical enough to talk her out of it, and Sis is practical enough to let herself be talked out of it. Mia Farrow's role is written so that she's like the frail, big-eyed waifs that Janet Gaynor and Loretta Young used to play, but she also has a sturdy, independent side. She can see that Tom Baxter, whom she spends some time with, is a romantic simp—she's drawn to him, but she knows he's all hollow gestures and couldn't survive in her world. She refers to him, quite simply, as "a wonderful man" but "fictional."

This is the first Woody Allen movie in which a whole batch of actors really interact and spark each other. It's the first time that he has written a large number of good comedy roles—even if most of them are, like Tom Baxter, only mock characters. When Tom impulsively pops out of the screen at the Jewel, he disappears from the story of the black-and-white movie, just as Emma Bovary disappeared from the novel when she went to the Plaza Hotel. The other characters on the screen at the Jewel —the rich sophisticates who met Tom at a tomb in Cairo and invited him for a "madcap" weekend in Manhattan—can't go on with the story, in which he is supposed to fall for Kitty Haynes (Karen Akers), a slinky, tall torch singer at the Copacabana. Kitty is stranded, and so are a dowager countess, played by Zoe Caldwell, and an assortment of swells, played by John Wood, Ed Herrmann, and Van Johnson, and several other characters, including a blond ninny (Deborah Rush) and the tubby black maid, Delilah (Annie Joe Edwards), who is reminiscent of Hattie McDaniel in the 1935 *Alice Adams*. Allen has written these roles so that each recalls a specific type of thirties-movie character. And when Tom Baxter (who's the juvenile lead, the perennial enthusiast in the mold of

Charles Starrett and David Manners) takes off with Cecilia, the others lose their high-toned diction and begin to bicker about their relative importance in the picture. They also bitch at the Jewel's crabby patrons, who want the story to continue, or their money back. The countess, who has a gilded baritone like Tallulah Bankhead's, gets down to a scary basso when she expresses her disgust at Tom's unprofessionalism. Zoe Caldwell's chest tones and her glare may remind you of such magnificent tough old broads as Constance Collier and Alison Skipworth. And John Wood is immaculately asexual in the hollow-head-under-a-top-hat Edward Everett Horton tradition. (He's funnier than Horton was, because he doesn't overdo it.) Van Johnson has a slightly decayed grandeur and raised eyebrows, and Ed Herrmann, of the aristocratic sloping head, is like an eternal preppy—he looks as if he should be standing next to Rudy Vallée, singing "The Whiffenpoof Song."

Much of the comedy is in the shifts and transactions of the characters on the screen at the Jewel, the townspeople, and the New York and Hollywood people who arrive to deal with the emergency—a group that includes Gil Shepherd (Jeff Daniels), the actor who played the role of Tom Baxter, and who wants to get Tom and his pith helmet back up on the screen where they belong. Gil quickly realizes that Cecilia is the key to the mystery—that Tom left the screen in order to court her. Woody Allen shows new verve as a director in his work with Jeff Daniels (he was Debra Winger's husband in *Terms of Endearment*). As the chaste, quixotic Tom, Daniels has a sequence in which he's picked up by a prostitute named Emma (a nod to "The Kugelmass Episode," perhaps?) and taken to the local bordello, where his good looks and romantic ideals are a big hit. Dianne Wiest is spectacularly touching and funny as Emma, and the bordello scene, though not in a strict sense necessary to the plot, adds to it—brings it some bright hues, some texture. When the girls offer Tom a free roll in the hay and he declines, because he's in love with Cecilia, Emma wants to know if there are "any other guys like you out there." She and the other girls get misty-eyed over Tom; they're far more naïve about his romantic appeal—his niceness—than Cecilia is.

As the skin-deep Tom and the shiny-eyed narcissist Gil, Jeff Daniels comes through with two unmistakably different satiric performances. Woody Allen's cinematographer, Gordon Willis, lights Gil to bring out his avidity for stardom; he's irradiated, like Gene Kelly at the première in *Singin' in the Rain*—his teeth, the whites of his eyes, and his polo coat and spiffy fedora all gleam. Gil is such an actory actor that when he humbly tells Cecilia he isn't really a star yet, you half expect him to spit flashbulbs. He's something of a challenge, and Cecilia livens up when she's with him. He speaks rather patronizingly of his responsibility for Tom, telling her that he "created" the character, and her tone is slyly ingenuous when she says, "Didn't the man who wrote the movie do that?" Of course, Gil is full of anxieties about his career; Cecilia, with her storehouse of movie trivia, advises him as if she were the editor of *Photoplay*. And he laps up her adulation.

The movie has been thought out with such graceful intelligence that its flaws seem minor. Cecilia's trip into the black-and-white world at the Jewel doesn't come to much. There's also a lapse in the way Woody Allen handles the film-industry people who show up in the town: except for Gil, they don't have satiric personality traits. The writer *didn't* create them —they're just lumpy walk-ons, and the energy leaks out of the scenes with Alexander Cohen as the producer. And by not making it clear how consciously manipulative Gil is, Allen leaves a gap that the audience experiences as a sense of dislocation. And though Gordon Willis's black-and-white images are exactly what's needed, his color cinematography —as well as the work of the production designer—seems too rich and shadowed for comedy. The Depression thirties was the era of Deco dishware in cheap and cheerful primary colors, of yellow oilcloth on kitchen tables and red-and-white plaids and checkerboard patterns wherever you looked. The deep *Godfather* browns here are too serious, and they link into a few problems of emotional tone.

There's a central piece of miscasting: as Cecilia's husband, Danny Aiello is too heavy and loutish. Probably he was selected for the incongruity of this big vulgarian's being married to the slight, fine-drawn Cecilia (and her supporting him), but we don't have a clue to why she married him or why he married her. Woody Allen has too much taste to let us see the husband smacking Cecilia around, but we hear about his having done it, and his physique is threatening. I waited for Aiello to become more stylized—for his oafishness to be made comic. (He does lighten up—but not enough—when Cecilia comes home and catches him with a giggly, voluptuous flooze.) I rather dreaded Cecilia's scenes with her husband, and after the flooze episode, when you see Cecilia trudging through town carrying her suitcase, and then, defeated, going back, because she has no place else to go, the film has a morbid, unfunny subtext. You don't want her to have to go home to this bruiser's surplus gut and his thick, Victor McLaglen arms. (Our image of him makes the resolution of the film cruelly harsh.) It's difficult to know how much of the subtext is intentional. Some of it is surprising: the fairy-tale man, the two-dimensional man from the black-and-white world, is the only one who treats Cecilia decently; the other men abuse her or betray her. (Does

Woody Allen believe that young women who claim that they've found someone "nice" are all deluded?)

There's something else that the crushing presence of the husband connects with. Woody Allen knows how to merge his modern sensibility with that of Buster Keaton. (The first step is that what was accounted for in *Sherlock Jr.* as a dream is now presented in a matter-of-fact manner, with the cunning capper that it's "fictional.") The film is far more Keatonesque than Chaplinesque. Mia Farrow has her plangency, but she's also a hardhead, like Keaton, and with something of his resilience and individuality. (She's the only beauty to have survived Diane Arbus's camera.) But though Woody Allen isn't like Chaplin—he doesn't make you cry—he has a naturally melancholic, depressive quality. It's his view of life; the movie casts a spell, yet at the end it has a bitter tang. It says that sweetness doesn't get you anywhere. And though in acting terms Mia Farrow carries off her Chaplinesque moment of reconciliation to fate, I think it's a mistake. Woody Allen's full vision here could take a less tidy, airier finish—he needed to pull something magical out of a hat. (He might even have carried through on the illogical plot turns of the movie within the movie.) Most of Buster Keaton's comedies ended happily, and when Chaplin wasn't being maudlin so did his. Woody Allen puts a strain on his light, paradoxical story about escapism when he gives it a desolate, "realistic" ending. The author's voice that emerges from his movies, and from this one in particular, is that of a winner who in his deepest recesses feels like a loser. Happiness and success aren't real to him; painfulness is the only reality he trusts. (Trusting it is his idea of integrity.) And so he sentimentalizes his own make-believe here by trying to give it "real" emotion.

But this *Purple Rose* has enough true poignancy for us to forgive it its fake poignancy. I watched this movie all but purring with pleasure. It's a delicate classic comedy. It's not a picture to go to with huge expectations; it doesn't have the daring or excitement of a great work. But it has a small, rapt quality, and I think it's Woody Allen's finest creation. It's scaled to Mia Farrow's cheekbones. And it has a surprising warmth.

The English comedy *A Private Function* is like an Ealing Studios comedy of the late-forties, early-fifties period as it might have been skewed by Joe Orton. The picture keeps adding greedy eccentrics and scatological jokes until everything is interconnected and the action seems on the verge of exploding into lewd farce. It never quite makes the final leap (there's something very English about that), but it's pretty funny anyway. The dialogue doesn't let you down. Alan Bennett, who wrote the script, was one of the Beyond the Fringe foursome, with Peter Cook, Dudley Moore, and Jonathan Miller, and has become perhaps the best known (and most prolific) of Britain's television playwrights. In *A Private Function*, he writes lines that make you laugh not just at the line itself but at the knotty mental state of the person who delivers it. The jokes seem to erupt out of the characters. Bennett and the young director Malcolm Mowbray, who worked up the story idea with him, are making their joint début in feature films, and the picture has a distinctive zest and virulence.

The action is set in a small Yorkshire town in 1947, during the worst of the postwar austerity, with rationing of bread and eggs, and all kinds of food shortages. The whole country seems to be steeped in petty vice, and for the sake of a chop or a roast just about every character engages in deceit and fraud and other species of moral turpitude. The plot involves the efforts of the local pillars of society—the proudly royalist doctor (Denholm Elliott), the solicitor (John Normington), and the pudgy accountant (Richard Griffiths)—to hold a subscription banquet celebrating the nuptials of Princess Elizabeth and Prince Philip. In order to serve something suitable for a patriotic feast, the three leading citizens have made a deal with a black marketeer—a local farmer—to fatten a hidden, "unlicensed" pig. The three, however, have tried to drive out a lowly newcomer to the town, a mild-mannered chiropodist named Chilvers (Michael Palin), who makes his house calls on a bicycle, and when, on a visit to the farmer's wife, he discovers their felonious secret he has an uncharacteristic vengeful impulse: knowing they can't complain to the police, he takes a notion to steal their pig. This material might seem rather basic, but the moviemakers have a streak of the higher insanity: when Chilvers tells his socially ambitious wife—played by Maggie Smith —she's ecstatic about the idea. Though the writing is rather shaky on this point, and it may not make a lot of sense to us in the audience, Mrs. Chilvers is convinced that stealing the pig will change her and her husband's lives and give them the social position she feels is her due. (And because of her maneuverings it does work out that way.)

This woman of steel who bosses and bullies her husband is an inspired parody of Lady Macbeth. Mrs. Chilvers gives piano lessons, and spends much of her time trying to keep her dotty old mother (Liz Smith) in line, but she has visions of herself as a woman of class and refinement —visions that have been severely tested by her marriage. Maggie Smith and Liz Smith (no relation) make a great mother-daughter comedy team; the mother is like a bleary, befuddled mirror image of the daughter's pretensions. And Maggie Smith can bring you up short by a devastating inflection. When Chilvers polishes the car that for want of fuel he has kept on blocks but will need for the kidnapping, he says, in satisfaction, "I can see me face in that." The mournfulness of all Mrs. Chilvers' disappointment in him comes out in her "So can I."

After Chilvers kidnaps the pig and brings it home, he lacks the callousness to kill it, and the pig, who snuffles like a chugging train and has an upset stomach in addition to normal piggy incontinence, uses the Chilvers living quarters as a pen. Maggie Smith proves herself a sovereign comedienne in the broadest of broad situations. When visitors to the Chilvers home are puzzled by the foul smell, Mrs. Chilvers wrinkles her skinny nose, tightens her mouth, and tries to blame it on her mother's advanced years. Soon the angry town leaders arrive to claim the main course of their banquet, and fall to arguing. The most reasonable is the accountant, whose resemblance to the pig makes him seem rather endearing—he's as dismayed as the tenderhearted Chilvers at the prospect of the animal's being butchered. (Chilvers offers the suggestion that the power-élite fellows should set her up somewhere in a sty.)

A Private Function is like *Volpone* set in a cabbage patch. The characters cheat and conspire at such a low level that at times you laugh helplessly. About the only person in town who abides by the egalitarian regulations is the inspector for the Ministry of Food (Bill Paterson), and he has no sense of smell or of taste, and seems deficient in other senses, too. At least, he does until his seductive landlady (Rachel Davies) gets him to paint stocking seams on her bare legs. When the bigwigs are shouting and carrying on at the Chilvers place, Mrs. Chilvers dresses up in a horrendous, tarty blue frock, wheels in a cocktail cart, and socks her body around—she's using her idea of feminine wiles. The scene begins promisingly but lasts a shade too long, and the final celebration dinner is too comfy. By not going into wild farce, the movie becomes trivial. It goes nowhere—no further than the Ealing comedies did. But it's alive and unruly; the humor keeps boiling up. The film has quick shifts of tone, and every once in a while there's an effect that's inexplicably, touchingly funny—like the deranged lyricism of a shot of the mother and the huge pink porker side by side looking out of an upstairs bedroom window.

March 25, 1985

CODDLED

As David, the L.A. advertising whiz who's the protagonist of *Lost in America,* Albert Brooks is only a slightly exaggerated specimen of a large number of rising young businessmen and professional men—the insecure successes, the swollen-headed worriers. He's the baby that we see inside those prosperous professionals. David has a bland moon-face surrounded by an aureole of tight, dark curls; it's as if he wore his brains on the outside. He looks soft; he isn't fat, though—he's just too well fed. If he were a contented man—say, a musician in a symphony orchestra who picked up extra income from the recording companies—he might be a likable dumpling. But David is an obsessive careerist who agonizes over every detail of his life. On the night before he expects to be made vice-president of the ad agency, he lies awake wondering whether he and his wife, Linda (Julie Hagerty), the personnel director of a department store, have done the right thing in putting down a deposit on a four-hundred-and-fifty-thousand-dollar house. He still harbors the dream of dropping out—of taking to the road, like the heroes of *Easy Rider.* He's torturing himself with anxieties, and he keeps waking the exhausted Linda to tell her his misgivings and be comforted by her reassurances.

David has got himself so keyed up for the vice-presidency and has put so much energy into worrying about whether he's picking the right house, the right Mercedes, and the right boat to go with the job that when he is finally in the boss's office and is offered a different kind of promotion (a big new account that involves a transfer to New York) he doesn't have the flexibility to deal with it. He becomes unhinged; he's like an outraged infant. He howls, he rants. If he can't have the title he wants, he doesn't want anything. His explosion comes in waves: he quiets down for a second or two, and then his nasal whine starts up again. By the time the scene is over, he has insulted the boss and been fired from his hundred-thousand-dollar-a-year job, and he's in a state of shock that's also a state of exaltation, of triumph. He rushes over to his wife's store, demands that she quit, too, and wants to celebrate this moment of liberation by having sex right this minute on her desk in her glass-enclosed office.

Lost in America is a satirical comedy about upper-middle-class infantilism and obnoxiousness—everything that Albert Brooks' David incarnates. Brooks, who directed the film and co-wrote the script (with Monica Johnson, who also worked on his two earlier pictures, the 1979 *Real Life* and the 1981 *Modern Romance*), has developed a cool, balanced attitude toward himself as performer. The self-absorbed, ingrown David is quite different from the characters that Albert Brooks has played in other directors' movies. Brooks was Cybill Shepherd's officious political co-worker in *Taxi Driver*; he was the unromantic bridegroom who collapsed on his wedding night in *Private Benjamin*; he was the driver in the prologue to *Twilight Zone—The Movie*; and he was close to inspired as the symphony conductor's manager in the 1984 *Unfaithfully Yours*. He's a remarkable comic actor—remarkable enough, perhaps, to delude people into thinking he's just playing himself in *Lost in America*. It's true that the camera often seems to be staring at David, revealing his innermost weakness. (He's always sorry for himself.) And Albert Brooks may have conceived this character because he saw the possibilities for this kind of maddening twerp in himself, but David is a fully created obsessive fool. He's a highly verbal jerk who half knows he's behaving like a jerk but can't stop himself—he's a self-conscious, pesky toddler at loose in the world. But though he's tiresome to everybody in the movie he isn't tiresome to us. David's lines have been sharpened to a fatuous fine edge—he keeps us laughing at him. And *Lost in America* doesn't dawdle; it's pleasantly snappy—it makes its comic points and moves on.

Julie Hagerty is an ideal choice for David's mate: you listen to Hagerty's Linda and you know why she puts up with him. Her little-girl breathiness tells you. And the dim stress and panic of her gaze suggest that somewhere in her past she has been frightened and David is the Teddy bear she clutches. (These two are endlessly apologizing to each other; they do it so automatically they might be apologizing in their sleep.) Linda is bleakly pretty; she's gaunt and hollow-eyed and wispy —she seems to be disappearing. David's aggressiveness and his near-loony dependence on her don't faze her. Life fazes her. She's bored to depression by being cooped up in her office in the department store; she's depressed by her whole conformist existence. But she's too timid and worn down to come right out and express her resentment. Curly-headed

David, who's crazy about her—kissing her and complimenting her ritu-
ally (if nothing else occupies his mind)—never guesses at her feelings.
When these two sell off their property, buy a luxury motor home, and,
with the security of a nest egg of roughly a hundred and forty-five
thousand, set out to find themselves and get in touch with the real
America, the picture has the promising overtones of a Preston Sturges
comedy.

The movie makes a honey of a transition—a cut from the farewell
party that David and Linda's friends give them to a shot of David looking
minuscule behind the wheel of the disproportionately large motor home
as they leave L.A. The best visual joke in the picture is simply the
recurring image of these two people who think themselves dropouts and
Easy Riders as they move across the country encased in their thirty-foot
Winnebago. Along the way, Brooks has a couple of sustained showpiece
scenes where he plays off someone who can't quite believe that this guy
is actually saying what he's saying. After the meek Linda blows their
nest egg at the Desert Inn Casino, in Las Vegas, David goes to see the
pit boss (well played by Garry Marshall, the director of *The Flamingo
Kid*) and, using his advertising-man skills—and here he's flexible—tries
to persuade this smart, tough fellow to give back the money. The most
ingenious of David's gambits is that returning Linda's losses can be
good for business—that the casino can thus be publicized as a casino
with heart, one that periodically plays Santa Claus to losers. Spritzing
one proposal after another, as if he'd been hired to prepare a campaign,
David beams at the pit boss, he cajoles him; he doesn't grovel, but you
know he would if he thought it would have any effect. And his adversary
is amused by the agility of David's thought processes. (In a Preston
Sturges comedy, the pit boss might have gone loco and actually adopted
the Christmas-casino idea.) David also has an interview scene with an
employment agent (Art Frankel) in a desolate small town in Arizona;
when David tells the agent how much he was earning, the old guy is
infatuated with the numbers and can't resist tweaking him by repeating
the amount over and over.

David and Linda's experiences in the real America turn out to be a
two-week vacation, and the movie has a nice, quick wrapup. In terms of
David's character, the end says all that needs to be said. And probably
there's no way for Brooks to develop the plot any further, because he
sees David as hopeless—as upper-middle-class in every soft fibre of his
anxious, coddled being. But the movie needs another turnaround, because although the ending is right for David, it isn't right for Linda.
Once she's away from her hated job, she becomes prettier and more

bouncy. She is perhaps even too adorable at times, but not glaringly. (Julie Hagerty may look like the old-fashioned girl that suitors would bring nosegays to, but she's a gifted, sexy comedienne.) Linda's losing the money seems to free the movie, to open it, and she herself relaxes a bit. David becomes more compulsive than ever. His worst terror has been realized, and his mind never shuts down. He tries to hold his anger in, but when he's looking out over Hoover Dam he can't help yelling about the money, and once again the joke is in the disproportion between him and the physical setting. David keeps going over what has happened. He picks at it; he bleeds. But Linda, having done the unthinkable, is able for the first time to laugh at him. And there's the suggestion that her blowing the money wasn't a totally subconscious protest: in her tiny, touching voice, she maneuvered David away from his plan that they go to the Silver Bell Chapel to renew their marriage vows, and got him to take her to the Desert Inn. Afterward, her only explanation to David is "I held things in for so long I felt like I was going to burst." By talking her into quitting her job, David has unloosed something in her that Brooks and his co-writer don't quite know what to do with.

The movie is so good that it needs to flower; it's like a Sturges idea that runs dry. But it's still a nifty, original comedy. The performances in the along-the-road vignettes are like a series of small presents to the audience. If the movie seems slight, that may be because we're essentially following just the one story—David's. It would be great if Albert Brooks could get to the point of showing the interaction of a group of these contemporary monomaniacs—which is essentially what Sturges did (though Sturges didn't rip the characters from inside himself). Brooks is on to something: satirizing the upper middle class from within, he shows the nagging terror along with the complacency. If he could pit a David against a few other people as driven and talkative as he is—if a David had to fight for screen time and space with people every bit as competitive—there's no telling what comedy heights Brooks could scale.

□

Most of *The Breakfast Club* takes place in the library of a suburban Chicago high school where, for various infractions of the rules, five students are serving a 7 A.M.–4 P.M. Saturday detention. Each of the five is a different type, and together they form a cross-section of

346

the student body. They are a champion wrestler (Emilio Estevez), a popular redhead "princess" (Molly Ringwald), a grind (Anthony Michael Hall), a glowering rebel-delinquent (Judd Nelson), who wears an earring, and a shy, skittish weirdo (Ally Sheedy). They walk in not liking each other and with their defenses in place. But they're like the homosexuals who gathered at the party in *The Boys in the Band* and played the "truth game." In the course of the day, under the prodding of the rebel and the mellowing effect of the marijuana he provides, they peel off layers of self-protection, confess their problems with their parents, and, after much shedding of tears, are stripped down to their true selves. When the doors are opened, they walk out transformed. They know who they are; they know who the others are. *The Breakfast Club* is *A Chorus Line* without the dancing. It's *The Exterminating Angel* as a sitcom. This is a very wet movie (and a very white movie), but it is a box-office hit, and has been widely praised for its seriousness. "It's the kind of mature teenage film I enjoy seeing" is one of the quotes used in the advertising.

The writer-director John Hughes, who made his directing début just last year, with the uneven but light and peppy *Sixteen Candles*, has gone the group-therapy route this time and has also fallen back on the standard device for appealing to teen audiences, the device of *Rebel Without a Cause* and *Splendor in the Grass*: blaming adults for the kids' misery. Each kid in turn tells the group of the horrors of home: the wrestler's father pushes him to compete, the princess is given *things* but not affection, the brainy grind is pressured to be a straight-A student, the (secretly sensitive) rebel is beaten and burned by his brute of a father, the shy girl—the basket case—has parents who ignore her. It's she who puts her finger on the source of all their troubles. "It's unavoidable," she says. "When you grow up, your heart dies." During the confessions, faraway synthesizer-organ sounds come toward you. And, as if the truths being uncovered in the library weren't enough, in the basement the janitor (John Kapelos) is doing a truth-telling number on the dean (Paul Gleason) who is proctoring the detention. The dean's heart is dead, all right—he hates the students. He's a bureaucrat who's in the school system strictly for the money. He tells the rebel that he's not going to let anyone endanger his thirty-one thousand a year.

Young audiences have always been suckers for this kind of flattery. They love hearing kids swap stories about how rotten their parents are, and no doubt they like to see all this viciousness loaded on the school official. The budding neuroses that made these kids antagonistic to one another are cured by their coming to see their parents and teachers as

347

the common enemy. Watching as each kid bared his psyche, I had the hopeful thought that maybe this script was something John Hughes had written several years earlier (long before *Sixteen Candles*). I would like to believe that, because he has another picture coming out in a few months. He does have talent, but in *The Breakfast Club* it's tucked in around the edges of his schematic plot.

Hughes' production unit is based in Chicago, and that seems to be good for his ear. When the kids are just killing time and being funny—when they're not being challenged by the rebel's probing—the dialogue has an easy, buggy rhythm. (There are stray bits of oddball parody when you can't tell exactly what is being parodied.) But the scenes involving the snotty, callous dean ring false right from the start, and though Paul Gleason seems miscast, maybe anybody playing this villain would seem miscast. Judd Nelson's role as the catalyst-rebel—the working-class kid who's good with his hands (he loves shop), and is also a hipster, and fearless—is a dud, too. And Nelson doesn't seem to have a speck of spontaneity. After his early scenes, he becomes too self-pitying, and he's given to tilting up his head and pointing his nostrils at the camera.

The four other leading performers fare a lot better. As the straight-arrow jock, Estevez (who was the kid in *Repo Man*) isn't particularly enjoyable—he's a little heavy on sincerity—but he does a creditably simple job, especially in his long monologue about his father's always telling him to "win, win." Molly Ringwald's role isn't as fresh or festive as her birthday-girl part in *Sixteen Candles*, but she slips into the well-heeled Miss Popularity languor without any unnecessary fuss. And Anthony Michael Hall, whose teeth are still in the braces he wore in the gleeful role of Geek in *Sixteen Candles*, delivers a thoughtful, nuanced performance. He's the pale, tall, thin boy who is an ace at book learning —he excels in math and is active in the Physics Club—but is a frightened, virtuous dork away from his books. The fine-featured Hall takes this traditional namby-pamby good-boy role and fills it out with fresh emotion. (He's prodigious—he comes close to flooding a role the way Debra Winger does.)

But the only performance that has a comic kick to it is Ally Sheedy's. She's a flip-out, a girl who hides in her clothes and thinks she's being a loner and a mysterious recluse. Bundled up in black shawls and layers of cloth, she's like a junior Madwoman of Chaillot; with her forehead hidden under her dark hair, and her chin held down, she's furtive yet bold. Her minx's face is a tiny triangle in the darkness. When she moves, she darts, and when you see her eyes they dart, too, and flash—they're the eyes of someone who's secretly grinning. Crazy sounds come out of her, and she does eccentric things—like drawing a picture of a winter scene and shaking her dandruff on it for snow. She's a marvellous comic sprite, a bag-lady Puck. And then John Hughes makes his soggiest mistake: the princess takes her in hand, scrubs all the black eye makeup off her, gets her out of her witches' wrappings, and brushes her hair back and puts a ribbon in it, and she comes forth looking broad-faced and dull. But she's supposed to be beautiful, and she captures the jock's heart.

The picture opens with an epigraph from David Bowie's "Changes": "And these children that you spit on/as they try to change their world/are immune to your consultations./They're quite aware of what they're going through." And the picture closes on the group leaving the school with all their new understanding, and the now smiling rebel flinging his fist straight up in the air, in a gesture of defiance, solidarity, triumph. But all that this encounter-session movie actually does is strip a group of high-school kids down to their most banal longings to be accepted and liked. Its real emblem is that dreary, retro ribbon.

April 8, 1985

PASSION

Eli (Nick Mancuso) and Blue (Peter Coyote), the two central characters in *Heartbreakers*, are inseparable friends, and it's easy to perceive their longtime affection for each other. It's in the half looks they exchange; it's in the way they move down the street together, and in the things they take for granted. The movie is about what's underneath their buddy relationship: their competitiveness, their jealousy of each other, their resentments—all the unresolved feelings that go into making them rivals. Women are their battlefield. The darkly handsome Eli takes over his father's business (a women's-apparel factory), and he lives in a swank little house, drives a neat car, and isn't short of funds, so maybe there's a natural balance in the fact that the women he likes are attracted to Blue, a driven, unsuccessful painter, always broke.

Bobby Roth wrote and directed this low-budget feature (his fourth), and it was photographed on locations in his home town, Los Angeles, by the Berlin-born cinematographer Michael Ballhaus, whose wide-ranging credits include seventeen Fassbinder films. When Eli and Blue are hanging out at places like Fatburger or the gym The Sports Connection, they fit right in. Both in their mid-thirties, they're like hip American versions of the men in Bertrand Blier's *Get Out Your Handkerchiefs*; they're attractive to women and they have no trouble making out, but women mystify them. At the beginning of the movie, Blue realizes that Cyd (Kathryn Harrold), who has been living with him for five years in a loft with few of the amenities—it doesn't even have a real bed—is "slipping away" from him. She wants something more substantial than his idea of an artist's life; she complains that when he's painting he forgets all about her. Blue is sick at the thought of losing her, and he expresses his anxieties to Eli. But all he says to Cyd is "If you're not happy, leave," and despite her feelings for him she takes up with the attentive, dependable Chuck King (Max Gail), an abstractionist who sells and isn't as passionately involved in his work as Blue. (The paintings in this movie seem exactly right: King's patterned canvases look like Blue's description of them as wallpaper. If Blue were more generous, he might call them agreeable, workmanlike wallpaper.) Cyd's leaving Blue precipitates the events of the movie. Desperate to win her back, he tries to pull his life together. He quits his crummy job at a printshop—he tells the boss he can't stand printing porno stuff anymore. And then he talks a gallery owner into giving him a show by capitalizing on his (somewhat embarrassed) attraction to fetishes: he produces a series of high-camp Pop paintings—porny pinups that feature a dominatrix, Candy (the late Carol Wayne), decked out in a wig, high heels, garter belts, merry widows, and leather.

Meanwhile, Eli, who is shorter and more muscular than Blue, and looks younger and healthier, loses his father, takes on heavier business responsibilities, and, after years of doing well with women but feeling empty because they don't mean more to him than casual sex, spots the girl he thinks is *the* girl. Liliane (played by Carole Laure, the willowy French-Canadian actress who was the pivotal figure in the Blier film) is an assistant at the gallery where Blue is to have his show, but her principal occupation appears to be doing calisthenics, aerobics, and dance movements. (The results seem worth every bit of the compulsive

350

effort.) When Liliane isn't working out, she's wiggling like an exotic temptress, with her long dark hair sheathing her snaky body. Carole Laure suggests a haunted, feverish sensuality, and she gets by with all of Liliane's sultry squirminess, even when the editing doesn't protect her and she's seen rolling her eyes like a latter-day Tondelayo (the sexy savage of *White Cargo* who drove men wild with lust). The key difference between Liliane and Tondelayo is that Liliane fancies herself a feminist. Her idea of controlling her life is to have sex with Eli in his car but refuse to go to bed with him; she's like a soulful dominatrix, and she keeps him spinning.

Roth doesn't quite sustain the Eli-and-Blue parallel-lives construction; he seems more involved with Blue—maybe because he dealt with a character in Eli's situation in his film *The Boss' Son*. And there could be another reason. In photographs, Roth looks like a cross between Coyote's Blue and Mancuso's Eli, and in an interview with the *Times* he said that the two characters "were actually two sides of myself—the political artist side and the businessman-Jewish-son side—and they were based on composites of all my male friends." But he must have identified much more strongly with the artist side; the film couldn't be so full of tension and temperament if he hadn't. Roth has an intuitive feeling for movement—movement that appears natural yet is heightened. The picture doesn't look as if it had been photographed in separate shots; the movement seems fluid, continuous. There's always something going on between Mancuso and Coyote; they're a good team, even though Mancuso on his own is a dark, polite blank—Heathcliff out to lunch. He suggests a generic businessman-son, with no specifics and little personality—just a faint disaffection. (Eli is smooth-faced and withdrawn even in the hospital scene where his dying father—played by George Morfogen, who's a fine physical matchup—expresses contempt for him.)

Sometimes the characters open their mouths and what comes out isn't dialogue—it doesn't deepen the scene or move it along. And sometimes the characters simply don't have enough to say, and the scenes feel muffled or hollow, as if the director wasn't quite sure what he was getting at—as if he was hoping for a revelation. (Roth may need to work with a writer.) *Heartbreakers* engages a viewer, but it doesn't hold together in the memory, because it's all moods and moments, and much of the emotion swirling about is inchoate—for example, Liliane's weeping after sex, and even in the wonderful scene where Eli asks Blue to dance with Liliane so he can watch and torment himself. It's a mood-poem movie. (At times, it's like a more realistic Alan Rudolph film; at other times it's a little like one of Cassavetes' drunken-buddy pictures.)

And the mood is basically set by Peter Coyote. He's more open to the camera than anyone else; his face and body say more. Mancuso's handsomeness is like a mask, but Coyote, who often looks ravaged, meets the other actors more than halfway. The women's attraction to him is convincing; their subsequent anger, disappointment, and depression are convincing, too.

Blue wants women to be around when he takes a break from his work; he doesn't want to be bothered when he's working. He expects the women he likes to be far more independent than they are—he is surprised to discover that he can't deal with them on his terms without hurting them. (The saddest is Candy, the hooker-model with the whips, who's a sweet, maternal pussycat.) The movie catches the confusion in the relations of the sexes without sentimentalizing that confusion. (Blue's name is the film's most sentimental touch, and it can be partly explained by the fact that his paintings are actually the work of the artist Robert Blue.) What binds the two guys is their bewilderment about women. They seem to blame each other for a good measure of their emotional frustration (and their rage erupts when they play racquetball).

The women in this movie are all likable, yet they're screwed-up and, from the men's point of view, utterly impossible. The women don't want the guys to be overprotective or to treat them as helpless, yet they expect to be taken care of. The men don't know which signals to follow, and the women don't know which signals they're sending out, because their feelings are contradictory. They want to be respected as modern, independent women, and they want to be cuddled like little girls. Courting Liliane, Eli keeps trying to tune in to whatever frequency she's operating on, but he never finds it. Blue can't believe that Cyd, who acknowledges that she loves him, will stay on with Chuck King. There's nothing dirty or spiteful or anti-woman in Roth's approach; it simply recognizes how insane all this is.

Heartbreakers deals with sex in a matter-of-fact way and in an American idiom—in our body language, with our shorthand, and in our lofts and apartments. The characters are frazzled in ways we recognize. Coyote's Blue looks like the kind of guy who has tended his boyishness over the years; he has the not-quite-grownup American look—an anguished boyishness. And when his sold-out show and his unaccustomed solvency don't bring Cyd back, his face takes on new expressions of uncertainty and pain. Blue's capacity for unconcealed suffering is what makes him Roth's hero. At the opening of the movie, when Blue is afraid he's losing Cyd, he goes to Eli's place to talk to him, and Eli and his date

(Jamie Rose), who are giddy and charged up and just about to have sex, forget about it and take him out to comfort him. He really cares about Cyd, and that's more emotionally involving for them than the flirty relationship they were engaged in.

It's Blue's depth of emotion—what Eli calls his "passion"—that Eli can never forgive him for. It's what, in the framework of this movie, distinguishes the artist from the businessman. There's an undeniable element of fanciness in the conception, and I wish the movie weren't awed by Blue. Are his glossy pinups an expression of his passion? Or of something lesser—a callow obsession, perhaps, or even a way of taking revenge on Cyd? There's an element of revenge in Blue's becoming successful—he's showing her what she passed up. (Generally, the kind of close relationship between men that *Heartbreakers* is about doesn't last after one of them marries, and this might suggest that Blue isn't as serious about Cyd as he wants to believe he is.) Roth doesn't go deep enough, but he succeeds in using the two men as a way into the American culture of sex, circa the mid-eighties, and he captures something of West Coast bohemianism. He characterizes everyone; people who nod at Eli or Blue in a breakfast spot turn up again, and you begin to get a sense of them as the regulars in the places Eli and Blue go to. Blue has no illusions about the kind of gallery he's showing at; it's the hot gallery of the moment, run by a dealer (James Laurenson) who takes sixty per cent. But this dealer knows what he's up to, and he's as happy as a baby boy when he puts over an unknown like Blue. He prances in triumph, and sings "For I Am a Pirate King." Roth uses time-lapse photography as a comic device to show us the gallery filling up for the opening of Blue's show. When things are in full swing, Blue's old boss from the printshop comes over to congratulate him and to twit him, too, about his having been fed up with porno stuff; it's a fine small exchange.

If the movie is a little unformed, that's because Roth is attempting to be truthful to his own experience and the lives of those around him. He's trying to express lives in flux. This is the sort of attempt that usually turns into an unreleasable picture, a straining-for-seriousness embarrassment. But Roth has his wits about him, and Peter Coyote rings true whether he's drunkenly razzing Chuck King or sobbing in a crowded diner. *Heartbreakers* becomes more involving as it goes on, and when it's over, you feel you've seen something (even if you're not quite sure what).

Desperately Seeking Susan is a mutant of some sort, an attempt at screwball charm that can make your jaw fall open and stay down until the rest of your head joins it. (A friend of mine says that this picture is for people who grow up on rotoscope animation and prefer it to the real thing.) The director, Susan Seidelman, pulps her actors; she wipes them out and turns them into cardboard. All their responsiveness is cut off—there's nothing going on in them. No subtext—nothing. This flatness must be part of what the admirers of the film (it's being widely praised) think is new. Seidelman doesn't show any interest in drawing us into the action, either. This can make the movie seem very postmodern. Set in the punk world, it's a mistaken-identity fantasy about doe-eyed Roberta (Rosanna Arquette), a suburban housewife in New Jersey who becomes fixated on a drifter named Susan (played by the rock star Madonna). Susan's lover communicates with her through the personals columns, and Roberta, imagining that Susan's life is full of the passion that's missing from her own, goes to lower Manhattan and tails her. And the picture chases after Roberta, who's meant to be adorably dopey. But with scenes that have no pulse or rhythm, and dialogue that makes you cringe, dopey is all that Rosanna Arquette can manage.

The movie doesn't have a story—just a story line. A klunk on the noggin turns Roberta into an amnesiac, she gets a job as a night-club magician's assistant, is pursued by a killer who thinks she's Susan, falls in love with the projectionist at the Bleecker Street Cinema, who also thinks she's Susan, is put in jail as a prostitute, and on and on. How did this script (by Leora Barish) ever get produced? Nobody comes through in the movie except Madonna, who comes through as Madonna (she moves regally, an indolent, trampy goddess), and the cinematographer, Edward Lachman, whose lighting gives the East Village shops and streets a funky prettiness—like an Expressionist painting of neon squalor and lollipops. Lachman and Seidelman and the production designer, Santo Loquasto, stir up a sense of visual activity, but the transactions between the people on the screen are stupefying (and often in woozy slow-motion, like a rock video going poetic).

When you come out of Desperately Seeking Susan, you don't want to know who the director is—you want to know who the perpetrator is. Susan Seidelman made a name with her first feature, the 1982 Smithereens, a moralistic view of a skinny young groupie (Susan Berman) whose tacky efforts to be part of the downtown, punk-rock scene were fun to watch until the picture started using her as a bad example. The movie didn't just set her up as a victim of false ideals; it also delivered the homiletic message that if you're not kind to other people you'll be left alone. The images got grubbier and grubbier as the selfish groupie was finally utterly humiliated and was on her bedraggled way to being a hooker and a junkie. *Smithereens* is one of those dismally naïve movies that make you pay for every smile or chuckle you had at the start, but it was brought in for only eighty thousand dollars (it was shot in 16 mm.), and Susan Seidelman, an N.Y.U. film-school graduate, was taken up as a public heroine. And now *Desperately Seeking Susan*, which cost five million dollars, is being treated as a fulfillment of the (dim) promise of *Smithereens*.

Essentially, Madonna's role as Susan is a continuation of the selfish bad example, but at least this picture is, technically speaking, a comedy, and so the character doesn't have to pay for her narcissism. And Madonna doesn't look as if she's about to, even if the script called for it. She has dumbfounding aplomb. In the scenes in which she's in New Jersey, vamping Roberta's square husband, who's in the hot-tub business, she luxuriates in suburban materialism as if she'd discovered the pleasures of imperial Rome. The film has its myth structure: Roberta is the good girl who gets mixed up with Susan the bad girl and is liberated. But its only promising moments are in the possibilities for a reversal—when Madonna suggests that suburban comfort might be just the ticket for a girl who's been hustling for her keep.

An example of the moviemaking technique here: Susan goes into one of her old, nocturnal haunts and runs into an acquaintance—the cigarette girl—who is presented to us in a shot that starts with her legs and travels up her body; we're appraising her flesh, like a roué. Susan says something to her, and moves on; the other girl is of no further consequence.

To quote Bernardo Bertolucci, who was quoting the Brazilian Glauber Rocha, "A film director is the man who finds the money to make a movie." That basic definition holds for women, too, and Susan Seidelman has met it—twice. She has also been lucky: the audiences at *Desperately Seeking Susan* seem willing to accept her amateurishness as a confirmation of the happy, new-wave innocence of the movie. ("See," Seidelman is saying, "I'm just as dopey as my heroine.") But actors ought to be cautious: what she does to Rosanna Arquette could happen to anybody.

April 22, 1985

THE MUDDLE AGES

here's some enticement in the idea of *Ladyhawke*, a medieval romance set in and around the walled city of Aquila, which is ruled by an evil bishop (John Wood). This tyrant secretly lusts after the matchlessly beautiful golden-haired Princess Isabeau (Michelle Pfeiffer), and when he discovers that she and his captain of the guard, the noble Navarre (Rutger Hauer), are in love, he reverts to sorcery and puts a curse on the couple to frustrate them forever. Each sunrise, Isabeau turns into a hawk; each sundown, Navarre turns into a black wolf. The movie is about the banished Navarre's attempt to fight his way back into Aquila to take vengeance, and how the spell is eventually broken, with the assistance of a boy thief called Phillipe the Mouse (Matthew Broderick), the only person who has ever escaped from the bishop's dungeons, and a swillbelly priest (Leo McKern), who was once the lovers' confessor. There's also some lure in the settings. Aquila, with its immense fortress, has been synthesized out of three castles, dating back to the twelfth and thirteenth centuries (with portions going back even further), that were part of Luchino Visconti's estates in the mountains north of Parma—inherited holdings that Visconti worked to restore. And the crumbling abbey on a mountain peak, where the priest lives alone, is actually Rocca Calascio, a castle built in the Dark Ages; it was more than four hundred years old when Richard the Lion-Hearted, on his way home from the Crusades, was imprisoned there. This is no little back-lot B picture. The interior of the bishop's Greco-Roman cathedral was built full scale on Cinecittà Studios' Teatro 5—the largest sound stage in Europe. A huge amount of effort was put into training hawks and wolves (and a malamute dog for some doubling), and the accoutrements have their own grandeur: Rutger Hauer sports black armor and a black visor with V-shaped stripes which makes his head look like a hood ornament for a medieval Rolls-Royce, and he sits on a round-rumped black charger whose hooves shake the earth.

Just about everything connected with *Ladyhawke* is big except the storytelling instinct of its director, Richard Donner. It's a mild and dreary movie. Donner—he also made *The Omen, Superman, Inside Moves,* and *The Toy*—doesn't build the scenes. There's no development; he just shuffles along, and frequently the audience seems to be a few plot devices ahead of him, numbly waiting for him to catch up. If there's one thing a movie about magical transformations needs, it's quick-wittedness. When, just before dawn, Isabeau (the name sounds like a transsexual Isabelle) falls from the tower of the mountaintop abbey, we expect the first rays of the savior sun to hit her dramatically—we expect her to turn into a hawk with a whoosh, like a parachute opening. But we have to wait too long, and the metamorphosis, when it comes, is drab and blurry. At almost every point in the movie where we might expect a little ping of surprise or mystery, Donner lets us down, and the cumulative disappointment can make what should be a glorious tale of enchantment seem depressing. Even the explanation of the vile bishop's curse on the lovers is a fizzle: it comes too late, after you've figured most of it out for yourself. And the climactic event (lifted from Mark Twain's *A Connecticut Yankee in King Arthur's Court*) has no dazzle or thrill. We wait for the big surprise to be sprung, and it's passed over so casually it hardly seems to have happened. There's a blah at the center of this movie.

Though the outdoor scenes have a good smoky clutter that gives you a medieval feeling of enchanted forests and murderous innkeepers, the picture has a tinted, muddied-up look. And, inexplicably, Michelle Pfeiffer, who, with her pale, almond-shaped eyes and her amazing porcelain cheekbones, has the beauty that the story calls for, is too often shrouded in shadows and darkness; you have to strain to see her. Pfeiffer hasn't yet had a role to give meaning or tenderness to her beauty; she's a bit remote (and not just visually), but she's lithe and graceful, and she moves fast. Compared with, say, Elizabeth Taylor and Joan Fontaine in *Ivanhoe,* she's a whirlwind, and though she doesn't affect us emotionally, as Taylor did, her modern physical freedom is in key with the mythological world of man into wolf, woman into hawk. Yet neither the director nor the screenwriters—Edward Khmara, Michael Thomas, and Tom Mankiewicz—do much with the theme of sensual deprivation. There is only one scene when we actually feel that Isabeau (by night) and Navarre (by day) are longing for each other: it comes in an instant of sunrise when they touch hands just before she turns into a hawk, and as she flies off he, though he is already in human form, lets out a wolflike howl of anguish. (It's the best scene they have—the only one that stirs the imagination.) But casting John Wood as the bishop cancels out the libidinous nature of the punishment inflicted on the lovers. Wood's bean pole of a bishop doesn't have the physical presence of a major villain. Thin-lipped and dry-mouthed, he speed-freaks through his lines, turning them into tongue twisters. Consumed with passion for Isabeau? Not this fellow. His only lust is for enunciation.

A strapping blue-eyed platinum blond, Rutger Hauer looks like the actor Adolf Hitler would have wanted to star in the movie of his life. This Dutch Siegfried (the hero in *Soldier of Orange,* the leader of the angry replicants in *Blade Runner*) has rid himself of his accent, and he gives a solid performance—too solid, maybe, and heavy-spirited. His Navarre is short on youthful dash, and we don't get much chance to cheer for him, because the director often cheats in the action sequences. When Navarre has no weapon except the short arrow that he has pulled out of his breast and he's up against knights with broadswords, the camera angles jump about and suddenly his enemies are vanquished, without our seeing how. We feel—almost subliminally—gypped. And the clumsiness in the construction of the script makes him seem obstinate and a little thick in the head. His quest is simply to kill the bishop, though if he does he and Isabeau can never be united. The priest has a plan to break the spell, but it requires Navarre to wait a day before entering Aquila. He insists on pushing ahead, and the priest has to conspire with Isabeau and Phillipe to delay him.

If Navarre doesn't quite click as a hero, it's essentially because the character we're meant to identify with is Matthew Broderick's Phillipe (that's how Philippe is spelled in the credits), who is like a contemporary American adolescent placed in the Middle Ages. It's a basic convention: Bob Hope used to be himself in the midst of costume pictures, and, of course, Twain's Connecticut Yankee brought his modern consciousness to King Arthur's court. But *Ladyhawke* isn't a comedy, and so the device doesn't feel integral. You may suspect that this kid is there for insurance—that he's meant to represent the young ticket buyers who (the producers are afraid) might not want to be in the thirteenth century without one of their own on hand. Phillipe is made too endearing; he falls into the category of impish lad. And Broderick, who has had considerable experience playing young Neil Simon characters on the stage and the screen, gives his "clever" lines urban inflections that sometimes turn the movie into a skit about a little Jewish wise guy and Aryan giants. The effect is something like putting, say, a boy Woody Allen at Robert Taylor's elbow in *Ivanhoe.*

Phillipe talks to God, like a standup comic with Him for an audience.

(And since the sound mix is poor, Phillipe's voice seems to be coming from an empty room in another country.) Yet even when the lines are irritating, Broderick isn't. Yearning and wistfulness may come to him too easily, but when he isn't chattering to God—when he's interacting with the other performers—he's a happy, ingenious actor. He knows how to play scared and make it funny. He has a touch of the giddy uninhibitedness of the great clowns—you can see the character carried away by his thoughts, the way you sometimes could with Bert Lahr or Joe E. Brown. Put up on the screen for comic relief, Broderick has more of a fairy-tale quality than anyone else, and he gives this limp movie with its disco-medieval score its only traces of inspiration.

The question may be raised of what accounts for the quotes in the ads: "Fabulous!" and "Don't Walk, Run!" and "Enchanted, enthralling, marvelous," "A rousing, old-fashioned adventure," and "It makes you drunk on films again." The answer may be that even in a period of drought people in the press and on TV are looking for something to praise—they don't want to be soreheads. And *Ladyhawke* doesn't look pop or junky or crude, and God knows it isn't "challenging." So it doesn't scare them off. Its limpness makes it respectable.

May 13, 1985

TIDAL

When Sergio Leone's epic *Once Upon a Time in America* opened here in June, 1984, in a studio-hacked-down version (cut from three hours and forty-seven minutes to two hours and fifteen minutes), it seemed so incoherently bad that I didn't see how the full-length film could be anything but longer. A few weeks later, though, the studio people let me look at it, and I was amazed at the difference. I don't believe I've ever seen a worse case of mutilation. In the full version, the

359

plot, which spans almost a half century, was still somewhat shaky, but Robert De Niro's performance as the Jewish gangster, Noodles, took hold, and the picture had a dreamy obsessiveness. I was excited about it and expected to review it a few weeks later, when it was to be released. But the opening was postponed, the weeks stretched into months, and by the time the full (or reasonably complete) epic showed at the New York Film Festival and began slipping into a few theatres, other films were making a more urgent claim.

There's a special reason it lacked urgency: like the rest of Sergio Leone's work, *Once Upon a Time in America* has no immediacy, no present tense. And being in many ways a culmination of his career it's probably the least anchored of his films. Leone, who grew up in the Italian studio world (his father, Vincenzo Leone, was a pioneer director), isn't interested in observing the actual world—it probably seems too small and confining. He's involved in his childhood fixations about movies—stories enlarged, simplified, mythicized. (He only makes epics.) There's no irony in the title: he uproots American Westerns and gangster pictures and turns them into fairy tales and fantasies. In this movie, a Jewish deli on the Lower East Side in 1921 is on a street as broad as Park Avenue and has a storeroom the size of a football field. Leone doesn't care about the fact that it was the crowded, constricting buildings that drove the kids into the streets. He directs as if he had all the time in the world, and he has no interest in making his characters lifelike; he inflates their gestures and slows down their actions—every lick of the lips is important.

After we've seen conventional gangster pictures, the characters may become enlarged in our memories because of what they do and how the actors look as they're doing it. Leone doesn't bother to develop the characters—to him, they're mythic as soon as he puts them on the screen. And in this movie, though he gives almost an hour to the childhood years of his gang of six Jewish boys (and a couple of girls), the camera solemnizes and celebrates these kids of ten and twelve and fourteen from the start. It's like watching the flamboyant childhood of the gods. In a sense, what Leone gives us is predigested reveries; it's escapism at a further remove—a dream-begotten dream, but a feverish one, intensified by sadism, irrational passions, vengeance, and operatic savagery. (In the genre he created, the spaghetti Western, the protagonist didn't wait for his enemies to draw; he shot first.) Leone has found the right metaphor here: the movie begins and ends in an opium den, where Noodles puffs on a pipe while episodes of his life of killings and rapes and massacres drift by and a telephone rings somewhere in the past. The action is set in 1921, 1933, and 1968—but not in that order.

In its full length, the movie has a tidal pull back toward the earliest memories, and an elegiac tone. Partly, I think, this is the result of De Niro's measured performance. He makes you feel the weight of Noodles' early experiences and his disappointment in himself. He makes you feel that Noodles never forgets the past, and it's his all-encompassing guilt that holds the film's different sections together. De Niro was offered his choice of the two leading roles—Max, the go-getter, the tricky, hothead boss of the group, and the watchful, indecisive Noodles, the loser, who spends the years from 1921 to 1933 in prison. I respect De Niro's decision, because he may have thought that the passive Noodles, whose urges explode in bursts of aggression against women, would be a reach, would test him. But I think he made a mistake in terms of what was best for the movie, which, despite its hypnotic bravura, lacks the force at its center that a somewhere-between-twenty-one-and-forty-five-million-dollar epic (depending on who is asked) needs. James Woods, who plays Max, dominated the short version; he actually provided its brighter moments, and it's a sad thing when you go to a movie and look forward to seeing James Woods, whose specialty is acting feral. In the full version, De Niro gives the film its dimensions. He keeps a tiny flame alive in his eyes, and his performance builds, but Leone doesn't provide what seems essential: a collision between Noodles and Max—or, at least, some development of the psychosexual tensions that are hinted at. (When Noodles and Max are young teen-agers and are murderously beaten by a rival gang, Noodles lies writhing and Max crawls toward him—it's like Jennifer Jones and Gregory Peck at the end of *Duel in the Sun*.) The film's theme is the betrayal of the immigrants' dream of America; Max —ever greedy for more money, more power—represents the betrayer. By leaving the two men's competition and love-hate as just an undercurrent, the film chokes off its dramatic core. And Noodles often seems to be contemplating his life instead of living it. He's at his most assured— he comes into his own—when Noodles is about sixty; there's something old about him from the start. (No one is less likely to be called Noodles.)

Leone wants the characters to be as big as the characters he saw on the screen when he was a child, and he tries to produce that effect with looming closeups and heroic gestures; the key thing for his actors is to have the right look. Yet, despite his having breathed and talked this movie for almost ten years before he started production, he made some flagrant mistakes when he got down to the casting. After you've seen his *Once Upon a Time in the West*, you can't get the iconographic faces (Henry Fonda, Charles Bronson, Jason Robards, Woody

361

Strode, Claudia Cardinale, Jack Elam, and all the others) out of your mind. But it's almost impossible to visualize all of the five adult gang members in *America*, even right after you've seen the movie. Worse, they don't have the basic movie-gangster characteristic: they don't emanate danger. And although Deborah, the dancer-actress that Noodles loves all his life, is marvellously vivid in her young girlhood, when she's played by Jennifer Connelly (who's so clear-eyed she walks away with the twenties passages), the role of the adult Deborah is taken over by Elizabeth McGovern, who's classically miscast. McGovern's hairstyle is ferocious, she's unflatteringly photographed, and she moves like a woman who has never got used to being tall. She looks dispirited, and the flair she shows in her comedy roles isn't visible— she's so bad you feel sorry for her. (She's also the victim of a glitch in the film's time scheme: Deborah goes off to Hollywood in 1933, and then we learn in 1968 that she's now a big star.) McGovern's inability to live up to the idea that she's De Niro's great love weakens the film's showpiece romantic sequence, set in a vast Art Deco oceanfront restaurant on Long Island—a restaurant that is closed for the season but that Noodles has rented for the evening, with a full staff and a dance orchestra. The scene is meant to reveal Noodles' yearning nature; it's clear that Leone was thinking about Gatsby and lost dreams.

The other actresses fare much better. Tuesday Weld is in peak form as a nympho moll who becomes Max's girl. She isn't doing that anomic acting that made her tedious in films like *Play It As It Lays* and *Who'll Stop the Rain*; she looks great, and she has a gleam of perversity. She brings the film some snap and humor, and Woods has his best scene when he's elated at showing the other guys how little she means to him —it may be the best scene he has ever played. And, as a young woman that Noodles takes up with, Darlanne Fleugel is Art Deco incarnate; streamlined and blond, she wears her sleek thirties gowns with spectacular ease. Her performance is simple and in beautiful control, and De Niro has a relaxed elegance around her. The film could have used much more of her; she sets off its architectural motifs—its arches and scallop shapes.

Unlike Westerns, where everything is even literally out in the open, gangster movies have a special appeal: we want to know more about the concealed lives of these hidden outlaws, and how they work. (That was part of the excitement of the *Godfather* pictures—the fullness of the crime-family details.) Leone doesn't have enough interest in the real world to make the gang's dealings with bigger mobs and its union tie-ins even halfway intelligible. That's a real disappointment. You can't figure

362

out the logistics of the crimes; you don't know what's going on. What's probably going on is that Leone, with his dislocated myths, is like Noodles amid the poppy fumes—he's running old movies in his head. There's nothing in the movie to differentiate Jewish crime from Italian crime or any other kind. Leone's vision of Jewish gangsters is a joke. As a friend of mine put it, "it wasn't just that you never had the feeling that they were Jewish—you never had the feeling that they were anything."

The movie isn't really about America or about Jewish gangsters. But you can see why Leone was drawn to the subject: it was to create his widescreen dreamland view of the Lower East Side. That setting, filmed partly on a Brooklyn street near the waterfront, with the Williamsburg Bridge in the background, partly in Montreal, and partly on constructed sets in Rome, made it possible for him to transmute the Lower East Side settings of American gangster films—to give the genre a richer, more luxuriant visual texture. It's typical of Leone's grandiloquent style that the opium den, in the back room of a Chinese theatre, is sumptuous and large. And the Long Island restaurant that we see is impossibly lyrical and grand (the building is actually the Excelsior Hotel in Venice); it has to be archetypal for Leone, and it has to have an aura. Even though some of what he shows you defies common sense, visually he justifies his lust for the largest scale imaginable. He uses deep focus to draw details from the backgrounds into your awareness. The film is drenched in atmosphere, and you see more and more in the wide frames. You see howlers, too. One of my favorites is the gang's storing its booty of a million dollars in a locker in Grand Central in the twenties and Noodles' going to retrieve it in the thirties. But I imagine that if anybody had explained to Leone that those lockers were cleared every seventy-two hours he'd have brushed the fact aside as mere realism.

Just about all the incidents (including the palatial rented restaurant and the loot in the locker) echo scenes in Hollywood's gangster movies. There's the heart-tugger: the youngest and littlest member of the gang is the first to be killed. There's the black-humor gag: Max drives a hearse to pick up Noodles at the penitentiary gates, with a hooker who's ready and waiting stowed in a coffin. About all that's missing is that Noodles, being Jewish, doesn't have a boyhood friend who becomes a priest. Leone reworks the old scenes and embroiders on them. Our group of gangsters meet Tuesday Weld (and Noodles rapes her) in the course of an out-of-town robbery, when they're wearing hankies over their faces; when they encounter her again in New York, they reintroduce themselves by tying their hankies on their faces. (The fellows ask her to guess which one raped her, and they unzip.)

The movie might seem a compendium of kitsch—in a certain sense, it is. But it's kitsch aestheticized by someone who loves it and sees it as the poetry of the masses. It isn't just the echoing moments that keep you absorbed. It's those reverberant dreamland settings and Leone's majestic, billowing sense of film movement; the images seem to come at you in waves of feeling. Despite the film's miscasting and its craziness, Leone sustains the moods for an almost incredible three hours and forty-seven minutes—most of it unusually quiet. The movie has a pulse; it's alive. But not now. It's alive in some golden-brown past of the imagination.

May 27, 1985

SLAPHAPPY AND NOT SO HAPPY

What Have I Done to Deserve This! deserves a more inviting title. It's a generally likable dadaist farce about working-class family life in Madrid's housing projects—huge block buildings of dinky, cramped apartments put up in the sixties, during Franco's modernization program. The heroine, Gloria (Carmen Maura), cooks and scrubs and irons for her taxi-driver husband, her two sons, and her crabby old mother-in-law, and goes out to work as a cleaning woman. Gloria drags herself through eighteen-hour days with the help of No Doz and an occasional sniff of glue or detergent. She's the slightly surreal Mother Courage of this feminist parable. She's also a housewife version of those mean-spirited, henpecked husbands that W. C. Fields played in the thirties. She's everybody's slavey, and she's sex-starved besides. At the opening of the movie, she is invited into a shower with a naked patron of the martial-arts academy that she cleans; this kendo master is no master of the erotic arts—he leaves her as frustrated as her lug of a husband does. She works off her anger by bashing the air with a club—and that's a kind of haiku version of the movie, in which Gloria swats her chief oppressor and shakes loose from her family.

Pedro Almodóvar is a bad-boy writer-director—an actor and novelist who also writes comic strips and songs that are takeoffs of other people's songs. In *What Have I Done to Deserve This!*—his fourth feature film in 35 mm. (he shot an earlier one in Super 8)—he turns the slum buildings into stage sets, and daily life into a series of deadpan skits. He casts a delighted eye at the drug dealing of Gloria's fourteen-year-old son and the hustling of her twelve-year-old, who seduces his schoolmates' fathers. Her illiterate husband has a gift for forgery and is involved in a scheme to fake Hitler's memoirs. His old mother is played by a young actress (Chus Lampreave) who doesn't bother to use aging makeup. A red-haired little girl who lives in the building is a miniature Carrie, with telekinetic powers. And a ham bone is used as a lethal instrument.

Everything that happens is prepared for (in a slaphappy way), and the director connects all the characters, but there's no internal logic to the movie. Gloria is a fierce fighting woman one moment and a dishrag the next. We never get the hang of her attitudes: why is she so sweetly concerned about the little red-haired girl when she's relieved to be rid of her own kids? When a homosexual dentist offers to "adopt" her younger son, she sells the kid and buys herself a curling iron. Yet after we've chuckled at how self-centered everybody is—except the pretty prostitute (Verónica Forqué), who is the building's resident humanitarian—there are last-minute indications that Gloria is a loving mother and her sons are basically good kids who worry about her. (It's too upbeat a development when the dope-dealer boy heads back to farm country.) The movie has something of the hit-or-miss, bombastic quality of a Lina Wertmüller picture, but it's a lot easier to take. It isn't gummed up with "art."

Almodóvar is an underground-theatre clown. He may not know how to make anything stay with you—he may not even care to. He just likes to put on a show. Some of the vignettes might be comedy classics if their timing weren't so sloppy. The dentist's proposition, for example—his indication that, with his VCR and Sony stereo, he can give the boy the advantages that the boy's parents can't—has no payoff. And the actor who plays the dentist is too frenzied to let the proposition scene get its laughs. With the main exceptions of Carmen Maura's Gloria and her older boy (Juan Martínez) and the prostitute, the roles are performed rather crudely and perfunctorily. But, at least, the acting is pleasantly dry; very little is labored, or even stressed.

The best things in the movie aren't attached to its characters;

they're interludes—a parody of a coffee commercial, pseudo–Kurt Weill songs. And I liked the casual effrontery of Almodóvar's presenting the young-faced grandmother—it gives the movie an Off-Off Broadway informality. The picture comes closest to true dadaist slapstick in the scenes featuring a blood-spattered pet lizard named Dinero (Money) who is the only witness to a killing; it's suggested that Dinero might give the killer away.

When the slum apartment buildings are seen from the outside, their checkerboard patterns fill the screen. The buildings are like squared-off anthills—they're dizzying backdrops to the scenes shot in the streets. No doubt it was economy that dictated the size of the rooms in these bughouses, yet when you see the people crowded inside them with their big beds and chests and chairs you feel they've been made fools of—deliberately, perversely. Almodóvar—and this is his link to Brecht and Weill— makes these breeding grounds of vice seem macabre and frolicsome. But he's much more flip than they were. Gloria's impulses go every which way, and you'll probably never see a woozier treatment of the breakdown of the family and the decay of the society. *What Have I Done to Deserve This!* is like a comic-strip version of *The Threepenny Opera*. Its not adding up is, maybe, what's tickling about it.

The Swiss picture *Dangerous Moves*, which took the 1984 Academy Award for Best Foreign-Language Film, is loosely based on the celebrated Karpov-Korchnoi chess games. It's about a world-championship match held in Geneva between the longtime titleholder, Liebskind (Michel Piccoli), a courtly and cagey gray-bearded Russian Jew from the Soviet Union, and his former pupil, the challenger, Fromm (Alexander Arbatt), a young Lithuanian who defected from the Soviet Union and now lives in France. I was eager to see how the filmmakers —the writer-director Richard Dembo and the cinematographer Raoul Coutard—would handle the intellectual gamesmanship of chess. Well, they don't. The winner or loser of each day's proceedings is determined by what happens in the players' lives in the days between the games, or by the tricks that they and their aides use to spook the opposition during the games themselves. The movie shows the efforts of Liebskind's earnest, attentive wife (Leslie Caron) to keep him calm, because his heart is bad, but he's seething with all kinds of rage, sparked by the Soviet officials' refusal to let the only cardiologist he trusts accompany him to Switzerland. (The doctor's sons are in Israel, and the officials feared he might try to join them.) And the movie shows the anxieties of the high-strung, somewhat paranoid Fromm, who doesn't know what's happening to his wife (Liv Ullmann), back in Moscow. Both contestants are being manipulated by the Soviet bureaucracy.

Dembo might say that if he didn't present these psychological stresses and maneuvers there'd be nothing to photograph. But why pick chess if you're going to negate what's fascinating about it—the mental concentration it requires? By showing us two grand masters who are at the mercy of their emotions, Dembo banalizes chess and turns the movie into anti-Soviet psychodrama. And though the film proceeds systematically, game by game, we're not told how many games must be won, so we don't have any peg for suspense or excitement.

At first, Fromm's tempestuousness and the way he angers Liebskind, by arriving late for the sessions without the slightest show of contrition, puts us in an expectant mood; the handsome, blond Arbatt, who resembles Nureyev, and is, in fact, a Russian defector (an actor who found asylum in France), gives some promise of fireworks to come. Instead, we get poor Liv, who has been sent from Moscow to Geneva to upset her husband, staring at him watery-eyed as she delivers lines like "They destroyed me so that I would destroy you." Even Piccoli, who gives a cunning, authoritative performance, has no chance to wing past the pedantry of the conception. Each time he smokes a cigarette or scratches his fingers nervously, Dembo all but clangs a fire bell. Yes, we see that Liebskind is feeling old and mortal, that he's feeling his powers slip away. But is there nothing specific to the guy, or to his wife, who serves him with standard devotion? After a while, we're not even waiting to see who will win—we're just waiting to see how soon Liebskind's heart will give out.

Only two images stayed with me: the wonderful greenish water as Liebskind's boat crosses the lake from his bungalow to the exhibition hall where the games are played, and the surprise slapstick moment when the hypnotist that Liebskind's aides have planted in the audience to distract Fromm and the mime that Fromm's aides have planted to distract Liebskind file out of the hall at the same time and their eyes meet. *Dangerous Moves* didn't need to cave in on itself so lugubriously. A chess movie might be high comedy if all kinds of irrationality broke loose in the players' lives and then they sat down to their matches with their minds clicking like computers (but better).

The James Bond series has had its bummers, but nothing before in the class of *A View to a Kill.* You go to a Bond picture expecting some style or, at least, some flash, some lift; you don't expect the dumb police-car crashes you get here. You do see some ingenious daredevil feats, but they're crowded together and, the way they're set up, they don't give you the irresponsible, giddy tingle you're hoping for. The movie is set mostly in Chantilly, Paris, and San Francisco, and it's full of bodies and vehicles diving, exploding, going up in flames. Christopher Walken is the chief villain; the ultra-blond psychopathic product of a Nazi doctor's experiments, he mows people down casually, his expression jaded. And the director, John Glen, stages the slaughter scenes so apathetically that the picture itself seems dissociated. (I don't think I've ever seen another movie in which race horses were mistreated and the director failed to work up any indignation. If Glen has any emotions about what he puts on the screen, he keeps them to himself.)

All that keeps *A View to a Kill* going is that it needs to reach a certain heft to fit into the series. As the villainess, Grace Jones, of the flat-top haircut and the stylized look of African sculpture, is indifferently good-humored the way Jane Russell used to be, and much too flaccid, and as the blond heroine Tanya Roberts (who has a disconcerting resemblance to Isabelle Adjani) is totally lacking in intensity—she goes from one life-threatening situation to another looking vaguely put out. About the most that can be said for Roger Moore, in his seventh go-round as Bond, is that he keeps his nose to the grindstone, permitting himself no expression except a faint bemusement. It used to be that we could count on Bond to deliver a few zingers, but this time the script (by Richard Maibaum and Michael G. Wilson) barely manages a little facetiousness. The film does come up with one visual zinger: in the small role of Jenny Flex, a stunning young model named Alison Doody comes up with a curvy walk that's like sex on wheels.

Stick—adapted from an Elmore Leonard novel, and set in and around Miami—shows its director and star Burt Reynolds at a low ebb. Whether he's ill or just drained, the fun has gone out of his acting; he seems unsure of himself, and his voice is hoarse and on the verge of fading away. He tries to make his general depressiveness work in terms of the character, but this Stick—an ethical tough guy with refined tastes —has no consistency, and the film is cursed with the philosophical insights that came to him during the seven years he just spent in the slammer. *Stick* has its lowest point in a scene with a cruelly suave gang leader who lives in an apartment that looks like Presley's Graceland. Wanting to impress Stick, this gangster prepares to punish the young owner of a bodega who hasn't paid enough protection money. The grocer sits in helpless terror as the gangster, using a pair of tongs, takes a scorpion from a tank and places it on his arm. Slowly, it crawls toward his face: Will Stick find a way to save him or will he be stung? There is a cut, and we never find out.

The picture also has a high point. An actor named Dar Robinson— he's famous as a stuntman—plays an albino killer with a sinister half smile and blurry yellow eyes. He's always on the verge of doing something memorably baroque, and finally he does—he falls off the balcony of a high building, and while plunging to his death he keeps firing his revolver all the long way down. Except for that, the only thing that makes *Stick* worth mention is that George Segal, in the broadly written role of a cigar-chomping millionaire who likes to pal around with hoods, is rip-roaringly manic. Some of his old joy in acting comes out, and each time he appears he gives the movie a shot of energy. As he plays the part, the millionaire is carried away by the pure ecstasy of being rich.

June 3, 1985

EXTREMES

T he first thing that charmed me about *The Shooting Party*, which is set in the English countryside in the autumn of 1913, was the swiftness and wit with which we are introduced to the characters. A large number of landed gentry, aristocrats, servants, gamekeepers, beaters, and loaders have gathered at the Nettleby estate for a three-day shoot, and the camera, flitting like a butterfly, hovers over a couple of people talking about someone else, whirls over to that person in conversation, and from there to whoever is being talked about, and so on. This Alan Bridges film isn't merely based on Isabel Colegate's 1980 novel; it's a film of the novel, a transcription in the literal sense—"the arrangement of a composition for a medium other than that for which it was originally written." It's a novel acted out for us. But by devices such as those hovering, whirling introductions, and by the quality of the performances, and the economy and fleeting elegance of the whole production, Alan Bridges carries the Masterpiece Theatre approach to the level of art.

The novel is highly compressed: it's a set of variations on the end-of-an-era theme, with dozens of characters in less than two hundred pages. Colegate sets them up, one by one, in a few sentences—deft, sneaky details of their backgrounds—and then lets them speak for themselves. The dialogue is sly and pithy. At times, it's reminiscent of Oscar Wilde, and the adapter, Julian Bond, hasn't tried to improve on it. Whole scenes have the Colegate verbal rhythms intact, and a viewer can bask in the beautiful bounce and precision of the dialogue, which is spoken by the kind of cast you assemble when you fantasize about who should be in the movie of a novel you've just read. It's a dream of a cast.

James Mason is the aging baronet Nettleby, the host, whose wife (Dorothy Tutin), we are given to understand, used to be a gregarious creature, always on the go. Now she's content to bicker with the head gardener, keep an eye on her grandchildren, and play a killer game of bridge. Nettleby is the central figure—the embodiment of the values that are already frayed and will disintegrate in the war to come. And James Mason, in his final movie (he died last July, at seventy-five), goes out in glorious style. His Nettleby is a supremely civilized man; he sees other people for what they are, but he also sees the reasons for it. He speaks harsh words to only one person, the cold fish Lord Hartlip (Edward Fox), whom he reprimands for "not shooting like a gentleman," and he does so in a tone of pained regret. Mason uses a mild, aging man's voice in this role, and his querulous, cracked inflections make us smile. His face and, especially, that plangent voice are so deeply familiar that when we see him in a role that does him justice there's something like an outpouring of love from the audience to the man on the screen.

Mason validates our feelings: he uses his own physical deterioration for the role, yet he never turns into a grand old man or indulges in a quaver that isn't a funny, integral part of the country squire who's conscious that he's ineffectual—that he's losing his grip. In a scene midway, Nettleby, who breeds game birds on the estate so that he can provide his guests with these splendid shooting sprees, is confronted by a protester, played by John Gielgud, who marches into the middle of the shoot carrying a placard that says "THOU SHALT NOT KILL," and the old squire and the old zealot—each, in his own way, disaffected—converse. The scene is right out of the novel, but Mason and Gielgud are like soft-shoe artists; they bring suavity to their teamwork, with Mason matching his melancholy warble to Gielgud's melodious whine. They're even more hilarious than Gielgud and Ralph Richardson were on the stage in *No Man's Land*, because that was just two great actors sparring; here the two can tease each other from inside the characters they're playing. They're so amused they're almost laughing—they're in actors' heaven. And when, toward the close of the film, Mason has a scene that's overladen with the possibilities of pathos and grandeur—it's a scene with Gordon Jackson as a poacher whose cussedness the squire has come to respect—he pulls back; he underplays, magically. No one could accuse James Mason of not acting like a gentleman.

Bridges, whose 1982 film *The Return of the Soldier* opened here in February, has a special gift for these evocations of a world seen in a bell jar, and now, with Geoffrey Reeve as producer and Fred Tammes as cinematographer, he has refined his techniques. A late bloomer (he was born in 1927), Bridges goes beyond being pictorial and literary. He sharpens the novel's wry observations on the Edwardian era and at the same time infuses a sensuous sweetness into the material. The film isn't Chekhovian, exactly (though Mason is); it's more like a distillation of what's alluring about the Masterpiece Theatre productions—wonderful actors, given the chance to speak a celebrated writer's lines. And it's brought off with a sovereign ease. On TV, a novel like *The Shooting Party* would be a six-part series, full of longueurs, and shorteurs, too. Here, after we've met the key members of the party, the movie puts us (as the novel does) among actions and conversations going on simultaneously. And as the events become more intense Bridges picks up the pace and tightens the film's emotional hold on us. Many of his performers are veterans of the prestigious series shows with which he has long been associated, but actresses such as Cheryl Campbell (who was Vera Brittain in "Testament of Youth") and Judi Bowker (who was in "The Glittering Prizes") make a stronger impression in their brief screen time than they do in their much longer stints on TV—maybe because the pictorial setups are held so long on TV that we tire of them, and the images don't stay with us. As Lady Aline, the flighty, adulterous wife of Edward Fox's Lord Hartlip, who disgraces himself in the shoot, Cheryl Campbell is at one moment a pert-faced, nosy gossip, and at the next a tantalizing sensualist being caressed by her own long, wavy blond hair. It's a quicksilver performance that recalls Joan Greenwood at her most seductive. And Judi Bowker as the guileless Lady Olivia, the wife of thickheaded Lord Lilburn (Robert Hardy), looks at the camera with a direct gaze that makes her seem infinitely beautiful. When the tall, slim young barrister Lionel Stephens (Rupert Frazer) declares his love for her, you think, Of course—how could he look into her clear eyes and not imagine depths of mystery?

The movie has a few misdirected elements. One is a small subplot involving a love letter that Stephens writes to Olivia and then tears up and tosses into a wastebasket, from which it's retrieved by a young footman, who copies it and gives it to the servant girl he's courting. (She's a prosaic soul and disapproves of it as tosh.) Somehow, this episode comes through confusingly. And there's also some fuzziness about the identity of several of the characters. Though it doesn't really matter which of the assembled people are related to the Nettlebys, we don't know that at first, and I kept wondering which of them were the Nettlebys' children. It turns out that they have only a son, who is a diplomat and is out of the country, and that his wife, Ida (Sarah Badel), is the mother of all four grandchildren, including the flirtatious nineteen-year-old Cicely (Rebecca Saire) and the ten-year-old Osbert (Nicholas Pietrek), who has a pet mallard named Elfrida Beetle. We—and several of the guests and servants—fear for Elfrida when she's loose on the grounds on the third day; that's the day the shooters, having dispatched hundreds of pheasants, rabbits, and woodcocks, go after ducks.

Does it seem arch or frivolous that the characters fuss over a little boy's possible loss of a pet duck in a movie that's ostensibly about the Twilight of the Empire? Actually, it's Elfrida and all the other singularities that form this vision of an aristocracy reduced to playing games of death. Yes, we can see that the advancing line of beaters and the line of shooters with their loaders behind them are like lines of soldiers, and we recognize that these expensively got-up people, who regard their class as the flowering of the social order, and the British Empire as the best there has ever been, are on the edge of oblivion. Once again, a shooting party is being used as a symbol for the greater violence to come. But Colegate's tone is lightly self-mocking. (The moviemakers didn't find a way to adapt one of the elements that link with the Gielgud character and round out Colegate's conception. She sees the pheasants as fed and protected from predators, then cast forth from their Eden and "forced to take to the air reluctantly—heavy birds, a flight of more than a few feet exhausts them—forced up and out to meet a burst of noise and a quick death in that bright air.")

What keeps the picture from abstractness and overfamiliarity is that it's full of the English affection for gentle lunacy. Gordon Jackson plays the poacher as Colegate described him: "His conversational manner had always tended towards the histrionic." Aline Hartlip, who sees herself as passion's plaything, also manages to cadge some money from her hostess. The wide-eyed Olivia, never having had a romantic thought about Lionel Stephens, responds to his avowal of love—and the news he brings that their souls knew each other before—with the sudden discovery that, yes, she loves him, too.

The movie is about the tight fit of the jacket worn by the Hungarian count (Joris Stuyck) and the way Nettleby refers—fondly—to the immensely rich Sir Reuben Hergesheimer (Aharon Ipalé) as "the Israelite." It's about the traditions, loyalties, and idiosyncrasies that bind a social order. It's about the ceremonies of dressing for dinner and becoming part of the procession to go into the dining room and being seated at the table, where conversation is a form of theatre. Most of all, it's about how, given the chance, actors can take us beyond what we read in a book. Edward Fox, a master of twisted psyches and gnarled vocal tones, can make us feel the loneliness inside the miserable, arrogant Hartlip, who has nothing to be proud of except his reputation as the best shot in England—a reputation that Lionel Stephens, without giving the matter much thought, challenges. And Dorothy Tutin wraps the role of Lady Minnie Nettleby around her like a dowdy old sweater. (I enjoyed even the unplanned things, like the way Robert Hardy's fatuous Lord Lilburn recalls Nigel Bruce as the stocky, expostulating Dr. Watson, and the way Gielgud from some angles is a ringer for I. B. Singer.)

The Shooting Party isn't likely to appeal to the teen-agers at the shopping mall. What would they make of the characters' allusions to Ruskin and to George Meredith's *The Egoist*, which have been retained from the novel, or of a remark (Julian Bond's addition) that Lady Minnie makes to Lady Aline—"I've always thought your men more Ibsenite than Chekhovian"? (I'm not sure I know what to make of that, either.) There's probably no more preciously literate scene in movies than the explanation of how Elfrida Beetle got her name, but the scene is consciously, whimsically silly. This is one of the rare movies that can be said to be for an educated audience without that being a putdown.

Rambo: *First Blood Part II* explodes your previous conception of "overwrought"—it's like a tank sitting on your lap firing at you. Jump-cutting from one would-be high point to another, *Rambo* is to the action film what *Flashdance* was to the musical, with one to-be-cherished difference: audiences are laughing at it. More specifically, they're laughing at its star and progenitor, Sylvester Stallone, who comes across as a humanoid Christ figure with brown leather skin and symmetrical scars. Rambo has been programmed with (a) homoeroticism, (b) self-pity, (c) self-righteousness, (d) sweat, and (e) an insatiable need to be crucified over and over. He has a sour pout on his face, and he's given to deep, enigmatic utterances, such as "To survive a war you have to become war."

According to *Rambo*, we didn't lose the war in Vietnam—the United States soldiers weren't allowed to win it. And when it ended, our government made a deal to pay war reparations of four and a half billion dollars to North Vietnam for the return of our captured men, then reneged on the deal and tried to forget all about the prisoners of war.* Rambo goes in and brings a bunch of survivors out. Of course, he has his moments of pleasure: he has bits of his flesh sliced off by a sadistic, Nazi-like Russian (Steven Berkoff), he's spread-eagled on an electrified rack by torturers who think they can make him talk, he's branded in the face with a red-hot knife, he's immersed in pig glop while hanging crucifixion style. And, boy-oh-boy, what this killer Christ does to those Commies! He shoots them with his bow and arrows—arrows with explosive points that send them up in fireballs.

The jungle greenery is very lustrous; the cinematographer, Jack Cardiff, gets something of the effect in color that Josef von Sternberg got in black-and-white in a studio-made jungle in his 1953 *Anatahan*—it's as if each leaf had been oiled and buffed. And with the bare-chested Stallone slipping through these leaves the effect is mighty odd: you're supposed to be intoxicated by his lumpy muscles. The way he's photographed, he's huge—our national palooka—and the small Vietnamese in their ill-fitting uniforms don't look as if they had a muscle (or a brain) among them. They just stand around stupidly, waiting to be blown up; you may want to yell at them "Take cover!" But who could be heard above the soundtrack alerting you to watch for the next killing, and the audience's catcalls and the giggly cheers for Rambo's Zen marksmanship and his gorgeous fireballs? (The film reaches climax when two boats

*There is some factual basis for this: in 1973, President Nixon promised President Pham Van Dong $3.25 billion in U.S. economic aid, but Congress refused to grant the money.

crash in flames.) The director, George P. Cosmatos, gives this near-psychotic material—a mixture of Catholic iconography and *Soldier of Fortune* pulp—a veneer of professionalism, but the looniness is always there. Rambo's old Green Beret colonel calls him "a pure fighting machine," yet, like Rocky, Rambo always has to have bigger guys in his movies—real bruisers, like the Russian giant here—to beat him up. We mustn't forget that his namesake is Arthur (*A Season in Hell*) Rimbaud: trying to explain Rambo to a corrupt official, the colonel says, "What you choose to call hell, he calls home."

What Sylvester Stallone chooses to call a movie is a wired-up version of the narcissistic jingoism of the John Wayne–Second World War pictures. Its comic-strip patriotism exploits the pent-up rage of the Vietnam vets who feel that their country mistreated them after the war, and it preys on the suffering of the families who don't know what happened to their missing-in-action sons or brothers, fathers or husbands. A Sylvester Stallone hit movie has the same basic appeal as professional wrestling or demolition derbies: audiences hoot at it and get a little charged up at the same time.

David Morrell, whose novel *First Blood* was the basis of the first Rambo picture, has written the novelization of this sequel, from the screenplay by Stallone and James Cameron. It's a love letter to Rambo's weaponry—his nasty serrated knife and his bow and exploding arrows. In the author's note at the front of the book, Morrell tells us who "created" the weapons and where we should write to order them. I can hardly wait for my set to arrive.

June 17, 1985

RIPENESS

I f John Huston's name were not on *Prizzi's Honor*, I'd have thought a fresh new talent had burst on the scene, and he'd certainly be the hottest new director in Hollywood. The picture has a daring comic tone—it revels voluptuously in the murderous finagling of the members of a Brooklyn Mafia family, and rejoices in their scams. It's like *The Godfather* acted out by The Munsters, with passionate, lyrical arias from Italian operas pointing up their low-grade sentimentality. The 1982 novel, by Richard Condon, is a lively, painless read. His riffs about the corruption of American business and politics have a rote paranoia—they have no sting—but the characters are entertainingly skewed, and the story moves along and keeps you smiling. The movie does something more. When it's over, you may think of slight resemblances to *Beat the Devil* and *The Maltese Falcon*, but its tone is riper. The behavior on the screen is bizarrely immoral, but it has the juice of everyday family craziness in it. And the zest that goes into the Prizzis' greediest swindles is somehow invigorating. You'd think this movie the work of a young director because of the elation you feel while it's on, and afterward, too. Even *The Man Who Would Be King* didn't have the springiness that this has. The only thing about *Prizzi's Honor* that suggests a veteran director, or even hints at Huston's age (he's seventy-eight), is the assurance of his control. He directed this movie (his fortieth) on pure instinct—on the sum of everything he knows. It's as if his satirical spirit had become irrepressible—the devil in him made him do it.

Huston has a cast of devil's helpers, who have been coached in the jerky rhythms and combative dialect of Sicilian Brooklynese by the actress-playwright Julie Bovasso. She played John Travolta's mother in *Saturday Night Fever* and its sequel, and that's who they talk like. They sound like truculent trolls. As Charley Partanna, the enforcer (i.e., hit man) for the brotherhood, Jack Nicholson has added a facial effect: his upper lip puffs out and curls under, which thickens Charley's speech. (When he's fully in character, he's frog-faced and fishy-eyed, like a blown-up Elisha Cook, Jr.) Charley is a loyal and dedicated company man, but he's not too sharp; he's like a hardhat who's only good at his trade—he needs to be cranked up to think. And Nicholson's performance is a virtuoso set of variations on your basic double take and traditional slow burns. At times, Charley is like Jackie Gleason's vain Ralph Kramden in "The Honeymooners": he seems to want to waddle and shake more rolls of flesh than he's got. (Like Kramden, he wants to occupy a bigger space in the world.) Then he'll go limp and lacklustre, like Art Carney's Ed Norton. Nicholson's Charley plugs the "Honeymooners" kind of ordinariness into this Mafia world. And when he falls for a West Coast girl—a Polish blonde, Irene (Kathleen Turner), whom he meets at the Prizzi wedding that opens the movie—he's like a man conked out by a truckload of stardust. He's gaga. But Nicholson doesn't overdo his blurred expressions or his uncomprehending stare; he's a witty actor who keeps you eager for what he'll do next. There are reasons for audiences' good will toward him: he'll do anything for the role he's playing, and he has a just about infallible instinct for how far he can take the audience with him.

Charley's essential average-guyness is the movie's touchstone: this is a baroque comedy about people who behave in ordinary ways in grotesque circumstances. The Condon book is a takeoff on *The Godfather*, and Huston follows it right down to putting a spin on the details (like the quick glimpse of the wedding couple, so you can see that the bridegroom is shorter than the bride), but the parody isn't too broad—not even with Nicholson's inflated upper lip complementing Brando's pushed-out lower lip. (In a scene in which Charley, the romantic clod, is told that he is to be the next head of the family, Nicholson produces a small, eye-rolling flourish: for an instant—a passing shade of thought—he sees himself as Brando, the don.)

The title is, of course, satiric. The movie is about what the Prizzis do in the name of honor. Old Don Corrado Prizzi (William Hickey) is a shrunken little man, ghouly and wormy, with tiny, shocking bright eyes. These slitted, almost closed eyes are so alive they jump out at you. (They're like the director's eyes—they're the soul of the movie.) At eighty-four, this slippery master chiseller snoozes most of the time, but he still runs the mob, and he's plotting his "monument"—a banking maneuver that should net the family some seventy million dollars. Hickey, an esteemed New York acting coach, actually in his fifties, has always had a special energy, and his mock seriousness here is just what the mummified old don needs. Don Corrado can barely walk anymore (he shuffles), but he lives to rook people, and Hickey makes you feel the mean joy he takes in it. When the don wants to say something, he doesn't speak, exactly—he is so much into his own rhythms that he singsongs his remarks. But age hasn't softened him. And an old don has an advantage that other oldsters don't have: when this little geezer gives orders to the members of his family, they obey.

Don Corrado's two sons are big men. The firstborn, Dominic (Lee Richardson), who's in his sixties, runs the dirty side of the operations; the younger, better-educated, and slicker Eduardo (Robert Loggia), who's in his fifties, handles the "legitimate" investments and mingles with financial leaders and high-ranking men in government. Richardson and Loggia play their roles just tilted enough for you to register what it's like for men Dominic's and Eduardo's ages to be dominated—

still—by their father: it keeps all their childhood tensions going.

The member of the family who is closest in spirit to the tricky old don is his granddaughter Maerose (Anjelica Huston), whose eyes are never at rest, either. Dominic, Maerose's rigid-minded father, has made her a family outcast, because some years earlier, when she and Charley were engaged and got into a scrap, she took off in a drunken rage and had an affair. She has been exiled to Manhattan, where she works as an interior decorator, but she's as busy plotting as the don himself. As Anjelica Huston plays her, the raven-haired Maerose is a Borgia princess, a high-fashion Vampira who moves like a swooping bird and talks in a honking Brooklynese that comes out of the corner of her twisted mouth. Anjelica Huston seems to have grown into her bold features: she's a flinty beauty here—she has the imperiousness of a Maria Callas or a Silvana Mangano. And, with that Brooklyn cabbie's diction, and Maerose's fixation on vengeance against her father, Anjelica Huston is an inspired comedienne, especially when she parodies penitence and sidles into a room dolorously, her head hanging on her shoulder. The stunning Maerose loves scandalizing the family, and comes to the wedding—the bride is her younger sister—in a scarlet-banded, one-shouldered black gown. Maerose has more in her face than anyone else has; she has irony and the strangeness of what's hidden. She's like a bomb ticking away in the background of the movie.

By contrast, Kathleen Turner's ravishingly pretty Irene seems pallid. Turner has built up a lot of audience good will, too, and she has her moments: Irene's intonations are hilariously ritualized when, after participating in a kidnap and a murder, she chirps "See you at dinner" to Charley and pecks him like a suburban housewife as he drives off with the kidnap victim. But her role doesn't really develop, and it suffers from an omission: Irene needs a scene to show the shift in her from the woman who's playing Charley for a sap—the woman who smiles to herself when she's got him hooked—and the woman who warms to the adoration of such a big man in the Mafia. (Charley is the kind of romantic who, after they've declared their love for each other, in a swank Mexican restaurant in L.A., takes note of what the orchestra is playing and says, "This is gonna be our song.") And Turner is at a disadvantage: Irene isn't from Brooklyn and doesn't have the chance to talk in the clan's comic lingo.

The central group is completed by Charley's father, Angelo "Pop" Partanna (John Randolph), who is the Prizzis' *consigliere* and Don Corrado's closest friend. As Condon described Pop, his "sweetness and amiable good cheer about murder and corruption were legendary in the environment," and that's how Randolph plays him. He's always beaming, and when he looks at Charley, the hit man, the crinkles around his eyes radiate all over his face: there never was a father who took greater pleasure in his son. When the two are together, we see the father-son relationship in its ideal form. These two confide in each other the way fathers and sons do in storybooks for boys. I don't think Randolph has ever done anything this mellow before: Pop is overflowing with happiness, and when, toward the end, the kidnap and killing (which are tied in with the banking maneuver) cause unforeseen troubles, the childlike anxiety in his face suggests a perturbed saint.

It's impossible to say who's happier—Pop, who dotes on his son, or Don Corrado, who has always had his own way. Or the audience. I found myself laughing all the way through. Though some people don't respond to the movie at all, laughter seems to bubble up in most of us. Probably that's because characters like Pop and the don are only slightly warped versions of other doting parents, other tyrants. It's the context of Mafia connivery that makes their happiness, like Charley's romanticism, seem blissfully silly. (Being a mobster appears to produce the same result as a lobotomy: some vital connection in the brain is severed.)

Huston has made a character comedy out of Condon's prankish satire of American corruption. He has been so confident and free that he has included moviemaking jokes, like the use of obvious stock shots of planes whipping back and forth across the country to represent Charley and Irene carrying on their coast-to-coast romance. The characters come equipped with certain eccentricities of the "environment," such as the habit—apparently developed among people who make inordinate amounts of money—of saying "a dollar" when they mean a thousand dollars. When they refer to seven hundred and twenty dollars, they're actually talking about heavy cash. Except for the failure to round out Irene's character, the script, by Condon and, later, Janet Roach (who worked on the structuring of the scenes), is a beauty, and the Alex North score, with its lush, parodistic use of Puccini, and some Rossini, a little Verdi, and a dash of Donizetti, too, actively contributes to the whirling texture of the scenes. Even the musical jokes that you're not quite conscious of work on you, and the music seems to bring out the lustre of Andrzej Bartkowiak's cinematography. Everything in this picture works with everything else—which is to say that John Huston has it all in the palm of his big, bony hand.

You can feel a prickly excitement in the theatre. It's the kind of excitement that makes you say, "God, I love movies"—or, at least, "God, I love this movie."

It's a different kind of love that Satyajit Ray's *Ghare-Baire*, or *The Home and the World*, brings out, but it's love all right. Adapted from a novel that Rabindranath Tagore wrote in 1912 (Ray prepared a script for it in the forties, long before he made his first film, *Pather Panchali*), it deals with a great modern subject that has come up in Ray's work over and over: the emancipation of women, and what it does to them and to the men who love them. This is central to *Ghare-Baire*, which is the story of the emergence of a young wife from the seclusion and ignorance of purdah into the complexities of becoming more fully human—or, at least, adult—and having choices. The core situation is much like the one in James Joyce's play *Exiles*—the husband, in his pride, wanting the wife to be free to be faithful—but that's only the film's starting point.

Victor Banerjee (the Dr. Aziz of *A Passage to India*) is Nikhil, a maharajah in Bengal with a Western education and liberal views. His wife, Bimala (Swatilekha Chatterjee), is conventional in her beliefs, and is content to live in the women's quarters of his palace and be visible to no man except him. But he loves her and is proud of her, and wants her to be a modern woman, able to move in the world. She first saw him at their wedding: how will he ever know whether she really loves him if she doesn't have the opportunity to choose him—to prefer him to other men? For ten years, Bimala is taught by an English governess and encouraged to think for herself and develop her creativity. At last, in 1907, Nikhil persuades her to take the momentous walk with him down the corridor that leads from the women's apartment to the main rooms of the palace. There, in the drawing room, he introduces her to his friend the handsome, fiery radical Sandip (Soumitra Chatterjee, the Apu of *The World of Apu*, and a principal actor in eleven other Ray films). And then the refined, uncoercive Nikhil watches passively—helplessly—as she becomes enthralled by Sandip's cocksure masculinity and his revolutionary rhetoric.

The movie is about the destruction of the marriage, and the riots and bloodshed caused by Sandip's terrorist supporters. It's a large theme—a double tragedy, in the home and in the world—presented in a formal style that owes almost nothing to the conventions of American or Western European films. The screen frame is almost square, and the scenes —most of them inside the rooms of the palace—are in deep, glowing colors. The main characters talk, and the camera just stays on them and waits until they finish, yet these conversations develop a heart-swelling intensity. In a sense, the method is like that of amateur moviemakers who think that all they need to do is put actors in a room and photograph them reading their lines as if they were on a stage. The difference is that Satyajit Ray, who has been making movies for thirty years, didn't start with this simplicity—he achieved it. His approach—the intimacy of his focussing on the actors in their setting—may be influenced by Ozu or late Dreyer, but it isn't remotely austere or ascetic. India takes care of that.

When you're inside the palace, there's a lot of India outside the windows. The home and the world are interpenetrating metaphors. The interiors seem to be lighted through stained-glass windows, and the colors, the fabrics, the way the actors move—everything is erotic, ambiguous, in the process of being transformed. The richness of the performances—those of Victor Banerjee and Swatilekha Chatterjee in particular—and the colors and textures of the interiors are like an electric field. The conversations in golden light and shadows have their own kind of voltage. You watch these graceful people in draped garments in their lethargic, patterned décor, and everything in the country seems draped, hanging, defeated—and hectic, too.

The story takes place during the chaotic aftermath of Lord Curzon's partition of Bengal into Muslim and Hindu states, when the nationalist movement that Sandip is part of is trying to impose a boycott against all foreign goods (by claiming that imports are at the root of Indian poverty). Yet Bimala is becoming educated—becoming free—by imbibing English traditions. When this Indian woman sings, in English, the song that she has been taught by her governess—"Tell me the tales that to me were so dear, Long long ago, long long ago"—the confusion of cultures is insanely poignant.

Bimala is girlish and coquettish in the early scenes in the women's quarters, and part of the fascination of the movie is that Swatilekha Chatterjee grows with her role, and becomes more absorbing the longer you see her. She's not a mere ingénue; she's a full-bodied, rounded beauty, and her Bimala has an earthy, sensual presence. But Bimala and Nikhil obviously have no children, and we don't see them in passionate embraces, either. Nikhil's love for her seems more spiritual than physical.

For much of their ten-year marriage, each time Nikhil suggests that Bimala leave purdah behind she looks down, smiling defensively. It isn't her compulsion; it's his. She doesn't want to come out of the women's quarters—all incense and silks, Arabian Nights cushions and English bric-a-brac. The rooms are stuffed—surfeited—with treasures; Bimala seems to emerge from inside a jewel. Maybe it's because the drive isn't hers that she's so overwhelmed by Sandip's fervor, and so easily taken in. Nikhil could guide her—could explain what the boycott is doing to the poor in the area. But he wants her to wise up by herself; he wants her to jump over the giant hurdle of growing up in ignorance, and see through the political line of a messiah like Sandip. He tells her to use her "woman's intuition"—surely the last thing she should trust in making a choice between his passive principles and Sandip's ruthless magnetism. This gracious, recessive maharajah (with zero carnality) is the innocent one.

Nikhil seems almost to will the destruction of his marriage. We never get inside his kindness, his virtue, his high-mindedness—or his weakness. Yet this doesn't seem a defect in the film but, rather, part of its richness and its mystery. Toward the end, Bimala, who was wheedled into independence by her husband, becomes desperate to express that independence—recklessly, heedlessly. When it comes to truthfulness about women's lives, this great Indian moviemaker Satyajit Ray shames the American and European directors of both sexes.

July 1, 1985

INDEX